Also in the Variorum Collected Studies

GERARD TROUPEAU
Etudes sur le christianisme arabe au Moyen Age

MICHAEL LECKER
Jews and Arabs in Pre-and Early Islamic Arabia

M.J. KISTER
Society and Religion from Jahiliyya to Islam

DAVID AYALON
Islam and the Abode of War: Military Slaves and Islamic Adversaries

MAJID FAKHRY
Philosophy, Dogma and the Impact of Greek Thought in Islam

WAEL B. HALLAQ
Law and Legal Theory in Classical and Medieval Islam

R.B. SERJEANT
Customary and Shari'ah Law in Arabian Society

C.E. BOSWORTH
The Arabs, Byzantium and Iran: Studies in Early Islamic History and Culture

A.I. SABRA
Optics, Astronomy and Logic: Studies in Arabic Science and Philosophy

DAVID A. KING
Astronomy in the Service of Islam

AMNON SHILOAH
The Dimension of Music in Islamic and Jewish Culture

SIDNEY H. GRIFFITH
Arabic Christianity in the Monasteries of Ninth-Century Palestine

WILFERD MADELUNG
Religious and Ethnic Movements in Medieval Islam

GEORGE MAKDISI
Religion, Law and Learning in Classical Islam

VARIORUM COLLECTED STUDIES SERIES

Power, Marginality, and the Body in Medieval Islam

Professor Fedwa Malti-Douglas
(Annalese Poorman)

Fedwa Malti-Douglas

Power, Marginality, and the Body in Medieval Islam

Routledge
Taylor & Francis Group
LONDON AND NEW YORK

First published 2001 by Ashgate Publishing

2 Park Square, Milton Park, Abingdon, Oxfordshire OX14 4RN
711 Third Avenue, New York, NY 10017

Routledge is an imprint of the Taylor & Francis Group, an informa business

First issued in paperback 2018

British Library Cataloguing-in-Publication Data
Malti-Douglas, Fedwa.
Power, Marginality, and the Body in Medieval Islam. –
(Variorum Collected Studies Series: CS723).
1. Marginality, Social–Religious aspects–Islam. 2. Body, Human–Religious aspects–Islam. 3. Power (Philosophy)
I. Title.
297' 0902

US Library of Congress Cataloging-in-Publication Data
Malti-Douglas, Fedwa.
Power, Marginality, and the Body in Medieval Islam/Fedwa Malti-Douglas.
p. cm. – (Variorum Collected Studies Series).
Includes bibliographical references and index.
1. Arabic prose literature–660–750–History and criticism. 2. Arabic prose literature–750–1258–History and criticism. 3. Islamic empire–Intellectual life. 4. Islamic Empire–Social conditions. 5. Islamic empire–Biography–History and criticism.
I. Title. II. Collected Studies.
PJ7575. M35 2001 2001022821
892. 7' 830809–dc21

ISBN: 978-0-86078-855-3 (hbk)
ISBN: 978-1-138-37543-7 (pbk)

VARIORUM COLLECTED STUDIES SERIES CS723

To the tats who generously grace my world

COPYRIGHT NOTE

Grateful acknowledgement is made to the following copyright holders for their kind permission to reproduce the papers included in this volume: G.-P. Maisonneuve-Larose, Paris (II, V); Editions du Centre National de la Recherche Scientifique, Paris (III, IV); The Darwin Press , Inc., Princeton, NJ (VI); Brill Academic Publishers, Boston, MA (VII, VIII, IX); Institut français d'Etudes Arabes, Damascus, Syria (X); The University of Chicago Press, Chicago, IL (XI); Dr Jonathan Rodgers, The American Oriental Society, University of Michigan, Ann Arbor, MI (XII); Eisenbrauns, Winona Lake, IN (XIII).

CONTENTS

This volume contains xxii + 290 pages

PREFACE AND ACKNOWLEDGMENTS

Power, marginality, sexuality, and the body: powerful words indeed that serve as guides into the rich and variegated world of the medieval Arabo-Islamic imaginary. This world is populated by rulers and criminals, uninvited guests and theologians, women and the blind. The map to this fascinating world is the medieval text. But to say "medieval text" is to speak of an enormous array of materials spanning many centuries and genres. *Power, Marginality, and the Body in Medieval Islam* proposes to take its reader on a journey into this textual world. The reader will delve into religious normative texts, literary texts, biographical texts, historical texts. Though the paths to be explored remain still largely uncharted, their directions have been suggested by Michel Foucault, Gérard Genette, Claude Bremond, and others.

How did medieval Arabic prose traditions deal with these at times sexually explosive issues? Certainly not by occulting them. On the contrary, power, sex, marginality, and the body were explored with a frankness that can still shock readers today. In fact, the intellectual freedom and the playful way with which medieval writers could engage with what too many today undoubtedly consider taboo topics have much to teach us in the twenty-first century. The investigation of these issues in *Power, Marginality, and the Body in Medieval Islam* is not only a road into medieval Arabo-Islamic mentalities but a way of coming to grips with the textual strategies that a society used for grappling with them. In the process, the analytical lessons from the volume should hopefully open rather than close new methodological highways through the rich culture of the Arabo-Islamic world.

Those of us who were lucky enough to know the late brilliant social historian of medieval Islam, Michael Dols, all have memories of special encounters with him. I for one will never forget the time when, in an off-moment at a conference, he turned to me and said: Why is it that you and I are the only ones so fascinated by marginals?" I do not remember my response to Michael's question but I do remember that we both laughed heartily at this strange intellectual coincidence. He was then working on lepers and madmen while I was pursuing uninvited guests, thieves, and the blind. Our work was crossing in mysterious ways as we found ourselves often dealing with the same sources. I had never really thought very much about whether the subjects to which I devoted so much of my time were "marginal." But the more I pondered Michael's words, the more I admitted to myself that he was right. I had been intrigued by topics of marginality all along. And yet for me, marginality was as much part of the mainstream of the culture as the leading authors who engaged with it. The marginal could inform us about the Arabo-Islamic textual world in ways that complemented and redefined the discourses that we might think of as dominant. Nor were the "marginal" isolated in my work from other issues that had also preoccupied me all along: issues of power, of the body, of gender and sexuality. All these surface and resurface in odd and unexpected ways in *Power, Marginality, and the Body in Medieval Islam*. Bodies there are aplenty: the physically handicapped, like the blind, the male tortured body or female dismembered body, or the uninvited guest who transgresses with his body. Bodies also become pawns in games of power, be it the power of the word or the power of politics.

A famous eleventh-century religious figure and historian, al-Khatîb al-Baghdâdî, is accused of homosexuality and plagiarism. The battleground for this verbal war over a theologian's reputation is the biographical dictionary ("Islamic Biography"). An Islamic indigenous genre, the biographical dictionary flourished in the central Islamic lands. Biographies of individuals could be organized in a multiplicity of ways: around a chronological period (such as a specific century), around a city (such as Baghdad), around a legal school (such as the Shâfiᶜîs), around a vocation (such as poets), or even around physical characteristics (such as the blind). "Controversy and its Effects in the Biographical Tradition of al-Khatîb al-Baghdâdî" asks how the biographical tradition of this leading figure dealt with tendentious information in his multiple biographies. The textual and sexual controversy surrounding this famous theologian and legist demonstrates the complexity of the biographical world in which medieval intellectuals were represented.

Sexuality and textuality defined the world in which al-Khatîb's written life circulated. And, in an interesting twist of literary fate, al-Khatîb's work itself becomes the basis of a later anecdotal collection by a prominent Hanbalî scholar (the legal school al-Khatîb had to flee!) ("Yûsuf ibn ᶜAbd al-Hâdî and His Autograph of the *Wuqûᶜ al-Balâ' bil-Bukhl wal-Bukhalâ'*"). But these are the ironies of the scholarly universes in which medieval intellectuals moved.

How fascinating all these intricacies of biography become when the biographical world is circumscribed by at once a physical deficiency, like blindness, and a biographical datum, like a dream. The most famous biographical dictionary of the blind, the *Nakt al-Himyân fî Nukat al-ᶜUmyân*, by the Mamlûk historian, al-Safadî, poses different challenges ("Dreams, the Blind, and the Semiotics of the Biographical Notice"). The visually handicapped were a visible part of the fabric of the medieval Arabo-Islamic textual universe, a prominent category among male intellectuals, yet at the same time marginal in certain textual discourses. Dreams were (and still are) a privileged medium in Islam, holding a special position in the normative literature (for example, the *hadîth*, the actions and sayings of the Prophet).

In the biographies of the blind, dreams are important narrative components that explore the boundaries of what constitutes an individual's life. Their complexity is increased by al-Safadî's discussion (in the introductory essays to the *Nakt*) about whether or not the visually handicapped are capable of seeing in dreams. In addition, the precise contents and location of a dream narrative are important semiotic markers. Is the dream in the biography of the dreamer or in that of the dreamed about? An individual's appearance in a dream after his death testifies to a conception of a life that englobes the afterlife. Other dreams speak to more earthly matters: the recovery of stolen items, the cure of a physical ailment, etc.

Dreams are only one way in which a discourse on blindness is created in the pre-modern Arabo-Islamic sphere. Michel Foucault and historians of medieval *mentalités*, like Jacques Le Goff, have made us all conscious of the importance of other types of texts in the creation of mental structures dealing with marginality. "Pour une rhétorique onomastique: les noms des aveugles chez as-Safadî" and "*Mentalités* and Marginality: Blindness and Mamlûk Civilization" carry the examination of blindness further, transcending the oniric and venturing into larger areas such as the onomastic as well as that of compensation. Here, sexuality plays an important role. Proverbs and cosmographical literature, to cite but two textual areas, tell part of the story. The blind are endowed with sexual prowess in a fascinating language that plays off upper and lower body parts against one another. The visually handicapped, we also discover, are quite capable of demonstrating their verbal superiority over their sighted colleagues. This verbal power is not far from something we shall see below.

A different sort of power, this time that of a ruler exercising his authority in fighting crime, exists in "The Classical Arabic Detective." A fisherman finds the dismembered parts of a woman's body in the Tigris. This case allows a caliph to become a detective in the classical mode of detection and uncover the criminal. Sexuality plays a role in the act of detection as well: the same ruler-detective uncovers an illicit sexual act between two men and punishes the culprit. The caliph-detective, not unlike some of his more modern counterparts (e.g. Sherlock Holmes), demonstrates his skills best when paired with a less talented character, who acts as foil to the detective's crime-solving abilities. The classical Arabic detective has literary cousins with whom he shares other properties, namely the classical Chinese detective.

Crime and criminals in the medieval Arabo-Islamic universe are also elements in the creation of a powerful discourse of the body and torture. What is the role of confession in the uncovering of a crime? If a criminal does not confess, what recourse does the law-enforcer have? The chapter "Texts and Tortures: The Reign of al-Muᶜtadid and the Construction of Historical Meaning," examines the many facets of a ruler. More than that, it shows the manipulation of the human body and its torture by a crime-fighting caliph, al-Muᶜtadid, familiar to us from the exploits that made of him a classical detective. The complex figure that is al-Muᶜtadid permits an examination of the various source materials that help create a personality in the rich Arabo-Islamic textual corpus, from chronicles and biographical dictionaries to those multi-discourse anecdotal collections called *adab* works.

And, of course, the medieval individual was delineated by more than merely anecdote and historical entry. The complex issue of naming, already familiar from the epithets used for the blind, will become even clearer in the examination of onomastic elements ("The Interrelationship of Onomastic Elements: *Isms*, *Dîn*-Names, and *Kunyas* in the Ninth-Century A.H."). How were various parts of people's names interrelated, and what do these relationships tell the reader about medieval *mentalités*?

The complexity of the name is derived primarily from that great repository, the biographical dictionary. But as the case of al-Muᶜtadid demonstrates, the literary anecdote is just as powerful an element in the medieval Arabo-Islamic textual ethos. And, sure enough, it turns out that the criminals subjected to torture (and whose bodies become pawns in the game of power with the ruler) are different from the petty thieves whose role in this complex textual world is more ludic than that of their violent cousins ("Classical Arabic Crime Narratives: Thieves and Thievery in *Adab* Literature"). Thieves operate, in the medieval *adab* corpus, as one of a group of character types who populate the anecdotal collections. These anecdotal character types have a special relationship to trickery, wit, and verbal eloquence. Sometimes they are victorious and get away with the loot, at other times they are outwitted by the individuals they attempt to rob. Women victims can be eloquent here as well, demonstrating the complexity of the gender dynamics of the anecdotes about thieves.

The thieves contribute to the creation of a discourse of transgression and violation. They are not the only anecdotal characters to be active participants in this discourse, however. Uninvited guests also transgress ("Structure and Organization in a Monographic *Adab* Work: *al-Tatfîl* of al-Khatîb al-Baghdâdî"). These marginal character types play a complex role in the medieval Arabo-Islamic textual world. Their actions are most often directed to the intimate sphere: family banquets, wedding receptions, private parties. It should then perhaps come as no surprise that they, too, will shamelessly resort to a sexual discourse when attempting to satisfy their role of uninvited guest.

The nexus of food and hospitality that dominates the anecdotal literature on uninvited guests is reversed in a literary genre with close relationships to the anecdotal texts: the *maqâma*. Loosely translated "séance," the *maqâma* is a genre distinguished by its discourse properties. The first *maqâmas*, those of Badîᶜ al-Zamân al-Hamadhânî (d. 398/1008), constituted a series of narratives, all in rhymed prose and all recounted by the same narrator expounding the adventures of a rogue hero, Abû al-Fath al-Iskandarî. Abû al-Fath, like his anecdotal cousins, lives by his wits and most often cheats the other characters. How interesting it then becomes to have this rogue hero become a victim of a host who outwits him. "*Maqâmât* and *Adab*: 'al-Maqâma al-Madîriyya' of al-Hamadhânî" examines one of the most famous of these narratives, "al-Maqâma al-Madîriyya." Named after a stew, the *madîra*, the *maqâma* describes the dilemma of Abû al-Fath, this time the guest of a miser. Abû al-Fath is invited to the home of his host and regaled with a description of the *madîra*, which remains the object of discourse, merely talked about and never served.

"Al-Maqâma al-Madîriyya" highlights the male host and his male guest. The setting may be the domestic sphere but the wife of the host is absent. Her voice is not heard. Fortunately, other women in the medieval Arabo-Islamic sphere are more visible than the host's wife. "Playing with the Sacred: Religious Intertext in *Adab* Discourse" explores the intertextual use of religio-normative materials. How are verses from the *Qur'ân* and traditions of the Prophet used in the prevalent anecdotal collections? And how does the intertextual exploitation of these materials help to redefine both the religio-normative materials and their anecdotal literary cousins? Women, it turns out, are major players here. And as such they testify to the diversity of this textual universe, and in *Power, Marginality, and the Body in Medieval Islam* they sit alongside major figures in the medieval Arabo-Islamic sphere.

When I think that Michael Dols left us in 1989, well over a decade ago, I realize that the studies that form the bulk of this volume have been with me even longer. It was in 1974, over a quarter of a century ago, that I ventured to France as a graduate student embarking on doctoral research. I had no idea then that this adventure would make such a lasting intellectual impact on all my work. I had gone to Paris having read and greatly admired the delightful autobiography *Among Arabic Manuscripts* by the Russian scholar Krachkovskii. That romantic notion of being buried under dusty tomes and discovering something rare accompanied me as I began my research at the Bibliothèque Nationale. But I quickly became cognizant of the fact that while I loved digging in and through medieval manuscripts, that was not enough. As luck would have it, as I was walking along the Boulevard Saint-Germain one day, I spotted the French translation of *The Morphology of the Folktale* by Vladimir Propp. I bought the book, inhaled it as fast as I could, and went on to look for more such sustenance. And Paris had it all: Roland Barthes, Claude Bremond, A. J. Greimas, Tzvetan Todorov, and many other names that were at that time largely alien to American academics. The revelation that was French criticism opened my eyes to a new world, the world of textual analysis and cultural criticism. I ventured forth into this area, hitherto unexplored in Middle Eastern studies, applying it to a wide corpus of medieval Arabo-Islamic texts. Dare I say that in the process I shocked some and scandalized yet others with the strange language of structuralism and semiotics, a language that was foreign to scholars of the Arabo-Islamic universe who had spent many years studying the foreign languages of the geographical area but not the foreign languages of criticism.

It was also in that same year, 1974, that my eyes would open to another world, the world of biographical dictionaries and onomastics. I was fortunate when I was but a graduate student, still in the excitement of intellectual discovery and exploration, to be taken under the wings of two most distinguished patrons, Georges Vajda and Jacqueline Sublet, at the Institut de Recherche et d'Histoire des Textes in Paris. I would work with them for an extended period as a Chercheur attached to the Centre National de la Recherche Scientifique where I was introduced to the secrets and pleasures of medieval Arabo-Islamic biographies. They and all the colleagues and friends in the international Onomasticon Arabicum project and in the *Cahiers d'Onomastique Arabe* (on whose editorial board I was privileged to serve) made the exploration into medieval names a truly pleasurable task.

Working in France around highly successful and prodigious scholars whose main pursuit in life was the intellectual journey was exhilarating. It was assumed that if I, as a graduate student, had something interesting to say, I could undertake the research, write it up as an article, and submit it to a journal, most likely also based in Paris. It was thus that I wrote one of my earliest studies, the one addressing controversy in the biographical tradition of al-Khatîb al-Baghdâdî. Georges Vajda and Jacqueline Sublet encouraged me to submit the study to Abdel Magid Turki, then (as now) co-editor of *Studia Islamica* with A. L. Udovitch. I was daunted by the prospect of publishing in such a prestigious venue. And many were the afternoons when I struggled with the article in the Bibliothèque Nationale, writing and rewriting the conclusion in those pre-computer days. The article was accepted in *Studia Islamica*, appearing in 1977. The sense of excitement at seeing my ideas in print and participating in a broader intellectual dialogue has never left me. And, after all these years, I still feel a debt of deep gratitude to Jacqueline Sublet, Abdel Magid Turki, and Georges Vajda for instilling in a young student the confidence to pursue scholarship and aim for the highest possible goals. It was Abdel Magid who would later invite me to become a member of his research team, the Equipe de Recherche 060302 at the Centre National de la Recherche

Scientifique and the Université de Paris-Sorbonne, an association I carried proudly, even as I pursued my career on the other side of the Atlantic.

But it was not only the Centre National de la Recherche Scientifique whose generosity facilitated my scholarly endeavors. I acknowledge with gratitude fellowships from the American Philosophical Society, the National Endowment for the Humanities, the Social Science Research Council and the American Council of Learned Societies, the American Research Institute in Turkey, and the American Research Center in Egypt. This support came at critical times in the development of many of these studies.

As I think back over the nearly quarter century that has seen the publication of the studies included in this volume, I cannot help but think of other people around the world without whose help and generosity I could never have published them. A scholar without a library is like a ship without an anchor. And I have been one of those lucky scholars who found incredible support and sustenance from the staff of the world's most famous libraries. The staff of the Bibliothèque Nationale in Paris spoiled me over the years I worked there and most of all it was Yvette Sauvan who helped me in ways too numerous to count. In Damascus, I was fortunate to have the cooperation of ᶜAlî Sandûq and Mâjid al-Dhahabî of the Majmaᶜ al-Lugha al-ᶜArabiyya, without whose generosity and kindness the work on Yûsuf ibn ᶜAbd al-Hâdî would never have been accomplished. The intellectual and physical hospitality of André Raymond and Thierry Bianquis at the Institut Français de Damas is impossible to repay. In Cairo, I would be privileged to work with the leading names in the Arab world at the Dâr al-Kutub, beginning with the late poet and luminary, Salâh ᶜAbd al-Sabûr, and ending with the prominent critics, ᶜIzz al-Dîn Ismâᶜîl and Jâbir ᶜAsfûr, cherished friends to this day. Stateside, it was George N. Atiyeh and his staff at the Library of Congress who always seemed to come to the rescue. I cannot possibly count the number of times I would call George in Washington, advise him that I was coming to D.C. for the day, and ask for his help in advance in locating materials. George would invariably have the multiple tomes waiting for me. I would then begin the mad dash to locate the right pages and photocopy them. None of it could have been accomplished without George, whose knowledge of the sources was only matched by his generosity and incredible kindness. George also facilitated my work with the Library of Congress office in Cairo and its then director, Michael Albin. The Library of Congress staff there, like the staff at the American Research Center in Egypt and those at the Fulbright offices under the generous care of Ann Radwan, became almost family and the various offices almost a home away from home, as I would sit sipping coffee while trying to learn about recent intellectual and publishing developments not only in Egypt but throughout the Middle East and North Africa.

Need I add that no work is ever complete without the input of friends and colleagues? I am grateful to all those who attended the lectures I delivered over the years, especially since many of those presentations were eventually revised to take the form of some of the published studies in this volume. Comments from colleagues at the American Research Center in Egypt, the University of California, Los Angeles, the University of California, Berkeley, the University of Chicago, Princeton University, and Yale University only improved my work.

But as I think over the several decades that produced these studies, I acknowledge with deep gratitude that there are individuals who have monitored my progress since my graduate student days and my early career until the present. These are scholars who stimulated me by their example and encouraged me by their friendship and unswerving support. Mohammed Arkoun, Bernard Lewis, George Makdisi, and Speros Vryonis: not one of them was my official teacher but they have all been superb mentors and guides. And it is perhaps one of life's ironies that all four never let gender issues get in the way. While all might not be of one mind on how to approach the medieval Islamic world, and while all might not agree about the politics of the Middle East, they are nevertheless formidable scholars whose deep knowledge and commitment to the most rigorous standards of scholarship can only be an inspiration to those fortunate enough to know them. Each of them taught me, in his own way, that to be a great scholar meant much more than simply to publish scholarly tomes. Being a great scholar, I learned, was also to possess an inordinate amount of intellectual generosity, an ability to share ideas, and a capacity to encourage younger scholars. Being a great scholar, I also learned, meant that one's life should be one of continuous learning and discovery, coupled with humility and modesty. And, most of all, being a great scholar, I also learned, was the ability to possess that all-too-rare commodity, a sense of humor and an ability to laugh at one's own foibles.

George Makdisi shepherded me in my early days as a graduate student. He was not my "official" teacher but he was much more. He was the type of mentor whose generosity is an ideal. I will never forget the first time I met George Makdisi at an American Oriental Society conference in Santa Barbara. He was the scholar who could question a speaker and show beyond the shadow of a doubt if that speaker did not know the materials under discussion. I and other members of the audience were stunned, when not afraid, watching this performance. After one of the panels, George engaged me in what I thought would be a quick conversation but which turned out to be a three-hour grilling session about my research interests and where I was heading intellectually (I had not yet even passed my Ph.D. Qualifying Examinations!). I knew that despite the friendly exterior, George Makdisi was testing me, something for which I am grateful to him to this day. He gave me a piece of advice that I still pass on to my students. "Read the text so many times," George told me, "that you can literally see the figure in the text walking before your very eyes." I always heeded this advice and would laughingly tell him years later that I could still see al-Khatîb al-Baghdâdî walking before my eyes.

But George's intellectual generosity would go way beyond this priceless advice. After completing the work on the autograph manuscript by Yûsuf ibn ᶜAbd al-Hâdî, I asked George if he would be willing to read over my study. There was no one in the world better equipped to give me criticism than George Makdisi who had not only worked with Yûsuf's absolutely atrocious and unreadable handwriting but who also was an international expert on Hanbalîs. Sure, George volunteered, why didn't I simply come up to the University of Pennsylvania. We would have lunch, he added, and then sit down in his office and do the work. I was then on the faculty of the University of Virginia and the relatively short distance made the suggested plan possible. On the day of the meeting, I awoke to a gigantic blizzard. I was undaunted and I set out in three feet of snow from Charlottesville with Allen Douglas, heading for Philadelphia. On arrival, we discovered that the university had closed its doors, and that George was not on campus. He had tried to call and cancel but could not reach us. No problem. He invited us to his home, where we were his honored guests. George and I went over the manuscript and I felt moved and privileged that a scholar of the stature of George Makdisi would open his home to a young assistant professor and her husband, have them spend the weekend with his family, and cook for them while they were his guests. He regaled us with meals that I still remember to this day.

Almost ten years later, George would invite me, this time to a colloquium he was organizing with Giles Constable on "Medieval and Renaissance Humanism" at the Bellagio Study and Conference Center on Lake Como. That was where I tried out my ideas on "Playing with the Sacred." The intellectual excitement from the group of scholars that George and Giles gathered was matched only by the absolutely idyllic environment at the Villa Serbelloni.

Another participant at the Bellagio conference was Speros Vryonis. I was a graduate student at U.C.L.A. when Speros was the Director of the University's Von Grunebaum Center for Near Eastern Studies. I was not by any means preparing to be a specialist in the field to which Speros had dedicated his life. How I would come to his attention as a mere graduate student he would only tell me years later: he was struck by the fact that I was the only graduate student to attend all the public lectures and scholarly events sponsored by the Center. He inquired about me, learned of my field of interest, and did nothing but encourage and support me in these endeavors. I found I could count on Speros for his generosity, and most of all for his honesty. He also extended numerous invitations to me to lecture and to participate in conferences. Speros had the idealism that comes from wanting to make sure that one does the best one can, with the hope that others will do the same. A giant in his field, Speros could move as easily in Islamic studies as he did in Byzantine studies. He invited me to Dumbarton Oaks, where in his company I shared the lunch table with some of the world's leading Byzantinists. He arranged a lecture tour for me at which I would deliver my study on the *tufaylīs*. But more importantly, Speros encouraged me when I was still a graduate student feeling my way forward. As I shyly handed him (it was before I received my Ph.D.) my first offprint (1976) and then my second (1977), he turned to me and said: "You've been bitten by the bug." His statement was a way of encouragement and an expression of his pride in a student. I was both flattered and honored. But I also felt the burden of responsibility that comes from any honor. Later, Speros would change that image and tell me that I had fire in my belly. Now, decades later, as I can still hear the voice of Speros Vryonis making these declarations, I am tempted to engage him in a discussion of corporal imagery, a discussion that he and I could surely laugh about. Over twenty years after that first offprint, when I gave Speros a copy of my satirical novel on the academy, he did me the greatest honor. He wrote back the funniest take-off on academic prose and exegesis I have encountered: I still derive great pleasure from reading that incredible missive. But more than anything, it is perhaps the qualities of Speros Vryonis as a human being that will always stay with me. His battle against cancer set a courageous example for me to follow as I battled my own physical limitations. His courage in the face of different sorts of adversities taught me more than books ever could. And this is nothing compared to the unbounded compassion that Speros seemed to possess. As he and I one day got into a conversation about the tragic death from AIDS of a colleague and one of his graduate students, I was overwhelmed by the pain and agony Speros was feeling. I appreciated even more then what an extraordinary human being he was. And as I sat very reluctantly in a wheelchair in the Milan airport after the conference at Bellagio, it was Speros who kept me company and advised me on how best to travel when one faces not just the usual agonies of displacement but those agonies multiplied by health problems.

It would be many years after my first invitation to Princeton University to lecture on "The Classical Arabic Detective" that Bernard Lewis would explain to me the motivations behind his having extended several invitations to me to lecture at Princeton, once as an Eberhard L. Faber lecturer. He confessed that he was concerned about his female graduate students and wanted them to have women role models. I was flabbergasted. Only recently did I discover that I shared this incredible tribute with another close friend, Wendy Doniger, something that made us both sensitive to the fact that perhaps more than any other senior scholar whom we knew, Bernard was incredibly conscious of gender issues and of the need to combat gender stereotypes. I also came to understand why it was Bernard who had recommended me to serve on important committees, like a visiting committee at Harvard or a panel at the National Endowment for the Humanities. As I embarked on my publishing career, I became aware that the invitations to Princeton had done more than allow me to benefit from the comments of friends and colleagues. They had opened doors to an equally precious commodity, a university press. Were it not for Bernard's invitations, I am certain that I would not be today an author with two Princeton University Press books to her name. Bernard's generosity extended beyond mere invitations, however. Over the years, he has shared his own publications and research, his unparalleled knowledge of the Middle East, and his guidance. When I needed a work that was unavailable in any library in the United States, I would call Bernard to find out if he by any chance had it in his own personal library. And more often than not he did. I did not have to ask Bernard to make the volume available to me. Invariably, and to my surprise, he would take charge of photocopying materials and make sure that a package would soon follow. But perhaps more than anything, Bernard's example has taught me not to be hampered by the intellectual boundaries that the academy often seeks to impose on its members. Bernard Lewis might seem a most unlikely person to call when seeking unorthodox advice. Many years ago, I was offered a position at a prestigious university where the chair of the department indicated to me that were I to join the faculty, I would have to stop being the *enfant terrible* of the profession, publishing on subjects like comic strips. I was completely taken aback. I called Bernard and will never forget his words of wisdom. If an academic department wishes to impede your intellectual growth and shackle your desire for intellectual exploration, you do not want to join it. Needless to say, I did not accept the position. To this day, I heed Bernard's words, no matter what the university and no matter what the department. And as I was sharing my plans with Bernard about *Power, Marginality, and the Body in Medieval Islam*, he responded in total surprise, adding that this sort of project was for people nearing retirement. Ah, the ironies of life. Nevertheless, this did not mean that Bernard's advice would not play a role in the title of the book.

And it was thanks to an invitation from Bernard Lewis to participate at a conference at the Institute for Advanced Study at Princeton that I would meet Mohammed Arkoun. I was long familiar with Arkoun's contributions on medieval philosophy, having read them as a graduate student. But this was a conference on mutual perceptions East and West that spanned the medieval and the modern and I, as a young assistant professor beginning her career, trained as a medievalist but speaking on modern intellectual movements would meet Mohammed Arkoun, who at that time was one of the few people in the world who could navigate the medieval and the modern with equal ease. It has been decades since that conference and Mohammed Arkoun has encouraged me and supported me and, simply put, been a part of our family's everyday life. Whenever I invited Mohammed for a lecture I would offer him what to me was the more luxurious option of staying in a hotel. But he always insisted that he would rather be with our family at home, surrounded by cats and trees. So whether in Austin, Texas, joking at a picnic with novelists and painters, or in Bloomington, Indiana, helping to push my car up a steep driveway in the mud and snow, Mohammed consistently graced our home with his wit and laughter. Although most of the time our telephone calls stretch over continents, I can always count on Mohammed's support, encouragement, and advice. Perhaps more than anything, however, it is Mohammed's position as a world-class intellectual with extensive knowledge of the wider languages of the humanities and social sciences that has made him an inspiration. I could always rely on him to call my attention to a book I should read — and one not necessarily in Middle Eastern studies. I will never forget Mohammed's insistence that I publish "The Classical Arabic Detective" in the journal he edited, *Arabica*, one of the premier international journals in the field. He paid me the highest compliment when he told me that he wanted to keep the journal up-to-date on the most current and exciting research. And when Mohammed was a visiting professor at a prestigious institution in the United States, many were the times that he would call me in frustration and tell me that he felt he was speaking a foreign language because no one seemed to understand his highly sophisticated analytical vocabulary. It was such moments that would bring my own French intellectual journey back to me and make me grateful for that walk I undertook all those years ago on the Boulevard Saint-Germain. Then when I served as moderator at a plenary session of the annual Middle East Studies Association several years ago, at which Mohammed was one of two featured speakers, I observed that it was Mohammed's eloquence and passion that kept the audience begging for more. But I also recognized then that wit and charm aside, only those few privileged to know Mohammed well know the extent of his commitment to free inquiry and freedom of expression, alas commodities all-too-rare in today's volatile academy.

If Speros Vryonis had mentioned to me many years ago that I should consider publishing a set of studies as a Variorum collection, it would be another friend, Wael Hallaq who would push me over the starting line. In one of our many conversations, Wael suggested I undertake this project, citing himself as an example and laughingly adding that I should delete my birth date from my c.v. so that the publisher would think me older than I am. Wael very generously put me in touch with Dr. John Smedley and the project was launched. John Smedley has been nothing short of amazing. From my phone calls to him from Paris, through my detailed letters, to my numerous emails, he has been the model of patience and support. Without him, *Power, Marginality, and the Body in Medieval Islam* would still be a figment of my imagination.

Nor could the last stages of the manuscript preparation and completion have been accomplished without Dr. Renate Wise. Colleague, friend, editor, professional indexer, and much much more, Renate's extraordinary skills were all brought to bear on the book preparation. Her knowledge of Middle Eastern and European languages combined with her meticulous eye for detail was a great boon as I entered the race to meet the publication deadline.

I have been fortunate over the decades as I first completed the individual studies and then the volume to have Allen Douglas by my side. It is only when I write acknowledgments for books that I officially thank him, in the process accumulating even more debt. But in fact my gratitude to him extends above and beyond published results to cover all the processes of intellectual discovery and creation. I have been spoiled by his acumen, intelligence, and deep knowledge of the humanities and social sciences. As I moved from philology through history to cultural studies, Allen was always there to inject his wisdom and unparalleled critical skills, sacrificing his time to help me complete whatever project needed completion. Only he knows how much I owe him, and more importantly only he knows that I can never repay him for all those moments when he made something that seemed impossible possible or when he brought laughter out of misery or when he would just not allow me to give up.

And, as always, I express my gratitude to the other individuals who populate my everyday world, those in the P.-T. family. S., D., and A. Nothing I do is ever done without them. Whether they help me write or they edit my writing, their presence has become a necessary part of my work. They are a source of inspiration, pleasure, calm, beauty, and affection. They also know, as Allen does, that words cannot express the depth of my feelings for them. In periods of pain, as in periods of pleasure, they are guardian angels.

FEDWA MALTI-DOUGLAS

Bloomington, Indiana
January 2001

PUBLISHER'S NOTE

The articles in this volume, as in all others in the Variorum Collected Studies Series, have not been given a new, continuous pagination. In order to avoid confusion, and to facilitate their use where these same studies have been referred to elsewhere, the original pagination has been maintained wherever possible.

Each article has been given a Roman number in order of appearance, as listed in the Contents. This number is repeated on each page and is quoted in the index entries.

I

ISLAMIC BIOGRAPHY

Islamic biographical dictionaries represent an indigenously Arabo-Islamic literature that appears to have no significant pre-Islamic antecedents and no parallel in the medieval West. The genesis of the biographical dictionary has often been linked to the science of *hadîth* criticism. Some scholars, however, prefer to relate this genre to Arab genealogical storytelling and poetic traditions. It would appear that the biographical dictionary, with its characteristic principles of arrangement, reflected basic Arab mental structures, since examples devoted to varied types of individuals appeared almost simultaneously.

The arrangement of these compendia is linked to the concept of *tabaqât*, or classes. In *tabaqât* works the biographies were divided into groups that could be based on generations (as with *hadîth* transmitters) or on levels of merit or skill (as with poets). In a possibly later development this term was also applied to compendia limited to a given type of individual but not divided into classes (for example, the *Tabaqât al-shu*ᶜ*arâ'* of Ibn al-Muᶜtazz, *d.* 908). Finally, in certain cases *tabaqât* simply seems to be synonymous with biographical dictionary. Although biographical literature may have originated in *tabaqât* format, it developed into a diverse and sophisticated historical and literary genre that saw its golden age under the Mamluk sultanate (*ca.* 1250-1500).

Compendia included general works stretching from the advent of Islam to the author's time (for example, the fourteenth-century *al-Wâfî bi'l-wafayât* of al-Safadî) and more specialized collections that could be devoted to cities (the eleventh-century *Ta'rîkh Baghdâd* of al-Khatîb al-Baghdâdî) or occupations ranging from scholar and Koran reciter to singer and dream interpreter. Specializations were not limited to occupations, but could be based on the interests of the biographers: al-Safadî complied collections both of the blind and of the one-eyed.

The number of individual notices, and hence the length of the compendium, could vary from relatively short works describing one hundred personages to multivolume texts comprising thousands of notices. Besides *tabaqât* arrangements, notices were also organized chronologically by death date or alphabetically by *ism* (first or given name, as distinguished from patronymics, nicknames, and the like) or by combination thereof.

The biographical notices themselves could vary sharply in length from a few lines to extended biographical or critical essays covering many pages. Most typically, however, notices ranged between about half a page and four or five pages. Most commonly the data presented include the date of birth (when available), the date of death, the genealogy of the subject, his education, his teachers, the books he wrote, and some anecdotal material (provided at the discretion of the biographer).

Almost invariably the notices began with an onomastic chain, a list of names, appellations, and titles, that provides genealogical and onomastic information, setting the subject in his social and professional context. Following this varied information the biographer could proceed to what he considered most significant in the subject's life. This might include character traits, important events, or more "academic" concerns, such as the biographee's education, his teachers, and his travels in search of knowledge. The materials relating to the death of the person, be they the circumstances of death, the cause of death, or his appearance in dreams after his death, can most often be found at the end of the notice. Clearly, this order is not accidental.

In those parts of the notice that follow the onomastic chain, the biographer could choose among several discourse styles. One was the simple declaratory presentation of biographically significant information. Another was the anecdote, a sophisticated literary form. Anecdotes could be included because they illustrated an important characteristic of the biographee, because they transmitted a noteworthy biographical datum, because they were entertaining, or because they met a combination of all three criteria. The third major discourse style was poetry, and since most educated Muslims were at least occasional poets, the verses could be those of the biographee, those composed about him, or even those of the biographer. The literary skill of the biographer, therefore, involved the balancing and arrangement of these different discourse types in the notice.

Obviously the relative weight given to different discourse styles reflected the preferences and tastes of the authors. Poetry, of course, was an especially important element in the biographies of poets, and some collections, like the tenth-century *Kitâb al-aghânî* of Abû'l-Faraj al-Isfahânî and the eleventh-century *Yatîmat al-dahr* of al-Thaʿâlibî, hovered between biographical dictionaries and what were essentially literary anthologies in biographical form. At the other extreme, some biographers limited themselves almost exclusively to the onomastic chain and a few items of dry data (for instance, the seventeenth-century *Shadharât al-dhahab* of Ibn al-ʿImâd).

Biographical compendia contain a great wealth of historical data, both about the subjects of the notices, and about the society in which they lived. The "reference" quality of these texts, however, should not lead us to forget that, at their best, they were finely crafted literary and biographical masterpieces. Muslim biographers copied freely from their predecessors, generally following a system of scholarly reference and citation. Each writer, however, took artistic and historical responsibility for the precise form and wording, as well as for the selection and arrangement of borrowed materials. One onomastic or honorific element added or deleted, one anecdote lengthened, shortened, or commented upon, could alter the image of the subject. Indeed, such biographical variations could lead to controversy and polemics. For this reason the proper understanding of the biographer's intent is often dependent on the deciphering of sets of codes ranging from the onomastic to the oneirocritical.

Different biographers, naturally, had their own styles, reflected in the tone and organization of their notices. In his *Wafayât al-aᶜyân*, for example, Ibn Khallikân not only follows a relatively consistent pattern of organization but also tends to paint his subjects as the "ideal type" of the appropriate social or personal category. He reinforces this quality by avoiding either a polemical tone or controversial incidents. The fifteenth-century Abû'l-Mahâsin Ibn Taghrîbirdî, by contrast, in his *al-Nujûm al-zâhira*, opts for the pithy phrase or description, seemingly avoiding intricate details but in fact providing the reader with a forceful portrait of the personages he treats (be the portrait negative, as in the case of the historian and *hadîth* authority al-Khatîb al-Baghdâdî, or more positive, as in the case of the Andalusian poet Ibn Zaydûn). Biographical peculiarities such as these are important not only directly, for the picture they provide of the biographee, but also indirectly, for what they tell us of the historical and literary preferences of the biographer.

BIBLIOGRAPHY

Hartmut E. Fähndrich, "The *Wafayât al-Aᶜyân* of Ibn Khallikân: A New Approach," in *Journal of the American Oriental Society*, 93 (1973); Ulrich Haarmann, "Auflösung und Bewahrung der klassischen Formen arabischer Geschichtsschreibung in der Zeit der Mamluken," in *Zeitschrift der Deutschen Morgenländischen Gesellschaft*, 121 (1971); Ibrahim Hafsi, "Recherches sur le genre '*Tabaqât*' dans la littérature arabe," in *Arabica*, 23 (1976) and 24 (1977); Donald Presgrave Little, *An Introduction to Mamlûk Historiography* (1970); Fedwa Malti-Douglas, "Dreams, the Blind, and the Semiotics of the Biographical Notice," in *Studia Islamica*, 51 (1980); Franz Rosenthal, *A History of Muslim Historiography*, 2nd ed. (1968).

II

CONTROVERSY AND ITS EFFECTS IN THE BIOGRAPHICAL TRADITION OF AL-KHAṬĪB AL-BAGHDĀDĪ*

The Medieval Arabic biographical notice was more than just a repository for onomastic and biographical data but was also a vehicle for praise and polemic. In the composition of a notice, the author was, at the least, presented with the opportunity of taking a position on the personage in question or certain aspects of his life. If a biographer were to become aware of some controversial information concerning a personage, would he exclude it or would he include it? And if he were to include it, how would he present it?

By tracing the biographical tradition of the noted scholar al-Khaṭīb al-Baghdādī, it will be possible to examine the appearance and treatment of certain controversial incidents in his life and the reactions or defenses these provoked in the biographical tradition. This study, though it will discuss the life of al-Khaṭīb al-Baghdādī, is not a biography. First of all, it is not biographically complete. More importantly, however, its goal is not the elucidation of a particular historical reality. Rather, it takes the text as the object of study and the biographical tradition, though this of course must be built around

(*) I would like to thank the Centre National de la Recherche Scientifique and the Institut de Recherche et d'Histoire des Textes in Paris, whose generosity made this, and much else, possible.

aspects of a person's life, as a potentially independent phenomenon, itself capable of development. For the purpose of this study, the biographical tradition is being considered as the totality of the biographical notices devoted to a given personage. This distinguishes it, thus, not only from studies which are biographical in aim but also from those which concern themselves with the work of one biographer be these either literary or historiographical in orientation. (1)

Abū Bakr Aḥmad ibn 'Alī ibn Thābit ibn Aḥmad ibn Mahdī, better known as al-Khaṭīb al-Baghdādī, was, to introduce him briefly, an eminent *ḥadīth* scholar and theologian, as well as author of numerous works, including the justly famed *Ta'rīkh Baghdād*. He died in the year 463/1071. (2)

As might be expected, the biographical tradition about al-Khaṭīb is extensive and there are numerous notices to be found. The following, which include all the most important, have been identified and used in this study. (3) For convenience, they have been arranged in chronological order.

1) Ibn 'Asākir (d. 571/1176), *Tabyīn Kadhib al-Muftarī* (4)
2) Ibn 'Asākir (d. 571/1176), *al-Ta'rīkh al-Kabīr* (5)
3) Ibn al-Jawzī (d. 597/1200), *al-Muntaẓam fī Ta'rīkh al-Mulūk wal-Umam* (6)
4) al-Bundarī al-Iṣfahānī (c. 623/1226), *Kitāb Zubdat an-Nuṣra wa-Nukhbat al-'Uṣra* (7)

(1) For some recent examples, see H. Fähndrich, "Man and Men in Ibn Khallikān, A Literary Approach to the Wafayāt al-A'yān," Doctoral Dissertation, U.C.L.A., 1972; D. P. Little, "Did Ibn Taymiyya Have a Screw Loose?" *Studia Islamica*, XLI (1975), pp. 93-111; and by the same author, "Al-Ṣafadī as Biographer of his Contemporaries," in D. P. Little, ed., *Essays on Islamic Civilization* (Leiden: E. J. Brill, 1976), pp. 190-210.

(2) The most extensive biography is Yūsuf al-'Ish, *al-Khaṭīb al-Baghdādī, Mu'arrikh Baghdād wa-Muḥaddithuhā* (Damascus: al-Maktaba al-'Arabiyya, 1945).

(3) See 'Umar Riḍā Kaḥḥāla, *Mu'jam al-Mu'allifīn* (Damascus: al-Maktaba al-'Arabiyya, 1957), v. II, pp. 3-4; Jacob Lassner, *The Topography of Baghdad in the Early Middle Ages* (Detroit: Wayne State University Press, 1970), note 28, p. 228. See also the editor's note on p. 92 of the *Wafayāt al-A'yān*, cited below.

(4) (Damascus: Maṭba'at at-Tawfīq, 1928), pp. 268-271.

(5) ed. A. Badrān (Damascus: 1911), v. I, pp. 398-401.

(6) (Hyderabad: Maṭba'at Dā'irat al-Ma'ārif al-'Uthmāniyya, 1940), v. VIII, pp. 265-270.

(7) MS. Paris, Bibliothèque Nationale, Arabe 2146, folio 32r.

5) Yāqūt (d. 626/1229), *Kitāb Irshād al-Arīb ilā Ma'rifat al-Adīb* (1)
6) Ibn al-Athīr (d. 630/1233), *al-Kāmil fī at-Ta'rīkh* (2)
7) Ibn al-Athīr (d. 630/1233), *al-Lubāb fī Tahdhīb al-Ansāb* (3)
8) Sibṭ ibn al-Jawzī (d. 654/1256), *Mir'āt az-Zamān* (4)
9) Ibn Khallikān (d. 681/1282), *Wafayāt al-A'yān* (5)
10) Abū al-Fidā' (d. 732/1331), *al-Mukhtaṣar fī Akhbār al-Bashar* (6)
11) adh-Dhahabī (d. 748/1348), *al-'Ibar fī Khabar man Ghabar* (7)
12) adh-Dhahabī (d. 748/1348), *Kitāb Tadhkirat al-Ḥuffāẓ* (8)
13) Ibn al-Wardī (d. 749/1349), *Ta'rīkh Ibn al-Wardī* (9)
14) aṣ-Ṣafadī (d. 764/1362-3), *Kitāb al-Wāfī bil-Wafayāt* (10)
15) al-Yāfi'ī (d. 768/1367), *Mir'āt al-Janān* (11)
16) as-Subkī (d. 771/1369), *Ṭabaqāt ash-Shāfi'iyya al-Kubrā* (12)
17) al-Asnawī (d. 772/1370), *Ṭabaqāt ash-Shāfi'iyya* (13)
18) Ibn Kathīr (d. 774/1373), *al-Bidāya wan-Nihāya fī al-Ta'rīkh* (14)
19) Ibn Qāḍī Shuhba (d. 851/1448), *Ṭabaqāt ash-Shāfi'iyya* (15)

(1) ed. D. S. Margoliouth (London: Luzac & Co., 1923), v. I, pp. 246-260.
(2) (Beirut: Dār Ṣādir, 1966), v. X, p. 68.
(3) (Cairo: Maktabat al-Qudsī, 1938), v. I, p. 380.
(4) MS. Paris, Bibliothèque Nationale, Arabe 1506, folios 130v-133v.
(5) ed. Iḥsān 'Abbās (Beirut: Dār ath-Thaqāfa, n. d.), v. I, pp. 92-93.
(6) (Cairo: al-Maṭba'a al-Ḥusayniyya, 1907), v. II, pp. 187-188.
(7) ed. Fu'ād Sayyid (Kuwait: Maṭba'at Ḥukūmat al-Kuwayt, 1961), v. III, p. 253.
(8) (Hyderabad: Maṭba'at Majlis Dā'irat al-Ma'ārif al-'Uthmāniyya, 1957), v. III, pp. 1135-1146.
(9) (Najaf: al-Maṭba'a al-Ḥaydariyya, 1969), v. I, pp. 520-521.
(10) ed. Iḥsān 'Abbās (Wiesbaden: Franz Steiner Verlag, 1969), v. VII, pp. 190-199.
(11) (Hyderabad: Maṭba'at Dā'irat al-Ma'ārif an-Niẓāmiyya, 1920), v. III, pp. 87-88.
(12) ed. 'Abd al-Fattāḥ Muḥammad al-Ḥulw (Cairo: Maṭba'at 'Īsā al-Bābī al-Ḥalabī, 1966), v. IV, pp. 29-37.
(13) ed. 'Abd Allāh al-Jubūrī (Baghdad: Maṭba'at al-Irshād, 1970), v. I, pp. 201-203.
(14) (Cairo: Maṭba'at as-Sa'āda, n.d.), v. XII, pp. 101-103.
(15) MS. Paris, Bibliothèque Nationale, Arabe 2102, folios 33r-33v.

20) Ibn Taghrī Birdī (d. 874/1470), *an-Nujūm az-Zāhira fī Mukūk Miṣr wal-Qāhira* (1)
21) Ibn Hidāya (d. 1014/1604), *Ṭabaqāt ash-Shāfi'iyya* (2)
22) Ibn al-'Imād (d. 1089/1679), *Shadharāt adh-Dhahab fī Akhbār man Dhahab* (3).

In a first group of notices, the biographical data are limited, on the main, to essential onomastic information coupled with some dates of birth and/or death. In addition, one may find in these notices some laudatory descriptions of the personage, perhaps a mention of his works or even where he died and who carried his bier. A general characteristic of these notices is an absence of anecdotal material. The first group is composed of numbers 4, 6, 7, 10, 11 and 13 above. These notices, thus, contain no controversial information or appreciations and need not be considered any further.

A second group of notices, while also containing no controversial elements, offers a fuller selection of biographical data including a measure of anecdotal material. This group consists of numbers 2, 19 and 22. These biographies, in addition to the data discussed above, also tend to include information concerning subjects like the places to which al-Khaṭīb traveled in quest of knowledge, the wishes he made at Zamzam, his religious affiliation, diverse pious actions or displays of scholarly erudition, and the circumstances concerning his death and burial. These last, though somewhat tangential to this study are not without interest. (4)

One further notice can be set aside at this time, that of al-Yāfi'ī. The bulk of this notice is the same as that of Ibn Khallikān and it contains the same essential information. The

(1) (Cairo: al-Mu'assasa al-Miṣriyya al-'Āmma lit-Ta'līf, n.d.), v. V, pp. 87-88.

(2) (Baghdad: Maṭba'at Baghdād, 1937), pp. 57-58.

(3) (Beirut: al-Maktab at-Tijārī liṭ-Ṭibā'a wan-Nashr wat-Tawzī', n.d.), v. III, pp. 311-312.

(4) In conformity with his wish, al-Khaṭīb was buried next to the grave of the famous Ṣūfī, Bishr al-Ḥāfī. This was done over the objections of another Ṣūfī who had dug his grave in that spot, and prayed there repeatedly. It was explained to the reluctant Ṣūfī that as al-Khaṭīb took precedence in life, so would he in death. See, for example, Ibn 'Asākir, *at-Ta'rīkh*, p. 299.

principal differences lie in the treatment of the laudatives and the dates of birth and death in the opening lines. The notice gives the appearance of having been copied either from Ibn Khallikān or from Ibn Khallikān's source, Ibn an-Najjār. (1)

The notices devoted to al-Khaṭīb are not, however, by any means all so anodyne. Yāqūt, for example, paints a much less flattering portrait of the man. He recounts the following story. While in Damascus, al-Khaṭīb used to frequent a handsome youth. People naturally spoke about this and the story reached the Rāfiḍī ruler of Damascus. He thereupon ordered his chief of police *(ṣāḥib shurṭatihi)* to kill him. The latter, a Sunnī (the Rāfiḍīs were Shī'īs), advised al-Khaṭīb to place himself under the protection of the Sharīf ibn Abī al-Ḥasan al-'Alawī. (2) This was done, and when the Amīr questioned the Sharīf about it, ibn Abī al-Ḥasan said that he did not approve of al-Khaṭīb but since al-Khaṭīb was an important person, his execution would lead to retaliation on the Shī'īs in Irāq. Al-Khaṭīb was thereupon expelled from the city and he moved to Ṣūr. (3)

Yāqūt relates another interesting story. Most of the works of al-Khaṭīb except the *Ta'rikh*, he says, made use of the works of one aṣ-Ṣūrī, (4) who would begin them and not finish them. After his death, aṣ-Ṣūrī left a large number of unfinished works with his sister and al-Khaṭīb exploited them. (5) Yāqūt also notes that al-Khaṭīb was accused of being drunk, which account is quoted by aṣ-Ṣafadī. (6)

The story concerning the works appears in Ibn al-Jawzī's notice in a shorter form which does not mention aṣ-Ṣūrī's sister.

(1) I have not been able to locate the notice by Ibn an-Najjār. The work described as the *Dhayl Ta'rīkh Baghdād* by Ibn an-Najjār, MS. Paris, Bibliothèque Nationale, Arabe 2130/1 is clearly something else. See E. Amar, "Sur Une Identification de deux Manuscrits Arabes de la Bibliothèque Nationale," *Journal Asiatique* (1908). Dixième Série, XI, pp. 237-242.

(2) See C. van Arendonk, "Sharīf," *EI*¹, v. IV, pp. 336-341.

(3) Yāqūt, v. I, pp. 255-256.

(4) For a biography of aṣ-Ṣūrī which also deals with this problem, see Ibn Taghrī Birdī, v. V, p. 63.

(5) Yāqūt, v. I, pp. 249-250.

(6) Yāqūt, v. I, p. 253; aṣ-Ṣafadī, v. VII, p. 194.

In addition, the *Ta'rīkh Baghdād* is not specifically excluded from the works taken over, though the ambiguity leans more towards the interpretation that it should be excluded. (1) This shorter form is also found in Ibn Kathīr, who cites Ibn al-Jawzī. Ibn Kathīr offers, however, two minor additions: he states that al-Khaṭīb borrowed the works from aṣ-Ṣūrī's wife, and he is noncommittal as to whether the works were copied by al-Khaṭīb or merely completed by him. (2)

The reason Yāqūt gives for al-Khaṭīb's leaving Damascus for Ṣūr is also to be found in aṣ-Ṣafadī. The latter's account is almost identical to that of Yāqūt. (3) Adh-Dhahabī, in his *Ḥuffāẓ*, also includes the story of the youth. He retells it, but with the essential elements unchanged. (4)

Sibṭ ibn al-Jawzī in his biography of al-Khaṭīb repeats not only the story with the boy but the story concerning the works as well. The latter is found in its shorter form, as it was in the *Muntaẓam*. (5) The incident with the boy however, is given but with two new variants which, when seen together, give the account a rather negative tone. The author of the *Mir'āt az-Zamān* states first that the youth had accompanied al-Khaṭīb when the latter came to Damascus from Baghdād. Sibṭ ibn al-Jawzī also adds that when the chief of police came to al-Khaṭīb, he found him alone with the youth. (6)

The biographical notice least charitable by far towards al-Khaṭīb is that of Ibn Taghrī Birdī. He, like Ṣibt ibn al-Jawzī, includes both the story about the boy and that about the works. The author of the *Nujūm* repeats the statement that most of al-Khaṭīb's works made use of those of aṣ-Ṣūrī, but not only does he not exclude the *Ta'rīkh Baghdād* from this number he also adds, so that there should be no doubt: "that is, he took them in their entirety" *(ya'nī akhadhahā birumma-*

(1) Ibn al-Jawzī, v. VIII, p. 266.
(2) Ibn Kathīr, v. XII, p. 102.
(3) Aṣ-Ṣafadī, v. VII, p. 195.
(4) Adh-Dhahadī, *Ḥuffāẓ*, v. III, pp. 1141-1142.
(5) Sibṭ ibn al-Jawzī, folio 131v.
(6) Sibṭ ibn al-Jawzī, folio 132v.

tihā). (1) With the youth however, Ibn Taghrī Birdī uses the opposite tactic. Rather than repeat the story, he contents himself with the devastating remark: "his story with the youth whom he loved is well-known," and that he himself has refrained from discussing it because al-Khaṭīb was considered to be a noted theologian and *ḥadīth* transmitter. Nonetheless he tells the reader where the story can be found and cites some of the poetry al-Khaṭīb wrote to his beloved. (2)

To round out his notice, Ibn Taghrī Birdī stated that in his *Ta'rīkh Baghdād*, al-Khaṭīb "spoke in ugly words about most of the learned men of Islām," *(takallama fīhi fī ghālib 'ulamā' al-islām bil-alfāẓ al-qabīḥa)*, and used faulty *riwāyas* and *isnāds*. As a consequence, he was himself subjected to ignominious treatment. (3)

This attack upon the *Ta'rīkh Baghdād* was not an original idea with Ibn Taghrī Birdī. It brings us to another element of controversy in al-Khaṭīb's life. This involves his switch from Ḥanbalism to Shāfi'ism, his fight with the Ḥanbalīs and the composition of the *Ta'rīkh Baghdād*. In fact, al-Khaṭīb's break with the Ḥanbalīs was embedded in, and led to, an extended polemic concerning Aḥmad ibn Ḥanbal, al-Khaṭīb al-Baghdādī and the *Ta'rīkh Baghdād.* (4) For the purposes of the discussion of the biographical tradition, only those elements which are significant for the tradition itself have been selected.

(1) Ibn Taghrī Birdī, v. V, p. 87.

(2) Ibn Taghrī Birdī, v. V, pp. 87-88. One of the sources given by Ibn Taghrī Birdī is the *Muntaẓam* of Ibn al-Jawzī. The story is, however, not in the edition at hand, though it may have been included in a manuscript to which Ibn Taghrī Birdī had access.

(3) Ibn Taghrī Birdī, v. V, p. 87.

(4) This polemic developed its own literature. Ḥājjī Khalīfa cites two works: *as-Sahm al-Muṣīb fī ar-Radd 'alā al-Khaṭīb* by 'Īsā ibn Abī Bakr, and *as-Sahm al-Muṣīb fī Naḥr al-Khaṭīb* by as-Suyūṭī. See *Kashf aẓ-Ẓunūn*, ed. G. Fluegel (London: 1842), v. III, p. 632. Polemic around the *Ta'rīkh Baghdād* has apparently continued to recent times. The work by Muḥammad Zāhid al-Kawtharī, *Ta'nīb al-Khaṭīb 'alā mā Sāqahu fī Tarjamat Abī Ḥanīfa min al-Akādhīb* (Cairo: Maṭba'at Tajlīd al-Anwār, 1942), is a defense of Abū Ḥanīfa and an attack on al-Khaṭīb and the *Ta'rīkh Baghdād*. These works, though necessarily containing much biographical information, are being considered as distinct from the biographical tradition, since they do not form part of biographical compendia.

The Ḥanbalī Ibn al-Jawzī is the earliest biographer to deal with this question, and in his notice on al-Khaṭīb he gives a lengthy expose of the fight which took place between al-Khaṭīb and the Ḥanbalīs. Ibn al-Jawzī relates that al-Khaṭīb was originally a Ḥanbalī but that the followers of this school turned against him when he adopted certain theological opinions. Ibn al-Jawzī even goes so far as to state that they were nasty to him. Not only did al-Khaṭīb change to Shāfiʿism, but he also, according to this biographer, was particularly unjust to Aḥmad ibn Ḥanbal in his biography of him (1) as he was to other noted Ḥanbalīs. Ibn al-Jawzī also accuses al-Khaṭīb of being unfair and dishonest in his treatment of *ḥadīths*. (2)

The account presented by Ibn al-Jawzī is reproduced in part and with a few unimportant changes by both Yāqūt and aṣ-Ṣafadī, the principal difference being that these two authors omitted the charges concerning the *ḥadīths*. (3) Ibn Kathīr limits himself to a vey brief account of the fight with the Ḥanbalīs. (4) As-Subkī, a Shāfiʿī, notes that there was a fight and adds, on his own authority, that al-Khaṭīb suffered because of lies spread against him. (5)

Sibṭ ibn al-Jawzī gives what is probably the fullest treatment of al-Khaṭīb's fight with the Ḥanbalīs. He repeats the greater part of the discussion by his grandfather, including all the elements discussed above. In addition, however, he also describes that which Ibn Taghrī Birdī clearly referred to as "ignominious treatment." The Ḥanbalīs would, for example, block al-Khaṭīb's door at night with clay so that if he needed to make his ablutions for the morning prayer, he would miss it! (6)

From the stories so far discussed it is abundantly clear that al-Khaṭīb al-Baghdādī was a controversial figure. His biographical tradition is filled with information scarcely designed

(1) For the biography of Aḥmad ibn Ḥanbal, see *Taʾrīkh Baghdād* (Cairo: Maktabat al-Khānjī, 1931), v. IV, pp. 412-423.

(2) Ibn al-Jawzī, v. VIII, pp. 267-269.

(3) Yāqūt, v. I, pp. 246, 251; aṣ-Ṣafadī, v. VII, pp. 191, 193.

(4) Ibn Kathīr, v. XII, p. 102.

(5) As-Subkī, v. IV, p. 34.

(6) Sibṭ ibn al-Jawzī, folios 131v-132r, 133v.

to enhance the reputation of a preacher and *ḥadīth* authority. As we have seen, the selection and treatment of this material could vary from notice to notice. Every controversy, however, has two sides, and the biographical tradition also contains a considerable number of elements tending to defend the reputation of the famous *ḥāfiẓ*.

The easiest way, of course, of handling embarrassing information is to avoid mentioning it altogether. To a certain extent, all those notices in the second group discussed above (numbers 2, 19 and 22) could be said to be following this policy. It is, however, impossible to draw any firm conclusions from negative data. In many ways, Ibn Khallikān resembles these notices, except that his remark, "if he had nothing but the *Ta'rīkh*, it would have sufficed," (1) should probably be understood in reference to the accusation about the works.

Another possibility would be to accept the historicity of an event or incident and yet try to excuse it or show that it is not blameworthy. Ibn al-Jawzī, after mentioning the report that al-Khaṭīb based some of his works on those of aṣ-Ṣūrī, adds that "someone may build a road and it is walked on, but in any case this was not a shortcoming on the part of al-Khaṭīb," *(waqad yaḍa' al-insān ṭarīqan faluslak wamā qaṣṣara al-khaṭīb 'alā kull ḥāl).* (2) This remark was repeated by Yāqūt and Sibṭ ibn al-Jawzī. (3) Adh-Dhahabī was also probably employing a defense of this sort when he noted that the Ḥanbalīs sided against al-Khaṭīb "until he inclined to what he inclined to" *(ḥattā māla ilā mā māla ilayhi).* (4) Adh-Dhahabī would seem to be referring to, on the one hand the actions taken against al-Khaṭīb, and on the other, his attacks on the Ḥanbalīs in the *Ta'rīkh Baghdād*, the former having caused, or justified the latter.

In all fairness, however, it should be noted that the authors who followed Ibn al-Jawzī's account (Yāqūt, aṣ-Ṣafadī, Sibṭ ibn

(1) Ibn Khallikān, v. I, p. 92.

(2) Ibn al-Jawzī, v. VIII, p. 266.

(3) Sibṭ ibn al-Jawzī, folio 131v; Yāqūt, v. I, p. 250. The edition reads "*waqad yaḍa' al-insān ṭarīqan fayaslukuhu,*" which is probably an error.

(4) Adh-Dhahabī, *Ḥuffāẓ*, v. III, p. 1142.

TABLE: APPEARANCE OF CERTAIN INCIDENTS

	Ibn 'Asākir	Ibn al-Jawzī	Yāqūt	Sibṭ ibn al-Jawzī	adh-Dhahabī	aṣ-Ṣafadī	as-Subkī	al-Asnawī	Ibn Kathīr	Ibn Taghrī Birdī	Ibn Hidāya
Boy			X	X	X	X				X	
Alternate for leaving Damascus								X	X		X
Works		X	X	X					X	X	
Drunkenness			X			X					
Ḥanbalis and *Ta'rīkh Baghdād*		X	X	X	X	X	X		X	X	
Dream 1	X				X	X	X				
Dream 2						X					
Dream 3						X	X				
Dream 4					X	X					

al-Jawzī) order the events in such a way that the Ḥanbalī attacks on al-Khaṭīb follow his theological deviations and precede his attacks on Aḥmad ibn Ḥanbal. Their accounts, while not necessarily morally excusing al-Khaṭīb's behavior, show an appreciation of the emotional logic behind it. Ibn Taghrī Birdī is, in fact, the only author who offers the opposite interpretation, making the actions of the Ḥanbalīs a consequence of al-Khaṭīb's attack upon them in the *Ta'rīkh Baghdād.*

A third possibility in dealing with controversial information, perhaps the most direct, would be to eliminate an unhappy episode in the life of the personage and replace it with another which, while entirely blameless, might explain the facts. This was done by three of the biographers at hand with the story of the boy and al-Khaṭīb's expulsion from Damascus. Ibn Kathīr relates in his notice that it so happened that one day al-Khaṭīb sang the praises of al-'Abbās in Damascus, as a result of which the Rāfiḍī followers of the Fāṭimids were furious and wanted to kill him. Al-Khaṭīb was able to plead with the Sharīf who thereupon protected him. Al-Khaṭīb then left Damascus and took up his residence in Ṣūr. (1)

Ibn Kathīr, interestingly enough, does not cite any sources for this version. The story that al-Khaṭīb publicly praised al-'Abbās does exist in adh-Dhahabī who cites Ibn 'Asākir for it. (2) In adh-Dhahabī's account however, this incident is not linked to al-Khaṭīb's exile from Damascus, for which event adh-Dhahabī gives the more conventional story with the boy. (3) Is Ibn Kathīr simply composing another explanation by taking known incidents in the life of al-Khaṭīb and linking them in a new way?

Two other authors take this tendency a step further, while exploiting the same political conditions. Al-Asnawī explains that while al-Khaṭīb was in Damascus, the *adhān* included the formula "*ḥayya 'alā khayr al-'amal*" (this is a Shī'ī formula), (4)

(1) Ibn Kathīr, v. XII, p. 102.
(2) This account is not in either of the notices by Ibn 'Asākir cited above.
(3) Adh-Dhahabī, *Ḥuffāẓ*, v. III, pp. 1141-1142.
(4) Th. W. Juynboll, "Adhān", *EI*², v. I, pp. 193-194.

the ruler got angry at him (al-Asnawī does not explain why) and intended to kill him, but then it was agreed that he should leave, whereupon he went to Ṣūr. (1)

Ibn Hidāya also gives this explanation, adding the missing causal link. He recounts that the ruler of Damascus used to order the *mu'adhdhin* to call out the formula, but that al-Khaṭīb would repudiate it with the result, as before, that with his execution imminent, he went out to Ṣūr. (2)

Neither al-Asnawī nor Ibn Hidāya gives any sources for their accounts. They, like Ibn Kathīr, rely upon the Shī'ī/Sunnī conflict to explain al-Khaṭīb's departure from Damascus. This is not without political plausibility since al-Khaṭīb was a noted Sunnī and the rulers were Shī'īs. It is worth noting, however, that the earlier versions of this incident rely on the same Shī'ī/Sunnī conflict to explain the Sharīf's recommendation of clemency.

These last three notices are chronologically fairly late in the biographical tradition. Ibn Kathīr, although he mentioned the problem with the works, was rather noncommittal and therefore his notice leans more towards the favorable. Both al-Asnawī and Ibn Hidāya, on the other hand, paint a faultless picture of al-Khaṭīb, a prolific writer who was exiled because of his Sunnī convictions.

All of the types of defense so far discussed, though they might be used to disculpate a personality and though they might form part of a notice whose general tone was favorable, address themselves to a specific incident or incidents in the life of the personage. There is, however, another type of information present in the biographical tradition which tends, by its very nature, to give a particularly authoritative judgment of the individual. These were dreams. Ibn Khallikān mentions that after the death of al-Khaṭīb, he appeared to people in many dreams, but does not recount any. (3)

Four dreams are described in the biographical tradition.

(1) Al-Asnawī, pp. 202-203.
(2) Ibn Hidāya, p. 57.
(3) Ibn Khallikān, v. I, p. 93.

The versions in aṣ-Ṣafadī will be presented first, since he is the only biographer to include all four.

Only one of the dreams is dated. Abū al-Qāsim Makkī stated that he had this dream on the twelfth of Rabīʿ al-Awwal in the year 463, which would seem to place it shortly before the death of al-Khaṭīb. (1) At dawn, he dreamed that he saw a group sitting with al-Khaṭīb in his house in the Bāb al-Marātib (2) for the study of the *Ta'rīkh* as usual. Al-Khaṭīb was sitting and on his right another person and on the latter's right yet a third person, whom the dreamer did not recognize. He inquired as to the identity of this person, who was not in the habit of attending these sessions. He was told: this is the Prophet who has come for the reading of the *Ta'rīkh.* Here the dreamer gives away the significance of his dream: "so I said to myself, this is indeed an honor for the *shaykh* Abū Bakr [al-Khaṭīb] that the Prophet attends his gathering, and it is also a refutation of those who find fault with the *Ta'rīkh* and state that is is biased against certain people." (3)

As-Subkī and Ibn ʿAsākir in his *Tabyīn*, who also relate this dream, add yet one more element. The dreamer, after making the observation about the *Ta'rīkh Baghdād*, says that thinking about all this kept him from "pouncing" *(an-nuhūḍ ilā)* on the Prophet and asking him all sorts of questions which he wanted to ask, and he woke up immediately. (4)

As was noted above, the dreamer himself explained the significance of his dream. There are however, other elements in his account which contribute to the importance of the dream. Dreams, of course, could be true or false. For the dream to transmit effectively a judgment on al-Khaṭīb, it would have to be true. One of the indications of the veracity of a dream is the presence of one of a number of figures, chief among them the Prophet. In addition, true dreams tended to be those whose interpretation was obvious, and what could be more

(1) Two different months are given for the death of al-Khaṭīb, *Dhū al-Ḥijja* and *Shawwāl.*

(2) See Yāqūt, *Muʿjam al-Buldān* (Beirut: Dār Ṣādir, 1955), v. I, p. 312.

(3) Aṣ-Ṣafadī, v. VII, p. 197.

(4) As-Subkī, v. IV, pp. 36-37; Ibn ʿAsākir, *Tabyīn*, pp. 268-269.

obvious than this, since the dreamer himself formulated the interpretation during the course of the dream. Finally, the time of the day at which a dream took place bore upon its veracity. The Prophet was quoted as saying that the dream which is most true is the one which is seen at dawn, and Abū al-Qāsim specified that he had this dream at dawn. (1) The dreamer, who was clearly a companion of al-Khaṭīb's, spared nothing to give the dream its maximum impact.

Adh-Dhahabī, who relates this dream as well, does not include either the comment about the *Ta'rīkh Baghdād* or the mention that the dream took place at dawn. (2) Thus, the dream account is deprived of two elements which contribute to its efficacity.

The Prophet appears in another dream with al-Khaṭīb. Here, the dreamer saw a Qāḍī of Baghdād, after his death, sitting on a chair. He approached him, greeted him and shook his hand. The dreamer then turned and saw al-Khaṭīb sitting on another chair. The Qāḍī told the dreamer a certain *ḥadīth* and al-Khaṭīb answered him with something the dreamer forgot. A disagreement ensued and al-Khaṭīb said, there is the Prophet, get up so we can ask him. The two *ḥadīth* authorities then went behind a green curtain, while the dreamer stayed outside. At that point, he awoke. (3)

As with the previous example, the presence of the Prophet is a witness to its veracity. The first dream, however, while clearly defending al-Khaṭīb, was also specifically directed at charges levelled against the *Ta'rīkh Baghdād*. This second, somewhat more general, would seem to be designed to defend al-Khaṭīb's reputation as a *ḥadīth* authority.

The two remaining dreams are of the same type and can be treated together. The third dream was related by a pious man who reported that when al-Khaṭīb died, this man saw him in a dream and asked him how he was. Al-Khaṭīb replied that

(1) Toufic Fahd, "Les Songes et leur Interprétation selon l'Islam," in *Les Songes et leur Interprétation*, Sources Orientales II (Paris: Éditions du Seuil, 1959), pp. 140-142.

(2) Adh-Dhahabī, v. III, p. 1145.

(3) Aṣ-Ṣafadī, v. VII, p. 197.

he was in rest, had all good things and was in Paradise. This dream also appears in as-Subkī. (1) In the fourth, the dreamer after the death of al-Khaṭīb saw someone standing in front of him and wished to ask him where al-Khaṭīb was. The person said to him, anticipating his question, he has been assigned a place in the center of Paradise where the pious meet. This dream also appears in adh-Dhahabī. (2)

Both these dreams show al-Khaṭīb in Paradise among the blessed. It was generally accepted in Medieval Islam that one could, through the vehicle of a dream, see the condition of a person in the afterlife. (3) Thus, these dreams provide a definitive judgment on the life of al-Khaṭīb. They, thus, comment upon his life as a whole. Implied within them, however, are the refutations of any specific objections.

The biographical tradition of al-Khaṭīb al-Baghdādī at times resembles a battlefield upon which the biographers marshalled their forces. It might be tempting to see the differences in the notices as reflecting the polemics between Shāfi'īs and Ḥanbalīs, between the followers of al-Khaṭīb and those of his opponents. Indeed, the two writers who make the greatest effort to clear al-Khaṭīb's name, al-Asnawī and Ibn Hidāya, are Shāfi'īs. Nevertheless, an attempt to divide the notices along these lines is not without difficulties. Ibn Kathīr and adh-Dhahabī, while Shāfi'īs, belong to that group Laoust describes as "chafiites hanbalisants". (4) Ibn al-Jawzī, a Ḥanbalī, includes many spirited criticisms of al-Khaṭīb, but is also the author of the oft-quoted remark defending al-Khaṭīb's behavior

(1) Aṣ-Ṣafadī, v. VII, p. 197; as-Subkī, v. IV, p. 37.

(2) Aṣ-Ṣafadī, v. VII, p. 197; adh-Dhahabī, v. III, p. 1145.

(3) G. E. von Grunebaum, "La Fonction Culturelle du Rêve dans l'Islam Classique," in Roger Caillois and G. E. von Grunebaum, eds., *Le Rêve et les Sociétés Humaines* (Paris: Gallimard, 1967), pp. 15-16. The information thus given did not have to be positive. See, for example, the dream at the end of al-Khaṭīb's long and controversial biography of Abū Ḥanīfa, *Ta'rīkh Baghdād*, v. XIII, p. 423. This author hopes to further elucidate the role of the dream in biographical literature in a study currently in preparation.

(4) For a discussion of the position of several Ḥanbalīs and Shāfi'īs, see the excellent study by H. Laoust, "Le hanbalisme sous les Mamlouks Bahrides (658-784/1260-1382)," *Revue des Études Islamiques* (1960), XXVIII, pp. 1-72, and especially pp. 57-58.

on the matter of the works. If in the second group, which contains no controversial information, one finds Shāfi'īs like Ibn 'Asākir, one also finds Ḥanbalīs like Ibn al-'Imād. Besides, it is only to be expected that notices devoted to al-Khaṭīb have a greater tendency to appear in *Ṭabaqāts* of Shāfi'īs.

Furthermore, as the case of Ibn al-Jawzī shows, many of the notices were neither all-white nor all-black. Aṣ-Ṣafadī, for example, who mentioned both the youth and al-Khaṭīb's drunkenness, also repeated all four dreams. It is perfectly clear that many of the writers did not feel under the obligation of including or excluding a story simply because it was flattering or unflattering to the subject. Nor did all of the sources. Abū al-Qāsim Makkī, who had the dream at dawn, is also the source for the story about the boy. (1)

In fact, it is only on the level of the tradition as a whole that the opposing tendencies of the controversy, attack and defense, can be distinguished. This is partially because, from the point of view of the controversy itself, the biographical tradition acts as an epiphenomenon. The obituary writers, unlike the polemicists, could, if they wished, place themselves above the controversy, the effects of which are nevertheless represented in their works.

When, on the other hand, the biographical tradition is considered as a phenomenon in itself, it becomes clear that the writers employed a certain number of techniques in dealing with the information that came to them from both the life and the controversy (and, of course, other biographers as well), and that in doing so they were able to give each notice that nuance or interpretation they desired. These techniques included mentioning or omitting incidents, offering excuses or asides, presenting longer or shorter versions or variants of a story or even replacing one story with another, and relating dreams in longer or shorter forms. The use of one or more of these techniques did not, of course, preclude the careful manipulation of the language.

(1) The sources give both Abū al-Qāsim Makkī ar-Rumaylī and Abū al-Qāsim Makkī al-Maqdisī, but they are the same person. See Ibn al-Athīr, *al-Lubāb fī Tahdhīb al-Ansāb*, v. I, p. 477.

The tradition taken as a whole does seem to display a certain development. The earlier notices tend to be composite and seem close to the controversy often reflecting both sides, and often using the same sources. It is only relatively late in the tradition that one finds the much more extreme notices of Ibn Taghrī Birdī, al-Asnawī and Ibn Hidāya, which are given over completely to the attack or defense of al-Khaṭīb.

Nevertheless, every one of the authors, early or late, favorable or critical, marshalled all his historical and literary talents to paint his own portrait of al-Khaṭīb. That these portraits should have been filled with praise and polemic, controversy and defense, would certainly not have surprised the author of the *Ta'rīkh Baghdād.*

III

THE INTERRELATIONSHIP OF ONOMASTIC ELEMENTS: *ISMS*, *DÎN*-NAMES AND *KUNYAS* IN THE NINTH CENTURY A.H.

In a discussion of names introducing his *Kitâb al-Wâfî bil-Wafayât*, aṣ-Ṣafadî presents the following anecdote:

Abû al-Farağ al-Mu'âfâ ibn Zakariyyâ' an-Nahrawânî related: I was performing the pilgrimage one year and was at Munâ during the days of the Tašrîq. I heard someone calling: "O Abû al-Farağ." So I said: Perhaps the person wants me, but then I said to myself that there are many people whose *kunya* is Abû al-Farağ, and did not answer him. Then he called out: "O Abû al-Farağ al-Mu'âfâ ibn Zakariyyâ'." and I did not answer him. So he called out: "O Abû al-Farağ al-Mu'âfâ ibn Zakariyyâ' an-Nahrawânî." So I said to myself: No doubt remains that he is calling me since he mentioned my *kunya*, my name, my father's name, and my place of origin. So I replied: "Here I am, what do you wish?" But then he said: "Perhaps you are from the Nahrawân of the East?" And I said, "Yes." So he said: "We want the Nahrawân of the West." So I marvelled at the coincidence of this[1].

The coincidence is, indeed, considerable. So much so, that the reader is tempted to wonder why Abû al-Farağ took so long to reply. Much of the interest of the anecdote and the surprise at its conclusion are based on the reader's perception of the probability of separate name elements appearing together in more than one case. For the Medieval Muslim, however, the probabilities are greater than would be the case were they determined by a calculation based on the total number of separate onomastic elements. In other words, Medieval Islamic names can be studied not only for the appearance or popularity of specific names at specific times[2] but also for the patterns of interrelationship, the systems of linkage, operating between different name elements.

In this study, attention will be directd to three name elements which exhibit varying degrees of linkage, that is, given examples of one name element tend to appear with matching examples of other name elements. The name elements in question are the *ism* or first name, the *laqab* with *dîn*, hereafter referred to as the *dîn*-name, and the *kunya*. The ninth islamic century has been chosen so that the data can be treated synchronically and because of the availability of large numbers of *dîn*-names as well as contemporary analyses for comparison.

The principal source has been the section devoted to the ninth century in the *Šadarât ad-Dahab fî Ahbâr man Dahab* of Ibn al-'Imâd (d. 1089/1679)[3]. In addition, a number of selective comparisons has been made with *aḍ-Ḍaw' al-Lâmi' li-Ahl al-Qarn at-Tâsi'* of as-Saḫâwî (d. 902/1497)[4].

The Dîn-Name and Its Transformations

Of the three name elements to be discussed, the *dîn*-name is the most elusive. This is because the name is capable of changing its form. The most common transformation is that between the form Fulân ad-Dîn and the form al-Fulân, grammatical definition by the *iḍâfa* being replaced with definition by the article. Curiously enough, while other transformations of the *dîn*-name have been noted by modern scholars, as will be shown below, this most common one has not. In addition, the ninth-century encyclopedist al-Qalqašandî (d. 821/1418), whose *Ṣubḥ al-A'šâ* contains the most important discussion of *laqabs* in Medieval Islam, also omits any reference to this correspondence[5]. It is possible that al-Qalqašandî did not bother to mention this because, as we will see shortly, it was so well established in the ninth century as to be obvious, and more recent scholars have merely unwittingly echoed this silence.

Not only can any *dîn*-name take the form with the definite article but the two forms can be used interchangeably for the same personage. This means that the relationship between these two forms is more than that of derivation. If the name is conceived as a sign, one can see that while the signifieds have remained the same (the signification, it should be remembered, is dual, referring both to the specific individual and to the values embodied in the *laqab*)[6], the signifier has changed.

Exemples are manifold. Writing shortly before our period, aṣ-Ṣafadî (d. 764/1363) in his *Nakt al-Himyân fî Nukat al-'Umyân* refers in the onomastic chain to one 'Izz ad-Dîn who becomes al-'Izz in an anecdotal setting within the same notice[7]. Similarly, Muḥammad ibn 'Abd al-'Azîz, who is Nûr ad-Dîn in the onomastic chain, becomes an-Nûr later in the same notice[8]. This might make it appear that the choice is one of context: the Fulân ad-Dîn form being reserved for the onomastic chain, while the al-Fulân form would be reserved for the anecdotal setting.

But it would seem that this choice of a name with *dîn* or a name with article is not strictly one of context but one of style as well. If one examines the *Šaḏarât aḏ-Ḏahab* of Ibn al-'Imâd and *aḍ-Ḍaw' al-Lâmi'* of as-Saḫâwî, one is immediately struck by the fact that Ibn al-'Imâd shows a clear preference for the compound name with *dîn*, whereas as-Saḫâwî favors the form with the article. Furthermore, these different forms of the *dîn*-name cannot be explained as being attached to different individuals. Instead, as Table I shows, the two biographers choose different forms when referring to the same individuals.

TABLE I

	Šaḏarât	*aḍ-Ḍaw'*
1.	*Badr ad-Dîn* Ḥasan ibn Šaraf ad-Dîn Abî Bakr ibn Aḥmad	al-Ḥasan ibn Abî Bakr ibn Aḥmad *al-Badr*
2.	*Zayn ad-Dîn* 'Abd ar-Raḥmân ibn Muḥammad al-Qazwînî as-Šâfi'î	'Abd ar-Raḥmân ibn Muḥammad *az-Zayn*....al-Qazwînî.... as-Šafi'î
3.	*Ǧamâl ad-Dîn* Abû al-Maḥâsin Muḥammad ibn Mûsâ....al-Makkî	Muḥammad ibn Mûsâ....*al-Ǧamâl* ....al-Makkî
4.	*Šaraf ad-Dîn* Abû al-Fatḥ Mûsâ ibn Muḥammad al-Ba'labakkî	Mûsâ ibn Muḥammad ibn Naṣr *aš-Šaraf* Abû al-Fatḥ....al-Ba'lî
5.	*Šihâb ad-Dîn* Aḥmad ibn Ism'îl... al-Ibšîṭî[9]	Aḥmad ibn Ismâ'îl ibn Abî Bakr *aš-Šihâb* al-Ibšîṭî[10]

As the above examples show, we are in the presence of a stylistic choice on the part of the author, and a researcher examining the *Šaḏarât* would discover a large number of names on the pattern Fulân ad-Dîn, while the student of *aḍ-Ḍaw'* would find a preponderance of al-Fulân. In addition, while there may be a tendency among some authors, like aṣ-Ṣafadî, to include the Fulân ad-Dîn in the onomastic chain while reserving the form with the definite article for an anecdotal context,this is clearly not a universal principle.Both Ibn al-'Imâd and as-Saḫâwîplace their chosen forms in the onomastic chains. Finally, it should be noted that there is a small number of exceptions in which each author employs the form more normally preferred by the other.

In effect, then, this choice represents a stylistic option for the biographer. When one wishes to describe the literary characteristics of a biographical work, the organizational and stylistic choices made by the author in creating his notice, attention must also be directed to the onomastic chain and to the forms of the elements within it.

This transformation of the *dîn*-name to another *laqab*, formed with the definite article, is not the only such variation. As Garcin de Tassy, van Berchem, Caetani and Gabrieli, and Ḥasan al-Bâšâ have noted, the *dîn*-name can also take the form of the *nisba*, that is, al-Fulânî[11]. Though the above mentioned scholars have left the matter vague, it is clear that the *nisba* form need not be reserved for a new individual but can be applied to an individual otherwise addressed with the al-Fulân or Fulân ad-Dîn forms. Ibn al-Aṯîr, in his *al-Lubâb fî Tahḏîb al-Ansâb*, consecrated this usage when he described al-Ǧamâlî as being the *nisba* of him who bears the *laqab* al-Ǧamâl[12]. Al-Qalqašandî, in his *Ṣubḥ*, extended this principle to the other *dîn*-names[13]. This can be seen clearly in the case of the Hanbalî scholar Yûsuf ibn 'Abd al-Hâdî ibn al-Mibrad (d. 909/1503) whose biographers regularly call him either al-Ǧamâl or Ǧamâl ad-Dîn[14]. Yûsuf's student, Šams ad-Dîn ibn Ṭûlûn, occasionally refers to his teacher in his own autobiography as al-Ǧamâlî[15]. Nevertheless, this form of the *dîn*-name seems to be comparatively rare.

Examining these three forms together, al-Fulân, Fulân ad-Dîn, and al-Fulânî, one can easily see that they form part of an onomastic system which can be said to govern a sphere of Arabic names. Within this sphere, the elements have a strictly paradigmatic relationship: they never appear together. In effect, then, if we were to look behind the three names, Ǧamâl ad-Dîn, al-Ǧamâl, and al-Ǧamâlî, for example, to see what they possess in common, what makes them all forms of the same name, we arrive at the word Ǧamâl. This constitutes what I should like to call the onomastic stem (Semiticists might prefer the term root, but the choice of botanical metaphor is not important). The name elements themselves could then be seen as morphological variations dictated by context or choice.

There is, however, one further possible transformation, that in which the stem appears by itself, without an article, taking the form of an *ism*. In the *Šadarât ad-Dahab*, we are told that a certain Aḥmad ibn Taqî ad-Dîn was known as Ibn Taqî[16]. In *aḍ-Ḍaw' al-Lâmi'*, as-Saḫâwî explains that the *laqab* of Yûsuf ibn 'Isâ Sayf ad-Dîn was shortened to be merely Sayf, and, for that reason, his biography was to be found under the letter *sîn*[17]. It could be said, thus, that Yûsuf's *laqab* had become an *ism*.

There is no evidence, however, that this transformation operated as a general rule. In other words, unlike the situation with al-Fulân or al-Fulânî, it does not appear that the Fulân form by itself could be used freely when referring to a Fulân ad-Dîn[18]. Thus, while such a usage is tied into the onomastic stem and, hence, the other *dîn*-name forms, it is linked only by a derivation which does not possess a power of generalization. Thus, we could describe the system of relationships around the onomastic stem of a *dîn*-name as being dual. On the one hand, we have those freely exchangeable alternative forms which do not need to be established for an individual before they are used, and, on the other hand, those forms created by derivation from the stem, used in specific cases, and attached to a specific individual[19].

Dîn-Names and Isms

It can be seen from the above discussion that *dîn*-names belong to a system which could be described as closed since it involves a series of transformations of the name which, though they may be influenced by general literary context or the level of address, do not seem to be affected by other, purely onomastic, elements. *Dîn*-names are, however, linked to another system, more generally onomastic. In this system, the *dîn*-name is seen as linked to a specific *ism*, or small variety of *isms*, or vice versa. Lists of *dîn*-names and their appropriate *isms* have been provided by al-Qalqašandî and have been noted with varying degrees of precision, detail, and comprehensiveness by more recent scholars[20]. Among the functions of this essay will be to compare these descriptive and normative statements with the corpora we have derived for the ninth century from the *Šadarât ad-Dahab* and *aḍ-Ḍaw' al-Lâmi'*. Having done so, it will then be possible to examine the structural properties of this linkage system, to investigate the relationships between these linkages and those governing *kunyas*, and, finally, to explore, synchronically, the principles involved in generating and mantaining these linkage systems.

To begin, what were the most common *isms* in the ninth century? Arranging the *isms* for this period in the *Šadarât* in descending numerical order, we arrive at Table II.

TABLE II

ISMS FROM THE *ŠADARÂT* (TOTAL: 953)

Ism	*Number*	*Percent of Total*
Muḥammad	278	29
Aḥmad	154	16
ʻAlî	76	8
Ibrâhîm	50	5
ʻAbd ar-Raḥmân	47	5
ʻAbd Allâh	42	4
Abû Bakr	32	3
Yûsuf	28	3
ʻUmar	25	3
Yaḥyâ	12	1
Ḥasan	9	1
ʻAbd al-Laṭîf	8	less than 1
Maḥmûd	7	"
ʻAbd al-Qâdir	7	"
ʻUṯmân	7	"
Ismâʻîl	7	"
ʻAbd al-ʻAzîz	6	"
Sulaymân	6	"
Ḥusayn	6	"
Mûsâ	5	"
ʻAbd al-Wahhâb	5	"
Ḫalîl	4	"
Yaʻqûb	4	"
ʻAbd ar-Raḥîm	4	"
Dâwûd	4	"
Qâsim	4	"

TABLE II (continued)

ISMS FROM THE *ŠADARÂT*

Ism	*Number*	*Percent of Total*
'Abd al-Karîm	3	less than 1
'Îsâ	3	"
'Abd al-Mun'im	3	"
Names appearing twice or less	101	11
No *ism*	6	less than 1

The most striking feature of this corpus is the dominance of Muḥammad (29 %) and Aḥmad (16 %) over all other names. Even 'Alî only reflects 8% of the corpus. The apparent Sunnî bias of this list is further reinforced when we notice that there are greater numbers of both Abû Bakr and 'Umar than either Ḥasan or Ḥusayn.

The general representativeness of this group can be better judged when a comparison is made with the *isms* from *aḍ-Ḍaw' al-Lâmi'*, devoted exclusively to the ninth century.

TABLE III[21]

ISMS FROM *AḌ-ḌAW' AL-LÂMI'* (TOTAL: 10,133)

Ism	*Number*	*Percent of Total*
Muḥammad	3077	30
Aḥmad	1312	13
'Alî	778	8
Ibrâhîm	377	4
'Abd ar-Raḥmân	303	3
'Abd Allâh	292	3
Abû Bakr	271	3
'Umar	242	2
Yûsuf	167	2
Yaḥyâ	135	1
'Abd al-Qâdir	135	1
Ismâ'îl	92	1
Ḥusayn	81	1
'Abd al-'Azîz	79	1
'Abd al-Laṭîf	74	1

TABLE III (continued)

ISMS FROM *AḌ-ḌAW' AL-LÂMI'*

Ism	*Number*	*Percent of Total*
Ḥasan	70	1
Maḥmûd	65	1
'Uṯmân	61	less than 1
'Abd al-Wahhâb	53	”
al-Qâsim	52	”
Ḫalîl	51	”
Names appearing less than 50 times	2366	23

The most striking feature of this table, based on a sample ten times as large as that of the *Šaḏarât*, is its virtual identity with Table II when expressed in percentages. The only major difference is the reversal of tha relative position of 'Umar and Yûsuf.

We can now examine the linkage between these *isms* and *dîn*-names in the *Šaḏarât*. Table IV shows the *dîn*-names which appear with specific *isms*.

TABLE IV

ISMS WITH CORRESPONDING *DÎN*-NAMES IN THE *ŠAḎARÂT*[22]

Ism	*Number*	*Dîn-Name*	*Number*
Muḥammad	278	None	47
		Šams ad-Dîn	119
		Badr ad-Dîn	16
		Ǧamâl ad-Dîn	13
		Kamâl ad-Dîn	10
		Nâṣir ad-Dîn	10
		Naǧm ad-Dîn	7
		Tâǧ ad-Dîn	5
		'Izz ad-Dîn	5
		Muḥibb ad-Dîn	5
		Taqî ad-Dîn	4
		Ǧalâl ad-Dîn	4
		Šaraf ad-Dîn	4

TABLE IV (continued)

ISMS WITH CORRESPONDING *DÎN*-NAMES IN THE *ŠADARÂT*

Ism	*Number*	*Dîn-Name*	*Number*
Muḥammad (continued)		Amîn ad-Dîn	3
		Maǧd ad-Dîn	2
		Muḥyî ad-Dîn	2
		Fatḥ ad-Dîn	2
		Quṭb ad-Dîn	2
		Raḍî ad-Dîn	2
		Names occuring once	16
Aḥmad	154	None	27
		Šihâb ad-Dîn	99
		Taqî ad-Dîn	3
		Muwaffaq ad-Dîn	2
		Muḥyî ad-Dîn	2
		Muḥibb ad-Dîn	2
		'Izz ad-Dîn	2
		Burhân ad-Dîn	2
		Tâǧ ad-Dîn	2
		Names occuring once	13
'Alî	76	None	19
		'Alâ' ad-Dîn	27
		Nûr ad-Dîn	21
		Muwaffaq ad-Dîn	5
		Ṣabr ad-Dîn	1
		Šams ad-Dîn	1
		Ṣadr ad-Dîn	1
		'Afîf ad-Dîn	1
Ibrâhîm	50	None[23]	14
		Burhân ad-Dîn[24]	32
		Ṣârim ad-Dîn	3
		'Imâd ad-Dîn	1
'Abd ar-Raḥmân	47	None	12
		Zayn ad-Dîn	24

TABLE IV (continued)

ISMS WITH CORRESPONDING *DÎN*-NAMES IN THE *ŠADARÂT*

'Abd ar-Raḥmân (cont.)		Ğalâl ad-Dîn	2
		Amîn ad-Dîn	1
		Asad ad-Dîn	1
		Fatḥ ad-Dîn	1
		Rukn ad-Dîn	1
		Tâğ ad-Dîn	1
		Taqî ad-Dîn	1
		Waḥîd ad-Dîn	1
		Walî ad-Dîn	1
'Abd Allâh	42	None	18
		Ğamâl ad-Dîn[25]	18
		Taqî ad-Dîn	3
		Hizabr ad-Dîn	1
		Šaraf ad-Dîn	1
		Ğalâl ad-Dîn	1
Abû Bakr	32	None	7
		Taqî ad-Dîn	13
		Zayn ad-Dîn	5
		'Imâd ad-Dîn	2
		Šaraf ad-Dîn	1
		Raḍî ad-Dîn	1
		Ṣadr ad-Dîn	1
		Zakî ad-Dîn	1
		Kamâl ad-Dîn	1
Yûsuf	28	None	11
		Ğamâl ad-Dîn	11
		Sinân ad-Dîn	3
		'Izz ad-Dîn	2
		Ṣalâḥ ad-Dîn	1
'Umar	25	None	2
		Zayn ad-Dîn[26]	11

TABLE IV (continued)

ISMS WITH CORRESPONDING *DÎN*-NAMES IN THE *ŠADARÂT*

Ism	*Number*	*Dîn-Names*	*Number*
'Umar (continued)		Sirâğ ad-Dîn	7
		Nağm ad-Dîn	2
		Ğamâl ad-Dîn	1
		Niẓâm ad-Dîn	1
		Rukn ad-Dîn	1
Yaḥyâ	12	None	5
		Šaraf ad-Dîn	3
		Amîn ad-Dîn	1
		Muḥyî ad-Dîn	1
		Niẓâm ad-Dîn	1
		Taqî ad-Dîn	1
Ḥasan	9	None	3
		Badr ad-Dîn	4
		Ḥusâm ad-Dîn	1
		'Izz ad-Dîn	1
'Abd al-Laṭîf	8	None	1
		Sirâğ ad-Dîn	2
		'Izz ad-Dîn	1
		Zayn ad-Dîn	1
		Mu'în ad-Dîn	1
		Nağm ad-Dîn	1
		Taqî ad-Dîn	1

It is already apparent that certain *isms* are heavily dominated by given *dîn*-names: Muḥammad by Šams ad-Dîn, Aḥmad by Šihâb ad-Dîn, 'Abd ar-Raḥmân by Zayn ad-Dîn, 'Abd Allâh and Yûsuf by Ğamâl ad-Dîn, and Ibrâhîm by Burhân ad-Dîn, while 'Alî is split almost evenly by 'Alâ' ad-Dîn and Nûr ad-Dîn. For the most part, these linkages correspond with those indicated by al-Qalqašandî, if one bears in mind that the principles used by the Medieval scholar were concerned with an analytical and causative approach and not a global and synchronic one. While the largest number of correspondences fit within that group of linkages which he describes both as historically based and as associated with *qâḍîs* and *'ulamâ'*, one name, however, cannot be fit into al-Qalqašandî's schemata, and that is Abû Bakr with its predominance of Taqî ad-Dîn[27]. An examination of Table IV also shows that, in every case, there is a significant number of *dîn*-names other than the principal, linked, name. Further, many *dîn*-names appear for more than one *ism*. For these reasons, certain patterns will be easier to see if Table IV is reversed, the *dîn*-names presented with their corresponding *isms*.

TABLE V

DÎN-NAMES WITH CORRESPONDING *ISMS* IN THE *ŠAḎARÂT*

Dîn-Name	*Number*	*Ism*	*Number*
Šams ad-Dîn	122	Muḥammad	119
		Aḥmad	1
		'Alî	1
		Šams	1
Šihâb ad-Dîn	103	Aḥmad	99
		Mûsâ	1
		Muḥammad	1
		Ni'mat Allâh	1
		Rasûl	1
Zayn ad-Dîn	55	'Abd ar-Raḥmân	24
		'Umar	11
		Abû Bakr	5
		'Abd ar-Raḥîm	2
		Muḥammad	1
		'Abd al-Laṭîf	1
		'Abd al-Qâdir	1
		'Abd al-Ḫallâq	1
		'Abd al-Muġîṯ	1
		Taġrî Birmiš	1
		Ša'bân	1
		Ḫâlid	1
		Ǧa'far	1
		Bilâl	1
		Ṭâhir	1
		'Ubâda	1
		Raḍwân	1
Ǧamâl ad-Dîn	45	'Abd Allâh	18
		Muḥammad	13
		Yûsuf	11

TABLE V (continued)

DÎN-NAMES WITH CORRESPONDING *ISMS* IN THE *ŠAḎARÂT*

Dîn-Name	*Number*	*Ism*	*Number*
Ǧamâl ad-Dîn (cont.)		Aḥmad	1
		'Umar	1
		Ǧamâl	1
Burhân ad-Dîn	35	Ibrâhîm	32
		Aḥmad	2
		Ḥaydara	1
'Alâ' ad-Dîn	29	'Alî	27
		Muḥammad	1
		No *ism*	1
Badr ad-Dîn	27	Muḥammad	16
		Ḥasan	4
		Maḥmûd	4
		Ḥusayn	2
		Aḥmad	1
Taqî ad-Dîn	26	Abû Bakr	13
		Muḥammad	4
		Aḥmad	3
		'Abd Allâh	3
		Yaḥyâ	1
		'Abd al-Laṭîf	1
		'Abd ar-Raḥmân	1
Nûr ad-Dîn	24	'Alî	21
		Aḥmad	1
		Maḥmûd	1
		Muḥammad	1
Šaraf ad-Dîn	23	Muḥammad	4
		Mûsâ	3
		Yaḥyâ	3
		'Îsâ	2
		Abû Bakr	1
		Ismâ'îl	1
		Ya'qûb	1
		'Abd Allâh	1
		'Abd al-Qâdir	1
		'Abd al-Mun'im	1
		Ša'bân	1
		Ṣadîq	1

TABLE V (continued)

DÎN-NAMES WITH CORRESPONDING *ISMS* IN THE *ŠAḎARÂT*

Dîn-Name	*Number*	*Ism*	*Number*
Šaraf ad-Dîn (cont.)		Mas'ûd	1
		Nu'mân	1
		Yûnus	1
'Izz ad-Dîn	17	Muḥammad	5
		'Abd al-'Azîz	4
		Aḥmad	2
		Yûsuf	2
		Ḥasan	1
		'Abd al-Laṭîf	1
		'Abd ar-Raḥîm	1
		'Abd as-Salâm	1
Tâǧ ad-Dîn	15	Muḥammad	5
		'Abd al-Wahhâb	3
		Aḥmad	2
		Isḥâq	1
		'Abd ar-Raḥmân	1
		'Abd ar-Raḥîm	1
		Bahrâm	1
		Tâǧ	1
Ǧalâl ad-Dîn	12	Muḥammad	4
		'Abd ar-Raḥmân	2
		Naṣr Allâh	2
		Aḥmad	1
		'Abd Allâh	1
		As'ad	1
		Ġânim	1
Nâṣir ad-Dîn	11	Muḥammad	10
		Aḥmad	1
Kamâl ad-Dîn	11	Muḥammad	10
		Abû Bakr	1
Sirâǧ ad-Dîn	10	'Umar	7
		'Abd al-Laṭîf	2
		Muḥammad	1
Naǧm ad-Dîn	10	Muḥammad	7
		'Umar	2
		'Abd al-Laṭîf	1

TABLE V (continued)

DÎN-NAMES WITH CORRESPONDING *ISMS* IN THE *ŠADARÂT*

Dîn-Name	*Number*	*Ism*	*Number*
Muḥyî ad-Dîn	10	'Abd al-Qâdir	3
		Aḥmad	2
		Muḥammad	2
		Maḥmûd	1
		Yaḥyâ	1
		No *ism*	1
Ṣadr ad-Dîn	8	Sulaymân	2
		Abû Bakr	1
		Aḥmad	1
		'Alî	1
		Muḥammad	1
		'Abd ar-Raḥmân	1
		'Abd al-Mun'im	1
Mağd ad-Dîn	7	Ismâ'îl	3
		Muḥammad	2
		Faḍl Allâh	1
		Sâlim	1
Muḥibb ad-Dîn	7	Muḥammad	5
		Aḥmad	2
Muwaffaq ad-Dîn	7	'Alî	5
		Aḥmad	2
Amîn ad-Dîn	7	Muḥammad	3
		Yaḥyâ	1
		'Abd ar-Raḥmân	1
		'Abd al-Wahhâb	1
		Sâlim	1
Faḫr ad-Dîn	5	'Uṯmân	4
		Sulaymân	1
Sayf ad-Dîn	5	Muḥammad	1
		Taġrî Birmiš	1
		Ḫošqadam	1
		Aynâl	1
		Sayf	1
Sa'd ad-Dîn	4	Sa'd	2
		Muḥammad	1
		Aḥmad	1

TABLE V (continued)

DÎN-NAMES WITH CORRESPONDING *ISMS* IN THE *ŠADARÂT*

Dîn-Name	*Number*	*Ism*	*Number*
Fatḥ ad-Dîn	4	Muḥammad	2
		'Abd ar-Raḥmân	1
		Fatḥ Allâh	1
'Imâd ad-Dîn	4	Abû Bakr	2
		Aḥmad	1
		Ibrâhîm	1
'Alam ad-Dîn	4	Aḥmad	1
		Sulaymân	1
		Muḥammad	1
		Ṣâliḥ	1
Sinân ad-Dîn	3	Yûsuf	3
Ṣârim ad-Dîn	3	Ibrâhîm	3

One of the more interesting features shown by Table V is a fascinating type of name linkage. For example, among the *isms* given for Šams ad-Dîn we find the name Šams for one personage, similarly, one Tâǧ ad-Dîn carries the *ism* Tâǧ, one Ǧamâl ad-Dîn is named Ǧamâl, one Sayf ad-Dîn is also Sayf, and two Sa'd ad-Dîn-s are also Sa'd. Other examples which did not appear on either table include one Humâm whose *dîn*-name is Humâm ad-Dîn, and the single Qiwâm ad-Dîn whose *ism* is Qiwâm. What we have here is clearly the pattern Fulân, Fulân ad-Dîn. It should be stressed that this is not the same phenomenon as the transformation of the *dîn*-name discussed in the first part of this study. That transformation was reflected paradigmatically: one form of a *dîn*-name replaced another. Here, by contrast, we have a syntagmatic relationship between the Fulân and the Fulân ad-Dîn. It is reasonable to assume, however, that the sense of the transformability of *dîn*-names helps to permit the creation of an *ism* based on a *dîn* stem. For this reason, we can speak here of a situation in which two different onomastic systems, each governing *dîn*-names, have come together: the system of *dîn*-name transformation, on the one hand, and the linkage of *dîn*-names with appropriate *isms*, on the other. At the same time, this pattern of linkage allows us to see at least one of the principles governing the relationship between *ism* and *dîn*-name, that of the semantic identity of the stem.

That this semantic identity of the onomastic stem is a significant linkage principle can be seen by its extension to cases where the form of the *ism* does not look like a transformation of the *dîn* form. The two individuals called Karîm ad-Dîn in this section of the *Šadarât* both carry the *ism* 'Abd al-Karîm, while the sole Fatḥ Allâh is also Fatḥ ad-Dîn. In these cases, the linkage is clearly based upon the identity of onomastic elements.

A comparison of Tables IV and V brings a number of points sharply into focus. While from the point of view of the *ism*, 'Alî might not seem a strong linkage since it is divided between 'Alâ' ad-Dîn and Nûr ad-Dîn (with few others), from the point of view of *dîn*-names, the link is much clearer. Twenty-seven of twenty-nine 'Alâ' ad-Dîn-s are 'Alî, as are twenty-one of twenty-four Nûr ad-Dîn-s. If one starts with the *dîn*-name instead of the *ism*, the linkage is almost perfect. The situation with Ǧamâl ad-Dîn is virtually the opposite. The Ǧamâl ad-Dîn-s are divided between 'Abd Allâh, Muḥammad, and Yûsuf, but the Yûsuf-s are dominated by Ǧamâl ad-Dîn, as are the 'Abd Allâh-s. In effect, therefore, there are three types of relationships between *isms* and *dîn*-names which can be seen operating in this corpus. In the first, and simplest, there is a direct link between an *ism* and a *dîn*-name: Burhân ad-Dîn dominates the Ibrâhîm-s, just as Ibrâhîm dominates the Burhân ad-Dîn-s. In the second type of linkage, a given *ism* may be divided between two *dîn*-names, though each *dîn*-name is dominated by that *ism*. Such is the case of 'Alî discussed above. Finally, a given *dîn*-name may be associated with several *isms*, several of which it may dominate. The first type of relationship is more common than either of the other two. The overwhelming majority of the more numerous *isms* have a linkage of the first type, as does the preponderant number of the most popular *dîn*-names. Only a few of either *isms* or *dîn*-names are divided in their linkages. It is only when we get to the less common *dîn*-names and the less common *isms* that less clear relationships (or no apparent relationships at all) emerge. For this reason, it would be incorrect to say that it is either the *isms* or the *dîn*-names which form the conceptual categories, generating or dominating the linkage relationships.

The complexity and interlocking nature of these relationships can best be seen through a careful investigation of the *ism* Muḥammad and its associated *dîn*-names. Muḥammad is, of course, the most popular name, and if the situation is examined from the viewpoint of the *ism*, there is a clear linkage with Šams ad-Dîn. No other *dîn*-name is remotely close to this one among the Muḥammad-s. Similarly, and not inappropriately, Muḥammad has been linked to virtually every *dîn*-name, including many which appear only once. Among the major *dîn*-names, only Burhân ad-Dîn shows no Muḥammad, and one has to descend to cases of seven or less for this absence of Muḥammad to become more common. Despite this, there are clear cases of the second type of relationship, that in which a given *dîn*-name is made up completely of a given *ism*, though it does not represent a majority of the examples of that *ism*. Of the eleven Nâṣir ad-Dîn-s, ten are Muḥammad, as are ten of the eleven Kamâl ad-Dîn-s. With a few other *dîn*-names, the preponderance of Muḥammad is somewhat less: seven of the nine Naǧm ad-Dîn-s, five of seven Muḥibb ad-Dîn-s, and sixteen of twenty-seven Badr ad-Dîn-s. In a few cases, the name of the Prophet has a simple plurality: Šaraf ad-Dîn, 'Izz ad-Dîn, Tâǧ ad-Dîn, Ǧalâl ad-Dîn, and Amîn ad-Dîn.

But what about the nature of the most common *dîn*-names associated with Muḥammad? The most numerous after Šams ad-Dîn is Badr ad-Dîn. Van Berchem has suggested that "pour Muḥammad et Badr, ce rapport se pose peut-être sur un jeu de mots entre *badr, pleine lune*, et la bataille de Badr, où s'illustra le Prophète."[28] While a reference to the battle of Badr cannot be excluded, it would hardly seem necessary, or in keeping with the other *dîn*-names, none of which refers to places or incidents. In fact, Badr as full moon fits perfectly into an onomastic/semantic context which includes Šams, sun, and Naǧm, star. To go a step further, it may be that such 'celestial' *dîn*-names have restricted usage, which can be seen when they are examined together. Of course, the Šams ad-Dîn-s, because of their large number and virtually exclusive identification with Muḥammad, would weigh any sample. If one combines, however, the only other celestial *dîn*-names, Badr ad-Dîn and Naǧm ad-Dîn, one arrives at the following list: of thirty-seven cases, twenty-three are Muḥammad, four are Ḥasan, four Maḥmûd, two 'Umar, two Ḥusayn, one 'Abd al-Laṭîf, and one Aḥmad. Clearly, Muḥammad dominates.

When we turn to the less common *dîn*-names, the situation is more complex. Not only are there relatively few strong linkages but the small size of the samples makes generalization difficult. It is probably not coincidental, however, that all Sinân ad-Dîn-s are Yûsuf, and all three Ṣârim ad-Dîn-s are Ibrâhîm. Few other patterns are apparent other than the general ubiquity of Muḥammad and Aḥmad.

Isms, Kunyas, and Dîn-Names

Of course, *dîn*-names are not the only onomastic elements linked to *isms*. It has been observed that *kunyas* are also linked to *isms*. It must be remembered here that *kunyas* are not simply names based on the oldest son of a personage, but are honorific forms of address reserved for special circumstances and frequently given to the child at birth[29].

TABLE VI

ISMS AND *KUNYAS* IN THE *ŠADARĀT*

Ism	*Number*	*Kunya*	*Number*
Muḥammad	278	None	206
		Abû 'Abd Allâh	21
		Abû Ḥâmid	6
		Abû al-Ma'âlî	5
		Abû al-Fatḥ	4
		Abû al-Barakât	4
		Abû al-Yumn	4
		Abû al-Maḥâsin	3
		Abû aṭ-Ṭâhir	3
		Abû aṭ-Ṭayyib	3
		Abû Bakr	2
		Abû al-Faḍl	2
		Abû al-Ḫayr	2
		Abû al-Qâsim	2
		Abû al-Baqâ'	2
		Kunyas occuring once	9
Aḥmad	154	None	118
		Abû al-'Abbâs	23
		Abû al-Faḍl	2
		Kunyas occuring once	11
'Alî	76	None	47
		Abû al-Ḥasan	26
		Abû al-Futûḥ	1
		Abû al-Ma'âlî	1
		Abû Zayd	1

TABLE VI (continued)

ISMS AND *KUNYAS* IN THE ṢA*D*ARÂT

Ism	*Number*	*Kunya*	*Number*
Ibrâhîm	50	None	38
		Abû Isḥâq	7
		Abû Muḥammad	2
		Abû al-Ḫayr	1
		Abû Sâlim	1
		Abû Bakr	1
ʿAbd ar-Raḥmân	47	None	32
		Abû al-Faḍl	3
		Abû al-Faraǧ	3
		Abû Muḥammad [30]	2
		Abû Hurayra	2
		Abû Zayd [31]	2
		Abû Ḏarr	1
		Abû al-Maḥâmid	1
		Abû Bakr	1
ʿAbd Allâh	42	None	35
		Abû Muḥammad	3
		Abû al-Maʿâlî	2
		Abû al-Fatḥ	1
		Abû Umm Sibṭ al-Mâridîn	1
Abû Bakr	32	None	35
		Abû al-Ṣidq	3
		Abû al-Manâqib	1
Yûsuf	28	None	25
		Abû al-Maḥâsin	2
		Abû al-Muẓaffar	1
ʿUmar	25	None	21
		Abû Ḥafṣ	3
		Abû al-Futûḥ	1
Yaḥyâ	12	None	10
		Abû Zakariyyâ	2
Ḥasan	9	None	7
		Abû ʿUmar	1
		Abû Aḥmad	1

The only clear cases of a linkage relationship of the first type, in this context categorical identity between *ism* and *kunya*, are Abû al-Ḥasan/'Alî, and, to a lesser extent, Abû al-'Abbâs/Aḥmad, and Abû Isḥâq/Ibrâhîm. If the material is examined by *kunyas*, these linkages stand out more clearly as does that of Abû 'Abd Allâh with Muḥammad.

TABLE VII

SELECT *KUNYAS* WITH *ISMS* IN THE *ŠAḎARÂT*

Kunya	*Number*	*Ism*	*Number*
Abû 'Abd Allâh	21	Muḥammad	21
Abû al-'Abbâs	24	Aḥmad	23
		Muḥammad	1
Abû al-Ḥasan	27	'Alî	26
		No *ism*	1
Abû Ḥâmid	6	Muḥammad	6
Abû Isḥâq	7	Ibrâhîm	7

In these cases, the linkage of the specific *kunya* with its *ism* is clear even though in the case of Muḥammad, the *kunya* could not pretend to dominate the *ism*. For the most part, our samples agree with the non-quantitative list of equivalences presented by Caetani and Gabrieli. There are, however, significant variations, as can be seen in Table VIII.

TABLE VIII

Kunya	*Number*	*Ism*	*Number*
Abû Ḥâmid	6	Muḥammad	6
Abû al-Ma'âlî	8	Muḥammad	5
		'Abd Allâh	2
		'Alî	1

First of all, Caetani and Gabrieli do not give Abû Ḥâmid as a *kunya* for Muḥammad, though the linkage between that *kunya* and its *ism* is complete in our sample. Similarly, the Italian scholars only give al-Ḥasan and Šukr as *isms* for Abû al-Ma'âlî, whereas our sample gives three other names, of which Muḥammad is by far the most important[32].

Far more significant than the possible additions or corrections that can be made to previous lists is the fact that we are now in a position to examine these two different linkage systems, that of *ism* to *dîn*-name and that of *ism* to *kunya*, and to see to what extent they influence each other, and whether, in fact, one can speak of a *dîn*-name/*kunya* linkage as an independent variable.

The problem of potential linkages between *dîn*-names and *kunyas*, or, stated another way, that of the relationships between the *ism*/*dîn*-name and *ism*/*kunya* linkage systems can best be examined in what we called above the second and third types of linkage systems, that is, where the two categories being linked do not coincide. If, for example, we were to look at the Aḥmad/Šihâb ad-Dîn/Abû al-ʻAbbâs linkages, we would find that since each series displays a linkage of the first type, the two series match perfectly. If A equals B and B equals C, than A will equal C. Instead, we will be able to examine linkages of the second and third types if we start with the appellations Nûr ad-Dîn, ʻAlâʼ ad-Dîn, and Ǧamâl ad-Dîn.

TABLE IX

SELECT *DÎN*-NAMES WITH *ISMS* AND *KUNYAS* IN THE *ŠAḎARÂT*

Dîn-Name	*Number*	*Ism*	*Number*	*Kunya*	*Number*
Nûr ad-Dîn	24	ʻAlî	21	None	15
				Abû al-Ḥasan	6
		Aḥmad	1	None	1
		Maḥmûd	1	Abû aṯ-Ṯanâʼ	1
		Muḥammad	1	Abû al-Maʻâlî	1
ʻAlâʼ ad-Dîn	29	ʻAlî	27	None	14
				Abû al-Ḥasan	12
				Abû al-Futûḥ	1
		Muḥammad	1	None	1
		No *ism*	1	Abû al-Ḥasan	1
Ǧamâl ad-Dîn	45	ʻAbd Allâh	18	None	15
				Abû Muḥammad	1
				Abû Umm Sibṭ al-Mâridîn	1
				Abû al-Maʻâlî	1
		Muḥammad	13	None	10
				Abû al-Maḥâsin	2
				Abû Ḥâmid	1

TABLE IX (continued)

SELECT *DÎN*-NAMES WITH *ISMS* AND *KUNYAS* IN THE *ŠADARÂT*

Dîn-Name	*Number*	*Ism*	*Number*	*Kunya*	*Number*
Ğamâl ad-Dîn(cont.)		Yûsuf	11	None	9
				Abû al-Maḥâsin	2
		Aḥmad	1	None	1
		'Umar	1	Abû Ḥafṣ	1
		Ğamâl	1	None	1

The first and most obvious point that can be made is that the *kunyas* do not respond in any way to the division among the 'Alî-s between Nûr ad-Dîn-s and 'Alâ' ad-Dîn-s; the *ism* remains the dominant category. Further, though one 'Alâ' ad-Dîn is Abû al-Futûḥ, none of the other *isms* which can be found under Nûr ad-Dîn or 'Alâ' ad-Dîn has a *kunya* other than Abû al-Ḥasan. The only case where we see an apparent connection between *dîn*-name and *kunya* is with the 'Alâ' ad-Dîn Abû al-Ḥasan, who has no *ism*. Here, we may speak of an *ism* whose nature would be dictated by other elements, or simply the fortuitous omission of the *ism* by Ibn al-'Imâd. In fact, given that the non-'Alî *isms* have other *kunyas*, we can say that the *ism*/*dîn*-name linkage (which is of the second type) and the *ism*/*kunya* linkage (which is of the first type) operate independently of each other.

With Ğamâl ad-Dîn, the situation, of course, is reversed, since there are three major *isms*, 'Abd Allâh, Muḥammad, and Yûsuf. With 'Abd Allâh, there are too few *kunyas* to be significant. It may be important, however, that two of the Muḥammad Ğamâl ad-Dîn-s are Abû al-Maḥâsin, as are two of the Yûsuf-s. This association of Abû al-Maḥâsin with Ğamâl ad-Dîn can best be seen in the following table.

TABLE X

ABÛ AL-MAḤÂSIN IN THE *ŠADARÂT*

Dîn-Name	*Number*	*Ism*	*Number*
Ğamâl ad-Dîn	4	Yûsuf	2
		Muḥammad	2
Badr ad-Dîn	1	Muḥammad	1
Zayn ad-Dîn	1	Taġrî Birmiš	1

Clearly, four of the six Abû al-Maḥâsin-s are Ğamâl ad-Dîn. If we remember that Ğamâl ad-Dîn is a relatively unimportant *dîn*-name for

Muḥammad while it is the dominant one for Yûsuf, then a strong relationship between Yûsuf, Ğamâl ad-Dîn, and Abû al-Maḥâsin is suggested. We can both get a better view of this relationship and obtain a limited cross-check of our data by examining the relatively large sample of Yûsuf-s in *aḍ-Ḍaw' al-Lâmi'* of as-Saḥâwî.

TABLE XI

YÛSUF IN *AḌ-ḌAW' AL-LÂMI'*

Dîn-Name	Number	Kunya	Number
Ğamâl ad-Dîn	73	None	54
		Abû al-Maḥâsin	17
		Abû 'Abd Allâh	1
		Abû Muḥammad	1
Salâḥ ad-Dîn	2	None	2
Zayn ad-Dîn	2	None	2
Dîn-Names occuring once	7	None	7

The majority of Yûsuf-s are Ğamâl ad-Dîn and the most common *kunya* for the Yûsuf Ğamâl ad-Dîn-s is Abû al-Maḥâsin. In addition, the two other *kunyas* present may be suggestive. Abû 'Abd Allâh is normally the *kunya* for Muḥammad, Abû Muḥammad that of 'Abd Allâh. The presence of these two *kunyas* may be a reflection of the fact that the three most common *isms* occuring with Ğamâl ad-Dîn are indeed Yûsuf, 'Abd Allâh, and Muḥammad.

For the most part, Table XI serves to confirm the data in Table X as well as the linkage between Yûsuf and Ğamâl ad-Dîn. Taken together, Tables IX, X, and XI do show the general independence of the *ism/dîn*-name and the *ism/kunya* linkages. There does, however, seem to be some tendency, apparently independent of the *ism*, to link Abû al-Maḥâsin and Ğamâl ad-Dîn, but the case of the Muḥammad Abû al-Maḥâsin Badr ad-Dîn shows the limits of this tendency.

Conclusions

In sum, therefore, we have a series of reasonably distinct onomastic systems which can be divided between transformation systems and linkage systems, and it has been shown that, in certain cases (like the Fulân Fulân ad-Dîn), these two systems overlap and appear to influence one another. The linkage systems can be divided into a *dîn*-name/*ism* system, on the one hand, and a *kunyalism* system, on the other.Though these two linkage systems do appear to influence one another to some degree, they do not do so to an extent that would permit us to speak of an independent *dîn*-name/*kunya* linkage system.

In the course of our discussion of both the linkage systems and their contacts with the transformation system, we have had occasion to refer to what were, in effect, explanations of the nature of these linkage systems. In addition, it should be apparent by now that these systems are in a certain sense languages or, more properly speaking, semiotic systems. As such, they are second order systems whose elements have their own independent significations. And, despite some similarities, their closest parallels are not language-like systems which tend to directly communicate a consciously perceived message but what can be called social and cultural organizational systems, like menus (and their seasonal distributions), interior decoration and house plans, or systems for the arrangement of clothing in a wardrobe[33]. This helps to explain not only the occasional lack of rigor in these systems but the more fundamental fact of the coexistence of at least three distinct systems in a state of semi-independence. A fourth system, barely touched upon in this study, would be the onomastic discourse system which determines which names or which forms of names should be used inwhich contexts, and which itself ties into other linguistic and literary codes[34].

We can, nevertheless, speak of significations attached to these systems, which significations can also be seen as the logic behind the linkage systems. The first signified, of course, is general: it is that of cultural order. Arranging names in multiple patterns reinforces the sense of an articulated and ordered universe. Onomastic systems like these are just as much a creation of intricate order out of chaos as is theology or the visual arts. Cultural order as a signified is only reinforced by the fact that the principles of order themselves reflect many of the society's values.

What then are these values? Or, to put it another way, what are the principles governing the linkage system? The most important is usually explained as a combination of history, precedence, and usage. For example, a famous individual took a *dîn*-name or (especially in the case of supra-historical figures like prophets) had a given *kunya*, and these practices were reinforced through usage. Similarly, a usage of unknown origin is often credited with the link. In effect, this is the only argument advanced by Caetani and Gabrieli for the *dîn*-name/*ism* linkage and is also used by these authors for the *kunya*/*ism* linkage[35]. There are, however, limits to the explanatory powers of this principle. Al-Qalqašandî shows, for example, that there is a bewildering variety of different precedents and usages. Even more important, he observes that by his time many people had become dissatisfied with accepted linkages simply because they were so common and had begun, therefore, to depart from them[36] (and this in a society which is often thought of as fundamentally conservative). For these reasons, one could argue that, while usage certainly is an essential element of any functioning system, precedence is not sufficient to maintain a pattern, unless this pattern expresses other cultural values.

This, of course, leads to other, extra-historical principles. The first, and most obvious, is what we have called semantic identity, i.e. Fulân Fulân ad-Dîn. We saw above the connection between 'Abd al-Karîm and Karîm ad-Dîn, and we do have one 'Abd al-Karîm who is not only Karîm ad-Dîn but also Abû al-Makârim. Here, rather than a pure semantic identity, we have a morphological shift easily recognizable by the audience of the period, and which preserves a relationship of signification. This sort of relationship is equally apparent in linkages like 'Izz ad-Dîn/'Abd al-'Azîz, and 'Alî/'Alâ' ad-Dîn[37]. It can be asked, however, whether euphony is not also playing a role. Thanks to the morphology of Arabic, these grammatically related words with similar meanings are generally considered euphonious combinations. An element of euphony may be present in the linkage Ibrâhîm/Burhân ad-Dîn (*b-r-h-m/n*), though a theological signification is also intended.

This brings us to the last of the major types of linkage. This is a linkage which establishes a relationship between a given name and a quality (or, in the case, of *kunyas*, another name) independent of any grammatical or phonological relationship. 'Alî and his *dîn*-names are a good example, though Muḥammad shows the potential flexibility of such a system. In these cases, since the link is purely one of signification, we can speak of cultural micro-systems, of which the celestial *dîn*-names of Muḥammad would be a good example. The relationship Yûsuf/Ǧamâl ad-Dîn can also be seen in this light, since Yûsuf was known for his beauty (Ǧamâl equals beauty). This might also explain the presence of Abû al-Maḥâsin in this context (derived from *ḥ-s-n*, to be beatiful) and its special relationship with Ǧamâl ad-Dîn.

What is most characteristic of these linkage systems as a whole is not simply that they articulate Islamic values but also that they are generated and maintained by different kinds of principles. One can even speak of rules that occasionally operate within the system itself, like the apparent potential reversibility of relationships between names. ʻAbd Allâh/Abû Muḥammad is balanced by Muḥammad/Abû ʻAbd Allâh. On the one hand, these interlocking, often partial, and sometimes contradictory principles and systems reflect the historically developed nature of Medieval Arabic names. On the other hand, they also define a larger onomastic system which both created some sense of order and articulated the values of the civilization while leaving room for variety, individual expression, and finally, individual identification. It is this ambiguity between the potential linkage and potential independence of name elements which provides the tensions exploited in aṣ-Ṣafadî's anecdote.

NOTES

1. Aṣ-Ṣafadî, *Kitâb al-Wâfî bil-Wafayât*, ed. H. Ritter (Wiesbaden, 1962), v. 1, p. 35.

2. For some recent studies of the shifting popularity of Islamic first names, see R. W. Bulliet, "First Names and Political Change in Modern Turkey", *International Journal of Middle East Studies*, IX (1978), pp. 484-495; Richard W. Bulliet, *Conversion to Islam in the Medieval Period, An Essay in Quantitative History* (Cambridge, 1979); R. Traini, *Sources biographiques des Zaïdites (années 122-1200 h.): lettres alif-ḥâ'* (Paris, 1977), pp. xiii-xxiii.

3. Ibn al-ʻImâd, *Šaḏarât aḏ-Ḏahab fî Aḫbâr man Ḏahab* (Beirut, n.d.), v. VII, in its entirety.

4. As-Saḫâwî, *aḍ-Ḍaw' al-Lâmiʻ li-Ahl al-Qarn at-Tâsiʻ* (Beirut, n.d.).

5. Al-Qalqašandî, *Ṣubḥ al-Aʻšâ* (Cairo, n.d.), v. V, pp. 438-506; and, also, v. VI, p. 5ff. Cf., however, the transformations attendant upon conversion, v. V, pp. 490-491.

6. For this dual signification of many Medieval Arabic name elements, see my "Pour une rhétorique onomastique: les noms des aveugles chez aṣ-Ṣafadî", *Cahiers d'Onomastique Arabe*, I (1979), pp. 7-19.

7. Aṣ-Ṣafadî, *Nakt al-Himyân fî Nukat al-ʻUmyân*, ed. Ahmad Zakî Bâšâ (Cairo, 1911), p. 142.

8. Aṣ-Ṣafadî, *Nakt*, p. 255.

9. Ibn al-'Imâd, *Šadarât*, v. VII, pp. 217, 217, 161, 162, and 336.

10. As-Saḫâwî, *aḍ-Ḍaw'*, v. III, p. 836; v. IV, p. 154; v. X, p. 56; v. X, p. 191; and v. I, p. 235.

11. Garcin de Tassy, "Mémoire sur les noms propres et sur les titres Musulmans", *Journal Asiatique*, sér. 5, III (1854), p. 461; Max von Berchem, *Matériaux pour un Corpus Inscriptionum Arabicarum* (Cairo, 1903), v. I, p. 449; Leone Caetani and Giuseppe Gabrieli, *Onomasticon Arabicum, ossia repertorio alfabetico dei nomi di persona...* (Rome, 1915), p. 196, note 1; Ḥasan al-Bâšâ, *al-Alqâb al-Islâmiyya fî at-Ta'rîḫ wal-Waṯâ'iq wal-Âṯâr* (Cairo, 1957), p. 153.

12. Ibn al-Aṯîr, *al-Lubâb fî Tahḏîb al-Ansâb* (Baghdad, n.d.), v. I, p. 290.

13. Al-Qalqašandî, *Ṣubḥ*, v. V, p. 504.

14. For a list of biographies and an onomastic discussion, see Fedwa Malti-Douglas, "Yûsuf ibn 'Abd al-Hâdî and his autograph of the *Wuqû' al-Balâ' bil-Bukhl wal-Bukhalâ*" *Bulletin d'Etudes Orientales*, XXXI (1979), pp. 17-24.

15. See, for example, Ibn Ṭûlûn, "al-Fulk al-Mašḥûn fî Aḥwâl Muḥammad ibn Ṭûlûn", in *Rasâ'il Ta'rîḫiyya* (Damascus, 1930), p. 17. See, also, as-Saḫâwî, *aḍ-Ḍaw'*, v. X, p. 322.

16. Ibn al-'Imâd, Šadarât, v. VII, p. 242.

17. As-Saḫâwî, *aḍ-Ḍaw'*, v. X, p. 327.

18. According to Garcin deTassy, "Au lieu d'exprimer en entier ces surnoms composés, on n'exprime souvent, pour abréger, que la première partie du composé." He gives, as examples, cases like Farîd for Farîd ad-Dîn, Kamâl Pâšâ for Kamâl ad-Dîn. His conclusions, however, are open to doubt from several points of view. First of all, he may have confused the replacement of definition by the *iḍâfa* by definition by the article, on the one hand, with a transformation to an *ism*-like form, on the other, especially since, in his discussion, he tends to cite *nisbas* without the article. Finally, given that the author has based his discussion on a manuscript in his exclusive possession, which he declined to identify, by author or title, we cannot be sure that he was not looking at a particular type of linkage in which the *ism* is identical to the onomastic stem of the *dîn*-name, to be discussed below. Garcin de Tassy, "Mémoire", pp. 468-469, 473. Of course, *dîn*-name stems underwent a general transformation (as opposed to a paradigmatic option) to *ism*-like forms under the Ottomans, influencing the modern forms. See J. H. Kramers, "Les noms musulmans composés avec Dîn", *Acta Orientalia*, V (1926), p. 66.

19. It is possible that this is the case with *kunyas* like Abû al-'Alâ', but the matter requires further study.

20. Caetani and Gabrieli, *Onomasticon Arabicum*, pp. 201-202, note 2; van Berchem, *Corpus Inscriptionum*, v. I, p. 124, note 4; Ḥasan al-Bâšâ, *al-Alqâb* (who tends to follow al-Qalqašandî); Ignaz Goldziher, " 'Alî b. Mejmûn al-Maġribî und sein Sittenspiegel des östlichen Islam", *Zeitschrift der Deutschen Morgenländischen Gesellschaft*, XXVIII (1874), pp. 306-307; Franz Babinger, "Schejch Bedr ed-dîn, der Sohn des Richters von Simâw", *Der Islam*, XI (1921), p. 20, note 3. For lists of *dîn*-names, without discussions of linkages, see, among others, O. Codrington, *A*

Manual of Musalman Numismatics (London, 1904), pp. 58-76; Kramers, "Noms musulmans", p. 67; Albrecht Dietrich, "Zu den mit *ad-dîn* zusammengesetzten islamischen Personennamen", *Zeitschrift der Deutschen Morgenländischen Gesellschaft*, CX (1961), pp. 45-54, which lists the names omitted by Kramers.

21. This table was formed from the various tables of contents of *aḍ-Ḍaw'*, which is, of course, organized by *isms*. Of the personages listed by names other than *isms*, arranged towards the end of the work, only the Abû Bakr-s were counted. The rest were treated as having no *ism*.

22. All *dîn*-names have been presented in the form Fulân ad-Dîn. In fact, there was only a handful of other *dîn*-name forms in the work.

23. One Ibrâhîm also had the *ism* Burhân.

24. Includes one doubled with Taqî ad-Dîn. In these cases, preference was given to the name listed first, or clearly preferred by the biographer.

25. Includes one doubled with Quṭb ad-Dîn.

26. Includes one doubled with Sirâǧ ad-Dîn.

27. Al-Qalqašandî, *Ṣubḥ*, v. V, pp. 488-491. Cf. Caetani and Gabrieli, *Onomasticon Arabicum*, pp. 201-202, note 2.

28. Van Berchem, *Corpus Inscriptionum*, v. I, p. 124, note 4.

29. Caetani and Gabrieli, *Onomasticon Arabicum*, p. 103ff., where the authors distinguish genealogical and metaphorical *kunyas*; Ignaz Goldziher, *Muslim Studies*, ed. S.M. Stern (Chicago, 1967), v. I, p. 242; George Makdisi, "Autograph Diary of an Eleventh-Century Historian of Baghdâd–III", *Bulletin of the School of Oriental and African Studies*, XIX (1957), pp. 16, 32.

30. Includes one doubled with Abû al-Faraǧ.

31. Includes one doubled with Abû Hurayra.

32. Caetani and Gabrieli, *Onomasticon Arabicum*, p. 111.

33. Roland Barthes, "Eléments de sémiologie", *Communications*, IV (1964), p. 117; Roland Barthes, *Mythologies* (Paris, 1957), p. 191ff.

34. Malti-Douglas, "Yûsuf ibn 'Abd al-Hâdî", p. 19.

35. Caetani and Gabrieli, *Onomasticon Arabicum*, p. 110, 201-202, note 2.

36. Al-Qalqašandî, *Ṣubḥ*, v. V, pp. 488-491.

37. Cf. Caetani and Gabrieli, *Onomasticon Arabicum*, p. 110, who discuss this principle with *kunyas*.

IV

POUR UNE RHETORIQUE ONOMASTIQUE
LES NOMS DES AVEUGLES CHEZ AṢ-ṢAFADÎ

Comme l'a noté Jacqueline Sublet dans "La prosopographie arabe", les noms propres arabes couvrent un champ onomastique qui s'étend des noms personnels et patronymiques (c'est-à-dire les *isms*, *kunyas*, etc.) jusqu'aux noms d'apparence attributive ou caractérisante (c'est-à-dire les *laqabs*, *nisbas*, etc.)[1]. Mais tous ces noms, et plus particulièrement ceux d'apparence attributive, possèdent une bipolarité fondamentale. D'une part selon Roland Barthes: "Le Nom propre dispose des trois propriétés ... le pouvoir d'essentialisation (puisqu'il ne désigne qu'un seul réferent), le pouvoir de citation (puisqu'il peut appeler à discrétion toute l'essence enfermée dans le nom, en le proférant), le pouvoir d'exploration (puisque l'on "déplie" un nom propre exactement comme on fait d'un souvenir)"[2]. D'autre part, ils gardent leur sens primitif et extra-onomastique d'attribution ou de caractérisation directe. Il est évident que le chercheur arabisant ou islamisant ne peut se fier aux significations littérales des *nisbas* ou des *laqabs* étant donné les possibilités presque illimitées de dérivation, linguistique ou autre[3]. En effet, le nom attributif crée un lien entre le personnage et l'attribution. Mais étant donné les ambiguïtés essentielles des noms arabes, on ne peut jamais délimiter d'avance la nature de ce lien. L'attribution définit-elle le personnage? Ou le personnage l'attribution? Ou quoi que ce soit d'autre? En termes linguistiques chaque nom attributif possède en tant que signifiant au moins deux signifiés, à la fois distincts et unis. d'une part le personnage lui-même, d'autre part le concept.

C'est cet aspect des noms propres arabes que nous allons examiner à travers les noms d'aveugles qui font référence à leur cécité: les noms par lesquels les aveugles sont appelés ou caractérisés comme étant aveugles. Le texte de base sera le *Nakt al-Himyân fî Nukat al-'Umyân* d'aṣ-Ṣafadî (m. 764 h.), oeuvre qui renferme la plus grande collection connue de biographies d'aveugles de l'Islam et qui est probablement le livre sur les aveugles le plus important qui nous soit parvenu.

L'appellation la plus répandue est aḍ-Ḍarîr (l'aveugle), qui est donnée pour 135 des 314 personnages. Dans tous les cas sauf deux, aḍ-Ḍarîr se trouve dans la liste des appellations, généralement en début de notice où se trouvent les informations onomastiques[4]. En effet, cette appellation est si fréquente que l'on se demande, dans certains cas, si elle faisait partie primitivement du nom du personnage ou si elle a été ajoutée postérieurement par aṣ-Ṣafadî. Il se peut que cette expression ait prédominé car elle était considérée comme la façon la plus polie de désigner un aveugle[5]. De plus, la fréquence de ce nom aḍ-Ḍarîr est attestée par aḏ-Ḏahabî dans son *al-Muštabih fî ar-Riǧâl* et par Ibn Ḥaǧar al-'Asqalânî dans son *Tabṣîr al-Muntabih bi-Taḥrîr al-Muštabih*, qui l'accompagnent d'un lapidaire: *aḍ-Ḍarîr kaṯîr*[6]. Finalement, aḍ-Ḍarîr est la seule appellation qui, dans le *Nakt*, soit tirée de la racine ḍ–r–r.

Tel n'est pas le cas des racines '–m–y et k–f–f. On trouve en effet dix exemples du surnom al-A'mâ, l'aveugle, tous dans la section onomastique des notices. Mais il y a aussi un homme qui porte la *šuhra* al-U'aymî[7], diminutif qui veut dire le petit aveugle[8]. A l'encontre de la racine ḍ–r–r, ni le *Muštabih* d'aḏ-Ḏahabî, ni le *Tabṣîr* d'Ibn Ḥaǧar ne donnent d'exemples de la racine '–m–y. Moins communes encore sont les appellations al-Kafîf (quatre fois, dont une se manifeste en *šuhra*) et al-Makfûf (trois fois). On ne trouve pas ces deux surnoms dans les oeuvres spécialisées citées plus haut[9].

La dernière appellation qui nous intéresse, mais qui néanmoins pose le plus grand nombre de problèmes, est al-Baṣîr. Parce que le sens ordinaire de ce mot est le "voyant" ou "celui qui voit", dérivé de la racine b–ṣ–r dont la signification de base est la vue (au sens propre ou figuré), sa présence chez les aveugles prête à équivoque[10]. Pour cette raison, ce phénomène a provoqué beaucoup de discussion, tant chez les Arabes du moyen-âge que chez les arabisants modernes. Avant d'aborder les données d'aṣ-Ṣafadî et pour mieux voir la facture de notre auteur, il nous faut examiner les études des lexicographes, grammairiens et chercheurs.

En effet, si le mot *baṣîr* pouvait avoir la signification d'aveugle, il serait un exemple de *ḍidd* (pl. *aḍdâd*), mot qui est censé avoir deux significations opposées. Dans ce cas, son utilisation chez les aveugles serait tout à fait normale. Saïd Boustany et David Cohen ont inclus *baṣîr* dans la liste des *aḍdâd* qui se trouve dans la collection d'études les plus approfondies sur les *aḍdâd* et les phénomènes connexes, *L'Ambivalence dans la culture arabe*[11]. Décision raisonnable étant donné que *baṣîr* est considéré comme tel dans les livres sur les *aḍdâd* de Quṭrub (m. 206 h.)[12], d'as-Siǧistânî (m. 255 h.)[13], d'al-Luġawî (m. 351 h.)[14], et d'Ibn Dahhân (m. 569 h.). Le dernier de ces auteurs, Ibn Dahhân, ne fait qu'indiquer que *baṣîr* veut dire: le voyant (*al-baṣîr*) ou: l'aveugle (*al-a'mâ*)[15]. Des trois autres sources, al-Luġawî est le plus explicite puisqu'il nous présente les arguments de ses prédécesseurs, Quṭrub et as-Siǧistânî. Il cite Quṭrub pour qui *al-baṣîr* est à la fois celui dont la vue est correcte et celui qui est aveugle. Al-Luġawî continue en notant d'après as-Siǧistânî que l'expression *baṣîra* est utilisée pour une femme aveugle. Al-Luġawî ajoute l'histoire rapportée par as-Siǧistânî: un homme lui dit qu'il avait une mère "baṣîra", voulant dire par là qu'elle était aveugle[16]. En somme, tout ce qu'on trouve dans ces livres spécialisés, ce sont quelques affirmations et une anecdote à titre d'exemple. D'autre part, notons le fait, moins significatif bien sûr, que *baṣîr* n'est pas mentionné dans toutes les oeuvres spécialisées ou collections d'*aḍdâd*[17].

Mais en dehors des problèmes associés avec la non-inclusion de *baṣîr* dans quelques collections d'*aḍdâd*, restent les problèmes posés par son inclusion même. Si le concept du *ḍidd* est limité aux vrais cas de polysémie ou d'homonymie des opposés, il se pourrait que *baṣîr* ne soit pas un vrai *ḍidd*[18]. Même le fait d'inclusion pourrait être équivoque. Car il semblerait que les auteurs arabes médiévaux, soucieux d'allonger leurs oeuvres et de les rendre plus touffues, avaient tendance à y ajouter des exemples dont l'appartenance à la classe était douteuse. Aṣ-Ṣafadî lui-même n'évite pas ce piège[19].

Pour mettre un peu d'ordre dans la variété des *aḍdâd* donnés, Cohen a créé la catégorie d'*aḍdâd* rhétoriques. Mais c'est quand on essaie de préciser le type ou la nature de la figure rhétorique que la situation se complique. Cohen qui considère *baṣîr* comme un cas d'euphémisme suit une tradition déjà ancienne[20]. Avant d'aborder la discussion sur ce point, notons que le terme "euphémisme" possède au moins deux usages qu'il faut distinguer et dont l'un est plus courant aujourd'hui. La définition la plus courante est: "expression atténuée d'une notion dont l'expression directe aurait quelque chose de déplaisant"[21]. L'autre définition que l'on qualifiera, d'après R.A. Lanham, de rhétorique est: "Prognostication of good; opposite of *Ominatio*."[22]. Il est évident que c'est cette dernière qui est la plus appropriée au cas de *baṣîr*[23].

Parmi les arabisants qui ont parlé d'euphémisme, Marçais, Kofler, Weil et Fahd le rapprochent du concept arabe de *tafâ'ul*[24]. Ce rapprochement est essentiellement correct si on se réfère à la définition "rhétorique" de l'euphémisme. Le *tafâ'ul* est une figure arabe qui indique le remplacement d'un mot ou concept par un autre de bon augure. Ce remplacement n'est jamais un adoucissement ou une circonlocution. Au contraire, il est souvent antiphrastique et suggère des procédés conjuratoires ou magiques[25]. Chez les Arabes, *tafâ'ul* est donc très distinct des usages simplement polis ou euphémistiques dans le sens d'une expression atténuée. Cette signification courante d'euphémisme semble beaucoup plus proche du concept arabe qui consiste à "exprimer le difficile par le facile ou le laid par la belle expression."[26]. Sous cette rubrique qui fait partie des sections sur la *kinâya*, on trouve beaucoup d'euphémismes (type expression atténuée), même pour les aveugles. Tous ces exemples s'écartent très nettement de l'idée de *tafâ'ul*[27].

En dehors de la question de rapport logique, la qualification de l'usage de *baṣîr* pour un aveugle comme étant un exemple de *tafâ'ul* est attestée par un passage très intéressant du *Lisân al-'Arab*. Le lexicographe cite le cas du Prophète qui a voulu aller chez tel *al-baṣîr*, lequel était aveugle. Abû 'Ubayd explique alors que par *al-baṣîr* le Prophète a voulu dire "le croyant". Mais selon Ibn Sîda, le Prophète aurait voulu se servir d'un *tafâ'ul* car exprimer la vue (*al-baṣar*) est mieux qu'exprimer la cécité (*al-'amâ*)[28]. L'auteur du *Tâǧ al-'Arûs* reprend ce passage auquel il ajoute un autre tiré du *Baṣâ'ir Ḏawî at-Tamyîz* d'al-Fîrûzâbâdî: on appelle l'aveugle *baṣîr* par voie de contraire (*al-'aks*) mais ce qui est juste c'est qu'on l'appelle ainsi à cause de la force de discernement de son coeur (*baṣîrat al-qalb*)[29].

A côté de la référence au *tafâ'ul*, ces explications lexicographiques montrent que le *baṣîr* onomastique peut être compris comme changement de référence ou même paronomase[30]. Au lieu de décrire la vision physique qui manque à l'aveugle, elles soulignent sa vision spirituelle ou intellectuelle. La citation d'al-Fîrûzâbâdî ajoute aux autres explications celle de la reférence par le contraire. Ce n'est rien d'autre que l'antiphrase occidentale et quelques arabisants ont remarqué le caractère antiphrastique de cet usage-là[31].

On a donc plusieurs systèmes explicatifs, plusieurs possibilités d'interprétation pour le nom al-Baṣîr donné à un aveugle. On peut le concevoir comme *ḍidd*, comme euphémisme, comme *tafâ'ul*, comme antiphrase, ou même comme paronomase.

Etant donné toute la discussion provoquée par cet usage de *baṣîr*, il est intéressant d'observer que son utilisation chez aṣ-Ṣafadî est plutôt restreinte. En effet, *al-baṣîr* n'y figure que cinq fois (dont une dans la section non-biographique de l'oeuvre). Et ce nombre se réduit-il encore à trois personnages. L'exemple tiré de la partie non-biographique, aussi bien qu'une référence (la seule) dans la notice d'un autre personnage, se rapportent à un troisième personnage qui a sa propre biographie, le poète Abû 'Alî al-Baṣîr, dont nous parlerons plus loin[32].

Cette rareté nous permet de commencer par quelques constatations négatives: d'une part si *baṣîr* est un *ḍidd*, pour aṣ-Ṣafadî c'est un *ḍidd* purement onomastique. Pour l'auteur du *Nakt*, *baṣîr* ne semble pas vouloir dire aveugle. Il n'existe pas un seul emploi extra-onomastique du mot *baṣîr* auquel on puisse donner le sens d' "aveugle". Néanmoins, *baṣîr* est un mot très commun dans le *Nakt*[33]. Dans la discussion sur les aveugles dans *al-Ġayṯ al-Musaǧǧam fî Šarh Lâmiyyat al-'Aǧam*, également de notre auteur, *baṣîr* ne figure même pas[34]. En outre, aṣ-Ṣafadî ne semble point estimer que ce terme constitue une forme polie pour désigner l' "aveugle", un euphémisme courant, un *tafâ'ul* qu'il serait de bon ton d'utiliser en parlant d'un aveugle. Il se peut qu'*al-baṣîr* ait été ajouté à un nom pour une des ces raisons par un prédécesseur d'aṣ-Ṣafadî. Mais il faut se rappeler que l'on doit établir la signification synchronique d'un mot avant de faire des comparaisons ou d'en tirer des conclusions diachroniques: les données synchroniques doivent avoir priorité sur les données diachroniques[35]. Etait-il possible qu'aṣ-Ṣafadî ignorât les usages polis, les euphémismes, le *tafâ'ul*, les *aḍdâd*, en somme une bonne partie de la tradition linguistique et littéraire des Arabes? C'est possible mais peu probable. Selon van Ess: "Ṣafadî ist nicht Traditionarier, er ist Literat. Daraus erklärt sich seine Vorliebe für Dichtung."[36]. A côté de cette préférence pour la poésie, aṣ-Ṣafadî a aussi écrit le *Faḍḍ al-Ḫitâm 'an at-Tawriya wal-Istiḫdâm*, une étude sur la figure arabe, la *tawriyya*, qui n'est pas sans relation avec le *ḍidd*: tous deux renfermant une ambiguïté de signification[37]. Ce qui importe plus encore ici, c'est de savoir qu'aṣ-Ṣafadî a aussi rédigé une étude sur la paronomase, le *Kitâb ǧinân al-ǧinâs*[38]. Même dans ses livres non-linguistiques, comme le *Nakt*, il arrive à introduire des discussions linguistiques ou grammaticales[39]. Selon toute probabilité, aṣ-Ṣafadî aurait pu employer ou discuter *baṣîr* comme *ḍidd*. S'il ne l'a pas fait, c'est qu'il ne l'a pas voulu. Il est tout à fait possible que la tradition des livres d'*aḍdâd* n'ait été (en réalité ou pour as-Ṣafadî) qu'une tradition savante et artificielle qui ne reflétait pas l'usage courant[40].

Pour revenir au problème de *baṣîr* onomastique, on doit se rappeler que les noms propres, comme tous les mots, tirent leur signification non seulement de leurs rapports paradigmatiques mais aussi de leurs rapports syntagmatiques. C'est dire qu'il faut les examiner dans le contexte de la notice biographique et même dans l'enchaînement des appellations qui constituent la section onomastique de la notice[41].

Dans l'une des trois notices où figure le terme *al-baṣîr*, son usage est expliqué par notre auteur. L'une des deux autres est libellé comme suit. "Bašîr ibn Mu'âḏ al-'Aqadî *aḍ-Ḍarîr al-Baṣîr*"[42], et la dernière: "Aḥmad ibn Muḥammad ibn al-Ḥusayn ar-Râzî *aḍ-Ḍarîr* wa-yuqâl lahu Abû al-'Abbâs *al-Baṣîr*."[43]. On voit que, dans les deux cas, al-Baṣîr est associé à aḍ-Ḍarîr. Si *al-baṣîr* voulait dire "l'aveugle" ou s'il suffisait pour désigner un aveugle, il y aurait redondance, faute qu'évite aṣ-Ṣafadî. En effet, ni al-Kafîf, ni al-Makfûf, ni al-A'mâ ne sont jamais accompagnés d'aḍ-Ḍarîr dans la même chaîne onomastique et ne se trouvent jamais ensemble. La seule exception n'est qu'apparente: aḍ-Ḍarîr voisine avec al-U'aymî mais cette dernière appellation peut être considérée comme ambiguë. Ces passages sont formulés comme si l'auteur du *Nakt* avait voulu nommer un aveugle qui était aussi *baṣîr*[44].

La clef du problème est dans le seul exemple où le terme *al-baṣîr* a été expliqué par l'auteur. C'est le cas du poète Abû 'Alî al-Baṣîr. Aṣ-Ṣafadî commence par indiquer qu'on lui a conféré le surnom d'al-Baṣîr par emploi du *tafâ'ul*. Or on rapporte qu'il reçut ce surnom parce qu'il avait l'habitude de se réunir avec des amis pour boire du vin, et lorsqu'il se levait et quittait la partie antérieure de l'assemblée pour uriner, il évitait les verres et tous les instruments qui s'y trouvaient, puis il regagnait sa place. Tout cela sans que quelqu'un lui prît la main[45]. Cet homme reçut ainsi le surnom de *baṣîr* parce qu'étant aveugle, il agissait presque comme s'il pouvait voir. Bien qu'il se réfère au *tafâ'ul* aṣ-Ṣafadî explique le nom comme décrivant un aspect du personnage dans le sens de voyant.

C'est sans doute aussi la façon dont aṣ-Ṣafadî a compris les autres emplois d'*al-baṣîr*, qui pouvaient représenter la vision intellectuelle ou spirituelle. En somme, ce qu'on trouve chez aṣ-Ṣafadî est une sorte de *ḍidd* strictement limitée à la sphère onomastique. Il y a certainement aussi antiphrase puisqu'un aveugle est appelé "voyant", antiphrase cependant sans ironie[46] et toujours optimiste, qui est étroitement liée à la paronomase, presqu'à un jeu de mot. En dépit de la référence au *tafâ'ul* il est difficile d'y voir un effet conjuratoire ou de neutralisation magique. Le mot aveugle reste non-déguisé; il n'y a pas remplacement d'un mot de mauvais augure par un mot de bon augure. A plus forte raison, il n'y a pas d'atténuation d'expression.

On voit mieux les éléments combinatoires là où l'antiphrase se dénoue en antithèse. Aṣ-Ṣafadî cite le cas d'un homme qui était aveugle mais baṣîr en adab (ḍarîr bil-adab baṣîr)[47]. Ici il y a contraste mais il y a aussi paronomase puisqu'on confronte la vision physique avec la vision intellectuelle. On trouve le même contraste dans d'autres exemples[48].

En somme, al-baṣîr chez aṣ-Ṣafadî est le point de rencontre de deux figures, antiphrase, ou ḍidd onomastique, et paronomase. Il veut dire aveugle par antiphrase et voyant par paronomase. Mais cette rencontre ne peut se produire qu'au niveau onomastique. Pour cette raison, on pourrait même parler de prosonomase (paronomase prosopographique)[49]. Cette superposition des figures crée une tension au niveau de la signification: baṣîr hésite entre "voyant" et "aveugle". Il n'est pas accidentel que cette tension se manifeste au niveau onomastique. Elle est liée à la bipolarité des noms propres arabes qui se réfèrent à la fois à la personne et au concept, créant un lien entre les deux. Quand un aveugle est appelé al-Baṣîr, ce nom signifie aveugle par référence à la personne qui porte ce nom à cause de sa cécité. Mais ce nom tient aussi une signification du concept de la vue. Et, puisqu'il dégage un lien entre le concept et la personne, cette personne participe au concept de la vue, au sens figuré s'il le faut.

Cette bipolarité, cette ambiguïté des noms attributifs arabes fait qu'un nom peut renfermer tout le mystère, toutes les subtilités littéraires d'un vers de poésie. On pourrait même parler d'une poétique des noms. Un nom arabe peut donc contenir par nature tous les niveaux de signification et d'association que le génie de Proust a mis, selon Barthes, dans les noms propres de son époque: "Autrement dit, si le Nom ... est un signe, c'est un signe volumineux, un signe toujours gros d'une épaisseur touffue de sens ... c'est donc, d'une certaine manière, une monstruosité sémantique, car pourvu de tous les caractères du nom commun, il peut cependant exister et fonctionner hors de toute règle projective. C'est là le prix — ou la rançon — du phénomène d' "hypersémanticité" dont il est le siège, et qui l'apparente, bien entendu, de très près, au mot poétique."[50]

APPENDICE

A. *Aḍ-Ḍarîr*

87
88
89 (deux personnages)
90 (deux personnages)
91
96 (trois personnages)
99 (quatre personnages)
110 (deux personnages)
113 (deux personnages)
114 (trois personnages)
115 (trois personnages)
117 (deux personnages)
119 (deux personnages)
122
123
124
125
130
133 (deux personnages)
138
139
142
144
145 (deux personnages)
146 (deux personnages)
147
148
149 (trois personnages)
150 (trois personnages)
152 (deux personnages)
153
154
157 (trois personnages)
160
167
174
175
178 (deux personnages)
182
186
191
192
194 (trois personnages)
198
203 (deux personnages)
204
208
211 (deux personnages)
212 (trois personnages)
213
214
215 (deux personnages)
218 (deux personnages)
219
220
223
225 (deux personnages)
227
228
230
231
237 (deux personnages)
244
246 (deux personnages)
247 (deux personnages)
252 (quatre personnages)
254 (deux personnages)
258 (deux personnages)
263 (deux personnages)
264
265
271
276 (deux personnages)
287
290
293
297
298
299
300 (deux personnages)
301
302 (deux personnages)
305 (deux personnages)
306
307
308
312
314

B. *Al-A'mâ*

123
153
195
197
221
223
230
293
295
316

C. *Al-Kafîf*

114
190
234
308

D. *Al-Makfûf*

184
237
252

NOTES

1. Jacqueline Sublet, "La prosopographie arabe", *Annales*, XXV (1970), pp. 1236-1239.

2. Roland Barthes, "Proust et les noms", dans *Nouveaux essais critiques* (Paris, 1972), p. 124.

3. Voir, par exemple, les possibilités pour al-Buḫârî dans Ibn al-Aṯîr, *al-Lubâb fî Tahḏîb al-Ansab* (Baghdad, s. d.), t. I, p. 125.

4. On ne parle ici que de l'appellation aḍ-Ḍarîr utilisée en référence à un personnage et non des autres manifestations de *ḍarîr*. La même procédure a été suivie pour les autres noms. La pagination des références est donnée ci-dessus. Il y a aussi deux cas d'aḍ-Ḍarîr dans la partie non-biographique de l'oeuvre. Aṣ-Ṣafadî, *Nakt al-Himyân fî Nukat al-'Umyân*, éd. Aḥmad Zakî (Le Caire, 1911), pp. 41, 73.

5. E.W. Lane, *An Arabic-English Lexicon* (Londres, 1874), t. V, p. 1777. La source de cette appréciation n'est pas donnée.

6. Aḏ-Ḏahabî, *al-Muštabih fî ar-Riǧâl* (Le Caire, 1962), t. II, p. 415; Ibn Ḥaǧar al-'Asqalânî, *Tabṣîr al-Muntabih bi-Taḥrîr al-Muštabih* (Le Caire, 1966), t. III, p. 856.

7. Aṣ-Ṣafadî, *Nakt*, p. 110.

8. On a trois exemples d'al-A'mâ dans la section non-biographique, aṣ-Ṣafadî, *Nakt*, pp. 69, 76.

9. Al-Kafîf se trouve une fois dans la section non-biographique, aṣ-Ṣafadî, *Nakt*, p. 73. Nöldeke a voulu voir dans le nom d'Abû al-'Aynâ' (personnage se trouvant dans le *Nakt*) une référence à sa cécité. Pour cette raison il l'a même considéré comme un euphémisme pour "aveugle". Mais il n'est pas certain que cette interprétation soit la bonne. Abû al-'Aynâ' n'est devenu aveugle que vers la quarantaine, et la *kunya* semble faire référence à une discussion grammaticale. Voir: Theodor Nöldeke, "Wörter mit Gegensinn", dans Theodor Nöldeke, *Neue Beiträge zur Semitischen Sprachwissenschaft* (Strasbourg, 1910), p. 88; aṣ-Ṣafadî, *Nakt*, pp. 265-

270, Ibn al-Mu'tazz, *Ṭabaqât aš-Šu'arâ'*, éd. 'Abd as-Sattâr Aḥmad Farrâǧ (Le Caire, 1968), pp. 414-415; Yâqût, *Kitâb Iršâd al-Arîb*, éd. D.S. Margoliouth (Le Caire, 1925), t. VII, pp. 61-73; Ibn al-'Imâd, *Šaḏarât aḏ-Ḏahab* (Beyrouth, s. d.), t. II, pp. 180-182; al-Bayhaqî, *al-Maḥâsin wal-Masâwî*, éd. M. Abû al-Faḍl Ibrâhîm (Le Caire, s. d.) t. II, p. 147. Pour l'explication de la *kunya*, voir, al-Ḫaṭîb al-Baġdâdî, *Ta'rîḫ Baġdâd* (Beyrouth, 1966), t. III, p. 172; Ibn Ḫallikân, *Wafayât al-A'yân*, éd. Iḥsân 'Abbâs (Beyrouth, s. d.), t. IV, p. 348.

10. *Baṣîr* est aussi un *ism* masculin. Voir, Ibn Manẓûr, *Lisân al-'Arab* (Le Caire, s. d.), t. V, p. 134. On trouve aussi la *kunya* Abû Baṣîr, qui a été considérée comme une *kunya* d'aveugle. Voir, az-Zabîdî, *Tâǧ al-'Arûs* (Le Caire, s. d.), t. III, p. 428; A. Fisher, "Arab. *baṣîr* 'scharfsichtig' per antifrasin = 'blind' ", *ZDMG*, LXI (1907), pp. 425-434, et pp. 751-754; Ibn Qutayba, *al-Ma'ârif* (Le Caire, 1969), p. 454; aḏ-Ḏahabî, *Muštabih*, t. II, pp. 643-644 et Ibn Ḥaǧar, *Tabṣîr*, t. IV, pp. 1419-1420. Fait curieux, cette *kunya* ne se trouve pas dans le *Nakt*.

11. "Essai de traduction des *ad'dâd*", dans *L'Ambivalence dans la culture arabe*, éd . Jacques Berque et Jean-Paul Charnay (Paris, 1967), p. 452.

12. Hans Kofler, "Das Kitâb al-Aḍdâd von Abû 'Alî Muhammad Quṭrub ibn al-Mustanîr", *Islamica*, V (1932), p. 256.

13. A. Haffner, *Drei Quellenwerke über die Aḍdâd* (Beyrouth, 1913), p. 139, cité dans D. Cohen, "*Ad'dâd* et ambiguïté linguistique en arabe", *Ambivalence*, p. 36.

14. Al-Luġawî, *Kitâb al-Aḍdâd fî Kalâm al-'Arab*, éd. 'Izza Ḥasan (Damas, 1963), t. I, p. 63.

15. Ibn Dahhân, *Al-Aḍdâd fî al-Luġa* dans *Nafâ'is al-Maḫṭûtâṭ*, éd. M.H. Âl Yâsîn (Baghdad, 1963), p. 94.

16. Al-Luġawî, *Aḍdâd*, p. 63.

17. Voir, par exemple, al-Anbârî, *Kitâb al-Aḍdâd*, éd. M. Abû al-Faḍl Ibrâhîm (al-Kuwayt, 1960); Ibn Sîda, *Kitâb al-Muḫaṣṣaṣ* (Beyrouth, s. d.), t. IV, pp. 258-267; as-Suyûṭî, *al-Muzhir fî 'Ulûm al-Luġa wa-Anwâ'ihâ*, éd. M.A.J. al-Mawlâ, 'A.M. al-Baǧâwî, et Abû al-Faḍl Ibrâhîm (Le Caire, 1971), t. I, pp. 387-402.

18. La délimitation ou même l'existence des *aḍdâd* a été un sujet de controverse chez les Arabes. Voir, par exemple, S. Jabbour, "Classification et explication des *Ad'dâd*", *Ambivalence*, p. 75 suiv. Il me semble que le problème fondamental est le suivant: à quel point une figure devient-elle un cas de polysémie? Pour une théorie des rapports entre figures et polysémie, voir, Tzvetan Todorov, "Figures", dans T. Todorov et O. Ducrot, *Dictionnaire encyclopédique des sciences du langage* (Paris, 1972), p. 351.

19. Pour aṣ-Ṣafadî, voir, par exemple, *Nakt*, pp. 219-220, 239. Pour les *aḍdâd*, voir, G. Weil, "Aḍdâd", *EI²*, p. 185.

20. W. Marçais, "L'Euphémisme et l'Antiphrase dans les dialectes arabes d'Algérie", dans C. Bezold, éd., *Orientalische Studien Theodor Nöldeke* (Gieszen, 1906), t. I, p. 433; Theodor Nöldeke, "Wörter mit Gegensinn", p. 88; Kofler, "Kitâb al-Aḍdâd", p. 411; Weil, "Aḍdâd", p. 185; R. Bla chère, M. Chouémi, et C. Denizeau, *Dictionnaire Arabe-Français-Anglais* (Paris, 1967), t. I, p. 646; D. Cohen, "*Ad'dâd*

et ambiguïté", pp 35-36. Cf. F. Giese, *Untersuchungen über die 'Aḍdâd* (Berlin, 1894), pp. 55-56; Toufic Fahd, *La divination arabe* (Leyde, 1966), pp. 459-460.

21. Paul Robert, *Dictionnaire*, "Le Petit Robert" (Paris, 1973), p. 641, qui ne donne pas d'autre définition, ce qui est aussi le cas de M. H. Abrams, *A Glossary of Literary Terms* (New York, 1971), pp. 55-56.

22. R.A. Lanham, *A Handlist of Rhetorical Terms* (Berkely, 1968), p. 47. Il est à noter que dans la définition principale l'auteur présente les deux significations et dans la notice secondaire il ne donne que le sens d'expression atténuée, p. 123. A l'encontre du "Petit Robert", le "Grand Robert" note, avant la définition citée dessus: "proprement 'emploi d'un mot favorable, pour un mot de mauvais augure' ", *Dictionnaire* "Le Grand Robert", t. II, p. 704. Voir aussi, Emile Benveniste, "Euphémismes anciens et modernes", dans E. Benveniste, *Problèmes de Linguistique générale*, I (Paris, 1966), pp. 308-314.

23. Parmi les auteurs qui ont parlé d'euphémisme, seul Kofler (p. 441) a clairement indiqué qu'il se référait à la définition rhétorique. Marçais a mis *baṣîr* parmi les euphémismes antiphrastiques et les a liés au concept de bon augure. Mais il a brouillé un peu la question en comparant *baṣîr* avec des euphémismes qui sont des formules adoucissantes (pp. 431-433 et note 4, p. 433). Enfin, Cohen (pp. 36-37) montre dans sa discussion une tendance à faire basculer ces exemples d'euphémismes du concept adoucissant vers le concept du bon augure.

24. Marçais, "L'Euphémisme", p. 432; Kofler, "Kitâb al-Aḍdâd", p. 441; Weil, 'Aḍdâd", p. 185; Fahd, *Divination*, pp. 452-460.

25. Ibn Manẓûr, *Lisân*, t. XIV, p. 27; az-Zabîdî, *Tâğ*, t. VIII, p. 54. Cf. Fahd, *Divination*, pp. 452-460.

26. Abû al-Baqâ', *al-Kulliyât*, éd. 'A. Darwîš et M. al-Miṣrî (Damas, 1976), t. IV, p. 110, aṯ-Ṯa'âlibî, *Fiqh al-Luġa* (Le Caire, 1964), p. 592.

27. Abû al-Baqâ', *Kulliyât*, t. IV, pp. 110-111; at-Ṯa'âlibî, *Fiqh*, pp. 592-594. Sans entrer dans la matière difficile de l'identification des figures arabes, on peut noter que la *kinâya* est le plus souvent comparée à la métonymie. Ces comparaisons sont rendues encore plus délicates par les ambiguïtés que renferme le système rhétorique arabe aussi bien que le système aristotélicien.

28. Ibn Manẓûr, *Lisân*, t. V, p. 131. Fischer cite une autre histoire où le Prophète appelle le même personnage al-Baṣîr, "Arab. *baṣîr*", pp. 425-426.

29. Az-Zabîdî, *Tâğ*, t. III, p. 48; al-Fîrûzâbâdî, *Baṣâ'ir Ḏawî at-Tamyîz* (Le Caire, 1965), t. II, p. 223.

30. Il semble que, bien que l'histoire du *Lisân* soit connue, l'interprétation paronomasique a été ignorée par les orientalistes.

31. Marçais, "L'Euphémisme", p. 433; Cohen, "*Ad'dâd* et ambiguïté", pp. 36-37; Fischer, "Arab. *baṣîr*", p. 425. A.J. Greimas a aussi remarqué le rôle de l'antiphrase dans la formation des *aḍdâd*, "Le problème des *ad'dâd* et les niveaux de signification", *Ambivalence*, p. 286.

32. Aṣ-Ṣafadî, *Nakt*, pp. 76, 225, 265.

33. Souvent l'usage est tel que si *baṣîr* signifiait aveugle le passage deviendrait tout à faite incompréhensible. Voir, par exemple, pp. 58 et 129.

34. Aṣ-Ṣafadî, *al-Ġayṯ al-Musaǧǧam fî Šarḥ Lâmiyyat al-'Aǧam* (Beyrouth, 1975), t. II, p. 319 suiv.

35. Voir, par exemple, Ferdinand de Saussure, *Cours de linguistique générale* (Paris, 1931), pp. 124-126; J. Culler, *Ferdinand de Saussure* (New York, 1977), pp. 30-32.

36. J. van Ess, "Ṣafadî-Splitter", *Der Islam*, LIV (1977), p. 104.

37. Pour une description et un sommaire de cet ouvrage qui n'est pas encore édité, voir, S.A. Bonebakker, *Some Early Definitions of the Tawriya and Ṣafadî's Faḍḍ al-Xitâm 'an at-Tawriya wa-'l Istixdâm* (La Haye, 1966), pp. 63-98. Pour quelques traductions de *tawriya*, voir, pp. 9-10.

38. Van Ess. "Ṣafadî", LIII, p. 251.

39. Aṣ-Ṣafadî, *Nakt*, p. 6 suiv.

40. En général, comme l'a très bien montré Kamal Abu Deeb avec le cas célèbre de la description de la *qaṣîda* par Ibn Qutayba dans son *Kitâb aš-Ši'r waš-Šu'arâ'*, il est dangereux d'investir des passages qui expriment un avis ou une tendance ou même parfois un idéal de trop de signification normative ou généralisatrice. Kamal Abu Deeb, "Towards a Structural Analysis of Pre-Islamic Poetry", *International Journal of Middle East Studies*, VI (1975), pp. 1, 79-80. En outre, comme dit Cohen, "La notion de *d'idd* ne relève pas de la conscience mais d'une élaboration abstraite de certains grammairiens, et que certains autres se sont toujours refusé à admettre". D. Cohen, "Ambivalence, indifférence et neutralisation de sèmes", dans *Ambivalence*, p. 292. Bien sûr, il est possible qu'aṣ-Ṣafadî soit en faire l'exception, mais pour établir ce point il faudrait en faire des études synchroniques.

41. Saussure, *Cours*, pp. 172-180. Ce qu'on introduit ici est, en effet, un principe de syntaxe sémiologique. Il y a plusieurs niveaux de syntaxe dans les notices biographiques, et je tâche d'approfondir le concept du notice biographique comme système sémiologique dans une étude, "Dreams, the Blind, and the Semiotics of the Biographical Notice", *Studia Islamica*, sous presse.

42. aṣ-Ṣafadî, *Nakt*, p. 130. Il y a, en effet d'autres *nisbas* pour '—q—d. L'éditeur a mis une *fatḥa* sur le *'ayn* et on a choisi ici al-'Aqadî sans prétendre donner une solution définitive au problème. Voir, Ibn al-Aṯîr, *Lubâb*, t. II, pp. 348-349.

43. Aṣ-Ṣafadî, *Nakt*, p. 114.

44. On trouve dans la partie non-biographique al-Baṣîr al-A'mâ, aṣ-Ṣafadî, *Nakt*, p. 76.

45. Aṣ-Ṣafadî, *Nakt*, p. 225.

46. Cette absence de sens ironique, qui est peut-être liée au caractère quasi-magique de *tafâ'ul*, devient particulièrement significative quand on l'ajoute à la tendance des oeuvres sur les *Buḫalâ'* d'éviter soigneusement toute ironie et toute fiction satirique. Est-ce que le mot chez les Arabes est trop sacré pour qu'il puisse perdre entièrement sa signification primaire? Seul une étude approfondie sur le *hiǧâ'* pourrait fournir une réponse à cette question. Voir, Fedwa Malti Douglas, "The *Bukhalâ'* Work in Medieval Arabic Literature", Thèse de Doctorat (Los Angeles, 1977), pp. 273-280.

47. Aṣ-Ṣafadī, *Nakt*, p. 150.
48. Aṣ-Ṣafadī, *Nakt*, pp. 119, 194.
49. Lanham, *Handlist*, p. 82.
50. Barthes, "Proust", pp. 125-126.

V

DREAMS, THE BLIND, AND THE SEMIOTICS OF THE BIOGRAPHICAL NOTICE

The dreams in aṣ-Ṣafadī's biographical dictionary of the blind, the *Nakt al-Himyān fī Nukat al-'Umyān*, stand at the crossroads of several perspectives. On the one hand, they illustrate the role of the dream in the biographical notice while, on the other hand, their context relates them to the world of the blind. Finally, in order to explore the functions of dreams in Muslim biography, it is necessary to develop a unified conception of the biographical notice, and for this purpose, a semiotic interpretation will be advanced.

Khalīl ibn Aybak aṣ-Ṣafadī (d. 764/1363) was a Mamlūk official, better known for his voluminous biographical compendium, *al-Wāfī bil-Wafayāt*. His evident interest in blindness and the blind manifested itself in his authorship of the *Nakt al-Himyān* which comprises 313 notices and a series of introductory discussions on blindness. [1]

Biographical dictionaries like the *Nakt*, and especially

(1) Aṣ-Ṣafadī, *Nakt al-Himyān fī Nukat al-'Umyān*, ed. A. Zakī Bāshā (Cairo, 1911). On this work, see Ahmed Zéki Pacha, *Dictionnaire biographique des aveugles illustres de l'Orient* (Cairo, 1911) and Fedwa Malti-Douglas, « Pour une rhétorique onomastique : les noms des aveugles chez aṣ-Ṣafadī », forthcoming in *Cahiers d'Onomastique Arabe*, I (1979). This author is also preparing a computer listing and analysis of the work. The most complete biography of aṣ-Ṣafadī is that of D. P. Little in "Al-Ṣafadī as Biographer of his Contemporaries", in D. P. Little, ed., *Essays in Islamic Civilization* (Leiden, 1976), pp. 206-210. See also the very informative "Ṣafadī-Splitter" by J. van Ess, *Der Islam*, 53 (1976), pp. 242-266, 54 (1977), pp. 77-108.

Mamlūk ones, have attracted considerable attention and have spawned a vigorous historiographical literature. (1) It is only natural, however, that the origins and purposes of this literature have often shaped its methods and its conclusions. Bent on the search for valid or useful historical data, a search that has become particularly ingenious in the case of quantitative historians, (2) many scholars, using these works primarily as reference works, have been tempted to conceive of them as such. Concommitant with this, has been the tendency to regard some of these works as collections of "dry data" tending to "...renounce any literary ambitions." (3)

(1) See, for example, D. P. Little, *An Introduction to Mamlūk Historiography* (Wiesbaden, 1970), pp. 100-136; Franz Rosenthal, *A History of Muslim Historiography* (Leiden, 1968), pp. 93-95, 100-106, 194-197; Ulrich Haarmann, "Auflösung und Bewahrung der klassischen Formen arabischer Geschichtsschreibung in der Zeit der Mamluken", *ZDMG*, 121 (1971), pp. 49-60; Tarif Khalidi, "Islamic Biographical Dictionaries: A Preliminary Assessment", *The Muslim World*, LXIII (1973), pp. 53-65; I. Hafsi, "Recherches sur le genre *Ṭabaqāt*", *Arabica*, XXIII (1976), pp. 227-265, XXIV (1977), pp. 1-41, 150-186; and most recently, J. H. Escovitz, "A Lost Arabic Source for the History of Early Ottoman Egypt", *Journal of the American Oriental Society*, 97 (1977), pp. 513-518. For the most part, these works have concentrated on the twin areas of organization (*ṭabaqāt*, necrologies, alphabetical or chronological organization, etc.) and source research. A major tendency of historiographical literature has been a genetic bias, describing Muslim biography in terms of its original function as an auxiliary of *ḥadīth* criticism. See Claude Cahen. "Notes sur l'historiographie dans la communauté musulmane médiévale," *Revue des Études Islamiques*, XLIV (1976), p. 87 and the quote by Rosenthal in note 3. However, by the Mamlūk period Muslim biographical literature had long abandoned the limits set by its origins.

(2) See J. H. Escovitz, "Vocational Patterns of the Scribes of the Mamlūk Chancery", *Arabica*, XXIII (1976), pp. 42-62; R. W. Bulliet, "A Quantitative Approach to Medieval Muslim Biographical Dictionaries", *Journal of the Economic and Social History of the Orient*, XIII (1970), pp. 195-211; Carl Petry and Stanley Mendenhall, "Geographic origins of the Civil Judiciary of Cairo in the fifteenth century", *Journal of the Economic and Social History of the Orient*, XXI (1978), pp. 52-74.

(3) "Biography, on the other hand, was originally a handmaiden of the religious sciences. *As such, it was expected to provide only a limited number of dry data. No matter how elaborate they were, biographies of scholars were inclined to renounce any literary ambition.* While biographies of political figures as a rule shared the characteristics of political historiography, and, especially, the panegyrics of Persian court historiography relied on magnificent rhetoric, *the artlessness of scholarly biography sometimes tended to affect them as well as to becloud in general the literary value of much of Muslim historical writing.*" Franz Rosenthal, "Literature", in J. Schacht and C. E. Bosworth, eds., *The Legacy of Islam* (Oxford, 1974),

In two interesting articles, Hartmut Fähndrich has reacted against this trend, seeking to restore to the biographical notices of Ibn Khallikān their integrity as literary works. Interestingly enough, Ibn Khallikān has always enjoyed a favored literary reputation among Orientalists. But Fähndrich's conclusions, based on an analysis of anecdotal style, were clearly meant to be applied to other biographers as well: "A comparison of different versions of such biographical entities, revealing modifications in the presentation of personalities, may, then, lead to conclusive results about the style of an author of a biographical dictionary." Indeed, the approach is promising but is limited by its emphasis on the "literarization" of the text. (1)

A more appropriate methodology would have to transcend this apparent dichotomy between content and form, between historical data and literary style. Recent studies, by examining what could be called the paradigmatic corpora of biographical notices devoted to a single personage, have drawn attention to the significance of the selection, presentation and arrangement of data within the notices. After a discussion of two notices devoted to the Caliph 'Uthmān, R. S. Humphreys concludes: "Using a common stock of anecdotes, each man elaborates distinctive themes through definable modes of selection, arrangement, style, and tone." My own work on the biographical tradition of al-Khaṭīb al-Baghdādī has led me to similar conclusions. (2)

pp. 327-328 (emphasis mine). "Scholars have customarily used biographical dictionaries as they were intended to be used by the author, as reference books." Bulliet, "A Quantitative Approach," p. 195.

(1) When discussing Ibn Khallikān in his *A Literary History of the Arabs*, R. A. Nicholson agreed with Jones that "... it is the best general biography ever written;" and compared the author to Boswell, R. A. Nicholson, *A Literary History of the Arabs* (Cambridge, 1969), pp. 451-452; cf. H. A. R. Gibb, *Arabic Literature* (Oxford, 1963), pp. 133-134. Fähndrich's two articles are: "The *Wafayāt al-A'yān* of Ibn Khallikān: A New Approach," *Journal of the American Oriental Society*, 93 (1973), pp. 432-445; and "Compromising the Caliph," *Journal of Arabic Literature*, VIII (1977), pp. 36-47. The anecdotal analysis is in the latter article and the quote is on p. 47. The theoretical discussion is in the earlier article, see, especially, pp. 433-435, 441. For an earlier discussion of this concept of literarization (*Literarisierung)* as applied to Mamlūk biographical literature, see Haarmann, "Auflösung", p. 53.

(2) R. S. Humphreys, "The Reign of 'Uthmān ibn 'Affān as Presented in

These conclusions, by emphasizing the significance of the presentation of data in the notices, show the pitfalls inherent in the attempt to distinguish between purely literary or purely historical effect. (1) A change in one aspect of the text most often represents a change in the other. This is because the Medieval Arabic biographical notice functions as a semiotic system, that is a system of signs. To be more precise, the biographical notices themselves should be understood as *parole*, while their *langue*, or system, would be the ensemble of semiotic codes which logically precede their composition. (2) A system, of course, as Jeanne Martinet explains, implies "...l'existence de certaines unités, entretenant entre elles certaines relations, en vue d'accomplir certaines *fonctions*. Un système se définira d'abord par la fonction ou les fonctions qu'il remplit et, ensuite, par les moyens mis en œuvre pour y parvenir." (3) In this case, the particular flexibility in the functions of the biographical notice is matched by a flexibility in the articulation of its codes. It is these codes which permit the authors to vary the interpretation of their notices through the manipulation of data. This process, of course, does not exclude direct appreciations given through the appropriate literary codes.

A sign, as Barthes and Martinet, among others, have stressed is not a signifier *(signifiant)* but the interface between the signifier and the signified *(signifié)*. (4) The latter, of course, is conditioned by syntagmatic and paradigmatic context. An attempt to interpret elements in the notices as pure 'information,'

Ya'qūbī and Mas'ūdī," Paper delivered at the annual meeting of the Middle East Studies Association, November 9, 1976. I would like to thank my colleague Prof. Humphreys for making this paper available to me and for permission to quote. Fedwa Malti-Douglas, "Controversy and its effects in the biographical tradition of al-Khaṭīb al-Baghdādī," *Studia Islamica*, XLVI (1977), pp. 115-131.

(1) For a discussion of the problems inherent in the distinction between form and content generally, see René Wellek and Austin Warren, *Theory of Literature* (New York, 1956), pp. 140-141.

(2) See Roland Barthes, "Éléments de sémiologie", *Communications*, 4 (1964), pp. 92-102 and, especially, pp. 97-102.

(3) Jeanne Martinet, *La sémiologie* (Paris, 1975), pp. 109-110.

(4) Barthes, "Éléments", p. 105; Martinet, *Sémiologie*, pp. 73-75, 94; cf. Tzvetan Todorov, "Signe", in O. Ducrot and T. Todorov, *Dictionnaire encyclopédique des sciences du langage* (Paris, 1972), pp. 132-133.

that is, to use the notices as reference works, by isolating the material from its semiotic context, hides the sign. Instead of the signified, the scholar may be left holding the referent, that is, according to Eco, the entire logical class which can be evoked by the signifier. (1) Thus, a semiotic understanding of biographical dictionaries is essential, even for the social historian primarily concerned with the extraction of data: signified and referent need not agree.

This perspective, however, is equally vital to a literary appreciation, in the largest sense of the term, since it permits a unified interpretation of the biographical notice and not merely the anecdotal material. The notices in the *Nakt*, like those of other Mamlūk biographical dictionaries, begin with a list of names, attributives and laudatives which I have referred to, elsewhere, as the onomastic chain. This chain, far from being insignificant or unrelated to the notice, possesses its own languages and is often semiotically rich, giving the reader his first introduction to the significance of that which is to follow. (2)

(1) Umberto Eco, *A Theory of Semiotics* (Bloomington, 1976), p. 66. This definition, of course, is not universally accepted but merely seems to this writer to be the only one which does not create insuperable theoretical difficulties. See Martinet, *Sémiologie*, pp. 89-94 and Todorov, "Signe", p. 133.

(2) For the onomastic chain, see Douglas, "Rhétorique onomastique". Fähndrich has distinguished between "factual" and "illustrative" material. He defines the "factual" in the following manner: "It is the information that is usually not changed, except in volume and arrangement, on its way from one historical work to another. This so to speak static character of the 'factual material' can be contrasted with the dynamic character of what will be called 'illustrative material..." Fähndrich, "Ibn Khallikān", p. 438. Nevertheless, the author refined this distinction later in his study when he recognized that, in practice, the distinction must remain purely formal and that the notice, as a composition, reflects an arrangement of both types of material, Fähndrich, "Ibn Khallikān," p. 445. One advantage of a semiotic approach would be that it bypasses this distinction, while permitting the re-introduction of certain formal elements, like anecdotal structure, as semiotically significant.

The semiotic importance of conventional laudatives or name elements in the onomastic chain can best be seen by the furor which was caused by the omission of the term *faqīh* or a similar reference to *fiqh* in al-Khaṭīb al-Baghdādī's biography of Aḥmad ibn Ḥanbal. See, al-Khaṭīb al-Baghdādī, *Ta'rīkh Baghdād* (Beirut, 1966), v. IV, p. 412; Ibn al-Jawzī, *al-Muntaẓam* (Hyderabad, 1940), v. VIII, p. 267. On the controversy caused by al-Khaṭīb's *Ta'rīkh*, see Douglas, "Controversy", pp. 121-122.

From a literary-critical point of view, the biographical notice is, of course, a text. But it can be so conceived semiotically as well. Christian Metz has noted that almost all communications are, in fact, texts. "A text", Metz explains, "represents the result of the coexistence of many codes (or, at least, of many subcodes)." (1) This is particularly true of biographical notices. Codes range from the linguistic system of classical Arabic with its attendant literary codes through codes associated with names and titles to religious and secular codes of behavior.

Dreams possess great semiotic potential. First of all, in the Medieval Islamic tradition, they are privileged signs. Of the various forms of divination of non-Islamic origin, oniromancy would seem to be the only one fully accepted by Orthodoxy. A glance at the *ḥadīth* material will show the level of integration. (2) Many studies have been made of dreams in the Islamic world and, most recently, Jacob Lassner has cited a number of dreams which are, indeed, political signs. (3) Dreams, however, are also important for their semiotic diversity, their ability to act as the focal point for the interaction of various codes. In the Greco-Islamic onirocritical tradition, best represented by Ibn Isḥāq's translation of Artemidorus' *Oneirocritica*, dreams are treated as signs to the dreamer which are analyzed with reference to a code which has its own syntax (the same dream dreamed by different individuals has different significance), and relies heavily on symbols and indices. (4) Indeed, many Medieval works on dreams, like the

(1) Christian Metz, quoted and discussed in Eco, *Semiotics*, p. 57.

(2) See, for example, al-Kirmānī, *Sharḥ Ṣaḥīḥ al-Bukhārī* (Cairo, 1938), v. XXIV, pp. 94-143.

(3) Jacob Lassner, "Foundations of Power", manuscript of a work to be published by Princeton University Press, Chapter I. I would like to thank my colleague Professor Lassner for making the manuscript available to me.

(4) Artémidore d'Éphèse, *Le livre des songes*, trad. arabe de Ḥunayn b. Isḥāq, ed. Toufic Fahd (Damascus, 1964). For some recent controversy over the identity of the translator, see, Toufic Fahd, "Ḥunayn Ibn Isḥāq est-il le traducteur des *Oneirocritica* d'Artémidore d'Éphèse?" in *Ḥunayn Ibn Isḥāq* (Leiden, 1975), pp. 270-284. Carl Alfred Meier has accurately characterized one of the major qualities of the Artemidorian semiotics as "... la *polarité* et l'*ambivalence* des motifs oniriques..." Carl Alfred Meier, "Le rêve et l'incubation dans l'ancienne Grèce", in G. E. von Grunebaum and Roger Caillois, eds., *Le rêve et les sociétés humaines*

Muntakhab al-Kalām fī Tafsīr al-Aḥlām, attributed to Ibn Sīrīn, and an-Nābulusī's *Ta'ṭīr al-Anām fī Ta'bīr al-Manām* are essentially dictionaries of symbols. (1) The dream, thus, can enjoy the status of a sign even before its incorporation in the notice. A dream in a biographical notice can, therefore, link two semiotic perspectives. First, it is a sign to the dreamer and then second, by its integration in a given notice, it becomes a sign within the semiotic system of the biography. At the risk of repetition, it should be stressed that the interpretation of a dream in the traditional Islamic manner (or in a Freudian or Jungian manner, for that matter) does not exhaust the significance of the dream in the notice as it does not account for the biographer's decision to include it.

Indeed, biographers certainly vary in the degree of their interest in dreams. There is evidence that aṣ-Ṣafadī may have had a considerable proclivity to use dreams in the composition of a notice. In an earlier study, I noted that of all the biographical notices devoted to al-Khaṭīb al-Baghdādī, aṣ-Ṣafadī was, in fact, the only biographer to present all of the dreams in the corpus. (2) Furthermore, aṣ-Ṣafadī gives ample discussion to the relations between dreams and the blind in his introduction to the *Nakt*. Our author discusses whether or not the blind see in their dreams, and whether or not they see the angel of death. More significantly for our purposes, however, aṣ-Ṣafadī also discusses what it means if one sees a blind man, or is himself blinded or loses an eye in a dream. This exposition is drawn from the Greco-Islamic onirocritical tradition. Most often, aṣ-Ṣafadī writes: "the interpreters said" *(qāla al-'ābirūn)*, but he does also cite Artemidorus directly, which probably indicates

(Paris, 1967), p. 298. Sigmund Freud described this system of dream interpretation as "the cipher method". Sigmund Freud, *The Interpretation of Dreams*, trans. A. A. Brill (New York, 1950), pp. 10-11. An attempt to construct a synthetic grammar or grammars of the Islamic dream books would undoubtedly be of considerable interest.

(1) Ibn Sīrīn, *Muntakhab al-Kalām fī Tafsīr al-Aḥlām* (Cairo, 1963); an-Nābulusī, *Ta'ṭīr al-Anām fī Ta'bīr al-Manām* (Cairo, n.d.). For an inventory of Islamic onirocritical literature, see, Toufic Fahd, *La divination arabe* (Leiden, 1966), pp. 329-363.

(2) Douglas, "Controversy", pp. 126-129.

that he had access to this classic of onirocriticism. [1] The author of the *Nakt* has also included a short section on dreams in his *al-Ghayth al-Musajjam fī Sharḥ Lāmiyyat al-ʿAjam.* [2]

Up to now, we have used the word "dream" in a general way. Yet, the religious content of some of these experiences might classify them in another context as visions. For the purposes of this study, any auditory or visual experience related as having taken place during a sleeping state, will be considered a dream. Such experiences are clearly indicated in the text with a reference to sleep using such phrases as *ra'aytu fī an-nawm*, *ra'aytu fī al-manām* or, in one instance, *'atāhu fī manāmihi.* [3]

The above phrases are used to introduce a corpus of fourteen dreams. [4] For convenience, they have been numbered in the order of their appearance in the text (see accompanying table). Conspicuously absent from this corpus are clear examples of the particular type of coded prediction dream which occupies so much of the attention of the dream books. The two essential, and semiotically vital, characteristics of this type of dream are:

1) that it predicts a future event or events. Artemidorus classifies such dreams as *óneiros* and distinguishes them from *enýpnion*, which deal with the present. These terms were

(1) Aṣ-Ṣafadī, *Nakt*, pp. 18-21.

(2) Aṣ-Ṣafadī, *al-Ghayth al-Musajjam fī Sharḥ Lāmiyyat al-ʿAjam* (Beirut, 1975), v. I, pp. 240-248.

(3) For the potential ambiguity in Arabic between vision and dream, see, Fahd, *Divination*, pp. 269-272. In "Ibn Khallikān", p. 444, Fähndrich characterizes such phrases as *topoi* in anecdotes as opposed to anecdotal *topoi*. This characterization was not developed and, therefore, communicates little more than that dreams were a frequent component in the *Wafayāt al-Aʿyān*. While it has the advantage of pointing to a recurring element, it has the disadvantage of taking this element out of its semiotic context, which, as will be shown, can generate a considerable variety of significations.

(4) The elements in this corpus, thus, possess the simultaneous affinity and dissimilarity which Barthes considers essential for the two structural activities of dissection and articulation. Roland Barthes, "The Structuralist Activity", in Richard and Fernande DeGeorge, eds., *The Structuralists: From Marx to Lévi-Strauss* (Garden City, 1972), pp. 151-152. On the importance of a corpus, see also Robert Scholes, *Structuralism in Literature* (New Haven, 1975), p. 94; Tzvetan Todorov, *Grammaire du Décaméron* (The Hague, 1969), p. 11.

rendered into Arabic as *ru'yā* and *aḍghāth*. The *Oneirocritica*, as the name implies, concerns itself with the former. ([1])

2) that it is encoded, usually in a symbolic manner, that is, that the dream's significance or message is not the same as the dream narrative which must be interpreted or translated to yield this message. Artemidorus describes this kind of dream as allegorical *(allāgorikoi)*. He distinguishes them from the theorematic *(theōrāmatikoi)*, or direct dreams, which do not need to be interpreted and which will take place exactly as they are seen. This distinction is rendered into Arabic by *dhawāt ta'wīl* and *ẓāhira*. The *Oneirocritica*, like the Islamic dream books, is essentially concerned with allegorical dreams. ([2]) This dearth of coded prediction dreams takes on greater significance if one remembers that aṣ-Ṣafadī showed his awareness of this tradition in his introduction to the *Nakt*. In addition, dreams typical of this type can be found in the works of other biographers. ([3])

There are, however, two dreams which at least fulfill the first criterion. The first dream (no. 12) came to Hishām ibn Mu'āwiya. Aṣ-Ṣafadī recounts the dream in the following manner: a certain Abū Naṣr explained that he had a passion for a young *ghulām*, and that Hishām knew this. The latter said to Abū Naṣr that he saw him in a dream having thrown the youth on the ground and mounting him. Abū Naṣr then replied that if Hishām's vision *(ru'yā)* was correct, his hope would be fulfilled, and, for this reason, he kept after the youth until he was alone with him. ([4]) Though the question of the dream's veracity is posed, it is a prediction of a future event. It is evident, however, that it has no need of a symbolic dictionary to be understood. The interpretation is limited to

(1) Artemidorus, *Oneirocritica*, trans. R. J. White (Park Ridge, 1975), p. 14. Ibn Isḥāq, *Songes*, p. 7. The Greek equivalents are provided by the editor in the notes.

(2) Artemidorus, *Oneirocritica*, pp. 15-16; Ibn Isḥāq, *Songes*, p. 10.

(3) See, for example, the dream in Ibn Khallikān's biography of al-Ḥajjāj ibn Yūsuf, Ibn Khallikān, *Wafayāt al-A'yān*, ed. Iḥsān 'Abbās (Beirut, n.d.), v. II, pp. 53-54. Interestingly enough, this dream can also be found in the introduction to the *Nakt*, p. 21.

(4) Aṣ-Ṣafadī, *Nakt*, p. 305.

Abū Naṣr's statement that if the vision is true, he will be successful. If the sign had to be described in terms of codes, we would say that it was mimetic. What is most important for the semiosis of the dream, however, is that that which is seen is destined to take place: vision will become reality.

A similar structure (1) can be found in the dream of Ibn al-Ghumr al-Adīb (no. 4), who dreamt that he saw the Faqīh Shīth ibn Ibrāhīm reciting a poem. The import of these verses was that he was eighty-eight years old and that little remained of his life. When the dreamer recounted the dream to the *faqīh*, the latter indicated that he was, in fact, eighty-eight years of age that day and that his soul was announcing his death to him. (2) Once again, a future event is predicted, the interpretation is present in the text, and the dream content and its message are virtually identical.

When the two above dreams are compared, it becomes clear that they are both embedded in narratives whose central purpose is the presentation and orientation of the dream. These micro-units should best be labelled dream anecdotes, and it is evident that the two above possess the same structure: 1) A dreams about B; 2) A recounts dream to B; and 3) B interprets dream.

These dream anecdotes are, in effect, syntagms. Within them, the dreams themselves are unities of signification *(unités significatives)* analogous to the words in a language while the actual Arabic sentences are unities of distinction *(unités distinctives)*, analogous to the phonemes in a natural language.(3) Nevertheless, when these dreams are seen in the context of the biographical dictionary, itself conceived as a collection of unities, the biographical notices, an important syntactic distinction emerges. The first dream (no. 12) was in the notice of the dreamer, Hishām ibn Muʿāwiya: his dream was in his biography. The dream of Ibn al-Ghumr al-Adīb (no. 4),

(1) For this concept of structure (or morphology), see, among others, Vladimir Propp, *Morphologie du conte* (Paris, 1970), pp. 29-34; Jean-Marie Auzias, *Le structuralisme* (Paris, 1975), pp. 13-14.

(2) Aṣ-Ṣafadī, *Nakt*, p. 170.

(3) Barthes, "Éléments", pp. 105, 116-117.

V

on the other hand, was in the biography of Shīth ibn Ibrāhīm. Thus, one dream was in the notice of the dreamer, and the other, in that of the dreamed. The presence of dreams in the notice of the dreamed indicates that dreams can be tied into the notice not only by the biographical fact that a certain person has dreamed them but by the content of the dream itself as well. The dream of Ibn al-Ghumr was in the notice of Shīth because Shīth was the subject of the dream. This shows that the dream is not merely subjective but objective as well. Were it merely subjective, its content would not be significant for another biography. Stated another way, the dream is not wholly internalized to the dreamer but has external existence as well. (1)

There are two other dreams which occur in the notice of the dreamed. In one (no. 5), Aḥmad ibn ʻAbd ar-Raḥmān dreamt that he saw the subject of the notice, Ṣāliḥ ibn ʻAbd al-Qaddūs, in a cheerful state and asked him what God had done with him and how he fared with the accusations which had been made against him. Ṣāliḥ answered that he had been received by a Lord from whom no secrets were kept and who met him with mercy explaining that He knew that Ṣāliḥ was innocent of the accusations. (2) Clearly, the dream is meant to show that the dreamed, Ṣāliḥ, had gone to his judgment, been found innocent by God and was in Heaven. Equally clearly, it was designed not only to show his status in the after-life but also to clear him of specific charges. In the notice itself, aṣ-Ṣafadī tells us that he was executed by the Caliph al-Mahdī for being a *zindīq*. (3)

(1) Of course, the radical internalization of psychic phenomena is a distinguishing characteristic of modern Western "scientific" thought, while other cultures have often externalized them. See C. G. Jung, *Psychology and Religion* (New Haven, 1969), pp. 12-13. Freud best reflects the modern attitude: "The pre-scientific conception of the dream which obtained among the ancients was, of course, in perfect keeping with their general conception of the universe, which was accustomed to project as an external reality that which possessed reality only in the life of the psyche." Freud, *Interpretation*, p. 5.

(2) Aṣ-Ṣafadī, *Nakt*, p. 172. Ibn al-Muʻtazz attributes the same dream to an Aḥmad ibn Ibrāhīm, whom he also calls al-Muʻabbir, which would imply that he was a dream interpreter. Ibn al-Muʻtazz, *Ṭabaqāt ash-Shuʻarā'*, ed. ʻA. S. Aḥmad Farrāj (Cairo, 1968), p. 92.

(3) Aṣ-Ṣafadī, *Nakt*, p. 171.

Certainly, as Georges Devereux points out, all dream work is subject to cultural influences, [1] and the Islamic cultural context is far from being an exception to this. More dramatically, Malinowski characterizes as "official" dreams those dreams which "...run on lines prescribed by tradition...," contrasting these with "free" dreams which do not. [2] As will be shown in the course of this discussion, few of the dreams in the corpus are uninfluenced by cultural patterns. Indeed, it may well be their cultural patterning, their relative lack of individuality, which permits their inclusion in biographical literature. It is difficult in the absence of a more extensive survey of dreams in biographical literature to determine precisely which dream formations represent well-established "official" dream patterns which can be defined at once by their form, their function and their placement. Such a determination can, however, be made with the dream at hand. In an earlier study, I showed that dreams communicating the state of a person in the after-life, as well as being directed against specific accusations, were a major tool of biographical controversy. Like the dream discussed above, these dreams were also in the notice of the dreamed. [3]

The last dream in this category (no. 1) also shows us the divine judgment. Someone, the text does not even tell us who, dreamt that he saw Daʿwān ibn ʿAlī in a dream twenty-five years after his death. Daʿwān was clothed in white and his face was radiant. He took the hand of the dreamer and they walked together to the Friday prayer. Upon being asked what God had done with him, Daʿwān replied that he had presented himself to God fifty times, that the Deity had asked him what he had done and that he had answered that he had recited the *Qur'ān* and taught it. To this, God said that he would take good care of him. [4]

(1) Georges Devereux, "Rêves pathogènes dans les sociétés non occidentales'," in von Grunebaum, *Le rêve*, p. 199.

(2) Bronislaw Malinowski, *Sex and Repression in Savage Society* (New York, 1955), pp. 89-90. Cf. Robert Van de Castle, *The Psychology of Dreamign* (Morristown, 1971), pp. 7-8.

(3) Douglas, "Controversy", pp. 127-129.

(4) Aṣ-Ṣafadī, *Nakt*, p. 151.

Clearly, this last dream shows that the subject of the notice was in Paradise. Since both dreams, in effect, show the status of someone in the after-life, this becomes a biographical datum and the 'life' of the Medieval Muslim could be said to include his after-life, information about which is presented when available. In both cases, as well, this description of the after-life immediately follows the mention of the personage's death. There are two points, however, which distinguish the dream about Daʿwān from that about Ṣāliḥ. First, there is no evidence of controversy, no reference to accusation. Since the notice tells us that Daʿwān was a noted *muqri'* (*Qur'ān* reciter), the dream may be intended to validate his career. The other major difference relates to the dream's nature as a sign, speaking here as a sign to the dreamer and not within the notice. While neither dream relies heavily on symbolic coding, the first tells us that someone is in Paradise while the second, though it includes some aspects of telling, also shows us this fact. (1) The showing, however, hesitates between pure mimesis (the radiant face, the white dress and, of course, the action of going to the mosque), and a transparent symbolism. The fact that explicit telling can be found in both dreams permits them to stand alone: functionally, they form a dream anecdote by themselves. In these cases, thus, the dream as an original sign is taken up directly as a sign in the semiotic system of the biographical notice. It is only conditioned by its position and the other, non-dream related, material in the notice. In the first two dreams discussed (no. 4 and no. 12), the dreams as original signs were modified by the other elements in the dream anecdote and were transformed into new signs when entering the semiotic system of the notice. Thus, the literary structure of the dream anecdote betrays a transformation in the nature of the sign. The sign to the dreamer and that in the notice are not the same.

Another aspect of these two dreams is that they provide authoritative judgments on certain questions. In a sense, one

(1) On showing and telling in narrative, see Wayne C. Booth, *The Rhetoric of Fiction* (Chicago, 1961), pp. 3-20.

could say that the authority is God since His actions or words are related to us. Significantly, however, the Deity Himself did not appear in the dream. The person seen is the subject and not really the authority. What permits the dream to pretend to an authoritative judgment is the assumption that we have actually seen the person who is really telling us or showing us that he is among the blessed.

In other dreams, these two elements, the "actual" presence of an individual and the making of a judgment or the answering of a question, are combined in a different way. These dreams, like all those which will follow, are in the notice of the dreamer.

In one example (no. 9), Muḥammad ibn Ya'qūb Abū al-'Abbās saw his father in a dream. The father told his son to use the book of al-Buwayṭī (1) since there was none like it among the books of the Shāfi'īs. (2) A judgment is made and the authority, the father, is present.

In another example (no. 7), a professional dream interpreter, 'Alī ibn Aḥmad al-Ḥanbalī al-Āmidī, had had some silk stolen from him. He thereupon dreamt that he saw his *shaykh*, al-Imām Majd ad-Dīn 'Abd aṣ-Ṣamad, who told him who had stolen the silk, where it was and that he sould go and get it. Upon awaking, 'Ali observed that since his *shaykh* had always been truthful in life, so must he be after his death, and proceeded to recover his silk. (3) Here, the authority is the *shaykh* and his veracity in this context is determined by the fact that he was (and is) a truthful man. Thus, just as in those dreams in which we saw a person in the after-life, the *shaykh* is actually present and has communicated to his former pupil. Obviously, the other elements in the dream anecdote carry the proof of this fact and help to define the dream as a sign in its new

(1) Yūsuf ibn Yaḥyā al-Buwayṭī, a companion of ash-Shāfi'ī, was a great Shāfi'ī legist and scholar who died in the year 231/846. See as-Subkī, *Ṭabaqāt ash-Shāfi'iyya al-Kubrā* (Cairo, 1964), v. II, p. 162 ff.

(2) Aṣ-Ṣafadī, *Nakt*, p. 279.

(3) Aṣ-Ṣafadī, *Nakt*, p. 206. The statement that a person who has given information in a dream must be truthful since he was truthful in life is, in fact, a recurring element, or *topos*, in dream anecdotes. That it can be exploited quite differently is shown in an amusing anecdote in Ibn 'Abd Rabbihi, *al-'Iqd al-Farīd*, eds. A. Amīn, I. al-Abyārī and 'A. S. Hārūn (Cairo, 1949), v. VI, p. 163.

context. Yet, even if we take the dream anecdote as a whole, the syntactic context of the dream is still important for the dream's semiotic value. Had this, for example, appeared in the notice of ash-Shaykh Majd ad-Dīn, it would have testified admirably to his truthfulness and his powers. However, in the notice of the dream interpreter, ʻAlī ibn Aḥmad, the entire dream anecdote appears to demonstrate the subject's mastery of and use of dreams.

Table

Dream No.	Page	Subject of Notice	Notice of Dreamer	Notice of Dreamed	Dreamer (If in Notice of Dreamed)
1	151	Daʻwān ibn ʻAlī	—	×	Not Given
2	159	Saʻīd ibn al-Mubārak	×	—	
3	161	Simāk ibn Ḥarb	×	—	
4	170	Shīth ibn Ibrāhīm	—	×	Ibn al-Ghumr al-Adīb
5	172	Ṣāliḥ ibn ʻAbd al-Qaddūs	—	×	Aḥmad ibn ʻAbd ar-Raḥmān
6	196	ʻAbd al-Karīm ibn ʻAlī	×	—	
7	206	ʻAlī ibn Aḥmad	×	—	
8	206	ʻAlī ibn Aḥmad	×	—	
9	279	Muḥammad ibn Yaʻqūb	×	—	
10	299	al-Mu'ammal ibn Umayl	×	—	
11	302	Hārūn ibn Maʻrūf	×	—	
12	305	Hishām ibn Muʻāwiya	×	—	
13	311	Yaʻqūb ibn Dā'ūd	×	—	
14	312	Yaʻqūb ibn Sufyān	×	—	

It is not surprising that the same ʻAlī is the only personage to have two dream anecdotes in his notice. In the second (no. 8), ʻAlī dreamt that someone gave him a cooked chicken to eat and he ate from it. When he awoke, he found the rest of the chicken in his hand. (1) First of all, it is evident that it is the entire dream anecdote and not the dream which constitutes a sign. In the notice itself, aṣ-Ṣafadī has grouped this dream anecdote with the other one discussed above and described

(1) Aṣ-Ṣafadī, *Nakt*, p. 206.

them both as "strange stories" *(ḥikāyāt gharība).* (1) The chicken dream, like the one with the silk, would seem to testify to this dreamer's unusual involvement with the world of dreams.

In all those cases where the dream was in the notice of the dreamed, the dream content itself was vital to the semiotic role played by the dream in the notice. With those in the notice of the dreamer, however, this does not have to be the case. In the chicken dream discussed above, the circumstances do more than define the dream, they give it its interest; in their absence the dream would have been a completely different sign or no sign at all.

'Abd al-Karīm ibn 'Alī reported that he composed a poem in his sleep (no. 6) about the Qāḍī al-Quḍāt Ibn Razīn who had been deposed. In these verses, 'Abd al-Karīm told the Qāḍī to be of good cheer, and stated that better times would come. (2) The dream is not in the Qāḍī's notice and functions chiefly to show the visionary or poetic powers of the dreamer. The fact that 'Abd al-Karīm composed a poem which itself contained a vague prediction becomes more important than whatever happened to the Qāḍī.

The potential unimportance of the dream content is most clearly shown in a dream anecdote in the notice of Sa'īd ibn al-Mubārak ibn ad-Dahhān (no. 2). Ibn as-Sam'ānī reported that Ibn 'Asākir had told him about a dream of Ibn ad-Dahhān's. In this dream, Ibn ad-Dahhān saw someone he knew reciting poetry to another person as though he were his lover. Ibn as-Sam'ānī in turn mentioned this to Ibn ad-Dahhān who said that he did not know the story. Ibn as-Sam'ānī thereupon concluded that Ibn ad-Dahhān must have forgotten since Ibn 'Asākir was such a reliable transmitter. Ibn as-Sam'ānī then transmitted the story to Ibn ad-Dahhān through dictation so that Ibn ad-Dahhān eventually transmitted a story of which he was the source on two authorities : "*wa-qāla akhbaranī Ibn as-Sam'ānī 'an Ibn 'Asākir 'annī fa-rawā 'an shakhṣayn 'an nafsihi.*" (3)

(1) Aṣ-Ṣafadī, *Nakt*, p. 206.
(2) Aṣ-Ṣafadī, *Nakt*, p. 196.
(3) Aṣ-Ṣafadī, *Nakt*, p. 159.

In this notice, the dream by itself is not a sign but a mere unity of signification. It gains its semiotic quality only through its syntagmatic relationship with the other elements in the dream anecdote, and in this relationship the content of the dream itself is of no importance whatsoever. The anecdote as a whole is a sign of Ibn ad-Dahhān's forgetfulness.

In all of the cases so far discussed, the dream, whether or not an autonomous sign, was always the focus for the anecdote, the other elements of which helped to define the significance of the dream for the biographical notice. In one case, however, a set of dreams is merely a series of links in a narrative chain. In the notice of Yaʿqūb ibn Dā'ūd it is reported that he was imprisoned in the bottom of a well and a dome was built over the well. At the beginning of his thirteenth year of imprisonment, a being (literally, *ātin*, a comer) came to him in his sleep (no. 13), and recited in a verse that God had rescued Joseph from a cistern. Yaʿqūb then thanked God and said that relief had come. But a year passed and nothing happened. Then the same being came to him and recited another verse suggesting that relief might be near. But yet another year passed and nothing happened. Then the being came again and recited a third verse stating that God was bringing relief. When Yaʿqūb awoke, he was called, a rope was lowered into the well and he was brought up. (1)

As far as Yaʿqūb was concerned, the dreams were signs of his impending deliverance. The narrative in which they are contained, however, is not really a dream anecdote since its purpose is not to present a dream. When this narrative is examined in the context of the notice, it can be seen that its principal function is to give the cause of Yaʿqūb's blindness since we are told that he was blind when he was taken out of the well.

(1) Aṣ-Ṣafadī, *Nakt*, pp. 311-312. In his "La fonction culturelle du rêve dans l'Islam classique"' in von Grunebaum, *Le rêve*, p. 14, von Grunebaum attributes the series of dreams to "... le vizir déchu de al-Madhī [sic] (775-785), Yūnus b. ar-Rabīʿ..." and cites the study of E. Köcher, "Yaʿqūb b. Dā'ūd, Wezir al-Mahdis". But, in fact, the personage in question is Yaʿqūb ibn Dā'ūd. See, Erika Köcher, "Yaʿqūb b. Dā'ūd, Wezir al-Mahdis", *Mitteilungen des Instituts für Orientforschung* III (1955), pp. 378-420; and for the dream, p. 408.

As the preceding narrative reminds us, the *Nakt* is a dictionary of the blind, and yet only one of the eleven dreams discussed so far bore any clear relation to blindness. One explanation for this lies in the composition of the *Nakt* itself. Aṣ-Ṣafadī included in his dictionary a great many individuals who became blind late in life or shortly before their death. For this reason, we frequently do not know whether a given dreamer was blind at the time he had a dream, and in many cases, this potential blindness was irrelevant to the semiotic role of the dream.

There are, however, dreams in the corpus which are directly related to blindness. Two of these represent miraculous cures. Simāk ibn Ḥarb, who had lost his vision, dreamt (no. 3) that he saw Abraham in a dream. Simāk said that his vision had gone whereupon Abraham told him to go down to the Euphrates and open his eyes with his head under the water and that God would return his sight to him. Simāk did this and his sight was restored. (1) Once again, the dream is valorized by the rest of the anecdote. Further, the dream anecdote has a clear religious message (surrounding an apparent purification with water). Simāk himself was quoted in the notice as saying that he had lost his vision but that he had prayed to God who had returned it to him. (2)

This motif of prayer and response can be found in another dream anecdote which also contains a miraculous cure (no. 14). Ya'qūb ibn Sufyān related that he had been copying late one night and continued copying until the night came to its end. He suddenly became blind and could not see the light and began to cry more and more heavily because of this. In the process, he fell asleep and saw the Prophet Muḥammad in a dream. The Prophet asked him why he was crying to which he replied: "O Messenger of God, my vision has gone and I am grieved by what has escaped me concerning the writing of your *sunna*, and by being cut off from my country." The Prophet then told him to approach him and passed his hand over Ya'qūb's eyes as if he were reciting over them *(ka-annahu*

(1) Aṣ-Ṣafadī, *Nakt*, p. 161.
(2) Aṣ-Ṣafadī, *Nakt*, p. 161.

yaqra'u 'alayhimā).(1) Ya'qūb awoke, his vision restored, and returned to his copying.(2)

Here, the dream is only the second element in a three-part narrative. First, Ya'qūb is blinded; second, he is cured in a dream and third, we see that the dream is veracious and the cure effective. In contrast to the cure dream with Abraham discussed above, however, Muḥammad does not make a recommendation but effects the cure which could then be said to have actually transpired while the subject was dreaming. When Ya'qūb awoke, he could see.

The motifs of blindness and pious scholarship receive an entirely different treatment in the following account. Hārūn ibn Ma'rūf reported that it was said to him in a dream (no. 11) that "He who prefers *ḥadīth* over the *Qur'ān* is punished," and Hārūn understood this to be an explanation for his having lost his sight.(3) The dream and its interpretation do not show us the immediate cause of Hārūn's blindness but its explanation and ultimate cause. It is a punishment: it is clear from the notice that Hārūn was an important *ḥadīth* transmitter.(4)

In the last case to be discussed (no. 10), the punishment is effected in the dream itself, that is, the dream is pathogenic.(5) The poet, al-Mu'ammal ibn Umayl, wrote a verse to his beloved complaining that seeing her emaciated him. The second hemistich concluded: "*layta al-Mu'ammal lam yukhlaq lahu baṣar*" (would that for al-Mu'ammal no vision had been created). That night, the poet saw a man who put two fingers in the poet's eyes and said to him: "This is what you hoped for." Al-Mu'ammal awoke blind.(6)

Obviously this punishment is condign: we could even call it "poetic justice." Though the supernatural agent is neither named nor described, a religious, or at least moral, basis for

(1) This would appear to be a reference to a curative practice which involves reciting the *Qur'ān* over an invidual and which, according to my colleague Prof. A. A. Sachedina, is still practiced in the Middle East today.

(2) Aṣ-Ṣafadī, *Nakt*, p. 312.

(3) Aṣ-Ṣafadī, *Nakt*, p. 302.

(4) Aṣ-Ṣafadī, *Nakt*, pp. 301-302.

(5) Devereux, "Rêves pathogènes", pp. 191-192.

(6) Aṣ-Ṣafadī, *Nakt*, p. 299.

the action is implied. In fact, these four blindness-related dreams act as the vehicles for the interaction of blindness and religio-moral considerations. In two cases, blindness was a punishment and in one of these, the fault was essentially religious. The two cure dreams have also been integrated into this context, one man is cured through the intervention of a prophet, Abraham. The other had his vision restored by Muḥammad partially so that he could continue writing the *sunna*. The orientation is consistent: blindness comes as a punishment and is removed as a mercy. These observations concerning the moral or religious context of blindness are, of course, limited to the corpus of fourteen dreams found in the biographical notices in the *Nakt al-Himyān.*

This corpus included a considerable and illuminating variety of dreams. (1) Yet, there are principles of order within this variety. The location of a dream in the notice of the dreamer or that of the dreamed acted as one element in the determination of its semiotic role by calling attention to the dream as form or the circumstances surrounding it, on the one hand, and the dream content on the other. While the content was vital in all of the dreams found in the notice of the dreamed, for some of the dreams in the notice of the dreamer, this ceased to be the case. This syntactic distinction also plays an important role in the four dreams in which individuals appeared after their death. In the two in which these personages appeared in their own notices, they were testifying about themselves and their state in the after-life. When deceased individuals appear in the notices of others, however, they themselves are not at issue. Instead, from controversial figures, they have been elevated to authorities.

(1) One way of measuring the interest and variety of these dreams would be to note that many of them do not fit within von Grunebaum's five categories. Though these categories are provocative, their usefulness is limited by a certain lack of consistency and an absence of mutual exclusivity, von Grunebaum, "Fonction culturelle", pp. 14-20. The dreams in the corpus are also quite different from those recorded in the diary of Ibn al-Bannā' which are almost all allegorical prediction dreams. George Makdisi, "Autograph Diary of an Eleventh-Century Historian of Baghdād", *Bulletin of the School of Oriental and African Studies*, XVIII (1956), pp. 9-31, 239-260; XIX (1957), pp. 13-48, 281-303, 426-443.

The position of the dream, or more precisely of the dream anecdote, in the notice itself provides another syntactic principle which can have semiotic value. In the majority of cases, the dreams are placed towards the end of the notice. Sometimes, this placement is particularly suggestive. The dream in which Shīth ibn Ibrāhīm recited poetry foretelling his own death is the penultimate item in the notice. It is followed by a statement to the effect that a quarter in the city of Qifṭ was named after him. (1) In this position, the dream anecdote would appear to take the place of a statement giving the cause or date of death of the personage, further implying that he died shortly after having been seen in the dream. Additionally, the dreams of those who were seen in the after-life are placed after the death of the personage. In the case of Ṣāliḥ, it follows the account of his execution and is the penultimate element in his notice. With Da'wān, it follows his death date and ends the notice. (2)

But as these examples show, the problem of the significance of anecdotal location is not merely syntactic but is syntagmatic as well. Often, the significance of the dream anecdote is conditioned by the other anecdotal structures which precede it or follow it. The dream anecdote about Ibn ad-Dahhān (no. 2), for example, is preceded by a statement that for all of his knowledge, Ibn ad-Dahhān had poor handwriting and made many mistakes. (3) The two dream anecdotes about 'Alī ibn Aḥmad (no. 7 and no. 8) are preceded by a statement that he was a great dream interpreter and had other virtues as well, and that he was blinded early in his life, and is followed by a story illustrating his divinatory powers. (4) The statement about his blindness which is associated with the remark about his many virtues magnifies the powers shown in the two dream anecdotes.

In all cases, the dream is located in the anecdotal section of the notice. Hence, it is only natural that its form is always

(1) Aṣ-Ṣafadī, *Nakt*, p. 170.
(2) Aṣ-Ṣafadī, *Nakt*, pp. 172, 151.
(3) Aṣ-Ṣafadī, *Nakt*, p. 159.
(4) Aṣ-Ṣafadī, *Nakt*, pp. 206-207.

anecdotal. But this literary form plays a variety of semiotic roles. As has been shown, the dream is often defined or its role altered by the other elements present in the syntagm which is the dream anecdote. But the relationship between the dream and the dream anecdote is subject to considerable variation and this variation reflects itself in the role played by the dream in the notice. In the two dreams in which the personages were shown in the after-life (no. 1 and no. 5), the dream anecdote consists of the dream itself. This is partly no doubt because the dream type is official and, thus, easily understood but also because the dream represented a datum which was already biographical. This functional identity between the dream and the dream anecdote can be found in two other cases as well (no. 6 and no. 9).

But even where other elements are present, they vary in their role. Sometimes they interpret the dream, removing any potential ambiguity, as, for example, in the two prediction dreams (no. 4 and no. 12) as well as the dream about preferring *ḥadīth* to the *Qur'ān* (no. 11). In other cases, these elements testify to the veracity of the dream, as in the dream of the stolen silk (no. 7), and the two cure dreams (no. 3 and no. 14). Or, sometimes the dream is an essential function in a narrative as in the chicken dream (no. 8) or the dream of al-Mu'ammal (no. 10). In the most extreme cases, like that of Ibn ad-Dahhān (no. 2), the dream is a mere object in the story, its content irrelevant.

The dream anecdotes display this morphological diversity because they constitute that part of the text in which the transformation is made from one semiotic perspective to another. In the dream anecdote, the dream, which was a sign to the dreamer (or at least an experience of the dreamer), becomes a unity of signification capable of redefinition. The dream anecdote achieves this redefinition by creating a new sign, this time in the semiotic system of the biographical notice.

As a sign, however, the dream hesitates between message (1)

(1) Message is being used here as an abstraction to characterize certain dreams and should not be confused with Oppenheim's use of this same term to describe a

and event (event is considered here as being distinct from the mere event of giving a message). The dream as event can be seen quite clearly with the story of the poet al-Mu'ammal (no. 10). Al-Mu'ammal is not told that he will be blinded, he is blinded during the course of the dream. But this action has not merely taken place in some parallel or totally subjective universe which is the person's dream. That this action has been done to the physical al-Mu'ammal is shown by the fact that he awakens blinded. Were we to try to interpret this dream as a pure message, as for example in the Greco-Islamic onirocritical tradition, the entire anecdote would lose its sense. As aṣ-Ṣafadī himself noted in the introduction to the *Nakt*, if one sees himself being blinded by someone, then this person is leading him astray. (1) The dream has to be seen as an event for the anecdote to be coherent. The dream of Ya'qūb ibn Sufyān (no. 14) must also be seen in this way. In fact, there is little discontinuity between waking and sleeping, the subject falls asleep crying and is crying in his dream.

And the dream can be an event for the dreamed as well. Those who were seen in the after-life are actually, and not symbolically, present. It is this which permits the dream to transmit an authoritative judgment. This is also the case with those who act as authorities. This notion of the presence of those who are seen is clearly shown in a problem which aṣ-Ṣafadī discusses in his *al-Ghayth al-Musajjam*. A learned man was asked about the saying of the Prophet that when he is seen in a dream, he is truly seen *(ḥaqqan)*, and how this could be since the Prophet was seen in the same hour by many different people in many different places. The answer was given that Muḥammad was like the sun whose light covers many countries East and West. (2) In this way, even the dreams in which the dreamer is told a piece of information or given advice

certain type of dream common in the Ancient Near East. A. Leo Oppenheim, "Rêves divinatoires dans le Proche-Orient ancien", in von Grunebaum, *Le rêve*, p. 331.

(1) Aṣ-Ṣafadī, *Nakt*, p. 19.

(2) Aṣ-Ṣafadī, *Ghayth*, p. 244.

or directions, like the dream with Abraham (no. 3), can also be seen as events.

The two prediction dreams (no. 4 and no. 12), on the other hand, act essentially as messages. Not only do they predict future events (hence they have not happened) but these are the only two cases in which dreamers saw other individuals who were clearly still alive. Shīth ibn Ibrāhīm even interpreted the dream (no. 4) in which he had appeared as indicating that his "soul" *(nafs)* was announcing his death to him. (1) The dream (no. 11) about preferring *ḥadīth* to the *Qur'ān* was also a message, though given directly, while the dream of ibn ad-Dahhān (no. 2) has the form of a message, though this becomes irrelevant. The dreams which came to Ya'qūb ibn Dā'ūd (no. 13) during his captivity were both messages and events. In all cases, the dream anecdotes turn these messages into events or connect them directly with events.

This distinction is an important one since it may be a distinguishing characteristic of the dream in the biographical notice. Allegorical prediction dreams tend to be pure messages and not events. For example, if a woman dreams that she gives birth to a serpent, this action has not taken place but is a message indicating that an analogous action will take place in the future.

Further, poetry is a frequent element in the dreams and this poetry usually contains a message. Yet, the dreamer does not dream the message but dreams that someone recites the poem, which recitation is an event. Hence the message is directly given and its delivery can be seen as the event of the dream. This distinguishes it sharply from the allegorical prediction dream which is a message disguised as an event.

When the dreams are combined with other elements in the dream anecdotes, these other elements reinforce the quality of the dream as an event. Thus, though some of the dreams came to the dreamers as signs or messages, in the biographical dictionary they all appear as events. Hence the dream, which may contain a message, is transformed when necessary into an

(1) Aṣ-Ṣafadī, *Nakt*, p. 170.

event. This event becomes part of an anecdote which is itself an event or series of events. This anecdote then is the literary form in which the event becomes a sign alongside the other events in the biographical notice.

To summarize, the dreams chosen for inclusion tended already to be events. Their placement in the anecdotes increased and oriented this event-status so that an event/sign was created.

Hence, in the notice, these events (until read) are signifiers. But what are the signifieds? And how are they conveyed? It is not surprising that the signifieds are biographical and often conventionally so. Nevertheless, they do emphasize certain themes. Five of the dreams (nos. 3, 10, 11, 13, and 14) explain the change in the blindness-status of the personage, either how he became blind or how he ceased to be blind. But in this context, they also do much more: they orient this change within a moral universe. The judgments thus made reflect on the entire life of the individual and his moral and religious status. Also, as in the case of the personage who preferred *ḥadīth* to the *Qur'ān* (no. 11), they provide a judgment on a specific practice and on a career. In the story of Ya'qūb (no. 13) who was rescued from the well, in which story they would be otherwise narratologically unnecessary, the dreams portray the rescue as an act of divine mercy.

Moral and religious judgments, however, were not limited to the blindness dreams, but obviously manifest themselves in dreams of those who were seen in the after-life (no. 1 and no. 5). Also judged are specific accusations, useful in controversy, and in the case of the *muqri'* (no. 1), professional activities. Fully half of the dreams, therefore, order the entire notice by conveying a judgment on the personage, distinct from the enumeration of his curriculum vitae.

The other major role of the dream anecdotes is to display the visionary, divinatory or otherwise magical powers of the dreamer (nos. 6, 7, 8, 9, and 12). Not surprisingly, the dream as a sign tends to be specialized for other-worldly concerns.

But the dream can play a more earthly and conventional

role. One gave us the circumstances of death (no. 4) and another, the personal trait of forgetfulness (no. 2).

What, then, is the relationship between signifier and signified? What kinds of codes are used in the semiotic system of the biographical dictionary? First of all, the codes are the established literary narrative ones. For those elements which were included because they may have been considered important biographical information, as, for example, circumstances of death or causes of blindness, these are the only codes used. Most of the other signs use a metonymic code of cause and effect. If someone is in Heaven, he was pious, if he was punished, he was not. If he displays certain powers, it means that he had them: we infer the cause from the effect. Or, as in the case of a personality trait, the general is inferred from the particular.

This figurative language is, of course, at once simple, flexible, and easy to read. Yet the dream anecdote is often a complex sign with many elements and more than one signified. It is the syntagmatic and syntactic contexts which make the crucial distinctions directing the reader to one aspect or another of the dream as sign.

VI

Mentalités and Marginality: Blindness and Mamlūk Civilization*

IN *Illness as Metaphor*, Susan Sontag has shown that diseases can transcend their biological realities and become the focus for other cultural concerns, and that they can become part of a language through which a given society articulates social and cultural values.[1] One can then agree with the cultural historian of medicine, Marcel Sendrail, that each epoch has "its own pathological style," consisting not so much of the specific maladies of any time and place as of the manner in which a society defines its relationship to disease, its concepts of illness and of health.[2]

But what is true of different epochs is certainly even more true of different civilizations. And what is true of disease is clearly also true of pathological conditions and physical handicaps, like blindness. Indeed, it will be the purpose of this study to show that the physical handicap of blindness serves as a kind of metaphor for a significant group of concepts, values, and ideals in medieval Islamic civilization. The conceptions that medieval Islamic civilization, and specifically Mamlūk civilization, held of the blind formed an important part of the *mentalités* of that civilization.

But what are *mentalités*? The term has been rendered into English as mentalities, mind sets, or, less frequently, mental structures. *Men-*

*I would like to thank the NEH, the SSRC/ACLS, and the ARCE, whose generosity made this work possible. An earlier version of this study was delivered as a public lecture at the University of Chicago on May 3, 1984, and in its present form is a contribution to the work of the Equipe de Recherche 06 0302 of the C.N.R.S. in Paris.

talités history can be understood as a school whose goal is the explanation of popular social attitudes and forms, and whose chief method is the exploration of the networks of structures through which social conceptions are conveyed. Structure, according to Patrick Hutton, "refers to all of the forms which regularize mental activity, whether these be aesthetic images, linguistic codes, expressive gestures, religious rituals, or social customs."[3]

For Jacques Le Goff, perhaps the foremost historian of medieval European *mentalités*, the first appeal of *mentalités* history resides precisely in its "imprecision," in its ability to designate that "je ne sais quoi" of history.[4]

But Le Goff does elaborate a more detailed, if not precise, definition of *mentalités* history: the blending of traditional history with other branches of the human sciences, notably ethnology and sociology. In this connection, Le Goff also emphasizes the special relationship that the history of *mentalités* enjoys with social psychology, noting the development of studies on criminality, marginals, and deviants. Le Goff adds that this type of history can be located at the juncture of the individual and the collective, the unconscious and the intentional, and the marginal and the general. Linked to this for the French medievalist is the additional area which distinguishes the historian of *mentalités*, the types of sources which he exploits, including literary and artistic documents. The latter sources remove the emphasis of the historical activity from the presentation of "objective" phenomena to the representation of these phenomena. The important element in a historical source is no longer the facts which it presents, but rather the manner in which the source presents them.[5]

But the history of *mentalités* is also associated with the work of Michel Foucault. His studies on insanity, the birth of the prison, and so on, have, to use Paul Veyne's expression, "revolutionized" history.[6] Foucault aims at the isolation of epistemes and their mutation in the course of Western history. Hayden White has characterized the Foucaultian episteme as the " 'total set of relations that unite, at a given period, the discursive practices that give rise to epistemological figures, sciences, and possibly formalized systems' of knowledge."[7] Hutton has pointed out that what makes Foucault's approach similar to that of earlier *mentalités* historians, such as Norbert Elias, is that he bases the search for common attitudes in the "common codes of knowledge through which the world is perceived." These codes, his "discourses," are "the verbal expression of the mental structures . . .

through which man organizes his activities and classifies his perceptions of the world."[8]

In fact, whatever the area of inquiry (madness for Foucault or the civilizing process for Elias), most historians dealing with Western mental structures have tended to follow the developmental mode. This, of course, must be seen in relation to the larger school from which *mentalités* history emerged, the *Annales* school. The *Annales* school is well-known for its emphasis on what Braudel called "social time," as opposed to "political time." For Braudel, the level of social time lies beneath that of political time. "Deeper still" for him is "geographical time, where change is barely perceptible."[9]

But the fact that political events may be set aside as markers of change has not meant an abandonment of diachrony. Historians like Philippe Ariès, in his studies of death, and Michel Foucault adhere to a diachronic framework. It is simply a framework which englobes greater periods of chronological time. When Foucault, for example, discusses the "carceral" mode in Western society, in his study of insanity or that of the penal system, he associates this with the development of new attitudes in the West, and development implies diachrony. As Hutton demonstrates, the emphasis in Foucault, as in Norbert Elias, is on a diachronic shift from external to internal codes of behavior.[10]

The developmental tendency of most, though not all,[11] *mentalités* historians is not logically necessary to the study of the history of mentalities. Such approaches have arisen to a considerable degree in response to preexisting historical problematics, like the rise of the modern West for Elias and Foucault or the sea-change from early medieval to late medieval culture for Radding.[12] Since such problematics are foreign to our study of Mamlūk civilization, we shall adopt a completely synchronic approach. Logically, synchronic examinations of Arabo-Islamic mentalities must precede diachronic comparisons. A synchronic examination of Mamlūk civilization does not, therefore, in any way imply an eternal Islamic cultural essence. Nor does it imply that nothing important changed in the two and a half centuries during which the Mamlūks ruled much of the Arab world. It merely seeks to delineate those cultural elements which remained constant during this period. Since all that can be attempted in the present study is the identification of the principal roles of blindness and the blind in Mamlūk mentalities, little scope is left for diachronic comparisons.

The synchronic bias of this study means that it draws as much from literary critical (especially structuralist) approaches as it does from purely historical ones. It is the text which provides the starting point for the analysis of mental structures, and it is the subsequent comparison between structures present in various texts which will then permit us to speak of mental structures in general.

A mental structure concerning blindness does not generally exist in isolation from the totality of a society's mentalities. Mental structures are usually articulated as part of discourses, that is, a specific language (or, to be more precise, semiotic system) which the society uses to articulate its values. Hence, we have moral discourses, discourses of the body, etc. In addition, blindness is integrated into these discourses under the sign of a particular mental operation or mode, that is, the relationship or conception impressed upon blindness to integrate it into that particular discourse.

This conception of social consciousness as articulated through discourses owes much, of course, to that of Foucault. So too does our understanding of the relationship between the facts of social life (institutions, social roles, etc.) and the ideas or values consciously articulated by a society. As Foucault has shown, it makes little sense to see ideas as either the causes of, or after-the-fact generalizations from, social institutions. Thus, institutional frameworks and social roles, just like literary images or proverbs, are direct reflections of basic mental structures. Social reality is just as much the seat of discourse and the articulator of values as are purely literary or textual phenomena.[13]

The nature of the textual sources for this study raises another issue evoked by historians of mentalities. Hutton makes it clear that in his view, history of mentalities "considers the attitudes of ordinary people toward everyday life."[14] And this point of view would be shared by many a *mentalités* historian. Insofar as "ordinary" here means "anonymous," or "collectively held," Hutton's proposition is implicit in the history of mentalities. But if "ordinary" means "non-elite," it is not. Our approach, based upon written sources, will, of necessity, tend to reflect elite positions. However, there is no reason to assume that the mental structures present in them are not shared by lower social strata. On the contrary, it is in the nature of many classical sources, like *adab* works, to include materials whose origins may be popular, or at least traditional, like proverbs. In addition, Arab scholars were alive to popular sayings and practices, and felt free to comment upon them.

Le Goff has mentioned the study of marginal groups as falling within the history of mentalities.[15] And here again, of course, the definition of marginality is important. In *Aspects de la marginalité au Moyen-Age*, several scholars of the medieval West have attempted to define marginality for that society. One can speak, for example, of statistical marginality; or one can speak of structural marginality, in which the marginal is someone outside the norm, someone who is not well integrated, or who is excluded from society. Thus, the study of a society's discourse on marginality can help us to understand the way this society conceives of the normal and of its relationship to the marginal, or to a plurality of marginalities.[16]

We have repeatedly spoken of historians of the medieval West and how they perceive that society. Yet, the problems posed for the historian of Islamic mentalities need not necessarily be the same. Although the methodologies exploited by historians of the West can shed light on the path to be followed, the area to which the path is leading need not be identical. We should not necessarily be led into the study of a concept or an area, simply because that concept has been studied in the West. Foucault's problematics need not be our own. Nor should we await a study by a Western historian before deciding that a given topic is worthy of scholarly investigation.

When we speak of a society's mentalities, we are talking not just about the attitudes that this society brings to different social facts. We are speaking also of the relative importance that the society in question gives to different components or concepts. Hence, automatically to shift categories from one civilization to another is, in a way, to prejudge the morphology of that society's mentalities.

Each society articulates its own concerns through concepts or issues that are central to it. And we must extract the key concepts and issues from within the society itself. Blindness is such a concept for Islamic society, one which acts as the focus for the articulation of a large range of social values.

Why blindness specifically for a study of Mamlūk mental structures? The question of blindness is an important one in Islamic civilization, and appears in virtually all of the major types of sources in the medieval period: from the theological and the legal through the historical to the literary and the philological.

This importance becomes more clearly visible under the Mamlūks, the slave soldiers who ruled Egypt and Syria from about 1250 until 1517. There is no question but that the visually handicapped formed part of the background of social life in the Mamlūk domains. Eye disease leading to blindness has been prevalent in the Nile Valley since antiquity.[17] While the physical presence of the blind is not sufficient to explain their ubiquity in texts, it is probably a condition of it.

In addition, the question of blindness transcends the mere problem of a physical handicap, to touch on the important area of vision, both physical and spiritual. Blindness also plays a central role in crucial debates in Islamic culture, as it touches on the problems of vision vs. hearing, and written vs. oral culture.

The Mamlūk period is distinguished by the richness of its sources. The most important for our purposes is the biographical compendium and general study on blindness and the blind, the *Nakt al-himyān fī nukat al-'umyān*, by the Mamlūk official Khalīl ibn Aybak al-Ṣafadī (d. 764/1361).[18] In addition, this period represents the culmination of a long tradition of learning in the Arabic and Islamic disciplines. As such, it includes within it sources from earlier periods, such as ḥadīths, the Qur'ān, proverbs, etc. Thus, the fact that a source may have been written before our period does not eliminate it from the texture of Mamlūk mental structures. To take an extreme case, even though the Qur'ān was revealed long before the Mamlūk period, it was still considered a normative document by most representatives of Mamlūk society, and had to be integrated into their mental structures. It is merely necessary in this case that we have some indication of how particular verses were understood at that time. Since medieval Islamic civilization had a considerable reverence for traditional materials of both a religious and a secular nature, a similar situation obtains with a large variety of written sources, provided that we have some reason to believe that these texts were still important in Mamlūk times. Hence, the historical or intellectual conjunctures which may have presided over the birth of a given text are no longer relevant to us. What is important is the place that this text, or any of its ideas, occupies in the systems of Mamlūk mentalities.

Despite the variety of literary sources, multiplied in turn by the composite nature of these sources, there are a limited number of ways in which blind individuals appear. These types of categories should be understood as being at once textual and social. They are social in that they do represent different social levels in Mamlūk society. But they are also textual because they represent the social types isolated textually, and not necessarily all those existing in the society at large. Nor, as we shall see, are they the result of a systematic attempt to paint blindness in different social classes. Each comes from a different kind of text and reflects different kinds of concerns with blindness.

The first, and most numerous, category is that of the individuals who inhabit the biographical dictionaries. A biographical dictionary can be organized around different principles, geographical, chronological, or occupational. The genre reached its apex in the Mamlūk period.[19] The *Nakt al-himyān* of al-Ṣafadī, our most comprehensive source on blindness, presents over three hundred biographical notices of blind individuals. Since this dictionary is organized around a specific physical characteristic, absence of vision, it covers a large range of individuals, from scholars to poets, Qur'ān reciters, ḥadīth transmitters, rulers, etc. But the visually handicapped appear in other types of biographical dictionaries, when they fit within the parameters of the work in question.

The personages who inhabit the biographical dictionaries are the individuals whose blindness is most often specified. In these works, we are normally told the cause of blindness: was it congenital, was it acquired through a disease or through blinding, was it a result of old age? It is also in this category that we find the famous blind personages of medieval Islam, the 'Abbasid poets Bashshār ibn Burd (d. 167 or 168/784–785) and al-Ma'arrī (d. 449/1057), the Andalusian lexicographer Ibn Sīda (d. 458/1066), and others.[20] Blind poets are represented not only in biographical literature but also through their poetry, and thus may appear in *adab* works, poetic compendia, etc.

Socially, the subjects of biographical notices, whether sighted or blind, are members of the elite, though an elite understood in the broadest sense. Hence, biographical literature presents us with the view of the elite blind: who they were, how they lived, etc. There are, however, other social/textual types of the blind; and the clearest of these, after the "elite," is its social opposite, the beggars. There is no doubt that blind beggars were prevalent in medieval Islam. Yet, we do not expect to find accounts of beggars in the biographical literature. Instead, this category has a tendency to appear in the literary sources: in *adab* works and in the *maqāmāt*. What is particularly interesting in this literature is that alongside the relatively small number of genuine blind beggars, we find a large number of falsely blind beggars, that is, beggars who feign blindness.[21] It is clear from this literature that blindness is considered not only an exemplary physical defect for a beggar but also one likely to be mimicked.

Of course, when we speak of the elite and of beggars, we are speaking of two categories which are reasonably easy to distinguish. They are at opposite ends of the social spectrum and rarely appear together in the sources. But, the literary world of late medieval Islamic civilization does not restrict itself to these two categories. What about the average blind individual, that common man of *mentalités* history? That category most often surfaces in the literary sources, specifically in the anecdotal material. These common individuals are not famous personages. The onomastic information pertaining to them is often absent, or restricted to a first name. In other words, their identity remains unknown. It is clear, however, that these individuals who inhabit the anecdotes are not beggars. We may be told their occupation: in one case, we know that the subject of the anecdote is a water carrier. We get glimpses at times of their marital situations. It is in this context that we find the anecdotes which relate the extraordinary feats of the blind; these extraordinary acts are most often attached to what we have called "common individuals." Here we read, for example, about a blind individual who, despite his handicap, could thread a needle and sew.[22]

Though blind individuals are represented through three social/textual types, the blind as a unified social group also have a place in medieval *adab* works. First and foremost, the blind are placed among the other handicapped, usually referred to as *ahl al-'āhāt*, those possessing a physical infirmity or defect. This category includes those whom we would consider handicapped, like the blind and the lame, but also many who are physically abnormal. Ibn Qutayba (d. 276/889), for example, included the blue-eyed, and those with bad breath, among others,[23] while the Damascene scholar Yūsuf ibn 'Abd al-Hādī (d. 909/1517) combined the blind with the hemiplegic, the wall-eyed, the flat-nosed, and the large-mouthed.[24] Al-Nuwayrī (d. 732/1332), in his *Nihāyat al-arab*, places the blind between women and beggars, and shortly after idiots.[25] Hence, the blind form part of a larger group, which is, at first sight, not easy to define. This group does, however, consist of the marginal. But how is this marginality defined? In fact, there are two discourses of marginality, one of which is purely physical. But this physical marginality is not that of a handicap, but merely one of physical difference, of a variation from the normal, and not one which excludes from society as a whole. Hence, in this schema, a blind individual is physically different but not necessarily handicapped. One could almost, in these cases, speak of a merely statistical marginality.

The other discourse of marginality is a social one. And here we see the blind placed with other social categories in Mamlūk society whose status could be defined as relatively unfavored, like beggars and women. The relationship between blindness and beggary has already been alluded to above, while that between the blind and women will be discussed later. Suffice it to say that the discourse of the blind as one among many marginal groups suggests the conception of blindness as a relative and not an absolute handicap. And by extension, blindness forms part of an integrated marginality.

Perhaps one of the best ways of seeing the mental structures of a given civilization on a given concept is to examine the terms which the civilization uses to express that concept. And for the visually handicapped, there is thus no better indication than the philological tradition itself. As Pierre Henri has shown, the terminology for blindness and the blind in the West is linked to the notions of darkness (for example, in the French word *cécité*), of being mixed-up or troubled (the German and English *blind*), to the notion of being hidden or closed (the Slavic languages), and to the concept of smoke, with the Greek *tuphlos*, from which we derive "typhlology," knowledge relating to blindness.[26]

Unlike the Western languages, where the available vocabulary for the concept of blindness is actually quite restricted, Arabic has a multiplicity of words. For the blind, the most common usages are *a'mā, kafīf, makfūf,* and *ḍarīr*. There is also a word applied to the congenitally blind, *akmah*. But, what do these words tell us? *A'mā* comes from the verbal root *'-m-y*, and according to the lexicographical sources, including the *Tāj al-'arūs* of al-Zabīdī (d. 1205/1791) and *al-Muḥkam* of Ibn Sīda, the verb expresses the disappearance of vision altogether.[27] But al-Ṣafadī, who is something of a *mentalités* historian himself, delves into the question of this verb in one of his introductions to the *Nakt al-himyān*. Al-Ṣafadī explores many verbs whose roots have the radicals *'ayn* and *mīm* in the first two positions, but whose third radical may be another consonant. This enables him to show that, in fact, these verbs all express the idea of covering and hiding or disappearance. He thus links them to the concept of *'amā*, or blindness.[28]

Interestingly enough, al-Ṣafadī limits himself to this one verb in his philological discussion. And this despite the fact that he does exploit the other synonyms in the rest of the work, be it in the remaining introductions or in the biographical notices themselves.

Although the word *a'mā* could be considered the generic term for a blind man, the appellation *al-ḍarīr* is the one which is most common in the onomastic chains, or lists of names, in the biographical notices themselves. This commonness is also attested in specialized works on names, such as the *Tabṣīr al-muntabih* of Ibn Ḥajar al-'Asqalānī (d. 852/1449).[29] *Al-ḍarīr* appears to have been the most polite way of designating a visually handicapped individual. *Ḍarīr* comes from the root *ḍ-r-r* whose basic meaning is "to harm" or "to injure." And, again, according to the lexicographical sources, it is used to signify one whose vision has gone, or one who has been injured by an illness.[30]

As for the two words *al-kafīf* and *al-makfūf*, they are both derived from the same verbal root, *k-f-f*, whose basic meaning has the sense of "filling" or "wrapping." The verb is used in the passive with the word *baṣar*, *kuffa baṣaruhu*, to signify that someone has been blinded or lost his sight.[31]

To these terms, we can add *akmah*, which refers to one who is born blind, as when it is said, *kamiha baṣaruhu*, which the lexicographers relate to darkness obliterating someone's sight.[32] There is yet one more term, and rare at that, used to refer to a blind individual, and that is *maḥjūb*. This word, whose basic meaning is "covered," is thus used with reference to someone who is blind.[33]

The term *baṣīr*, or "sighted," is also sometimes presented as referring to the blind. However, as I have shown elsewhere,[34] even though *baṣīr* is generally listed in the *aḍdād* works as possessing the meaning "blind," it did not really have this usage in the Mamlūk period, and was only used with specific individuals when referring to an aspect in which they could be said to be sighted.

It is clear that there are tendencies in the lexicographical tradition which relate to blindness. *Akmah*, used for the congenitally blind, is not exploited nearly to the same extent as the words derived from the other verbal roots. In fact, al-Ṣafadī, when he provides information about congenital blindness, almost always writes *wulida a'mā* (he was born blind) rather than *akmah*.[35] Furthermore, in the appellations used for blind personages, al-Akmah does not appear at all. And yet, as we have seen, this term is, in the philological tradition, the only one with a clear connection to darkness. The three other terms, which are also the more common ones, provide a connection between blindness and the physiological problem of the loss of sight: that the sight may be covered or that it may disappear, without any overt connection between this loss of sight and darkness. It would seem that the connection of blindness with darkness, a connection which clearly exists in the West,[36] is shunned in the medieval Islamic tradition.

The terms for blind and blindness carry two general associations: one, the most common, with the idea of covering, and one with the idea of injury or defect. The notion of defect is already familiar to us. But when we compare both these ideas with the Western philological associations with darkness or confusion, we perceive that the Arabic concepts remain more closely attached to the physical reality of the absence of sight. They do not expand the idea of blindness into a larger world of darkness or the even more general notion of confusion. The relatively down-to-earth aspects of the Arabic terminology, therefore, reduce the separation between the blind and the sighted. The blind are injured or defective, to be sure, but their injury is not projected outward into a more general state. This is a mental structure which we shall see again and again: blindness remains in the physical realm and does not escape into mental or spiritual differences.

Blindness thus plays a role in philology, in the discourse of words and their ultimate meanings. But, how the blind actually lived also reflected itself in the consciousness of Mamlūk civilization. The living patterns of the blind were taken up as part of a larger discourse of daily life.

The aspect of the daily life of the visually handicapped which receives the greatest attention in the written sources is that of mobility. This vital aspect of daily life appears in virtually all the sources, from the legal to the anecdotal. Most of the anecdotes relating extraordinary feats by blind individuals involve mobility. We are told, for example, about al-Faḍl Abū 'Alī, who in the midst of a gathering would get up to fulfill a need and would navigate a room full of people without ever falling. Al-Ṣafadī tells us that he once saw a blind man walking with his wife. He was guiding her by the hand and warning her about pitfalls in the road.[37]

But these stories are clearly meant to be extraordinary. They are included because they run counter to the norm. The texts make it clear that blind individuals were quite commonly led by guides. The question of guiding a blind individual receives attention in the various types of sources. The legist Anas ibn Mālik said that he who guides a blind man for forty steps will not be touched by Hellfire, obviously an injunction which encourages the guiding of the blind. The issue of a guide also enters into the question of the religious duties of a blind individual. Is the Friday prayer, for example, incumbent upon him? The advice in this area is that if he has a guide or can afford one, then he should attend. Other questions arose from this as well. In one case, for example, a man was guiding a blind individual, and they both fell into a well. The blind man fell on top of his sighted guide and killed him. Who was responsible? In fact, there was a well-developed jurisprudence to deal with legal questions arising from the interdependence of the blind man and his guide.[38]

That the guide was the preferred mode of mobility for the visually handicapped is also attested to, for example, by the fact that the eighth-century caliph, al-Walīd I, ordered that a companion be provided to guide every blind individual in the kingdom.[39]

The role of the guide can be seen as more than simply one of facilitating the mobility of the blind individual. More importantly, he played a mediating role between the visually handicapped and his physical and social environment. The blind poet al-Khuraymī mentions in one of his poems that his guide would also tell him whom to greet.[40]

But of course, the visually handicapped moved about on their own, be it with the help of a stick or otherwise.[41] This seems, however, to have been much less the preferred technique, and receives far less attention in the sources.

Hence, the mobility of the blind seems to be one of the central concerns in the texts at hand, with emphasis placed on the guidance of the blind. However, how does this help us to understand the mental structures about the visually handicapped? On the one hand, one can construe the information on mobility as deemphasizing the independence of the visually handicapped. But concomitant with this is the more significant fact that the blind are encouraged to circulate, when necessary, with another individual, a guide. This, of course, places the stress on the communal aspect, the visually handicapped individual being conceived as part of the social system. Hence, this emphasis on the mobility of the blind person and his relationship with his guide is integrative. But the mode of integration is that of dependence. Dependence, in this context, could be defined as inferiority plus integration.

That this association of the blind with their guides along the mode of dependence reflects a basic mental structure can be seen in the way it is exploited in the onirocritical literature. We are told, for example, that one who dreams that someone is blinding him will be led astray by that person.[42] Even more interesting is the interpretation provided for the individual who dreams that his two eyes are someone else's eyes. This indicates that the dreamer will become blind and that someone will show him the way.[43] Hence, blindness represents a dependence on someone else's eyes—not darkness, but dependent vision.

The other area of the daily life of the blind which is noted by the medieval sources is that of eating. The Qur'ānic verse from Sūrat al-Nūr: "There is no fault in the blind, and there is no fault in the lame, and there is no fault in the sick, neither in yourselves, that you eat of your houses, etc.," is interpreted by al-Qurṭubī (d. 671/1273) in his commentary as an injunction to eat with the blind, the lame, and the sick. Al-Qurṭubī further noted that people had an aversion to eating with the blind. In this period, people usually ate from a common dish, which explains al-Qurṭubī's remark that the sighted were disturbed by the blind whose hands had a tendency to roam over the food.[44] The difficulty which the visually handicapped normally encountered while eating can be seen from another perspective. Al-Tha'ālibī (d. 429/1038) notes that after Ḥassān ibn Thābit became blind, he would ask if the food before him was "of one hand" or "of two hands" before reaching out to it.[45] Though this anecdote is positive rather than negative, it testifies, as much as al-Qurṭubī's commentary, to the difficulties experienced by the blind when eating. Yet, in both cases, the emphasis is on the blind and the sighted eating together, which activity is presented as a laudable one. Partaking of a common meal was, and remains, one of the most important social activities of Islamic civilization. Thus, the problems encountered with eating, like the linked notions of mobility and dependence, must be seen in the context of social integration. And in the consciousness of Islamic society, the two greatest problems to be overcome in this quest for integration were mobility and table manners.

Perhaps one of the most fascinating areas for the understanding of the mental structures about the blind in medieval Islam is what we can call a discourse on the body. In his extremely interesting study, "En Marge du monde connu: Les Races des monstres," Bruno Roy isolates conceptions about unusual physical types in the medieval West. According to Roy, these classifications represent an attempt on the part of Western European man to confirm his own normality.[46] By extension from Roy's analysis, we can argue that the discussions of the physically unusual in the Mamlūk sources also help to define what society considered normal. When society discusses the physically unusual, it is, in effect, articulating values about the physically normal and its significations, that is, a discourse on the body.

We have already noted in the philological discussion that blindness was treated as an essentially physical state. But what kind of physicality are we dealing with? There is no doubt that one of the most significant aspects of this physicality is its link to the notion of physical imperfection. Part of this, of course, can be seen in one of the terms used for the visually handicapped individual, *al-ḍarīr*, someone who has been injured, and hence someone whose physical integrity has been called into question.

But this mental structure of physical imperfection is present on a deeper level. It is well known that one of the practices used to dethrone a ruler in Islam was to blind him. This procedure, which began in the tenth century, was accomplished in order to make the individual physically imperfect, and hence improper for holding office.[47] This practice, of course, testifies to the connection between blindness and physical imperfection.

If physical perfection or integrity was a qualification for the status of ruler, how much more might it be so for that of prophet. The concern with the physical integrity of prophets lies at the root of the debate on whether or not a prophet could be blind. For the medieval Muslims, the problem was provoked by the "fact" of the blindness of the prophet Jacob, attested in the Qur'ān (Sūrat Yūsuf, verse 84). The controversy manifests the difficulty of integrating the Qur'ānic story with the conception of the physical integrity of prophets. The fact that some Muslim scholars attempted to deny the blindness of Jacob,[48] thus flying in the face of the more obvious meaning of the Qur'ānic story, testifies to the importance of the idea that a prophet could not be blind, and its attendant mental structure that blindness represents a serious physical imperfection.

The question of whether a visually handicapped individual was fit for other legal and theological functions receives a great deal of attention in the sources. Most of these issues are quite complicated and arguments were, as a rule, adduced for both sides. The legists, for example, discuss the issue of whether a blind individual could be an appropriate witness. Another controversial area is the ability of the visually handicapped to be reliable transmitters. In both issues, the problem can be seen to be linked to the possibility of confusion arising from the hearing process.[49] But it is the argument in favor of acceptability which is striking in this context. It is noted that when the wife of the Prophet, 'Ā'isha, and other holy women in early Islam transmitted, they did so from behind a curtain. Their hearers would then transmit on their authority. It is well known, al-Ṣafadī adds, that, in this case, the state of the sighted woman is the same as that of the blind man.[50] What this example points to is a relationship between blind men and sighted women. In fact, in legal works, one can also observe this close relationship between the blind and women. In cases where the visually handicapped are not treated like the sighted, their status is sometimes specified as being similar to that of women. We can see this, for example, in the discussion which al-Suyūṭī (d. 919/1505) devotes to the blind in his compendium of Shāfi'ī *fiqh, al-Ashbāh wa'l-naẓā'ir.*[51]

That this relationship between women and blind men is not accidental and that it forms in fact an integral part of the mental structure of physical imperfection, can be seen when we examine other types of texts. I have shown in other studies the significance of the arrangement of medieval encyclopedic *adab* works.[52] The arrangement of topics in these multi-subject works reflects a social arrangement presented in descending order, with the most important topics preceding the less important ones. Women are usually discussed toward the end of the text, and have a tendency to appear along with children and the insane, among others. For our purposes, it is what this arrangement tells us about the blind that is significant. The visually handicapped in these encyclopedic *adab* works invariably find themselves allied to the women. This is the case in the prototypical encyclopedic *adab* work, the *'Uyūn al-akhbār* of Ibn Qutayba, as well as in the fourteenth-century encyclopedia, the *Nihāyat al-arab* of al-Nuwayrī.[53] And insofar as the women are also most often linked to the notions of physicality and sexuality, the blind, by extension, are also associated with these notions.

But the placement of the visually defective alongside women can also tell us about the attitude to this defect in general. Women are, of course, an integral part of Islamic society, whether or not one approves of the mode of integration. Mentally associating the blind with women is an integrative attitude to the visual defect. One could argue from this comparison that the blind are not even being treated as abnormal. Theirs is a state of physical inferiority that is as much a normal part of society as is the state of womanhood. And, as we shall see shortly, the blind also share with women associations with physicality and sexuality.

A defect, of course, can be conceived as a loss or a lack. But a lack poses the question of compensation, the idea that this unusual absence may be balanced by an unusual presence. It is, therefore, no surprise that we find the mode of compensation associated with the blind. We are familiar with one form of compensation: spiritual vision replacing physical vision. In the West, examples of this abound: Oedipus, the blind seer Teiresias, the poet Homer, and so on.[54] It is noteworthy that this particular form of compensation does not exist in the Islamic tradition. In fact, it is so alien to the mental structures governing blindness in Islam that we find the sources fleeing from it, as in the discussions centering around the blindness of Jacob. After his vision is restored, Jacob says to his doubting sons: "Did I not tell you I know from God that you know not?" referring to knowledge he gained while he was blind.[55] And, yet, no attempt is made to connect physical blindness with spiritual vision. In effect, the absence of an argument in this direction, along with the attempt to deny Jacob his visual handicap, attests to the fact that this mode of compensation did not form part of the mental structures of blindness.

An area where compensation is developed, however, is the sexual, the blind man being given special qualifications in this sphere. A proverb states *ankaḥ min aʿmā*, "more virile than a blind man."[56] This is, of course, meant to indicate that the blind individual possesses that characteristic to such a degree that he becomes the model against which other individuals are measured. The geographer and cosmographer al-Qazwīnī (d. 682/1283), in his *ʿAjāʾib al-makhlūqāt*, notes that the blind individual is the most virile of people, just as the eunuch is the one whose vision is the most correct. And that is because, in fact, the two functions, vision and sexuality, represent two opposite but complementary poles: what is missing from one is increased in the other.[57] Al-Qazwīnī, by setting the blind individual against the eunuch, makes the mode of compensation even clearer. But what is equally significant in this application of the mode of compensation is its socially integrative conclusion.

Here, of course, it is the blind man who is in question. The sexuality of the blind woman is another matter altogether. In fact, blind women receive scant attention in the sources. A discussion of the blind means a discussion of blind men.[58] The principal reason for this would seem to be that women are, themselves, already a specialized category of humanity. Thus, we do not find, for example, *adab* sections on handicapped women. This entire problem of the degree to which women can take on the properties associated with specific groups in Mamlūk civilization lies beyond the scope of this study.

But the relationship between blindness and sexuality is not peculiar to medieval Islamic civilization. The mental structures governing blindness in the West exploit it as well, but with a crucial difference.

Blindness in the West is linked to sexual transgression: Oedipus plucks out his eyes because of his incestuous relationship with his mother. Concomitant in the Western tradition is the notion of castration: blindness being seen as castration and the blind individual as one whose sexual abilities have been called into question. First of all, blinding, when used as a punishment for a sexual offense, can be, as with Oedipus, understood as a symbolic castration. Second, there seems to be in the modern West, as shown by Kirtley and Henri, a general association of blindness with castration and a general perception that the blind are desexualized or lacking in sexual interest or abilities.[59] Thus, in the West, blindness has an adverse relationship with sexuality.

In the Islamic tradition, on the other hand, the opposite is the case. Al-Qazwīnī expressed this well when he paired off blindness and sexuality and contrasted them with castration and vision.

The medieval Islamic position on the sexuality of the blind is thus the opposite of the Western one. Where the West uses equivalence, the East uses compensation. This should lay to rest the notion that such conceptions derive in any direct manner from the physical realities of blindness. It should also call into question the Freudian variant of this position, that such notions are based upon universal psychological laws.

This idea of compensation, when it is carried to the sexual sphere, is, of course, related to the notion of the physicality of the blind, mentioned above. Thus, the physicality which flows from the nature of the blind as defective also influences the mode of compensation.

Blindness in the West forms part of the moral discourse of crime and punishment, the crime being some form of sexual transgression. This moral discourse is also present in Islam, but free of the sexual connection. Blindness represents a punishment, and its removal a mercy. This is clear in the oniric material present in the biographies of blind individuals in the *Nakt al-himyān*. The removal of the defect invariably takes on religious significance, as when Simāk ibn Ḥarb, who lost his vision, saw Abraham in a dream. Simāk said that his vision had gone, whereupon Abraham told him to go down to the Euphrates and open his eyes with his head under the water, and that God would return his sight to him. Simāk did this and his sight was restored.[60]

Perhaps even more significant for our purposes are the examples in which the Prophet restored sight to blind individuals. These accounts of miracles include, for example, the case of a believer who came to the Prophet with his sight gone. The Prophet asked him what had befallen him, to which he replied that he had been feeding one of his camels and inadvertently put his foot on a snake egg, so his eyes became white, a euphemism for the onset of blindness. The Prophet breathed on his eyes and he was able to see again.[61] These cases show the removal of blindness as a mercy.

When blindness appears as a punishment, the punishment is often connected to theological or religious issues. For example, Qur'ānic verses in Sūrat Ṭāhā (verses 124–126) state that on the resurrection day, the individual will be raised blind because he did not heed God's signs. The dream interpreters adduced this verse to show that he who dreams that he is blind will forget the Qur'ān.[62] There is also the case of Hārūn ibn Ma'rūf, a famous ḥadīth transmitter, who lost his sight and was told in a dream that he who preferred the ḥadīth over the Qur'ān would be punished. Hārūn understood this as an explanation for his having lost his sight.[63]

Clearly, we are dealing with a spiritual transgression which is punished by physical blindness. Hence, blindness can, though it need not always, have a moral significance. When it does, it is as a punishment for a particularly Islamic type of religious fault.

We have seen that blindness can play a role in discourses on the body and physicality as well as in moral ones of crime and punishment. But it is perhaps blindness as a discourse on society which is the most provocative. The blind played a number of visible roles in Mamlūk society. We are speaking here, of course, not necessarily of the actual living conditions of the majority of blind individuals, but of the social roles set out for them by the society, and associated with them by that society. These form as much a part of the *mentalités* of blindness as do religious-legal prescriptions or textual treatments.

The principal professions of the blind were Qur'ān reciter, *mu'adhdhin*, scholar, and poet.[64] What is important for understanding the relationship between these professions and the role of the blind is that these careers were neither specifically reserved for the blind nor exceptional for them. The visually handicapped represented a minority in all these roles, though this minority could become very large, as, for example, with Qur'ān reciters.[65] This means that the blind poet or scholar worked alongside his sighted colleague. It was not generally assumed that a blind man made a better Qur'ān reciter or poet than a sighted individual.

What role do these blind personages then play? If a blind individual can recite the Qur'ān, it means that Qur'ānic recitation is an essentially oral activity, that an oral rendering of the Qur'ān is a full and correct rendering. The same can be said of the blind poet: he testifies to the essential orality of poetry.

Thus, the blind functioned as constant reminders that some of the most central aspects of Islamic culture contained an irreducible oral component. This extends even to scholarship. And it should be remembered in this context that since classical Arabic was rarely written with vocalization, the oral transmission of a text could be vital to its proper understanding. To say the least, an individual's seeing and reading a written Arabic text does not have the decisive advantages over an individual's hearing it, such as he would have, for example, in English.

This problem of oral vs. written forms of cultural transmission and their respective reliance on hearing and vision did not go unnoticed in the Mamlūk sources. We have already alluded to the problems raised by a visually handicapped transmitter; arguments in favor of such a transmitter were linked to the fact that early pious women such as 'Ā'isha transmitted from behind a curtain, and hence without seeing the source of a given statement. This controversy, however, went beyond the specific question of transmission, and provoked a lively debate over the questions of the superiority of sight vs. hearing, deafness vs. blindness.[66] Al-Ṣafadī, in his usual balanced way, presents both sides of the argument. But he includes an argument which demonstrates very well the selectivity that could be employed in the citation of Qur'ānic evidence. In Sūrat al-Baqara, the Qur'ān lists handicaps in the following order: deaf, dumb, blind. Al-Ṣafadī adduces this as evidence of the superiority of hearing, since "deaf" precedes "blind."[67] Yet, in Sūrat al-Isrā' (verse 97), the order is blind, dumb, deaf.

Perhaps the strongest evidence adduced in this argument is that relating to the question of whether a prophet can be blind or deaf. No prophet, al-Ṣafadī argues, was ever deaf; but the blindness of certain prophets was a known fact. In addition, deafness brings along muteness: the mute individual cannot speak because he cannot hear. But if sight disappears, it does not obliterate the faculty of speech. All of this permits our Mamlūk author to conclude that the evidence for the superiority of hearing is stronger than that for the superiority of vision.[68]

It is clear from al-Ṣafadī's discussion that his position did not command universal assent. But it is the very presence of this debate in the tradition which testifies to the role of blindness as a central concern in medieval Islamic civilization; and that because blindness and the blind articulate the values of oral vs. written culture.

When we speak of "oral" and "written," we should keep in mind that in the context of Islamic civilization, this distinction does not have the associations often linked to it of "low" vs. "high" culture. The oral component in classical Islamic civilization is intimately linked to high culture, and forms part and parcel of that civilization. In effect, Islamic culture balances between written and oral concepts of culture and cultural transmission. The division between high and low culture in medieval Islam which forms an equivalent to the Western dichotomy of written and oral culture lies in the diglossia between proper classical Arabic and more dialectical forms of language. Oral high culture is classical Arabic culture. And it remains an elite culture, even if some of its elements may ultimately have had a popular origin.

The oral component was clearly dominant in Islamic civilization at its inception. The backbone of early Arabic secular culture was *jāhilī*, or pre-Islamic, poetry; and even if this poetry was occasionally written down, it was conceived of as having been orally composed and transmitted.[69] Likewise with the Qur'ān: the revelation was a quintessentially oral one, and was only codified in writing at a later stage.

After the conquests, and subsequent greater contact with the older civilizations of the region, written culture became more important. But cultural values of the earlier period survived, and with them the importance of oral culture. It is well known, for example, that the philological tradition relied heavily on oral transmission, and that the oral authority of the bedouin continued long after the rise of urban centers.[70] It is the sanctity of this oral philological tradition which permits someone like the great Mamlūk scholar al-Suyūṭī to discuss the question of the oral transmission of language in his philological compendium *al-Muzhir*.[71]

Hence, we can speak of at least two highly valorized cultural traditions: a secular one based on poetry, and a religious one based on the Qur'ān. Both center on the oral component. It is no accident, therefore, that the blind play a major role in both traditions, as poets and Qur'ān reciters. Nor is it accidental that the proverbial literature gives us *aḥfaẓ min al-'umyān*, or "more capable of retaining in memory than the blind,"[72] on the one hand; while a word from the same verbal root, *ḥāfiẓ*, is employed for someone who has memorized the Qur'ān in its entirety. Memorization is a sacred activity.

This discussion also shows that the distinction between the nature of the oral and the written, as explored in the West from Plato to Paul Ricoeur (and recently "deconstructed" by Jacques Derrida)[73] cannot automatically be applied directly to Islamic civilization. Oral discourse in Islam is not necessarily more contextual than written. It partakes, for example, of the textual property of "autonomy" associated by Ricoeur with the written.[74]

We have seen that blindness and the blind appear in a variety of discourses, and through a variety of modes. There is one final area through which Mamlūk civilization took a global view of its relations with its blind members. This area is humor. Blindness was a fit subject for humor, and we find humorous anecdotes about blind individuals in a variety of medieval Arabic sources. These anecdotes, almost without exception, conform to a general literary model and reflect the same mental structures.

For us, however, two anecdotes will have to suffice. The first concerns the famous eighth-century blind poet, Bashshār ibn Burd. The anecdote was popular and appeared in sources from the 'Abbasid biographical compendium, the *Ṭabaqāt al-shu'arā'* of Ibn al-Mu'tazz, to Mamlūk texts like the *Nihāyat al-arab* of al-Nuwayrī and the *Nakt* of al-Ṣafadī.

Someone said to Bashshār ibn Burd: "God has never removed the two eyes of a believer without substituting some good for them. So with what did He compensate you?" So Bashshār replied: "With not having to see disagreeable people like you."[75]

The second anecdote has an anonymous hero:

Someone relates that he alighted at a village and went out at night to answer a call of nature. And, behold, there was a blind man on whose shoulder was a jar and who was carrying a lamp. So the sighted man said to him: "You there! As far as you are concerned, night and day are the same. So what is the meaning of the lamp?" The blind man replied: "O busybody! I carry it with me for the blind at heart like you to be guided by it so they do not stumble upon me and make me fall and break my jar."[76]

These anecdotes are superficially different: the protagonist in one is well known, the poet Bashshār ibn Burd; in the other, he is an anonymous blind individual. The anecdote with Bashshār is brief, being composed of a question and an answer. The second anecdote, on the other hand, is more complicated. But both anecdotes display the same functions (understanding a function in the Proppian/Bremondian sense[77]) and, hence, the two anecdotes display the same structure. In both, we have a question posed to a blind individual which puts him on the spot, and in both this blind individual provides a clever reply, ending the anecdote.

It might seem that we are dealing with the cleverness of blind individuals, as opposed to their sighted colleagues. And we might subsequently wish to interpret these actions as indicators of compensation.

But these anecdotes must be seen in the context that generates such stories in the Arabic literary tradition: that of *adab*. *Adab* works abound in anecdotes which display cleverness, and whose protagonists range from misers to party crashers, from thieves to the insane, etc. Verbal cleverness is one of the leitmotifs of medieval Arabic *adab* literature.[78]

If the message of these two anecdotes is thus not primarily that of cleverness, then what is it? To answer this question, we must examine the anecdotes from the point of view of blindness. In both anecdotes, the questions posed to the blind individuals call attention to their state of being different. They are both attempts to set blind individuals apart, to segregate them. However, the two replies, which literally leave the questioners speechless, confound this attempt at segregation. They effectively invert the situation created by the question, by directly involving the questioner and making him the butt of the joke. In one case, he becomes the disagreeable person whom God has spared the blind individual from seeing; in the other, he is the busybody who could conceivably cause the blind man to fall and break his jar. By inverting the situation, both replies call attention to the outlandish nature of the attempt to set the blind individual apart. The anecdotes, in fact, argue for an integrative attitude toward the visually handicapped.

In these anecdotes, and in many others in the literary sources, the sighted person is trying to call attention to, and hence to strengthen, the marginality of the blind individual. Associated with this on the part of the sighted person is a feeling of superiority. The blind man reverses this relationship of normality/marginality and superiority/inferiority by casting the sighted person into the marginal, inferior category. He is disagreeable or blind at heart. This role reversal is, of course, a familiar literary humoristic technique.[79] It is being used here to encapsule a dialogue between the sighted and the blind. And this dialogue represents Mamlūk society's overview of the problem of blindness and the blind. This is a view which recognizes the fundamental difference of the blind, along with their marginality, as seen in the reaction of the "normal" sighted individual. At the same time, this view cautions against the drawing of segregative conclusions from this difference. Finally, it is clearly no accident that this integrating, or in this case we had better say desegregating, message is placed not in the mouth of some benevolent sighted authority but in that of the blind individual himself.

NOTES

1. Susan Sontag, *Illness as Metaphor* (New York, 1978).

2. Marcel Sendrail, *Histoire culturelle de la maladie* (Toulouse, 1980), p. XIII.

3. Patrick H. Hutton, "The History of Mentalities: The New Map of Cultural History," *History and Theory*, XX, 3 (1981), p. 238.

4. Jacques Le Goff, "Les Mentalités: Une Histoire ambigüe," in Jacques Le Goff and Pierre Nora, eds., *Faire de l'histoire*, vol. III, *Nouveaux Objets* (Paris, 1974), p. 76.

5. Le Goff, "Les Mentalités," pp. 77–86.

6. Paul Veyne, "Foucault révolutionne l'histoire,'" in Paul Veyne, *Comment on écrit l'histoire* (Paris, 1978), pp. 201–42.

7. Hayden White, "Michel Foucault," in *Structuralism and Since: From Lévi-Strauss to Derrida*, ed. John Sturrock (Oxford, 1979), p. 92.

8. Hutton, "History of Mentalities," p. 252. Norbert Elias' most important works in this context are: *The History of Manners, Power & Civility*, and *The Court Society*, both translated by Edmund Jephcott (New York, 1982 and 1984).

9. Hutton, "History of Mentalities," p. 240. On the *Annales* school, see, also, Traian Stoianovich, *French Historical Method: The Annales Paradigm* (Ithaca, 1976).

10. Hutton, "History of Mentalities," p. 256. See, also, Philippe Ariès, *L'Homme devant la mort* (Paris, 1977); Michel Foucault, *Histoire de la folie à l'âge classique* (Paris, 1972); idem, *Surveiller et punir: Naissance de la prison* (Paris, 1975).

11. Jean Delumeau would be an exception. See, for example, Jean Delumeau, *La Peur en Occident* (Paris, 1978).

12. Charles M. Radding, "Superstition to Science: Nature, Fortune, and the Passing of the Medieval Ordeal," *American Historical Review*, LXXXIV (1979), pp. 945–69.

13. Veyne, "Foucault révolutionne l'histoire."

14. Hutton, "History of Mentalities," p. 237.

15. Le Goff, "Les Mentalités," p. 78.

16. Guy-H. Allard et al., *Aspects de la marginalité au Moyen-Age* (Montreal, 1975).

17. Ronald Hare, "The Antiquity of Diseases Caused by Bacteria and Viruses, A Review of the Problem from a Bacteriologist's Point of View," p. 128, and A. T. Sandison, "Diseases of the Eye," p. 457, both in Don Brothwell and A. T. Sandison, eds., *Diseases in Antiquity: A Survey of the Diseases, Injuries and Surgery of Early Populations* (Springfield, 1967); Folke Henschen, *The History and Geography of Diseases*, trans. Joan Tate (New York, 1966), p. 270.

18. Al-Ṣafadī, *Nakt al-himyān fī nukat al-'umyān*, ed. Aḥmad Zakī Bāshā (Cairo, 1911).

19. On the medieval Islamic biographical dictionary, see, for example, Fedwa Malti-Douglas, "Biography, Islamic," in the *Dictionary of the Middle Ages*, ed. Joseph R. Strayer, vol. II (New York, 1983), pp. 237–39; Ibrahim Hafsi, "Recherches sur le genre '*Ṭabaqāt*' dans la littérature arabe," *Arabica* XXIII (1976), pp. 227–65 and XXIV (1977), pp. 150–86.

20. See, for example, al-Ṣafadī, *Nakt*, pp. 125–30, 101–10, 204–5. Ibn al-Mu'tazz, *Ṭabaqāt al-Shu'arā'*, ed. 'Abd al-Sattār Aḥmad Farrāj (Cairo, 1968), pp. 21–31; Ibn Qutayba, *Al-Shi'r wa'l-shu'arā'* (Beirut, 1969), pp. 643–46; Ibn Khallikān, *Wafayāt al-a'yān*, ed. Iḥsān 'Abbās (Beirut, n.d.), III, 17–18; Yāqūt, *Mu'jam al-udabā'*, ed. D. S. Margoliouth (London, 1923–31), V, 84–86. For the numerous notices on al-Ma'arrī, see Moustapha Saleh, "Abū'l-'Alā' al-Ma'arrī, bibliographie critique," *Bulletin d'Etudes Orientales*, XXII (1969), pp. 133–204 and XXIII (1970), pp. 197–274.

21. See, for example, al-Jāḥiẓ, *al-Bukhalā'*, ed. Ṭāhā al-Ḥājirī (Cairo, 1971), p. 53; al-Bayhaqī, *al-Maḥāsin wa'l-masāwī*, ed. Muḥammad Abū l-Faḍl Ibrāhīm (Cairo, n.d.), II, 415–16; Al-Tanūkhī, *Nishwār al-Muḥāḍara*, ed. 'Abbūd al-Shālijī (Beirut, 1971–73), II, 358; al-Hamadhānī, *al-Maqāmāt*, ed. Muḥammad 'Abduh (Beirut, 1968 pp. 78–81. See also the excellent study by C. E. Bosworth, *The Medieval Islamic Underworld: The Banū Sāsān in Arabic Society and Literature* (Leiden, 1976), vol. I, especially p. 39 f.

22. Al-Ṣafadī, *Nakt*, pp. 86, 85; al-Nuwayrī, *Nihāyat al-arab fī funūn al-adab* (Cairo, n.d.), IV, 22.

23. Ibn Qutayba, *al-Ma'ārif*, ed. Tharwat 'Ukāsha (Cairo, 1969), pp. 578–79.

24. Yūsuf ibn 'Abd al-Hādī, *Kitāb al-ḍabṭ wa'l-tabyīn li-dhawī al-'ilal wa'l-'āhāt min al-muḥaddithīn*, MS. Ẓāhirīya. For similar mildly abnormal categories, see al-Jāḥiẓ, *Kitāb al-burṣān wa'l-'urjān wa'l-'umyān al-ḥūlān*, ed. 'Abd al-Salām Muḥammad Hārūn (Baghdad, 1982).

25. An-Nuwayrī, *Nihāya*, IV, 16–23.

26. Pierre Henri, *Les Aveugles et la société* (Paris, 1958), pp. 7–15.

27. See, for example, al-Zabīdī, *Tāj al-'arūs* (Beirut, n.d.), X, 255; Ibn Sīda, *al-Muḥkam wa'l-muḥīṭ al-a'ẓam fī al-lugha* (Cairo, 1958), II, 190; Ibn Manẓūr, *Lisān al-'arab* (Cairo, n.d.), XIX, 329. On the appellations of the blind

in al-Ṣafadī, see Fedwa Malti-Douglas, "Pour une Rhétorique onomastique: Les Noms des aveugles chez aṣ-Ṣafadī," *Cahiers d'Onomastique Arabe*, I (1979), pp. 7–19.

28. Al-Ṣafadī, *Nakt*, pp. 6–12.

29. Ibn Ḥajar al-'Asqalānī, *Tabṣīr al-muntabih bi-taḥrīr al-mushtabih*, eds. 'Alī Muḥammad al-Bijāwī and Muḥammad 'Alī al-Najjār (Cairo, 1966), III, 856; Malti-Douglas, "Pour une Rhétorique," p. 6.

30. See, for example, al-Zabīdī, *Tāj*, III, 348–49; Ibn Manẓūr, *Lisān*, VI, 153–54.

31. See, for example, al-Zabīdī, *Tāj*, VI, 234–36; Ibn Manẓūr, *Lisān*, XI, 211–14.

32. See, for example, al-Zabīdī, *Tāj*, IX, 409; Ibn Manẓūr, *Lisān*, XVII, 433.

33. See, for example, al-Zabīdī, *Tāj*, I, 203; Ibn Manẓūr, *Lisān*, I, 290.

34. Malti-Douglas, "Pour une Rhétorique," pp. 7–19.

35. Al-Ṣafadī, *Nakt*, pp. 114, 127, 145, 209, 212, 312.

36. Donald D. Kirtley, *The Psychology of Blindness* (Chicago, 1975), pp. 20–21; Henri, *Les Aveugles*, pp. 7, 37–38.

37. Al-Ṣafadī, *Nakt*, pp. 225, 86. See also al-Tanūkhī, *Nishwār*, III, 49.

38. See, for example, al-Ṣafadī, *Nakt*, pp. 39, 48, 58–59, 138, 305; al-Suyūṭī, *al-Ashbāh wa'l-naẓā'ir fī qawā'id wa-furū' fiqh al-shāfi'īya* (Cairo, n.d.), p. 274. Cf. *Kitāb Kalīla wa-Dimna*, ed. Louis Cheikho (Beirut, 1969), p. 54.

39. See, for example, Ibn al-Ṭiqṭaqā, *Ta'rīkh al-duwal al-islāmīya (al-Fakhrī)* (Beirut, 1960), p. 127. See also Michael Dols, "The Leper in Medieval Islamic Society," *Speculum*, 58 (1983), p. 899.

40. Al-Ṣafadī, *Nakt*, p. 71; Ibn Qutayba, *'Uyūn al-akhbār* (Cairo, 1963), IV, 57.

41. See, for example, al-Tanūkhī, *Nishwār*, III, 49.

42. Al-Ṣafadī, *Nakt*, p. 19; Ibn Sīrīn, *Muntakhab al-kalām fī tafsīr al-aḥlām*, printed on the margins of al-Nābulusī's *Ta'ṭīr al-anām fi ta'bīr al-manām* (Cairo, n.d.), I, 86; al-Nābulusī, *Ta'ṭīr*, II, 85.

43. Al-Ṣafadī, *Nakt*, p. 21. Cf. Artemidorus, *Kitāb ta'bīr al-ru'yā*, trans. Ḥunayn ibn Isḥāq, ed. Tawfīq Fahd (Damascus, 1964), p. 66.

44. The verse is from Sūrat al-Nūr, verse 61. A. J. Arberry, *The Koran Interpreted* (New York, 1974), II, 54; al-Qurṭubī, *al-Jāmi' li-aḥkām al-qur'ān* (Cairo, 1967), XII, 313. The same denial of fault can be found in Sūrat al-Fatḥ, verse 17, but without the reference to eating.

45. Al-Tha'ālibī, *Thimār al-qulūb fī 'l-muḍāf wa'l-mansūb*, ed. Muḥammad Abū 'l-Faḍl Ibrāhīm (Cairo, 1965), pp. 608–9.

46. Bruno Roy, "En Marge du monde connu: Les Races des monstres," in Allard et al., *Aspects de la marginalité*, pp. 71–80, and especially p. 76.

47. Adam Mez, *The Renaissance of Islam*, trans. Salahuddin Khuda Bukhsh and D. S. Margoliouth (London, 1937), p. 9. Cf. al-Ṣafadī, *Nakt*, p. 56.

48. Al-Ṣafadī, *Nakt*, pp. 42–44; al-Qurṭubī, *al-Jāmi'*, IX, 248. Cf. the arguments over whether an *imām* could be blind, al-Ṣafadī, *Nakt*, pp. 43–44; al-Suyūṭī, *al-Ashbāh*, p. 275; al-Shāfi'ī, *al-Umm* (Beirut, 1973), I, 165.

49. Al-Ṣafadī, *Nakt*, pp. 44–62; al-Suyūṭī, *al-Ashbāh*, pp. 274–75; al-Shāfi'ī, *al-Umm*, I, 165, VII, 46.

50. Al-Ṣafadī, *Nakt*, p. 62.

51. Al-Suyūṭī, *al-Ashbāh*, pp. 273–76.

52. Fedwa Malti-Douglas, *Structures of Avarice: The Bukhalā' in Medieval Arabic Literature* (Leiden, 1985), pp. 12–16.

53. Ibn Qutayba, *'Uyūn*, IV, 1–147; al-Nuwayrī, *Nihāya*, IV, pp. 18–22.

54. See, for example, Kirtley, *Psychology*, pp. 20, 53.

55. Arberry, *Koran*, I, 265.

56. Al-Ṣafadī, *Nakt*, pp. 21–22; al-Maydānī, *Majma' al-amthāl* (Beirut, n.d.), II, 412.

57. Al-Qazwīnī, *'Ajā'ib al-makhlūqāt wa-gharā'ib al-mawjūdāt*, ed. Fārūq Sa'd (Beirut, 1981), p. 348. Cf. al-Ṣafadī, *Nakt*, p. 54.

58. The principal exception would be the discussion over whether a nurse-maid can be blind. See al-Ṣafadī, *Nakt*, pp. 54–55; al-Suyūṭī, *al-Ashbāh*, p. 274.

59. Kirtley, *Psychology*, pp. 21, 27–30, 39, for example; Henri, *Les Aveugles*, pp. 36–37, 56, 61, for example.

60. Al-Ṣafadī, *Nakt*, p. 161. On the dreams of the blind in the *Nakt*, see Fedwa Malti-Douglas, "Dreams, the Blind, and the Semiotics of the Biographical Notice," *Studia Islamica*, LI (1980), pp. 137–62.

61. Al-Ṣafadī, *Nakt*, pp. 227–28.

62. Al-Ṣafadī, *Nakt*, p. 19. Cf. Ibn Sīrīn, *Muntakhab*, I, 86; al-Nābulusī, *Ta'ṭīr*, II, 85.

63. Al-Ṣafadī, *Nakt*, p. 302.

64. This can be seen not only in the *Nakt* but also in biographical compendia devoted to Qur'ān reciters, scholars, etc.

65. See, for example, the notices in Ibn al-Jazarī, *Ghāyat al-nihāya fī ṭabaqāt al-qurrā'*, ed. G. Bergsträsser (Beirut, 1980).

66. Al-Ṣafadī, *Nakt*, pp. 17–18. Cf. André Roman, "À Propos des Vers des yeux et du regard dans l'oeuvre du poète aveugle Baššār b. Burd," *Mélanges de l'Université Saint-Joseph*, XLVI (1970–71), p. 481.

67. Sūrat al-Baqara, verse 18; al-Ṣafadī, *Nakt*, p. 17.

68. Al-Ṣafadī, *Nakt*, pp. 17–18.

69. Of course, modern scholars have debated the authenticity and orality of pre-Islamic poetry, but for the medieval Arabs, neither was really in question. See, for example, Gaudefroy-Demombynes, "Introduction" to Ibn Qutayba, *Introduction au livre de la poésie et des poètes*, trans. Gaudefroy-Demombynes (Paris, 1947), p. XXXI.

70. See, for example, Anwar G. Chejne, *The Arabic Language: Its Role in History* (Minneapolis, 1969), pp. 48, 150.

71. Al-Suyūṭī, *al-Muzhir fī 'ulūm al-lugha wa-anwā'ihā*, eds. Muḥammad Aḥmad Jād al-Mawlā et al. (Cairo, n.d.), I, 137 f.

72. Al-Ṣafadī, *Nakt*, p. 83; al-Maydānī, *Majma'*, I, 318. Here also we find the mode of compensation, but it is not developed to the same degree that sexual compensation is. In addition, memorization is not spiritual vision. It is an intellectual activity of the most mechanical sort.

73. Paul Ricoeur, *Hermeneutics & the Human Sciences*, ed. and trans. John B. Thompson (Cambridge, 1981), pp. 139–40, 199–201; Jonathan Culler, "Jacques Derrida," in Sturrock, ed., *Structuralism*, pp. 166–73.

74. Ricoeur, *Hermeneutics*, pp. 139–40.

75. Al-Ṣafadī, *Nakt*, p. 66. With slight variants in Ibn al-Mu'tazz, *Ṭabaqāt*, p. 22; Abū 'l-Faraj al-Iṣbahānī, *Kitāb al-aghānī* (Beirut, 1970), III, 34; al-Nuwayrī, *Nihāya*, IV, 420–21.

76. Al-Ṣafadī, *Nakt*, p. 67. With slight variants in al-Nuwayrī, *Nihāya*, IV 22; Ibn al-Jawzī, *Akhbār al-adhkiyā'*, ed. Muḥammad Mursī al-Khawlī (Cairo, 1970), p. 154.

77. Vladimir Propp, *Morphologie du conte*, trans. Marguerite Derrida (Paris, 1970); Claude Bremond, *Logique du récit* (Paris, 1973).

78. See, for example, Malti-Douglas, *Structures of Avarice*; idem, "Structure and Organization in a Monographic *Adab* Work: *al-Taṭfīl* of al-Khaṭīb al-Baghdādī," *Journal of Near Eastern Studies*, 40 (1981), pp. 227–45; idem, "Classical Arabic Crime Narratives: Thieves and Thievery in *Adab* Literature," *Journal of Arabic Literature*, forthcoming.

79. See, for example, Henri Bergson, *Le Rire: Essai sur la signification du comique* (Paris, 1972), p. 73; Malti-Douglas, *Structures of Avarice*, pp. 108–37.

VII

THE CLASSICAL ARABIC DETECTIVE*

Detective fiction, which has long entertained readers, has also spawned a rapidly growing critical literature of its own. The questions addressed include the paternity of the detective genre, the nature of the characters exploited in detective fiction, and the implications of that literature, social or otherwise. This study will address itself to the detective figure in medieval Arabic literature, specifically as he appears in that branch of prose texts referred to as *adab* texts, texts composed predominantly of anecdotes and whose dual aim was to entertain and to educate. As part of our investigation, we shall examine the nature of the character of the detective, and its implications. The investigation will lead us to compare the figure of the detective in the East with that of his counterpart in the West.

Al-Muʿtaḍid, Detective.

Nowhere are the qualities of the detective more clearly present than in the character of the ninth-century caliph, al-Muʿtaḍid bil-Lāh. The first case we shall outline is one I should like to call «The Case of the Painted Hand.»

One of the servants of this celebrated caliph came to him one day and told him that he had been standing on the banks of the Tigris River, when he saw a fisherman cast his net. When the fisherman felt something in the net, he pulled it in and took it out of the water, and, lo and behold, it contained a leather bag. So the servant gave the fisherman money for his catch and took the bag, opened it, and discovered that it held some bricks and between the bricks was a human hand, dyed with henna. These objects he brought to al-Muʿtaḍid, who was horrified. He told the servant to go and tell the

---

* Earlier versions of this study were presented as public lectures at Princeton University on February 2, 1984, and at Yale University on November 12, 1984.

fisherman to cast his net once again «above, below, and around the same area.» This the fisherman did and he brought out another leather bag in which was a foot. The operation was repeated but nothing else emerged. Al-Mu^{c}taḍid was grieved by this and he exclaimed: «There is someone in this country who, without my knowledge, kills a person, cuts off his limbs, and scatters them? That is not sovereignty!» He did not eat for the entire day and on the morrow, he called one of his trustworthy agents, gave him the empty leather bag, and told him to go around to the bag makers in Baghdad, and if one of them recognized this bag, to ask him to whom he had sold it. Then he was to go to the buyer and to see, in turn, who had bought it from him. The man was to follow these directions without telling anyone.

After three days, the agent returned and explained what he had done. He had asked the tanners and the bag makers until he found out the manufacturer and then had asked about him. The manufacturer said that he had sold the bag to a perfumer in such and such a market. Al-Mu^{c}taḍid's agent then went to the perfumer and showed him the leather bag. The perfumer wondered how that particular item had fallen into the hands of the caliph's agent. The agent asked him if he knew the item, to which the perfumer revealed that, indeed, a certain Hashemite, three days earlier, had had ten of these bags purchased for him, the perfumer ignoring why he had bought them. The agent then asked who this Hashemite was, to which he was told that he was a descendant of ^{c}Alī ibn Rayṭa, that he was a huge man, and that he had a reputation for being the most evil and unjust of men, as well as being the most immoral vis-à-vis women. No one had informed al-Mu^{c}taḍid about him for fear of his evil doings. And the perfumer continued relating unfavorable stories about this man to al-Mu^{c}taḍid's agent until he finally mentioned that this evil character had several years ago become enamored of a certain singing slave girl. Her beauty was extraordinary, as was her singing. So he bargained with her owner over her but she would have nothing to do with him. But a few days ago, the Hashemite heard that the slave's owner wanted to sell her to a buyer, who had offered thousands of dinars for her. So the Hashemite went to the owner and told her that the least she could do was to send the slave girl to him to say her farewells. So after the Hashemite paid to rent the slave girl for three days, the owner left her in his custody. After the three days had passed, the evil man kept the slave girl hidden from her owner and no news was had of her. He claimed that she had run away from him, the neighbors claimed that he had killed her, and others believed that she was still with him. The owner, however, held funeral services for the girl and came and cried at the Hashemite's door and, in fact, made a disgrace of herself, but to no avail.

When al-Muʿtaḍid heard this, he thanked God for the revelation of the affair to him, and he called immediately for someone to take the Hashemite by surprise, and he had the owner of the slave girl brought in. Then al-Muʿtaḍid took out the hand and the foot in front of the culprit. When he saw them, his color changed and he realized that the game was up, so he confessed. Al-Muʿtaḍid ordered that the owner of the slave girl be paid the price of the girl from the treasury and he dismissed her. Then he imprisoned the Hashemite. Some say that he killed him, others that he died in prison[1].

The essential components of the anecdote are: A part of a corpse is discovered in the Tigris, which event angers al-Muʿtaḍid. He gives a set of directions to his agent, who dutifully follows them, and the guilty party is discovered. Al-Muʿtaḍid confronts him with the evidence, the hand and the foot, and the culprit confesses. Al-Muʿtaḍid then gives everyone his due, including payment to the victim's owner and punishment to the evil doer. In other words, we are dealing with the apprehension of a criminal, and this following the directions of the caliph himself. Put another way, we can say that when al-Muʿtaḍid sees what is obviously the evidence of a foul deed, he takes steps to uncover the murderer. In short, he behaves as a detective.

What we have here is, indeed, a detective story. The standard elements of a whodunit are present: the corpse (implied in the dismembered parts), the detective, the detection, and the murderer.

The existence of this medieval Arabic detective story leads directly to a number of questions. First, what is the relationship of this text to its Arabic literary context? Second, how do the Arabic texts themselves compare with other traditional or non-Western detective stories? Third, how does the Arabic detective literature

[1] Ibn al-Jawzī, *Akhbār al-Adhkiyā'*, ed. Muḥammad Mursī al-Khawlī (Cairo: Maṭābiʿ al-Ahrām al-Tijāriyya, 1970), pp. 47-48.

compare with the modern Western detective novel? And, fourth, can we speak of this literature as part of the origin of the modern Western novel? The best place to begin is with an in-depth discussion of the Arabic detective tradition.

To return to what we have called «The Case of the Painted Hand,» there are other elements which help to bring this anecdote within the frame of the detective story. The critical literature on detective fiction distinguishes between the «classical detective» and the «hard-boiled detective.» The classical detective is an intellectual sleuth, represented by such figures as Edgar Allan Poe's C. Auguste Dupin, Conan Doyle's Sherlock Holmes, Agatha Christie's Hercule Poirot and Miss Marple, Dorothy Sayers' Lord Peter Wimsey, and so on. The hard-boiled detective, on the other hand, represents a more recent development in the genre, and is characterized by such figures as Raymond Chandler's Philip Marlowe, Dashiell Hammett's Sam Spade; and so on[2]. As we shall have occasion to demonstrate, al-Muᶜtaḍid, as detective, fits more closely into the classical model.

Hence, with «The Case of the Painted Hand,» we are dealing with a «classical detective story.» The story line is restricted to the events relating directly to the crime and its investigation; and it follows the standard format beginning with the discovery of a corpse or misdeed, and leading to the uncovering of the culprit.

And, yet, we are dealing with a specific anecdote whose hero happens to be a caliph, and this anecdote is not an isolated literary phenomenon appearing by itself or in a collection of other «detection» stories. This story about al-Muᶜtaḍid appears in the *Akhbār al-Adhkiyā'* (Stories of the *Adhkiyā'*) of Ibn al-Jawzī (d. 597/1200). The *dhakī* (pl. *adhkiyā'*) is a character type defined by his *dhakā'*. This term, whose basic meaning is fullness or completion, can best be rendered in this context as acumen, intelligence, or cleverness[3]. The work by Ibn al-Jawzī, like similar *adab* works on character types, illustrates the characteristic or the character type through sets of actions. This anecdote about al-Muᶜtaḍid, by its very

---

[2] On the distinction between these two types of detective, see, for example, John G. Cawelti, *Adventure, Mystery and Romance* (Chicago: The University of Chicago Press, 1976), pp. 80-191.

[3] See, for example, Ibn Manẓūr, *Lisān al-ᶜArab* (Cairo: al-Dār al-Miṣriyya lil-Ta'līf wal-Tarjama, n.d.), v. XVIII, pp. 314-315; al-Zabīdī, *Tāj al-ᶜArūs* (Beirut: Dār Ṣādir, n.d.), v. X, p. 137.

presence in this text, is clearly meant to illustrate the concept of *dhakā'*.

But the *dhakī* is, in the *adab* tradition, a relatively complex figure because he is divisible into a number of more specialized character types, some of whom, like the party crashers (in Arabic, *ṭufaylīs*) or the thieves, can stand on their own as *adab* character types and have their own literary works devoted to them[4]. Hence, we have a variety of different types of *dhakā'*, ranging from that of the caliph or sultan to that of physicians, thieves, and even women.

What is *dhakā'* for al-Muᶜtaḍid in this anecdote? Or, more precisely, what is the particular kind of caliphal *dhakā'* herein illustrated? To arrive at this, we must rephrase this question and ask ourselves, what are the characteristic actions in this anecdote which we could interpret as demonstrating the quality of *dhakā'*? What al-Muᶜtaḍid does in this story is, of course, to initially tell his agent how to go about discovering the culprit, and, once this culprit is found, to redress the wrongs brought about by the guilty man, which includes punishing him for his crime. Therefore, the two essential qualities embodied in the type of *dhakā'* that this anecdote about al-Muᶜtaḍid demonstrates are, on the one hand, sagacity, and, on the other hand, providing justice. In other words, the anecdote, to properly transmit an evaluation of caliphal *dhakā'*, does not simply conclude with the discovery of the criminal, but includes the meting out of justice. This is an important component to which we shall have occasion to return below.

For our purposes, therefore, al-Muᶜtaḍid as *dhakī* is, in effect, al-Muᶜtaḍid as super-sleuth. And his dual actions which define his detecting role include the discovery of the guilty party and the punishment. That this is not an isolated phenomenon but represents an essential structure for the anecdotes involving the medieval Arabic detective can be seen when we examine the other literary units involving this caliph and his adventures with crime.

---

[4] Ibn al-Jawzī, *Adhkiyā'*, pp. 88-193, 214-217. There is, of course, the famous work on thieves by al-Jāḥiẓ, which is not extant. See Charles Pellat, «Nouvel essai d'inventaire de l'oeuvre ǧāḥiẓienne,» *Arabica*, XXXI (1984), p. 146. For the *ṭufaylīs*, see al-Khaṭīb al-Baghdādī, *al-Taṭfīl wa-Ḥikāyāt al-Ṭufayliyyīn, wa-Akhbāruhum wa-Nawādir Kalāmihim wa-Ashᶜāruhum*, ed. Kāẓim al-Muẓaffar (Najaf: al-Maktaba al-Ḥaydariyya, 1966). On this work, see Fedwa Malti-Douglas, «Structure and Organization in a Monographic *Adab* Work: *al-Taṭfīl* of al-Khaṭīb al-Baghdādī,» *Journal of Near Eastern Studies*, XL (1981), pp. 227-245.

Our caliph got up in the middle of the night to answer a call of nature, and he happened to see a male slave jumping off the back of another slave, then crawling on all fours, and slipping himself back between the other slaves. So al-Muʿtaḍid started to put his hand on one heart after another until he put his hand on the heart of the culprit, which was throbbing violently. Al-Muʿtaḍid kicked the slave and the latter rose. Then the caliph had the torture machines brought out, the slave confessed and was killed[5].

In this very concise anecdote, we see that the caliph has happened upon a slave who, having had illicit intercourse, had disappeared back into the group. To uncover the culprit, al-Muʿtaḍid employed the stratagem of checking the heartbeats of the slaves.

In this anecdote, the caliph is again portrayed as a giver of justice, in that the slave is duly executed. But, in fact, the focus of the anecdote is on the investigate powers of al-Muʿtaḍid, who, in order to discover the criminal, checked the heartbeat of the various slaves. His skills are clearly shown by his having known enough about human reactions and having been sufficiently quickwitted to conceive of the test before the culprit would have had the opportunity to calm himself.

This quality or faculty is the one for which a critical concensus has adopted the term ratiocination, and which finds its fullest description in the opening pages of Poe's «The Murders in the Rue Morgue.» It is a characteristic exemplified in the investigations of an Auguste Dupin or a Sherlock Holmes, one combining a knowledge of human nature and behavior with observation and analytical skills. After all, the process of discovery in Poe's «The Purloined Letter» is similar to the one found in the anecdote with al-Muʿtaḍid. It comes from asking what the culprit's behavior will be in a given situation[6]. It is al-Muʿtaḍid's knowledge that one of

---

[5] Ibn al-Jawzī, *Adhkiyā'*, p. 47.

[6] See, for example, David I. Grossvogel, *Mystery and Its Fictions: From Oedipus to Agatha Christie* (Baltimore: The Johns Hopkins University Press, 1979), p. 93; Cawelti, *Adventure*, p. 80; Michael Holquist, «Whodunit and Other Questions: Metaphysical Detective Stories in Postwar Fiction,» in Glenn W. Most and William W. Stowe, eds., *The Poetics of Murder: Detective Fiction and Literary Theory* (New York: Harcourt Brace Jovanovich, 1983), p. 154. Edgar Allan Poe, «The Murders in the Rue Morgue,» in *The Short Stories*, Greenwich Unabridged Library Classics (New York: Chatham River Press, 1981), pp. 246-249; Poe, «The Purloined Letter,» in Poe, *Short Stories*, pp. 465-477. Some contemporary semioticians, following Peirce, employ the term abduction for the most common form of detective reasoning. See, for example, Thomas A. Sebeok, «One, Two,

the consequences of sexual excitement will be a faster heartbeat and his application of this knowledge that permit him to discover the culprit.

But to return to the two stories of al-Muᶜtaḍid, both begin with the knowledge that a crime has taken place, proceed to the solution of the mystery (that is, the identification of the criminal), and the punishment of the guilty party.

Both these narratives, «The Case of the Painted Hand,» and the second, which we can call «The Case of the Excited Slave,» conform to the characterization which Michel Butor presents of the detective genre. In *L'Emploi du temps*, a mystery writer speaks of the detective narrative as possessing two superimposed temporal series: the days of the investigation, which begin with the crime, and the days of the drama which lead to it[7]. Developing this fundamental insight, Tzvetan Todorov argues that the detective novel contains two stories, that of the crime and that of the investigation. The first story, that of the crime, is usually completed before the second one starts. And, according to Todorov, the characters in the second story do not perform, they merely learn. Furthermore, the story of the crime is an absent one, it cannot be presented in the narrative as it took place; whereas, the second story, insignificant in and of itself, only serves to mediate between the reader and the story of the crime. It is these aspects of the narrative which, according to Todorov, permit the two stories to coexist in the narrative[8]. It can be questioned whether the story of the investigation can really be called insignificant. It is, in a sense, of course, parasitic on the original story. But it is more than a transparent narrative transmitting knowledge of the original story/crime. That conception would make the crime the essence of the detective story, whereas the character of the detective and the nature of his ratiocination are equally essential parts of the text. If the in-

---

Three Spells UBERTY,» pp. 1-10, Thomas A. Sebeok and Jean Umiker-Sebeok, «'You Know My Method',» pp. 11-54, and Gian-Paolo Caprettini, «Peirce, Holmes, Popper,» pp. 135-153, all in Umberto Eco and Thomas A. Sebeok, eds., *The Sign of Three: Dupin, Holmes, Peirce* (Bloomington: Indiana University Press, 1983). I prefer to use the term, and concept of, ratiocination because it can cover all the intellectual activities of the detective.

[7] Michel Butor, *L'Emploi du temps* (Paris: Les Editions de Minuit, 1957), p. 171.

[8] Tzvetan Todorov, «Typologie du roman policier», in Tzvetan Todorov, *Poétique de la prose* (Paris: Editions du Seuil, 1971), pp. 57-59.

vestigation is a means for gaining knowledge of the crime, it is also a means for displaying the virtuosity of the detective. This is, of course, as true of al-Muᶜtaḍid as it is of modern detectives.

With these slight reservations taken into account, it is easy to see that this Butorian/Todorovian schema applies perfectly to «The Case of the Painted Hand.» It also applies to «The Case of the Excited Slave,» though here, reduced to its barest minimum. The two temporal sequences are extremely brief, but the investigation does begin immediately after the crime has been committed.

The essential qualities of this schema are also applicable, but with one change to the following story:

Al-Muᶜtaḍid was sitting one day in a house under construction, watching the workers. He saw among them a black slave, who was rather disagreeable looking but quite merry, climbing the steps two at a time, and carrying twice what everyone else was carrying. The caliph had the slave brought and asked the reason for his behavior. But the slave simply stuttered. The caliph then asked his companion, Ibn Ḥamdūn, what he thought about this. Ibn Ḥamdūn's first reply was to ask who this was that the caliph should bother thinking about him, and then went on to opine that perhaps the slave had no family, a fact which would account for his lightheartedness. The caliph simply replied that he had already made an assessment of this case, of which he was quite confident: either this was someone who had somehow gotten money which did not belong to him, or he was a thief disguised as a workman. So the black slave was beaten until he revealed that he used to work in the limekilns and had one day happened upon someone with money. He had then taken the money and murdered its owner, and buried him in a pit. Some time later, he returned, dug up the bones, and threw them in the Tigris. It was the possession of the dinars, the slave admitted, which accounted for his lightness of heart. So the caliph had the money brought, and it was identified as belonging to a certain individual, whose name was on the money-bag. This person's wife was located and she certified that her husband had indeed gone out with this sum of money and had disappeared. So she was given the money, the black slave was killed, and al-Muᶜtaḍid ordered that his corpse be carried to a kiln, one supposes to be burnt there[9].

[9] Ibn al-Jawzī, *Adhkiyā'*, pp. 46-47.

In this anecdote, which we will dub «The Case of the Merry Slave,» there is clearly a foul deed, and, just as clearly, al-Muʿtaḍid recompenses the victim and punishes the culprit, as he did in «The Case of the Painted Hand.» But despite these similarities, there are significant differences. In «The Case of the Merry Slave,» the story does not begin with clear evidence that a crime has been committed. Thus, the investigation does not go from a known crime to an unknown criminal. In effect, the crime and the criminal are uncovered at the same time. Nevertheless, the «days of the drama,» to use the phrase from Butor, do precede the investigation.

From a strictly literary point of view, a difference between the two cases also manifests itself on the narrative level. In the «Painted Hand,» al-Muʿtaḍid's agent returns with his findings and relates the entire story in his own words. In other words, the culprit's actions are given in the third person, and that twice removed, and not directly by the guilty party. With the «Merry Slave,» on the other hand, the crime is related in the first person, with all the gruesome details that one might only expect from the murderer himself. This gruesomeness in narration replaces the gruesomeness represented in «The Case of the Painted Hand» by the physical discovery of the dismembered hand and foot.

But the role of al-Muʿtaḍid as detective is not only emphasized by his having smoked out this otherwise unknown crime but also by the presence of the second character in the narrative, Ibn Ḥamdūn, in a standard classical detective device. This relationship between detective and sidekick is, of course, also that of Sherlock Holmes and Watson, of C. Auguste Dupin and his narrator. It involves the reader and provides him with someone either to identify with or to feel superior to, as the case may be. Furthermore, if the reader is at a loss and is unable to untangle the story or guess at what is going on, the presence of this companion, who is usually also at a loss, gives the reader confidence. But, more importantly, this structure calls attention to the superiority of the detective figure by having him interact with someone inferior to him in ratiocinative skills. When al-Muʿtaḍid asks Ibn Ḥamdūn what he thinks is the matter with the slave, he is doing exactly what Dupin or Sherlock Holmes would do in that situation. And Ibn Ḥamdūn's answer, which seems logical on the surface, is, of course, the radical opposite of the explanation provided by the caliph, and which proves to be the correct one. The difference in the two levels of interpretation of the slave's behavior only serves to emphasize al-Muʿtaḍid's sagacity, and this, at Ibn Ḥamdūn's expense.

These anecdotes, hence, clearly demonstrate al-Muʿtaḍid's abilities as a detective. But they tie into the classical detectives genre in yet another way. As critics of the genre have pointed out, the detective story invariably begins with a calm or normal environment, against which the corpse is discovered or the crime made known. Thus, the initial order is destroyed and it is not restored until the investigation is completed and the culprit discovered[10]. In these anecdotes with al-Muʿtaḍid, we have much the same phenomenon. In the «Painted Hand,» the servant is standing by the banks of the Tigris watching a fisherman, an almost bucolic scene. In the anecdote with Ibn Ḥamdūn, al-Muʿtaḍid is sitting in one of his homes watching the men at work. The subsequent criminal development is not hinted at by the calm beginning. This development sequence is not as clearly laid out in «The Case of the Excited Slave,» though elements of it are implicitly present. The crime was discovered against the backdrop of a sleeping household.

Al-Muʿtaḍid and Other Arabic Crime Fighters.

Although these anecdotes all display the ratiocinative abilities of the caliph al-Muʿtaḍid, Ibn al-Jawzī, in his *Akhbār al-Adhkiyā'*, has not confined these abilities to al-Muʿtaḍid alone.

Three women came in to see the judge Iyās ibn Muʿāwiya[11]. He thereupon said: one is a wet nurse, the second, a virgin, and the third, separated from her husband. So he was asked how he knew this, to which he replied that when the one who was a wet nurse sat down, she held her breasts with her hands, as for the virgin, when she entered the room, she did not look at anyone, whereas when the woman separated from her husband entered the room, she glanced both to the right and to the left[12].

In this anecdote, Iyās identifies the types of women who have entered the room, based on their behavior. But, of course, in order

[10] See, for example, Cawelti, *Adventure*, pp. 82-83; Grossvogel, *Mystery*, p. 52; Holquist, «Whodunit,» p. 172; F. R. Jameson, «On Raymond Chandler,» in Most and Stowe, eds., *Poetics*, p. 126.

[11] Iyās ibn Muʿāwiya was a *qāḍī* of Baṣra who died in 121/739. See Charles Pellat, «Iyās b. Muʿāwiya,» *EI²*.

[12] Ibn al-Jawzī, *Adhkiyā'*, p. 68.

to do this, he must possess considerable knowledge of human behavior.

This very same judge in another anecdote looked at a crack in the ground and announced that there was a reptile under it. People looked and, indeed, there was a snake. When he was asked how he knew, he explained that there was a moist spot between the two bricks in that area and he knew that underneath was something that was breathing[13].

The skills that Iyās portrays in these anecdotes did not pass unnoticed in the medieval period. For example, al-Maydānī and al-Zamakhsharī, in their proverb collections, include the proverb, «Azkan min Iyās,» which should best be rendered as «more understanding» or «more sagacious than Iyās.» This is, of course, meant to indicate, as proverbs on that pattern do, that Iyās possesses that characteristic to such a degree that he becomes the model against which other individuals are measured. And, in order that the reader interpret the proverb properly, al-Maydānī in his *Majmaᶜ al-Amthāl* and al-Zamakhsharī in his *al-Mustaqṣā fī Amthāl al-ᶜArab* cite more anecdotes that follow the pattern that we have already observed[14].

Iyās' skills, needless to say, are very much those that we have come to associate with Sherlock Holmes. When asked how he knew the solution, it is a wonder that Iyās did not reply: «Elementary, my dear Muḥammad.»

But ratiocination does not a detective make. Although these abilities are important to the detective figure, they are not sufficient to define him. In many of the examples demonstrating exceptional sagacity and powers of reasoning, the demonstration itself serves as the be-all of the anecdote. Hence, unlike the stories with al-Muᶜtaḍid, the reasoning process does not possess implications beyond its own existence. Ratiocination in the absence of a crime does not become detection.

And yet, al-Muᶜtaḍid is not the only individual presented by Ibn al-Jawzī as working with crime or criminals or as meting out

---

[13] Ibn al-Jawzī, *Adhkiyā'*, p. 69.

[14] Al-Maydānī, *Majmaᶜ al-Amthāl* (Beirut: Dār Maktabat al-Ḥayāt, n.d.), v. I, pp. 457-458; al-Zamakhsharī, *al-Mustaqṣā fī Amthāl al-ᶜArab* (Beirut: Dār al-Kutub al-ᶜIlmiyya, 1977), v. I, p. 148.

justice. To take but one example, we possess stories about the powerful Buyid ruler, ʿAḍud al-Dawla[15].

ʿAḍud al-Dawla heard about a group of thieves who were robbing travelers on remote mountain passes. So he called a merchant and gave him a mule carrying two cases, in which delicious-smelling sweets had been placed. These had been filled with poison and wrapped very nicely. ʿAḍud al-Dawla gave the merchant some money and told him to travel with the caravan and make it appear as though he were carrying gifts for the wife of a prince. So the merchant did this, and he traveled in the front of the caravan. The thieves held up the caravan and took the travelers' provisions, clothing, and money. When one of the thieves opened the two cases, he was astounded by the sight and smell of the sweets. But realizing that he could not appropriate the entire two cases for himself, he called his companions and they, in turn, were completely amazed at the sight. They began to devour the sweets and died, down to the last one. Then the merchants retrieved their goods and money[16].

This anecdote obviously involves a crime and just as obviously involves the punishment devised by a ruler for that crime. But ʿAḍud al-Dawla, as the instigator of the solution, is not behaving as a detective. While his ruse does indeed show his *dhakā'* and fully entitles him to be included in Ibn al-Jawzī's *Adhkiyā'*, the unfolding of the narrative is quite different from that in the anecdotes involving al-Muʿtaḍid. Most important, there is no process of discovery. The crime appears at the beginning of the anecdote, in the form of a complaint to the ruler. The bulk of the anecdotes involving ʿAḍud al-Dawla follow this pattern of a complaint or problem raised initially, which is then solved by a ruse in the anecdote itself. But there is no actual process of uncovering during the course of which the criminal is made to appear. ʿAḍud al-Dawla's *dhakā'* is not used to discover the identity of a criminal but rather to effect the punishment of criminals who are outside the ruler's power. In a somewhat similar story, ʿAḍud al-Dawla tricked a merchant into releasing a necklace he was unfairly holding[17]. And

---

[15] ʿAḍud al-Dawla was a Buyid ruler who died in 372/983. He is «generally regarded, with justice, as the greatest *amīr* of the Buwayhid dynasty,» H. Bowen, «ʿAḍud al-Dawla,» *EI²*.

[16] Ibn al-Jawzī, *Adhkiyā'*, p. 55.

[17] Ibn al-Jawzī, *Adhkiyā'*, pp. 53-54.

this release, in turn, becomes evidence and leads to the merchant's punishment. In this story, the identity of the criminal is known and the ruler's cleverness consists in tricking him into showing his hand. In neither story, therefore, do we have a true detective narrative, which would begin with the knowledge of a crime, and then proceed to the identification of the criminal. Instead, the bulk of the stories of ʿAḍud al-Dawla[18], when combined with those of al-Muʿtaḍid, belong to a larger set, which could be called crimefighting anecdotes; and in which a ruler uses his exemplary cleverness to see that crime does not go unpunished.

This, in turn, brings us to an important question, and that is, why al-Muʿtaḍid? When we say that al-Muʿtaḍid is the literary personification of the detective we are saying that narratives involving detection tend to cluster around that caliph. Indeed, in Ibn al-Jawzī's *Adhkiyā'*, there are few narratives which can be construed as detective stories, and which are associated with other rulers. One such is built around another ʿAbbāsid caliph, al-Manṣur[19]. A more complex case is presented by Solomon, the Biblical ruler, and a prophet in the Islamic tradition. Stories which show his ratiocinative skills range from the famous Biblical story of how he determined the real mother of a child to the following story, which functions virtually as a detective anecdote. A man tells Solomon that geese have been stolen from him. During a sermon, the king addresses the crowd, saying: «And one of you steals his neighbor's geese and then comes to the mosque with a feather on his head!» The guilty party, of course, then gives himself away by reaching on top of his head[20]. Though we do not, properly speaking, have an investigation, the ruler does use his ratiocinative powers to find the author of a crime which had previously been denounced to him. Not all of the Solomonic crime-fighting anecdotes come this close to the detective pattern. As a result, Solomon's identity and his *dhakā'* are not as clearly linked to detection as are those of al-Muʿtaḍid[21].

---

[18] There is one story in which ʿAḍud al-Dawla uncovers the criminal as well. Ibn al-Jawzī, *Adhkiyā'*, pp. 55-56.

[19] Ibn al-Jawzī, *Adhkiyā'*, p. 41. Al-Manṣūr, as caliph, ruled from 136-158/754-775. See C. E. Bosworth, *The Islamic Dynasties* (Edinburgh: Edinburgh University Press, 1967), p. 7.

[20] Ibn al-Jawzī, *Adhkiyā'*, pp. 15, 16.

[21] Solomon, for example, was known in the Islamic tradition for his mastery of *jinn*. See *al-Qur'ān* (Cairo: Muṣṭafā al-Bābī al-Ḥalabī, 1966), Sūrat al-Naml, verse 17. See, also, al-Qurṭubī, *al-Jāmiʿ li-Aḥkām al-Qur'ān* (Cairo: Dar al-Kitāb al-

This literary situation is not unusual. As we mentioned earlier, these anecdotes form part of *adab* literature, an anecdotal literature composed largely of texts which deal with various character types. These are most normally social types, and can range from the witty and the insane to misers and party crashers. As I have shown in other studies, this literature portrays a given type of character through typical actions which that character, given his nature, is likely to perform. The character literature has a tendency, furthermore, to portray a given character type through the actions of different individuals[22]. Yet, despite this tendency, *adab* literature often provides an archetypical individual to portray a given type. And, interestingly enough, these archetypical figures are presented as historical. In the literature on *taṭfīl* (loosely translated, party crashing), for example, many individuals are shown performing characteristic *taṭfīl* actions. There is, nevertheless, an archetypical *ṭufaylī*, Bunān, who is presented as a kind of champion of *taṭfīl*[23].

We have a similar phenomenon with al-Muʿtaḍid. The principal difference is that al-Muʿtaḍid dominates the detective category to a greater degree than does Bunān with the *ṭufaylīs*. The most important reason for this is probably that with the detective, we are looking at a subdivision of the larger category of the ruler as *dhakī*, in turn a subdivision of the *adhkiyā'*.

One can ask, however, why this caliph should have been chosen for this particular narrative role? In this case, the literary al-Muʿtaḍid is supported by the historical one. Al-Muʿtaḍid, as caliph, ruled from 279/892 to 289/902. Although the medieval chroniclers and biographers vary in the amount and nature of the information they present about al-Muʿtaḍid, a clear picture nevertheless emerges, a picture which can help us to understand the literary image. For example, the caliph's virtuous nature is noted by al-Khaṭīb al-Baghdādī, in his *Ta'rīkh Baghdād*, and by Abū al-Fidā', in his *al-Mukhtaṣar*[24]. The ruler was so preoccupied with the

---

ʿArabī lil-Ṭibāʿa wal-Nashr, 1967), v. XIII, pp. 167-169; J. Walker, «Sulaimān b. Dāwūd,» *EI*².

[22] Fedwa Malti-Douglas, *Structures of Avarice: The Bukhalā' in Medieval Arabic Literature* (Leiden: E. J. Brill, 1985); Malti-Douglas, «Structure and Organization.»

[23] Al-Khaṭīb al-Baghdādī, *al-Taṭfīl*, pp. 83-111; Malti-Douglas, «Structure and Organization,» p. 230.

[24] Al-Khaṭīb al-Baghdādī, *Ta'rīkh Baghdād* (Beirut: Dār al-Kitāb al-ʿArabī, n.d.), v. IV, p. 404; Abū al-Fidā', *al-Mukhtaṣar fī Akhbār al-Bashar* (Cairo: al-Maṭbaʿa al-Ḥusayniyya, n.d.), v. II, p. 59.

affairs of his citizenry, according to Ibn al-ᶜImād, that he would wear the same clothing for a year[25]. But alongside this image of a concerned and just ruler, other features emerge. Al-Muᶜtaḍid had the reputation for having fortified the caliphate and restored order in the government and in the country at large, as well as reorganizing the police. He was also noted for being perspicacious and awesome[26]. Al-Masᶜūdī, in his *Murūj al-Dhahab*, explains quite clearly that al-Muᶜtaḍid had a penchant for torture and had elaborate torture machines used to extricate confessions from various individuals. Abū al-Fidā', Ibn al-Wardī, and Ibn al-Athīr, for example, note that even the caliph's friends abstained from performing misdeeds out of fear of him[27].

Therefore, the historical al-Muᶜtaḍid appears as a personality whose reputation supports the anecdotal al-Muᶜtaḍid. It would be a mistake, however, to attribute the literary figure directly to the historical one. The character al-Muᶜtaḍid the detective owes his existence essentially to literary causes. He fits within the literary schemata and satisfies the aesthetic demands articulated in this branch of *adab* literature. His position in the *Akhbār al-Adhkiyā'* is sufficient evidence for that. The historical character of this caliph merely made him an excellent candidate for adoption into an essentially literary system.

Thus, al-Muᶜtaḍid appears, on the literary level, as a good detective figure. And as we have already had ample opportunity to indicate, the fact that he fights crime is only one component in his literary existence as a detective. And the fact that an individual fights crime does not make him a literary detective.

---

[25] Ibn al-ᶜImād, *Shadharāt al-Dhahab fī Akhbār man Dhahab* (Beirut: al-Maktab al-Tijārī lil-Ṭibāᶜa wal-Nashr wal-Tawzīᶜ, n.d.), v. II, p. 200.

[26] See Abū al-Fidā', *al-Bidāya wal-Nihāya fī al-Ta'rīkh* (Cairo: Maṭbaᶜat al-Saᶜāda, n.d.), v. XI, p. 86; Ibn al-ᶜImād, *Shadharāt*, v. II, pp. 173, 199; Ibn al-Wardī, *Ta'rīkh Ibn al-Wardī* (Najaf: al-Maṭbaᶜa al-Ḥaydariyya, 1969), v. I, p. 340; al-Ṭabarī, *Ta'rīkh al-Mulūk wal-Umam* (Cairo: al-Maṭbaᶜa al-Ḥusayniyya, n.d.), v. XI, pp. 340, 341; Ibn al-Jawzī, *al-Muntaẓam fī Ta'rīkh al-Mulūk wal-Umam* (Hyderabad: Maṭbaᶜat Dā'irat al-Maᶜārif al-ᶜUthmāniyya, 1357 A.H.), v. V, p. 122; al-Masᶜūdī, *Murūj al-Dhahab wa-Maᶜādin al-Jawhar*, ed. and trans. C. Barbier de Meynard (Paris: Imprimerie Nationale, 1874), v. VIII, pp. 113-114; Jacob Lassner, *The Shaping of ᶜAbbāsid Rule* (Princeton: Princeton University Press, 1980), p. 296; K. V. Zetterstéen, «al-Muᶜtaḍid bi'llāh,» *EI*[1]. Our caliph was also credited with the suppression of gambling. See Franz Rosenthal, *Gambling in Islam* (Leiden: E. J. Brill, 1976), p. 145.

[27] Al-Masᶜūdī, *Murūj*, v. VIII, pp. 115-116, 141-142; Abū al-Fidā', al-*Mukhtaṣar*, v. II, p. 59; Ibn al-Wardī, *Ta'rīkh*, v. I, p. 340; Ibn al-Athīr, *al-Kāmil fī al-Ta'rīkh* (Cairo: Idārat al-Ṭibāᶜa al-Munīriyya, 1353 A.H.), v. VI, p. 101.

VII

74

The Thousand and One Nights and Arabic Detective Literature.

Critics in their never-ending search for literary antecedents have bypassed al-Muʿtaḍid, and turned their attention instead to *The Thousand and One Nights.* In a recent work on the Arabic novel, Roger Allen points to *The Tale of the Three Apples*, as «an almost classic detective novel: the dead body is found at the beginning of the story, the Caliph wants to find out who the culprit is, and in the end, the entire sorry tale is unravelled»[28]. In a later article devoted to a detailed analysis of this story, Allen even characterizes it as «a quintessential murder myster,» and «a finely crafted mystery story»[29]. Inded, from these remarks, the reader might imagine that he is dealing with a «classic detective novel»[30]. Hence, an examination of *The Tale of the Three Apples* is in order, if only to help us shed better light on the exact literary perimeters of a detective story, which, in turn, will help us to better understand the detective figure.

The story of «The Three Apples» involves the caliph Hārūn al-Rashīd and his vizier Jaʿfar. The caliph pays a poor fisherman for his catch which turns out to be a locked chest, containing the dismembered body of a beautiful woman. The caliph cries out in horror and asks himself whether people are going to be murdered in his reign and be a burden and a responsibility for him on Judgment Day. He concludes that they must avenge the woman. Hārūn al-Rashīd then orders Jaʿfar to find the murderer, stating that if he does not he will be killed instead. Jaʿfar asks for three days' delay, and out of fear of not finding the right culprit, he keeps to his house for the three days. On the fourth, the caliph sends for him, and since he has not found the murderer, Hārūn al-Rashīd orders his execution. On the way to the gallows, a young man confesses to the murder. Jaʿfar rejoices. But then an old man comes forth and he too confesses to the murder. The young man belittles the old man's confession and Jaʿfar takes them both before the caliph, and explains what happened. Both men confess again and the caliph

---

[28] Roger Allen, *The Arabic Novel: An Historical and Critical Introduction* (Syracuse: Syracuse University Press, 1982), p. 16.

[29] Roger Allen, «An Analysis of the 'Tale of the Three Apples' from *The Thousand and One Nights*,» in Roger M. Savory and Dionisius A. Agius, eds., *Logos Islamikos: Studia Islamica in honorem Georgii Michaelis Wickens* (Toronto: Pontifical Institute of Mediaeval Studies, 1984), pp. 52, 58.

[30] Of course, the story is not a «novel,» but this slip of the critic's pen is not really relevant for his analysis or ours. In the article cited above, «The Tale of the Three Apples» is referred to as a story, not a novel.

decides to execute them both. But Jaʿfar dissuades him, arguing that he will thereby be killing an innocent man. The young man further insisted on his guilt, describing the way that he had murdered the woman, down to the objects which had been found in the locked chest. So the caliph asked him why he had done this.

The young man then explained that the woman was his wife and that she had taken ill and wanted an apple. There were no apples to be had so he traveled to Baṣra to procure some for her. On his return, his wife was too ill to eat the apples, so he left all three of them by her bedside. He then went back to his shop and saw a black slave with an apple. He asked the slave about the apple, to which the latter replied that his mistress had given it to him, and that she had gotten the apples from her husband, who had procured them in Baṣra. So the young man went home, to find only two apples. He asked his wife about this and she answered that she did not know. So he killed her and threw her body into the Tigris.

At this point in the story, the young man entreated the caliph to hang him quickly, for fear that his wife would seek vengeance on Judgment Day. He continued the story. After having disposed of his wife, he returned home to find his oldest son crying. Upon being asked the reason for his tears, the boy revealed that he was afraid of what his mother would do to him because he had taken one of the apples, only to have it taken from him by a big black slave who asked him where he got it. The boy had disappeared out of fear. Of course, at this point, the young man realized his mistake, and he began to mourn his wife. His paternal uncle, his wife's father, was told the story and the two mourned together. This man is actually the old man who also confessed to the crime. The young man then told the caliph that the entire affair was the fault of the black slave. The caliph then asked Jaʿfar to find the slave and bring him within three days, stating that if he did not do so, he would be killed. Jaʿfar went home and said to himself, that craft and cunning would be of no avail. He stayed home for the three days and made his will, and when the messenger of the caliph came for him on the fourth day, he bade his family farewell. When saying good-bye to his youngest daughter, which he did last, he felt something round inside her dress, and asked her what it was. It was an apple which Rayḥān, their slave, had brought for her. Jaʿfar rejoiced, took out the apple, and asked for the slave. The slave then confessed and Jaʿfar marvelled at this entire story. He was saddened over the fate of the slave but quite glad for himself. He then took the slave to the caliph and told him the entire story. The caliph «marvelled with extreme astonishment, and laughed till he fell on his back.» Ja^cfar then said that this was really not as strange as the story of Nūr al-Dīn, and the caliph asked him to tell it. But Ja^cfar would only do so on condition that the caliph pardon his slave. The caliph agreed.

Then follows the story of Nūr al-Dīn and his son. After this long tale, *The Thousand and One Nights* text returns briefly to the tale of «Three Apples» to tell us that the caliph marvelled at this last story, and that he set the slave free, gave the young man one of his slaves and a monthly stipend, and made him a boon companion[31].

«The Tale of the Three Apples» is not, however, a detective story. Over twenty years ago, Mia Gerhardt, in her excellent study, *The Art of Story-Telling: A Literary Study of The Thousand and One Nights*, clearly demonstrated as much, and her arguments are still extremely cogent. Gerhardt noted that the modern mystery story possessed «a structural feature: its curious inverted chronology. Beginning with the more or less gory discovery of a murder, it subsequently presents a gradual reconstruction of the past, to show how and by whom the murder was committed»[32]. Here, we recognize, of course, the Butorian/Todorovian schema. But Gerhardt goes on to add «a second characteristic, this reconstruction depends on the activity of a particular sort of hero, the detective»[33].

Gerhardt, thus, classifies «The Tale of the Three Apples» as only «half» a detective story[34]. Gerhardt is absolutely correct in this assessment because the second criterion, the detective, is, as she points out, missing[35].

---

[31] Richard F. Burton, trans., *The Book of the Thousand Nights and a Night* (Burton Club Edition, reprinted U.S.A., n.d.), v. I, pp. 186-254.

[32] Mia I. Gerhardt, *The Art of Story-Telling: A Literary Study of The Thousand and One Nights* (Leiden: E. J. Brill, 1963), pp. 169-170.

[33] Gerhardt, *Story-Telling*, p. 170.

[34] Gerhardt, *Story-Telling*, p. 170.

[35] Gerhardt presents other stories which include detective figures but not the «inverted chronology,» arguing that «the two characteristics are never found in one and the same story. Separately, though, they do occur.» She subsequently identifies two stories «that show the prototype of our modern detective at work; but these do not attempt to set up a mystery.» Gerhardt, *Story-Telling*, pp. 170-171. In effect, though both figures display some skills associated with detection, neither really acts as a detective. One actually fills the then familiar role of repentant thief (see my "Classical Arabic Crime Narratives: Thieves and Thievery in *Adab* Literature," *Journal of Arabic Literature*, forthcoming) and the other is proving a point, not solving a mystery.

If there were a detective, who would it be? Is it the caliph, as our other examples would suggest? Like al-Muʿtaḍid, Hārūn al-Rashīd does react with indignation to the fact that a heinous crime has sullied his jurisdiction. Yet, he does not conduct an investigation; instead, instructing Jaʿfar to find the murderer. But unlike al-Muʿtaḍid, Hārūn al-Rashīd does not give his agent precise instructions on how to find the murderer. The only means he can think of to speed the investigation is to threaten to kill the investigator.

Is Jaʿfar then the detective? But, Jaʿfar is as far from being a detective as anyone could imagine. He goes home and sits for the three days during which he is supposed to be searching for the criminal. In fact, he gives up without even trying. Lest the reader think that this is accidental, the pattern of Jaʿfar's behavior is repeated. The first time, he is asked to find the murderer, but he remains at home instead. The second time, the caliph commissions him to find the slave, and, again, he remains at home. And, of course, in both cases, Jaʿfar's life was in danger, so one cannot say that he had no personal motive for finding the culprits. One of Jaʿfar's remarks is even more revealing. At one point, he said to himself that craft and cunning would be of no avail. No attitude could be farther from that of the true detective, who relies on his intellectual skills.

Hence, there is no detective in the story. And, that means that there is no detection either. The young man confesses, but that not at the urging of a force of justice but of his own free will. Furthermore, during the process of confession, he is not instigated to reveal more material by the questioning of the caliph, for example. Thus, one cannot say that the confession is extorted from him, as happens in one of the al-Muʿtaḍid anecdotes.

Of interest also is the caliph's reaction at the end of the story. When Jaʿfar tells him about the slave, Hārūn al-Rashīd breaks out in laughter. This is in contrast to what one would normally expect from a detective. Generally, the uncovering of the identity of the criminal is a solemn act. But even were it to be otherwise, Hārūn al-Rashīd's laughter is not that of triumph: the story indicates that he marvelled at the tale, and he is, in fact, laughing because the explanation is far from anything he might have imagined. There is also the fact that Hārūn al-Rashīd metes out no justice, no one is punished. Although this reaction is consistent with a repeating structure of *The Thousand and One Nights*, in which lives are saved by stories[36], it does not fit the detective mode[37]. Even modern detective stories, which do not necessarily present the punishment of the criminal, assume that crime will be followed by punishment.

In fact, if we must see this story in relation to detective literature, we would have to conclude that it represents, on one level, an anti-detective or even a counter-detective narrative, if not a parody of the type. The standard components of a detective story are reversed, or, perhaps, even mocked. Ja^cfar, whom we have to see as the supposed detective, since he is to find the culprits, remains at home and makes no effort to do so, though his life is in danger. The guilty young man is rewarded, and the guilty slave is set free. The caliph, who vowed to avenge the victim and whose first reaction in the text was that of anger, ends the narrative with laughter, and not having performed the threatened retribution.

What this almost parodic treatment of a criminal investigation does show is the existence in the medieval Arabic literary psyche of an association between the caliph and the role of investigating and punishing crimes.

The Tale of the Three Apples is perhaps an extreme case in this regard, because of its parodic elements. But it does remind us that, as John Cawelti, among others, has shown for modern literature, crime and corpses do not by themselves create detective fiction[38]. A detective and an investigation are essential components. Non-detective crime narratives are rampant in *The Thousand and One Nights*, as they are also in *adab* literature[39].

But it is not merely the criminal component of *The Thousand and One Nights* which has attracted the attention of critics in search of antecedents for the detective. Régis Messac, in his *Le «Detective Novel» et l'influence de la pensée scientifique*, characterizes the story of

---

[36] Gerhardt, *Story-Telling*, pp. 401-416; Tzvetan Todorov, «Les Hommes-Récits,» in Todorov, *Poétique*, pp. 86-91.

[37] Indeed, in the course of his analysis, Roger Allen recognizes the limitations of the «mystery story» model, declaring: «It is not so much a matter of 'whodunit?'...» In fact, his article contains may interesting and important points about how the story is crafted, which would not be invalidated but would, indeed, be strengthened by the omission of the «mystery story» label. Allen, «Analysis,» pp. 51-60.

[38] Cawelti, *Adventure*, pp. 51-105.

[39] Gerhardt discusses many of them in her chapter on «Crime Stories.» Gerhardt, *Story-Telling*, pp. 167-190. See Malti-Douglas, "Classical Arabic Crime Narratives."

«The Sultan of al-Yaman and His Sons» as presenting the ancestor of the Western detective. The story is, however, not a detective story, nor are the three sons really detectives. All that they do is to display the type of ratiocination also used by detectives, putting them and their story into the kind of non-detective ratiocination literature that was associated, for example, in the *Akhbār al-Adhkiyā'*, with Iyās ibn Muᶜāwiya[40].

Detective Literature East and West.

Even after eliminating from consideration, as I believe we must, related Arabic stories that are not true detective stories, we are still left with a group of stories which fit any modern Western definition of a detective story. It has become evident, however, that these stories also contain features which are distinctive to, and form part and parcel of, their Arabic literary environment. There are clearly differences in the way that the narrative of the detective is articulated in the East versus its presentation in the West. These can be seen more clearly if we reexamine «The Case of the Painted Hand» in its context and ask ourselves what the functions in the anecdote would be, using the concept of the Proppian function but modifying it along the lines suggested by Claude Bremond[41]. The functions in the anecdote would then be:

1. the discovery of the crime
2. the process of detection
3. the discovery of the criminal
4. the apprehension of the criminal and extraction of the confession
5. the punishment.

There are two functions in this list which tend to distinguish it from the classical Western detective narrative: the extraction of the confession and the punishment. Western detective stories do often contain confessions by the wrongdoers, but this is far from an

---

[40] Régis Messac, *Le «Detective Novel» et l'influence de la pensée scientifique* (Paris: Librairie Ancienne Honoré Champion, 1929), pp. 22-29. Fereydoun Hoveyda, in *Petite histoire du roman policier* (Paris, n.d.), pp. 40, 45, simply follows Messac's argument here. Richard F. Burton, *Supplemental Nights to the Book of the Thousand Nights and a Night* (Burton Club Edition, reprinted U.S.A., n.d.) v. IV, pp. 1-9.

[41] See, for example, Vladimir Propp, *Morphologie du conte*, trans. Marguerite Derrida (Paris: Editions du Seuil, 1970); Claude Bremond, *Logique du récit* (Paris: Editions du Seuil, 1973).

essential requirement. Even when they are present, they generally act as a literary mirror to the explanation of the crime which has just been given by the detective, though there are exceptions even to this. In no case, however, would the confession be extracted, for example, by torture, as it is in the Arabic tradition. But, does not this forceful extraction of the confession argue against the investigative skills of the detective? Has not torture replaced ratiocination as the means to identify the criminal? Two points are in order here. First of all, the confession is only extracted, or, in certain cases, torture resorted to, after the identity of the criminal has been intellectually established. The confession is only an added confirmation, superfluous from a strictly investigative point of view, and whose necessity seems to stem from moral and ethical, and not intellectual, concerns. As much as anything, it appears to answer an essentially literary demand for proof of the correctness of the caliph's judgment.

But there is a second aspect to the extraction of the confession. Its extraction often demands cleverness on the part of the caliph. As such, it does not necessarily demand torture. In «The Case of the Painted Hand,» for example the sight of the dismembered hand and foot is sufficient to provoke the confession. Sometimes, torture is not enough. In an al-Muʿtaḍid story in the *Murūj al-Dhahab* of al-Masʿūdī, a criminal insists upon his innocence, even under repeated torture. To trick him, our caliph declares himself satisfied of his innocence and prepares a lavish meal and a comfortable bed for the suspect. At the moment when the criminal was going to collapse into a contented slumber, the caliph shook him awake and asked him exactly how he committed the crime. The thief then gave himself away by explaining how he accomplished his deed[42]. Similarly, the «Merry Slave» was only led to confess by a combination of trickery and torture. In judging these incidents, we have to remember that torture was not considered the heinous act it is today, and, therefore, could be more easily assimilated to other techniques for tricking criminals into confession. It is also an instrument of justice, in that we hear in this literature of no innocent people being tortured.

Judicial torture is, of course, related to the caliph's accumulation of roles. That is, that he is at once detective and judge. The same

---

[42] Al-Masʿūdī, *Murūj*, v. VIII, pp. 151-161.

can be said of the last of the functions we mentioned, punishment, which clearly differentiates al-Muʿtaḍid from his Western colleagues. He is the detective and the law enforcer at one and the same time. In the Western equivalent, the classical detective type, the detective is set off against the police or the legal establishment. This does not necessarily imply an antagonistic relationship between the two. We are simply referring to the fact that the detective, in his Western garb, has a literary existence independent from that of the police. This, however, does not prevent him from cooperating with them (as Dupin does, for example), or calling them in to apprehend the criminal.

But though this function of punishment serves to differentiate al-Muʿtaḍid from his Western counterpart, it does, on the other hand, bring him in line with an Eastern counterpart, the figure of the classical Chinese detective. In the Chinese detective literature, the detective figure is also presented as the embodiment of the detective and the law enforcer. And this is the case with the stories told both about Judge Dee and Judge Pao. Both of these characters were also historical individuals, Dee having died in 907 and Pao in 1062. Although Pao's cases were recorded not long after his death, those of Judge Dee, according to Van Gulik, had to wait until the eighteenth century to take their present shape. Nevertheless, it is clear from the Chinese narratives that their literary figures, who are presented in their official capacities as redressers of wrongs, perform the same functions as al-Muʿtaḍid, including the extraction of confessions by various tortures, and the subsequent punishments. The principal structural difference between the Chinese stories and their Arabic counterparts is that the Chinese audience is told the identity of the criminal at the beginning of the story. However, the judge/detective does not receive this information and, hence, must, like other detectives, determine the author of a crime which has been presented to him[43].

[43] Robert H. Van Gulik, trans. and ed., *Celebrated Cases of Judge Dee (Dee Goong An)* (New York: Dover Publications, 1976); Leon Comber, trans. and ed., *The Strange Cases of Magistrate Pao* (Hong Kong: Heinemann, 1972); George A. Hayden, *Crime and Punishment in Medieval Chinese Drama: Three Judge Pao Plays* (Cambridge: Harvard University Press, 1978); George A. Hayden, «The Courtroom Plays of the Yüan and Early Ming Periods,» *Harvard Journal of Asiatic Studies*, 34 (1974), pp. 192-220. Continuing Hayden's studies, Ching-Hsi Perng, in *Double Jeopardy: A Critique of Seven Yüan Courtroom Dramas*, Michigan Papers in Chinese Studies, No. 35 (Ann Arbor: Center for Chinese Studies, 1978),

The Chinese detectives are also wont to exercise a great deal of ratiocination. In one of Judge Dee's celebrated cases, he smokes out a crime, in much the same way that al-Muʿtaḍid did in «The Case of the Merry Slave.» The judge had found the behavior of a particular character to be suspicious and, following his instincts, he uncovered not only what we would normally have expected from him as a detective, i.e. the culprit, but also the crime. And, as with the case of al-Muʿtaḍid, this was a heinous crime which would have gone unpunished, indeed unnoticed, had it not been for the judge's sagacity[44]. In this application of the ratiocinative skills, the Arabic and the Chinese figures come close to one another.

Although the two Eastern detective types bear many similarities, such as the ratiocination in detection, the meting out of justice, and so on, there is an important distinction between the Arabic and the Chinese detectives, and one which is significant for the portrayal of that figure in the Arabic tradition. As Van Gulik, Comber, and Hayden have pointed out, the supernatural plays a distinctive, if not a major, role in Chinese detective fiction. Both Judges Dee and Pao commonly utilize various supernatural signs or mantic systems to aid them in their detection. Judge Dee, for example, resorts to incubation to bring on a dream, which is instrumental in helping him solve a crime[45]. This element is almost completely absent in the corresponding Arabic literature. There, the detective is not

---

discusses a variant in which one courtroom judgment is reversed by another. The argument has been raised by numerous Chinese scholars (often writing from a Marxist perspective) that these Yüan dramas represent a form of political and social protest against the rule of this foreign dynasty. Both George Hayden and especially Ching-Hsi Perng show the weaknesses of these arguments. Hayden, «Courtroom,» p. 202; Ching-Hsi Perng, *Double Jeopardy*, pp. 10-15. A political argument based on social protest would be even less tenable applied to the Arabic sources. The criminals are not members of the upper classes and there is no suggestion of corrupt officialdom. On the contrary, these stories obviously support the dominant ideology of medieval Islamic civilization, by showing the ruler carrying out his role in the suppression of criminality. He is presented as font of justice and guarantor of order.

44 Van Gulik, *Judge Dee*, p. 30 ff.

45 Hayden, *Crime*, pp. 10-11; Comber, *Magistrate Pao*, pp. 15-16; Van Gulik, *Judge Dee*, pp. 78-87, which includes the use of other mantic systems. As Van Gulik, *Judge Dee*, pp. II-III, expresses it, «the Chinese have an innate love for the supernatural. Ghosts and goblins roam about freely in most Chinese detective stories; animals and kitchen utensils deliver testimony in court, and the detective indulges occasionally in little escapades in the Nether World, to compare notes with the judges of the Chinese Inferno. This clashes with our principle that a detective novel should be as realistic as possible.»

generally in need of the supernatural or of oniromancy, as the case may be, to help him fulfill his duties. This fact becomes more significant when viewed in the broader context of Islamic civilization. Dreams are a very common element in Islamic literature, and could be used to answer a large variety of questions, including some which might otherwise have been relegated to a «detective.» Thus, in one case, ʿAlī ibn Aḥmad al-Ḥanbalī al-Āmidī had some silk stolen from him. He thereupon dreamt that he saw his *shaykh*, who told him who had stolen the silk, where it was, and that he should go and get it. Upon awakening, ʿAlī did exactly as his *shaykh* told him and retrieved his stolen silk[46]. The theft, of course, represents a crime, but its solution was made through the oniric medium. And it is in much this same way that dream material helps the Chinese detective solve his cases.

Yet, in the cases we discussed, al-Muʿtaḍid used neither dreams nor any other suprarational devices in his investigations. Oniric material is attributed to al-Muʿtaḍid in the biographical and historical literature but it is generally the same kind of political dream material which we so often find associated with other rulers[47]. There is one case, located characteristically not in *al-Adhkiyā'* but in the chronicle, *al-Bidāya wal-Nihāya fī al-Ta'rīkh*, of Abū al-Fidā', in which al-Muʿtaḍid awakens from a dream terrified and insists that a certain sailor be brought to him. It turns that the sailor in question had committed a murder[48]. This overlapping of dream material and detective material is actually exceptional in the Arabic tradition, Indeed, none of the crime-fighting anecdotes made use of supernatural agencies. Hence, that part of al-Muʿtaḍid's persona as ruler which is concerned with solving crimes is kept essentially distinct from the world of dreams and mantic systems. This, of course, strengthens the purely ratiocinative and, hence, detective quality of his characterization.

We noted earlier that literary critics of the detective genre have frequently pointed out the importance of the beginning of the detective story. We are usually presented with a calm beginning

---

[46] Aṣ-Ṣafadī, *Nakt al-Himyān fī Nukat al-ʿUmyān*, ed. Aḥmad Zakī Bāshā (Cairo: al-Maṭbaʿa al-Jamāliyya, 1911), p. 206.

[47] See, for example, Ibn al-ʿImād, *Shadharāt*, v. II, p. 173; Lassner, *Shaping*, pp. 26-31; Ibn Khallikān, *Wafayāt al-Aʿyān*, ed. Iḥsān ʿAbbās (Beirut: Dār al-Thaqāfa, n.d.), v. II, pp. 53-54.

[48] Abū al-Fidā', *al-Bidāya*, v. XI, p. 88.

which in the Western format is typified by the countryside or the peaceful country village, or even by the comfortable environment of the detective's own living quarters, as with Sherlock Holmes. We noted the presence of this element in the anecdotes involving al-Muʿtaḍid, and even Judge Dee's cases begin with him sitting in his office, quietly attending to some «routine business»[49].

As a corollary to this, in both the Eastern and the Western modes of detective fiction, the intrusion of murder, crime, or the corpse, represents, on the literary plane, a breakdown of the order presented in the initial situation. And, subsequently, the detective who ventures into the investigation and solves the crime or the mystery is a character who restores order to a textual world which has temporarily lost it.

This restoration of order is equally true whether it be by al-Muʿtaḍid, or Judge Dee, or Hercule Poirot, or any of the standard classical detective figures. But, there is one crucial difference in the way the texts portray this restoration of order.

We already mentioned that in the Eastern detective story, the punishment formed a crucial part of the unfolding of this narrative. Whereas in the Western narrative, once the identity of the criminal is disclosed, once the puzzle is solved, every one lives happily ever after. The reader does not follow the criminal on his various adventures with the judicial system and its legal battles! Is he convicted? Does he receive a life sentence? etc. These are questions in which the classical Western detective narrative is not interested[50].

And yet, the classical Western detective restores order, as does his Eastern counterpart. But there is clearly a distinction in the conception of order as it is portrayed in these works. As we noted above, in the Eastern literature, we saw first the discovery of the crime, followed by the process of detection leading to the identification of the criminal, his confession, and, finally, the meting out of justice. In the Western narrative, on the other hand, we have first the discovery of the crime and, second, and last, the process of detection leading to the identity of the criminal. The final step does not exist on the literary level. But since both types of narratives are concerned with the restoration of order, this difference means that

---

[49] Van Gulik, *Judge Dee*, p. 10.

[50] Ernst Kaemmel, «Literature under the Table: The Detective Novel and Its Social Mission,» in Most and Stowe, eds., *Poetics*, p. 59.

we are dealing with two different visions of what constitutes order in the detective narrative. In the Western one, order comes through knowledge, whereas in the Eastern one, order is perceived through the meting out of justice. That is, in the last analysis, for the West, order *is* knowledge, whereas, for the East, order is justice. Of course, for the traditional society, justice depends upon knowledge. Hence, knowledge plays a crucial role, and is, of course, a prerequisite for the detective figure. Yet, in terms of restoring order, this knowledge is instrumental and order has not been restored until justice has been done.

We can see the same phenomenon if we look at the personality of al-Muᶜtaḍid. The caliph in these anecdotes appears, in a sense, as an arrogant and egotistical individual. This, of course, only brings him closer to the smug self-assurance, bordering on arrogance, of a Sherlock Holmes or an Hercule Poirot. But al-Muᶜtaḍid's egotism is distinct. His reaction when he hears of the corpse in «The Case of the Painted Hand» is a case in point. He is outraged that such an act could take place without his knowledge and outside his control. His ego is engaged by the mere existence of crime. The ego of the Western detective is bound up with his ability to solve a crime. He would never be upset to hear that a crime has taken place without his knowledge. What is a challenge for the Western detective is almost *lèse-majesté* for the Eastern one. This is, of course, because, as a ruler, he is responsible for order and justice. Order, in his literary system, involves his application of his justice.

It is easy to see in this contrast between order as knowledge and order as justice a testimony to the greater Western faith in reason and science acting alone. It is necessary to note, however, that this distinction is only wholly valid for the classical detective novel and is not fully applicable to the hard-boiled detective novel.

The Problem of Origins.

Given all the similarities which we have, nevertheless, shown between the medieval Arabic and modern Western detectives, we are naturally led to ask: can the medieval Arabic material be seen as the antecedent of the modern Western detective novel?

The author most closely associated with this theory and whose argumentation is normally used as a source in later discussions is Régis Messac, in the work already mentioned, *Le «Detective Novel» et l'influence de la pensée scientifique*. Messac is, in fact, arguing two different points. The first is the connection between *The Thousand and One Nights* story, which we already mentioned above, and Voltaire's *Zadig* and, thence, to the modern detective. The second point in Messac's work is that this development is related to the scientific spirit, specifically physiognomy, with its origin among the ancient Greeks[51].

We can analyze Messac's points one at a time. Messac begins by arguing that Voltaire's *Histoire orientale* is the progenitor of the modern Western detective figure created by Poe. He then shows, quite correctly, that Voltaire's tale was clearly influenced by the story presented in *The Thousand and One Nights* as the story of «The Sultan of al-Yaman and His Sons.» Messac then demonstrates that one of the components of this story has been located in still earlier texts in still earlier literatures, like the *Midrash* and Indian literature[52]. But, as we noted earlier, this tale is exclusively concerned with ratiocination and not with true detection. The famous incident in *Zadig* is the one in which the hero gives a detailed description of both the king's horse and the queen's dog, solely on the basis of their tracks. In *The Thousand and One Nights* tale, the three young men describe a camel from similar evidence[53].

Insofar as one traces Poe's detective figure back to Zadig, then Messac's argument is sound, since the relationship between Zadig and the Oriental tradition is unquestionable. There are, of course, important, if not crucial, differences between Zadig and C. Auguste Dupin. Nevertheless, the possibility of some filiation cannot be excluded. Nor can the possibility be excluded, however, that Poe was directly inspired by the tale in question. It is well known that Poe was greatly interested in the East and the author of «The Thousand-and-Second Tale of Scheherazade» was clearly familiar with the Middle Eastern classic[54]. Even if we argue this filiation, however, we would have to note that it is from one ratiocinative literature to another, which second literature subsequently evolved a detective figure. There would be no direct con-

---

[51] Messac, *Le «Detective Novel»*, pp. 17-58.

[52] Messac, *Le «Detective Novel»*, pp. 26-29.

[53] Voltaire, *Zadig ou la destinée* in Voltaire, *Romans et contes* (Paris: Garnier-Flammarion, 1966), pp. 34-36; Burton, *Supplemental Nights*, v. IV, pp. 4-5.

[54] He is, for example, the author of «Some Words with a Mummy,» and «The Thousand-and-Second Tale of Scheherazade.» See Poe, *Short Stories*, pp. 491-513.

nection between one detective figure and the other, merely a link, logical or coincidental, between each ratiocinative literature (or one literature, if we accept a Poe/*The Thousand and One Nights* connection) and a detective figure. What we would then have would be two linked ratiocinative literatures which each separately spawned a detective figure. If, on the other hand, one rejects the connection between Zadig and C. Auguste Dupin, which is anything but evident, then we have simply two independent inventions. The existence of an apparently separate Chinese case would further strengthen this interpretation.

Messac's second point was the relationship between this particular tradition of ratiocination and the Greek science of physiognomy. Whatever the relationship between Greek physiognomy and the ultimate origins of this tradition, there is no question but that the physiognomic tradition has a relationship to the Arabic detective.

In the introduction to his work, Ibn al-Jawzī notes, among other points, that the *dhakī* judges from external form and from physical behavioral traits. For example, someone whose eyes move quickly is a swindler and a thief[55].

The close relationship between *dhakā'* and physiognomy is also shown by the fact that al-Nuwayrī, in his *Nihāyat al-Arab fī Funūn al-Adab*, included «The Case of the Merry Slave» under the heading of *al-Firāsa wal-Dhakā'*[56]. The Arabic *firāsa* is used to translate the Greek science of physiognomy. But it represents more than just this learned tradition. Its basic meaning, as given, for example, by the lexicographer, al-Zabīdī, in his *Tāj al-ʿArūs*, is that of the close examination of something, or, in effect, perspicacity and penetration[57]. Clearly, in its broader, if not also in its narrower, meaning, *firāsa* is an attribute of the *dhakī* and especially of the detective.

The relationship between the acumen of the Arabic detective and this Graeco-Arabic scientific tradition is not, however, a completely clear one. If we look, for example, at the rules in the *Kitāb al-Firāsa* of the twelfth-century physician and philosopher, al-Rāzī, we can see that they represent a type of reasoning distinct from the forms of ratiocination most commonly employed by the detective,

---

[55] Ibn al-Jawzī, *Adhkiyā'*, pp. 11-14.

[56] Al-Nuwayrī, *Nihāyat al-Arab fī Funūn al-Adab* (Cairo: al-Mu'assasa al-ʿĀmma lil-Ta'līf wal-Tarjama wal-Ṭibāʿa wal-Nashr, n.d.), v. III, p. 150.

[57] See T. Fahd, «Firāsa,» *EI²*; al-Zabīdī, *Tāj al-ʿArūs*, v. IV, p. 207.

Eastern or Western. For example, al-Rāzī states that a beautiful voice is an indication of stupidity and weakness of intellect, while a large forehead is an indication of laziness[58].

The type of reasoning most commonly used by al-Muᶜtaḍid, as well as by the other ratiocinators of the *Adhkiyā'*, involves the discovery of past or present facts from distinctive elements in the behavior of individuals, or the extrapolation of what individuals in a given situation are likely to do, what will be the effects of given actions. Such reasonings are also characteristic of the modern detective. Physiognomy, on the other hand, is essentially concerned with the identification of a person's basic character, not his specific actions[59]. Hence, the two processes of detection and physiognomy are distinct.

There is one case of truly physiognomic reasoning in the «Merry Slave» story. Al-Muᶜtaḍid noted from the slave's visage, that is physiognomically, that he had a disagreeable temperament. And it was this knowledge that made the slave's cheerful behavior seem all the less normal. Since such cheerfulness was not caused by the slave's disposition, it had to be caused by something else. Even here, however, the physiognomic conclusion forms the premise for the analysis of behavior which itself had to be interpreted on non-physiognomic grounds. Hence, though physiognomy was clearly one of the techniques possessed by the medieval Arabic detective, it is far from representing the essence of his skill.

The Detective in Social and Cultural Context.

But once we begin to examine the relationship between physiognomy and detective literature, we are, in fact, entering a different area altogether, and that is the relationship of detective literature to its social or literary contexts.

The majority of Western critics writing on detective literature see the genesis of that literature in the nineteenth century and its

---

[58] Al-Rāzī, *Kitāb al-Firāsa*, in *al-Firāsa ᶜind al-ᶜArab*, ed. Yūsuf Murād (Cairo: al-Hay'a al-Miṣriyya al-ᶜĀmma lil-Kitāb, 1982), pp. 150, 161.

[59] On the Greek physiognomic tradition, see Elizabeth C. Evans, *Physiognomics in the Ancient World*, Transactions of the American Philosophical Society (Philadelphia: The American Philosophical Society, 1969). *Firāsa* in the Islamic tradition is also related to mystical knowledge, T. Fahd, «Firāsa,» *EI*². Cf. Carlo Ginzburg, «Clues: Morelli, Freud, and Sherlock Holmes,» in Eco and Sebeok, eds., *Sign*, pp. 110, 118.

paternity in Edgar Allan Poe. About Poe's primacy, John Cawelti, Geraldine Pederson-Krag, and Boileau, to cite but three, are all in agreement with Thomas Narcejac that: «Là-dessus, tout le monde est d'accord, et le fait est indiscutable»[60]. Once the genesis of the detective story is attributed to a historical period, theories are developed to account for its presence in this period. In this regard, critics are generally in accord that the society that permitted the development of the genre was an urban, industrialized capitalist society, which possessed a developed police force. As Boileau-Narcejac and Lacassin note, in addition, the period was one in which physiognomy was in fashion[61].

There are certain similarities in the situation with medieval Islam. The civilization with which we are dealing had an urban sector, as well as scientific developments. Elements of a police force were also present in the larger cities[62]. Nevertheless, the degree of urbanization should not be exaggerated. We are still comparing a medieval, essentially traditional, society with a modern, rapidly industrializing one. This explains the features which the Arabic detective shares with his equally pre-industrial Chinese counterpart. In both the Eastern models, the detective/crime relationship has been fitted into the traditional intellectual environment. So that while urbanization does seem to have some relationship with detective fiction, the necessary degree of this urbanization or modernization should not be exaggerated.

One of the differences between the traditional and modern conceptions which has already been noted is the emphasis upon execution, playing an almost ritual role, in both the Arabic and Chinese

---

[60] Cawelti, *Adventure*, p. 80; Boileau-Narcejac, *Le roman policier* (Paris; Presses Universitaires de France, 1982), p. 7; Thomas Narcejac, *Une machine à lire: Le roman policier* (Paris: Denoël/Gonthier, 1975), p. 23; Geraldine Pederson-Krag, «Detective Stories and the Primal Scene,» in Most and Stowe, eds., p. 19. Jorge Luis Borges went so far as to say that Poe even created the reader of the genre. See Jorge Luis Borges, «Le conte policier,» in Uri Eisenzweig, ed., *Autopsies du roman policier* (Paris: Union Générale d'Editions, 1983), pp. 289-291.

[61] Francis Lacassin, *Mythologie du roman policier* (Paris: Union Générale d'Editions, 1974), v. I, pp. 11-12, 91-92; Boileau-Narcejac, *Roman*, pp. 14-15, 18; Narcejac, *Machine*, pp. 31-32; Kaemmel, «Literature,» pp. 57-58.

[62] Al-Ṭabarī, *Ta'rīkh*, v. XI, p. 341. See, for example, Ira M. Lapidus, *Muslim Cities in the Later Middle Ages* (Cambridge: Cambridge University Press, 1984), p. 156. Both Messac, *Le «Detective Novel»* (pp. 56-57) and Hoveyda, *Histoire* (p. 41) note the urban character of medieval Islamic civilization and connect this with *The Thousand and One Nights*.

detective stories. In *Surveiller et punir*, Michel Foucault has noted the relationship between the role of execution in the pre-modern European penal system and a particular type of literature which he calls the «*discours d'échafaud.*» This literature was replaced in contemporary society, he argues, by detective literature, itself characterized by a battle of minds between detective and criminal[63]. In this way, of course, Foucault is putting himself in agreement with those critics who associate the detective novel with the modern Western police system. The Arabic example, however, clearly shows that there is no necessary contradiction between a traditional judicial and penal system, with its emphasis on execution as a crucial symbolic act, and the detective. Nonetheless, the comparison between the traditional Eastern and the modern Western detective narratives does support Foucault's general contention of the importance of execution as a central ritual in judicial practice.

The association of the detective novel with distinctive features of modern Western society and the explicit contrast with traditional values are also central to the theological interpretation of Siegfried Kracauer. For Kracauer, the whole system of the detective novel replaces that of Christianity, and the major elements of the novel can be understood in precise Christian ritual terms, with the detective replacing the priest[64]. The coexistence which we have seen of the detective and a flourishing Abrahamic religion makes Kracauer's associations more difficult to demonstrate.

There are, of course, clear differences between the literary importance of the medieval Arabic and the modern Western detective narrative. Most notably, modern detective fiction has become a genre of mass literature. The elite character of the medieval Arabic detective anecdotes, and indeed of the *adab* literature of which they form a part, is clearly shown by the sophisticated and occasionally *recherché* language which characterizes them. Such anecdotes were, after poetry, perhaps the most prestigious classical Arabic literary form. As such, they were more highly regarded than the relatively popular stories in *The Thousand and One Nights*[65].

---

[63] Michel Foucault, *Surveiller et punir: Naissance de la prison* (Paris; Editions Gallimard, 1975), pp. 9-72, and especially p. 72.

[64] Siegfried Kracauer, *Le roman policier: Un traité philosophique*, trans. Geneviève and Rainer Rochlitz (Paris: Petite Bibliothèque Payot, 1971).

[65] See, for example, Franz Rosenthal, «Literature,» in Joseph Schacht and C. E. Bosworth, eds., *The Legacy of Islam* (Oxford: Clarendon Press, 1974), p. 322.

But, of course, the greatest difference between these narratives and the modern detective story is length. The medieval Arabs developed a detective figure whose methods of detection were not dissimilar from those of his Western, or even Chinese, counterparts. They did not, however, develop a detective novel. This is not for the lack of a detective but because the novel, as a literary form, was foreign to the aesthetic concerns of the medieval Arabs. Instead of making their detective the hero of a novel, the Arabs characterized him in concise anecdotal narratives, and placed him along the other clever men and tricksters who people so much of the literature of the medieval Arab world.

VIII

TEXTS AND TORTURES: THE REIGN OF AL-MU'TAḌID AND THE CONSTRUCTION OF HISTORICAL MEANING*

INCREASINGLY, historians and literary critics find themselves converging upon historical texts, examining them as constructed literary artifacts, rather than as depositories of information. This attention to form and composition is motivated by the awareness that the literary modes of historical texts are frequently the most potent purveyors of ideological content, that one needs to understand the former in order to properly appreciate the latter. In this study, we will be concerned with the relationships between literary form and historical meaning in classical Arabic chronicles, biographical compendia, and largely anecdotal collections known as *adab* works. We shall focus on the treatment of the reign of the 'Abbasid caliph, al-Mu'taḍid bi-l-Lāh, and then, in a further discussion, on his association with torture and punishment.

Approaching Classical Arabic Historical Writing

Recent decades have seen a revolution in the approach to Western historical writing. Concern with the literary basis of Western historiography has led to an increased focus on history as narrative. Hayden White's 1973 *Metahistory: The Historical Imagination in the Nineteenth Century* is clearly the most important, if not the most unproblematic, contribution to this discussion. Paradoxically, this attention to literary narrative

* An earlier version of this study was presented as a plenary lecture at the Middle East History and Theory Workshop, "Literature as History/History as Literature," The University of Chicago, April 30, 1987.

as the dominant form of historical writing has taken place during precisely those years when the "story" has lost its dominance in conventional academic history, replaced by what we might call the anti-narratives of the *Annales* school.[1]

For students of Islamic historical writing, the problems have been posed in a somewhat different way. The introduction of literary critical approaches to the understanding of historical writing, the "literarization" of historical criticism, has been directed to the alterity of Islamic historical material. The relative strangeness of much Islamic historical writing led some to see many aspects of historical writing as lacking both literary grace and historiographical sophistication. In its extreme form, the absence of precisely those narrative forms and continuities familiar to the Western scholar was seen as the sign of a fundamental lack in the Islamic comprehension of history. Atomized writing came from atomized thinking and led to atomized history.[2]

The reaction against this point of view has grown almost imperceptibly. Historians, like Marshall Hodgson and H. A. R. Gibb, argued the significance of the exclusion, inclusion, and arrangement of material in medieval Islamic historical sources.[3] It has become increasingly

[1] See, for example, Hayden White, *Metahistory: The Historical Imagination in Nineteenth-Century Europe* (Baltimore: The Johns Hopkins University Press, 1973); Hayden White, "The Value of Narrativity in the Representation of Reality", in W. J. T. Mitchell, ed., *On Narrative* (Chicago: The University of Chicago Press, 1981); the studies in Robert Canary and Henry Kozicki, eds., *The Writing of History* (Madison: University of Wisconsin Press, 1978); Allen Douglas, "al-Mu'arrikh wa l-Naṣṣ, wa l-Nāqid al-Adabī", trans. Fu'ād Kāmil, *Fuṣūl*, 4, 1 (1983), p. 95-105. On the *Annales* school, see Traian Stoianovich, *French Historical Method: The Annales Paradigm* (Ithaca: Cornell University Press, 1976).

[2] The clearest statement of this position is perhaps that of Nadav Safran who links it to Aš'arī theology: "It is vain to look for causes and effects . . . Works of history are thereby reduced to the chronicle of events and the narration of wonders without any unity or connection beyond their tacit, common reference to God's will." Nadav Safran, *Egypt in Search of Political Community* (Cambridge: Harvard University Press, 1961), p. 17. Even the assumptions behind this argument are faulty, since the conceptual/discursive modes of a given society do not have to be derived from one of its theological schools, even an orthodox one. Lewis and Holt, for example, have drawn opposite (and far more reasonable) historiographical conclusions from the same religious tradition. See Bernard Lewis and P. M. Holt, "Introduction", in Bernard Lewis and P. M. Holt, eds., *Historians of the Middle East* (London: Oxford University Press, 1964), p. 3. For a discussion of this problem as it relates to biography, see Fedwa Malti-Douglas, "Dreams, the Blind, and the Semiotics of the Biographical Notice", *Studia Islamica*, LI (1980), p. 137-162. Conceptions of medieval Islamic historiography are also reflections of modern Western conceptions of medieval Western writing as well, as can be seen in White, "Value . . .", cited above.

[3] H. A. R. Gibb, "The Arabic Sources for the Life of Saladin", *Speculum*, XXV (1950), p. 58-72. Marshall G. S. Hodgson, "Two Pre-Modern Muslim Historians: Pitfalls

clear, however, that the full understanding of Arabic and other Islamic historical texts is dependent on the delineation of their literary codes, in effect, upon their comprehension and analysis as literary texts.[4]

Appreciating (in the largest sense of the term) Arabic historical literature, however, leads to the same problems as appreciating most other classical Arabic literary genres. It is no longer as acceptable as it once was to speak of the disunity or tiresomeness of classical literary texts. To arrive at these results, however, it has often been necessary to discard traditional Western literary categories and models. The same must be done for Arabic historical writing. Hayden White's approach will be of little use to us here, as his debate with Marilyn Waldman in *Critical Inquiry* revealed.[5]

The literary patterns of Arabic historiography must be sought in the genres of Arabic historical writing itself: not only the more or less annalistic chronicles but also the closely related biographical compendia and other non-fictional materials, like those loosely referred to as *adab*. Some of these forms, like biography, have already spawned a considerable

---

and Opportunities in Presenting them to Moderns," in John Nef, ed., *Towards World Community* (The Hague: Dr. W. Junk N.V., Publishers, 1968), p. 53-68.

[4] For an approach based upon the problem of literary appeal, see, for example, Hartmut Fähndrich, "*The Wafayāt al-A'yān* of Ibn Khallikān: A New Approach" *Journal of the American Oriental Society*, 93 (1973), p. 432-445; Hartmut Fähndrich, "Compromising the Caliph", *Journal of Arabic Literature*, VIII (1977), p. 36-47. For a generic/organizational approach, see I. Hafsi, "Recherches sur le genre *Ṭabaqāt*", *Arabica*, XXIII (1976), p. 227-265, XXIV (1977), p. 1-41, 150-186. For the historiographical implications of modes of discourse, see Fedwa Malti-Douglas, "Controversy and Its Effects in the Biographical Tradition of al-Khaṭīb al-Baghdādī" *Studia Islamica*, XLVI (1977), p. 115-131; Malti-Douglas, "Dreams"; Marilyn Robinson Waldman, *Toward a Theory of Historical Narrative: A Case Study in Perso-Islamicate Historiography* (Columbus: Ohio State University, 1980). Jacob Lassner's *Islamic Revolution and Historical Memory: An Inquiry Into the Art of 'Abbasid Apologetics* (New Haven: American Oriental Society, 1986) pays careful attention to the historiographical implications of textual strategies but he does not carry the implications of this approach to their fullest conclusions, arguing instead that "there are circumstances when rubbish is actually rubbish", p. 31. R. Stephen Humphreys includes a chapter on "Bayhaqi and Ibn Tahgribirdi: The Art of Narrative in Islamic Historical Writing during the Middle Periods," in his *Islamic History: A Framework for Inquiry* (Princeton: Princeton University Press, 1991), p. 128-147. The first part of this chapter is a survey of the major historical genres, the second part a comparative reading of passages by the two authors. Focusing, thus, on the Middle Eastern sources themselves, Humphreys has chosen not to exploit the evolving discussion of historical narrative.

[5] Applying Hayden White's approach to classical Arabic materials would demand two assumptions: that the discursive modes of historical writing parallel those of other literature and that modern Western forms would still be applicable in a medieval Islamic context. See White, *Metahistory*; White, "Value . . ."; and Marilyn Robinson Waldman, "'The Otherwise Unnoteworthy Year 711': A Reply to Hayden White", *Critical Inquiry*, 7, 4 (1981), p. 784-792.

critical literature.[6] Others, like the chronicle, have received somewhat less literary attention.[7] Yet, these texts possess marked affinities. The genres themselves often seem to melt, through intermediate forms, from one into the other. Many of the constituent elements, such as onomastic chains, anecdotes, and verse selections, are common to all the historical genres.

To what extent then are the operative codes of these different forms similar? To what extent are they different? Perhaps the most direct way of approaching this problem would be to examine a given unit of the Arabo-Islamic historical field, as it is articulated in a variety of forms of historical writing. The reign of the ʿAbbasid caliph, al-Muʿtaḍid bi-l-Lāh (279/892-289/902), is an ideal focus.[8] Not only is it extensively treated in chronicles but the monarch himself is well represented in biographical compendia. Slightly more unusual is the distinctive role that this ʿAbbasid caliph plays in *adab* works.

Indeed, a characteristic theme cuts through much of the Arabic historical writing on al-Muʿtaḍid: his association with a punishment/torture nexus. As a result, this thematic complex can help us to isolate the principles and codes used to situate historical meaning in different texts.

Organization I: The Chronicle

The texts whose organizational forms are at once most variable and most flexible are those which generally fit under the term chronicle.[9] By a chronicle, we mean a historical text whose dominant principle is the organization of material as events in time — in chronological order. Though there are deviations from strict chronological order within chronicles (and subordinated materials like obituaries/biographies), their dominant event/time organization distinguishes them from the biographical compendia of which the personal biographical notice is the fundamental unit of organization.

---

[6] See, for example, Ulrich Haarmann, "Auflösung und Bewahrung der klassischen Formen arabischer Geschichtsschreibung in der Zeit der Mamluken", *ZDMG*, 121 (1971), p. 49-60; Fähndrich, "*Wafayāt*" and "Compromising"; Malti-Douglas, "Controversy" and "Dreams". For further references, see Malti-Douglas, "Dreams", p. 137-140.

[7] The sole important study is that of Waldman, *Toward a Theory*. In his *Al-Kitāba l-Taʾrīḫiyya wa l-Maʿrifa l-Taʾrīḫiyya: Muqaddima fī Uṣūl Ṣināʿat al-Taʾrīḫ al-ʿArabī* (Beirut: Dār al-Ṭalīʿa, 1982), Aziz Al-Azmeh includes some hitherto understudied subgenres, like the *awāʾil*, but the work is essentially traditional in its approach.

[8] For the reign of this caliph, see Rainer Glagow.

[9] Cf. Franz Rosenthal, *A History of Muslim Historiography* (Leiden: E. J. Brill, 1968), p. 71.

Al-Muʿtaḍid appears in virtually every chronicle that deals with the ʿAbbasid period. Our problematic, however, necessitates concentration on a limited number of sources, which are both representative and historiographically interesting.

As a caliph, al-Muʿtaḍid can be defined by his reign, understood as a unit of time. This reign then becomes an event/time around which material in a chronicle can be organized. But the chronicler is at liberty to define this event as he sees fit. For example, Ibn al-Ṭiqṭaqā (d. 701/1301), in his *Taʾrīḫ al-Duwal al-Islāmiyya (al-Faḫrī)*, deals with the reign of al-Muʿtaḍid in a succinct but very interesting manner. After a brief onomastic presentation, followed by the date of the caliph's accession (279 A.H.), the text presents a brief (and favorable) description of al-Muʿtaḍid and his reign, emphasizing his good characteristics and the positive acts he undertook to rectify the caliphate. This is followed by his death date. The text proceeds to a discussion of the vizierate in al-Muʿtaḍid's days, including who was appointed vizier, as well as some biographical information about a vizier, when appropriate. We are then informed that our caliph died in the vizierate of al-Qāsim ibn ʿUbayd Allāh. The section on "The Caliphate of al-Muʿtaḍid" ends with the statement that the days of al-Muʿtaḍid and his viziers came to an end and that his son al-Muktafī bi-l-Lāh ruled after him.[10]

Clearly, Ibn al-Ṭiqṭaqā's text conceives of the caliphate as a complex unit, one involving an interrelationship of caliph and vizier(s). Each is defined through the other. The caliphate, while in a sense superior, since it is the primary principle of order, is, however, placed alongside another, and important, regnal category, that of the vizierate. In fact, two event/time units are present, that of the caliph and that of the vizier, and the two need not correspond neatly (by equivalence or by inclusion) with one another.

The complexity of the relationship becomes more evident if we also examine the reign of al-Muʿtaḍid's predecessor, al-Muʿtamid, who ruled

---

[10] Ibn al-Ṭiqṭaqā, *Taʾrīḫ al-Duwal al-Islāmiyya* (*al-Faḫrī*) (Beirut: Dār Ṣādir, 1960), p. 256-257. Franz Rosenthal, in his article on this famous historian in the *Encyclopaedia of Islam*, second edition, v. iii (Leiden: E. J. Brill, 1979), p. 956, notes that the work "consists of... biographies of the caliphs down to al-Muʿtaṣim, followed in each case by biographies of the viziers of the caliph." Though these texts are unquestionably biographical in the largest, adjectival, sense of the term, they are less than full biographies in the classical Muslim (or Western) sense. In the case of al-Muʿtaḍid, for example, no birth date is provided. Other strictly biographical data, such as one might find in a biographical compendium (e.g. the caliph's historic marriage to Qaṭr al-Nadā or his children), are also missing. The same is true for the "biographies" of the viziers. Other limitations of this view of the text will become evident below.

from 256/870 to 279/892. Al-Mu'tamid's last vizier, 'Ubayd Allāh ibn Sulaymān ibn Wahb, was also al-Mu'taḍid's first vizier. The description of him as a character, including poetry written about him, and his death date (288 A.H.) is given under the reign of al-Mu'tamid, even though he will reappear as vizier under al-Mu'taḍid. And it is in this same section (under the caliphate of al-Mu'tamid) that we read an anecdote involving this vizier and his response to al-Mu'taḍid when one of the latter's slavegirls died.[11]

The location of this anecdote is significant for several reasons. First, it witnesses to the interrelationship of vizier and caliph in the text of Ibn al-Ṭiqṭaqā. Second, the fact that an anecdote about a caliph, al-Mu'taḍid, is present in an account of a vizier increases the importance of the vizierial position. Perhaps most important, this anecdote represents a chronological intrusion. In Gérard Genette's terms, it appears in the narrative (the sequence in which events are reported in the text) before it does in the story (the sequence of events as they took place) thus creating a prolepsis. But, as the French critic further notes, prolepses (and their opposites, analepses) are of two types, repeating and completing.[12] This story of 'Ubayd Allāh and al-Mu'taḍid is a completing prolepsis because it is not also present in its normal chronological location, during the caliphate of al-Mu'taḍid.

The presence of this completing prolepsis makes clear, on a close textual level, the complex interplays in Ibn al-Ṭiqṭaqā's history. These anecdotes are not isolated, interchangeable units, written one without concern for the composition of the other. Their chronological imbrication, like the overlapping units of event/time, creates a network of interrelationships. Far more than a series of biographies, the *Ta'rīḫ al-Duwal al-Islāmiyya* embodies a vision of the political world of the 'Abbasids. The message of its organization is clear. The caliphate is a dyarchy. Power is shared, and history is made, by both caliph and vizier.

Not all chronicles, however, emphasize the dyarchy invoked in *al-Faḫrī*. A different, and more representative, case is the account of al-Mu'taḍid's reign in *al-Bidāya wa l-Nihāya fi l-Ta'rīḫ* by Ibn Kaṯīr (d. 774/1373). This annalistic work is organized around the principle of years.[13] Under a given year, the text presents first the incidents which took place in that year, be they natural or historical, followed by obit-

---

[11] Ibn al-Ṭiqṭaqā, *Ta'rīḫ*, p. 250-255.

[12] Gérard Genette, *Figures III* (Paris: Éditions du Seuil, 1972), p. 77-120.

[13] See, for example, George Makdisi, "The Diary in Islamic Historiography: Some Notes", *History and Theory*, XXV, 2 (1986), p. 180; Rosenthal, *A History*, p. 71-86.

uaries of individuals who died in that year.[14] This principle of organization is by no means peculiar to Ibn Kaṯīr. But, the annalist, like his colleagues the biographer and the *adab* writer, was at liberty to present fuller or briefer accounts, just as he could vary the principles of organization themselves. As much is evident from a comparison of Ibn Kaṯīr's text with similarly organized works, like *al-Muḫtaṣar fī Aḫbār al-Bašar* of Abū l-Fidā' (d. 732/1331), the *Ta'rīḫ* of Ibn al-Wardī (d. 749/1349), and the *Šaḏarāt al-Ḏahab fī Aḫbār man Ḏahab* of Ibn al-'Imād al-Ḥanbalī (d. 1089/1679).[15]

But, the annals function as more than a set of natural or historical incidents and obituaries given year by year. There are, at least, two discourses, two discursive forms, and, hence two modes of organization, that of the incidents and that of the obituaries. Nevertheless, both incidents and obituaries must also be understood as corresponding narrative units. Both types of events are normally introduced by the words *wa fīhā* (and in it), alluding to the year in which they took place. In addition, the "biographical" interest of the annalist is stimulated by the demise of a personage, itself an event. Hence, the natural disaster, the historical act, and the death of a character become equivalents in the annalistic scheme. Nor are even the bare events listed randomly, despite the organizational break of the *wa fīhā*.

For example, under the year 280/893-894, Ibn Kaṯīr mentions: "And in it (*wa-fīha*), the waters dried up in Rayy and Tabaristan so that water was sold three *ratl*s for a dirham, and the prices also rose there."[16] Under the year 281/894-895, we read. "And in it (*wa-fīha*), the drying of the waters in the territories of Rayy and Tabaristan was completed. And in it (*wa-fīha*), the prices rose, to the point that a man would eat his son and his daughter."[17]

These two series of events encapsule with extraordinary succinctness a complete chain of historical causation, running from a natural occurrence (drought) through its economic effects to its ultimate social consequences. A father eating his children evokes not only the extremes of

---

[14] Ibn Kaṯīr, *al-Bidāya wa l-Nihāya fī l-Ta'rīḫ* (Cairo: Maṭba'at al-Sa'āda, n.d.), v. XI, p. 66-94.

[15] Abū l-Fidā', *al-Muḫtaṣar fī Aḫbār al-Bašar* (Cairo: al-Maṭba'a l-Ḥusayniyya, n.d.), v. II, p. 56-59; Ibn al-Wardī, *Ta'rīḫ Ibn al-Wardī* (Najaǧ: al-Maṭba'a l-Ḥaydariyya, 1969), v. I, p. 334-340; Ibn al-'Imād al-Ḥanbalī, *Šaḏarāt al-Ḏahab fī Aḫbār man Ḏahab* (Beirut: al-Maktab al-Tiǧārī li-l-Ṭibā'a wa l-Našr wa l-Tawzī', n.d.), v. II, p. 172-202.

[16] Ibn Kaṯīr, *al-Bidāya*, p. 68-69.

[17] Ibn Kaṯīr, *al-Bidāya*, p. 70.

starvation but also the complete breakdown of that most fundamental of social ties, that between parent and offspring. From a literary point of view, pathos and conciseness are one.

Clearly, the incidents in 281 A.H. are related to those in 280 A.H. Yet, if we look at 281 alone, the historical causation seems to be lacking, since the drought and the price rise are listed as two independent events, each introduced by *wa fihā*. But this does not show an atomistic, non-causal view of reality, since, in the related series in 280, the drought and price rise form part of the same incident, while in 281, the price rise and social breakdown are linked within the same *wa fihā* phrase. And the phrase "was completed" links this series back to the preceding one. This play of variable juncture and separation shows the interrelationship both between the events in a given year and between those in successive years.

In effect, the events in the chronicle of Ibn Kaṯīr (as all annals) are organized both syntagmatically and paradigmatically, that is, in their mutual position in a series and in their relation to equivalent events in another series. In terms of historical contextualization, they are defined by both synchronic and diachronic patterns of causation.

A more thematic organization of al-Muʿtaḍid's reign can be found in the *Murūǧ al-Ḏahab wa Maʿādin al-Ǧawhar* of al-Masʿūdī (d. 345/956). The historian begins his account of the caliphate of al-Muʿtaḍid with an introductory section: first, giving basic statistical and family information, and then a synchronic overview of the character of both the caliph and his reign. The remainder of the notice is devoted to the events of this period. But, within this main body of the account, a thematic principle of organization is also in operation. Here, subjects under discussion seem to give rise to other subjects, related to the ones under consideration. Thus, for example, the murder of al-Muʿtaḍid's father-in-law, Abū l-Ǧayš Ḫumārawayh, by his palace eunuchs is followed by an elaborate discussion of eunuchs.[18] Or, for example, when discussing the geographical provenance of certain gifts offered the caliph by ʿAmr ibn al-Layṯ al-Ṣaffār, the text delves into an aside about the present state (that is in 332 A.H.) of the areas in question.[19]

Perhaps a by-product of this thematic predominance in al-Masʿūdī's

---

[18] Al-Masʿūdī, *Murūǧ al-Ḏahab wa Maʿādin al-Ǧawhar* (Beirut: Dār al-Kutub al-ʿIlmiyya, 1986), v. IV, p. 278-279.

[19] Al-Masʿūdī, *Murūǧ*, v. IV, p. 267.

text is the use of the anecdote as prime purveyor of information. For example, a drought in Basra is evoked in the course of an anecdote relating the arrival to court of a group of dignitaries from that city and the complaints they raised before the caliph. The purpose of the narrative seems to be to testify to the insight and intelligence of a member of the Baṣrian elite, Abū Ḫalīfa l-Ǧumaḥī, itself exemplified by the intellectual duel he fights with the ruler's vizier. That this is the intent of the story is shown by the fact that it is followed by more material on Abū Ḫalīfa.[20]

One result of this approach is to render the historical/natural event, the drought in Baṣra, subservient to the anecdote in which it is embedded. Furthermore, the drought is only one complaint among many that the dignitaries present to the caliph, and, as such, its importance as a natural disaster is reduced. This deemphasis of the "historical" is also strengthened by the absence of any chronological indication of when the drought took place or even when the visit to the ruler occurred.

This does not mean, however, that the text of al-Mas'ūdī is devoid of chronological markers. Simply, chronology is not foregrounded, as it is in the other chronicles. Further, though the *Murūǧ* follows a general chronological order, there are anachronies in the account. For example, the gifts presented by al-Ṣaffār in the year 286 A.H. precede events in the year 280 A.H.[21] Finally, within the yearly divisions, al-Mas'ūdī includes noteworthy personages who died in the years in question. A second, completing, set of death notices terminates the section on al-Mu'taḍid.[22]

Perhaps most intriguing in the *Murūǧ al-Ḏahab* are numerous asides in the text to the time of writing.[23] In narrative terms, these are prolepses, but it is what they do to the nature of the text as historical narrative that is important. We already noted the presence of one such aside in the discussion of al-Ṣaffār's gifts, when the text describes the present state of the areas in question. In the course of relating how Ṭuǧǧ ibn Šabīb Abū l-Iḫšīd led his armies out from Damascus in 281 A.H.,

---

[20] Al-Mas'ūdī, *Murūǧ*, v. IV, p. 268-271.
[21] Al-Mas'ūdī, *Murūǧ*, v. IV, p. 267-275.
[22] Al-Mas'ūdī, *Murūǧ*, v. IV, p. 307-308.
[23] See Tarif Khalidi, *Islamic Historiography: The Histories of al-Mas'ūdī* (Albany: State University of New York Press, 1975), p. 155-156. Cf. Ahmad M. H. Shboul, *Al-Mas'ūdī and His World: A Muslim Humanist and His Interest in Non-Muslims* (London: Ithaca Press, 1979), p. 302.

al-Mas'ūdī adds after the mention of al-Iḫshid's name that he is presently (that is, the mid 330s) the ruler of Egypt.[24] Or, when identifying Ḥamdān ibn Ḥamdūn, we are told that he is the grandfather of Abū Muhammad al-Ḥasan ibn 'Abd Allāh, whose honorific is presently Nāṣir al-Dawla.[25]

These prolepses, geographical, historical, or onomastic, redefine earlier events through later results or developments in the diachronic historical sequences of which these events form a part. Historical events become less circumscribed within their annalistic perimeters and form part of larger configurations. Even in the absence of anachrony, the thematic/syntagmatic organization of the text has the same general effect: dissolving the unilinear narrative into broader fields of multi-directional signification. Instead of a privileging of the chronological, as in Ibn Kaṯīr, or dyarchically political, as in Ibn al-Ṭiqṭaqā, al-Mas'ūdī's approach implies a totalizing, global, historical vision. Al-Mu'taḍid, then, is almost completely submerged within this description of his epoch.

Al-Mas'ūdī did not indiscriminately incorporate available data. On numerous occasions he sends the reader for further information to his *Aḫbār al-Zamān* or his *al-Kitāb al-Awsaṭ*.[26] We can only conclude that material is included when and where the historian judges it apposite.[27] As much also can be seen from the organization of the regnal account. Obituaries are organized in two different locations. Some are interspersed into the main sequence of events and anecdotes, others are reserved for the new chronological sequence of death notices at the end of the account. This dual arrangement permits the insertion of obituaries either thematically when relevant or at the end of the notice when not. These two principles of organization are united at the end of the regnal account. There, the chronological series of obituaries is completed by a discussion of the circumstances of the death of the caliph al-Mu'taḍid himself. This event both terminates the second chronological series and thematically closes the discussion of the reign of al-Mu'taḍid.

Organization II: Biography

If chronicles, by their nature, foreground the event/time unit of the reign of al-Mu'taḍid, there are other historical sources organized not

[24] Al-Mas'ūdī, *Murūǧ*, v. IV, p. 277.

[25] Al-Mas'ūdī, *Murūǧ*, v. IV, p. 277.

[26] See, for example, al-Mas'ūdī, *Murūǧ*, v. IV, p. 290, 294, 299, 308. Cf. Khalidi, *Islamic Historiography*, p. 154-155.

[27] See Khalidi's discussion of al-Mas'ūdī's view of "the historian's craft" in *Islamic Historiography*, p. 5-14.

around the event but the character. Such is the case with the well-established Islamic genre of biographical dictionaries.

We shall concentrate our analysis on the biographical notice devoted to al-Muʿtaḍid in the *Kitāb al-Wāfī bi-l-Wafayāt* of the Mamluk official, Ḫalīl ibn Aybak al-Ṣafadī (d. 764/1363). The organization of this notice can be understood both in terms of literary discourse and in terms of content, that is the arrangement of material by subject. In discursive terms, the notice consists of series of brief statements and descriptions separated by three anecdotes, placed after one third, after two thirds, and at the very end of the notice. The principle of discursive variety, familiar from *adab* works, is evident.[28]

But, the notice is also organized by content, and can be outlined as follows:

1) introductory material (onomastic data, birth, and death)
2) activity preceding accession
3) accession
4) activities as caliph
5) death
6) accession of successor
7) length of al-Muʿtaḍid's reign
8) relations with other individuals
9) closure of notice.

Like most biographical notices, that of al-Ṣafadī begins with an onomastic chain. The notice then provides the birth date (242 A.H.) and the date of death with a variant in the months. All this information operates as an introduction to the personage, and both the onomastic data and the birth and death dates sum up an entire life. This introduction is followed by al-Muʿtaḍid's military activity preceding his accession to the throne.

Section 3 of the notice, like the combination of Sections 6 and 7, acts as a divisional marker introducing the caliphal or regnal phase of al-Muʿtaḍid's life. It is logical, therefore, that the pre-caliphal activities (Section 2) precede the accession but follow the introductory material which defined the whole biography and not just the reign. In effect, there are two caliphal segments in the notice, synchronically arranged, both internally and in relation one to the other. The first is introduced by the marker of the accession (Section 3), while the second is signalled

---

[28] See, for example, Fedwa Malti-Douglas, *Structures of Avarice: The Buḫalāʾ in Medieval Arabic Literature* (Leiden: E. J. Brill, 1985), p. 53-55.

by the accession of al-Muʿtaḍid's successor (Section 6). The principal difference between these two regnal segments is thematic. The first (Section 4) concerns essentially the politically relevant actions and characteristics of the caliph, and an appreciation of his achievement as ruler. This segment terminates, logically enough, with his death (Section 5). After the accession of al-Muʿtaḍid's successor (Section 6), the biographer returns us again to the reign of al-Muʿtaḍid, conceived synchronically, by indicating the length of his reign (Section 7).

The second regnal segment of the biographical notice operates as an overview which also sets al-Muʿtaḍid in context, but this time, in his relations with other individuals. Mention is made of his mother and her death. Notice is also given that he is one of four caliphs, one of whom is al-Saffāḥ, whose fathers were not caliphs. It is in this section that his viziers are listed, as are the seals he had inscribed on his ring. The marriage to Qaṭr al-Nadā is mentioned along with the dowry.

The biography of al-Muʿtaḍid closes with verses of poetry he composed and an anecdote related by his companion, Ibn Ḥamdūn. We shall return to this anecdote below, but it can be noted here that by its nature, it brings thematic closure to the notice.[29]

This sketch brings out some essential features of the biographical notice as historical narrative. It does not, for example, begin with the birth and end with the death of al-Muʿtaḍid. Instead, his life is examined from several angles and from both synchronic and diachronic perspectives. The introduction frames the entire notice, but the progress from Sections 2 through 5 is essentially diachronic. Sections 7 and 8 are, again, synchronic, as is Section 9, which provides a thematic historical closure to the life and the notice. The synchronic, thematic tendencies of the notice are reinforced by the paucity of specific dates.

Organization III: Adab

The tendency for the individual to become less implicated in an extra-personal historical context, as one moves from the chronicle to the biographical dictionary, is even more evident in the transition from biography to *adab* work. *Adab*, defined briefly, refers in the context of medieval Arabic literature to those predominantly anecdotal texts whose dual aim was to entertain and to edify, and which were normally organized by topic. Yet, their mixed anecdotal discourse and entertaining

---

[29] Al-Ṣafadī, *Kitāb al-Wāfī bi-l-Wafayāt*, v. VI, ed. Sven Dedering (Wiesbaden: Franz Steiner Verlag, 1972), p. 428-430.

nature do not classify most *adab* works as fiction. It is not just that much of the material comprised in *adab* works ostensibly concerned historical or allegedly historical individuals. More important, information in *adab* works was presented as factual, frequently with the benefit of the evidentiary scholarly apparatus of sources and transmitters. For their audience, they were, therefore, historical works of a sort. The appearance of al-Mu'taḍid in these works should come as no surprise.

The *Aḫbār al-Aḏkiyā'* of Ibn al-Ǧawzī (d. 597/1200) is the most important *adab* source for our caliph.[30] The *ḏakī* (pl. *aḏkiyā'*) is a character defined by his *ḏakā'*. This term, whose basic meaning is fullness or completion, can best be rendered in this context as acumen, intelligence, or cleverness.[31] Ibn al-Ǧawzī's work, like similar *adab* works on character types, illustrates the characteristic or character type through sets of actions.[32]

But the nature of the *ḏakī* in the Arabic *adab* tradition gives a special complexity to the organization of the *Aḫbār al-Aḏkiyā'* and, hence, to the position of al-Mu'taḍid within it. Ibn al-Ǧawzī's book is an example of a type of intermediate *adab* work.[33] On the one hand, it shares with the monographic *adab* work the focus on a single character type, the *ḏakī*. On the other hand, like encyclopedic *adab* works, it is divided into content-defined sections whose ordering is also reminiscent of that in encyclopedic works. Further, many of these topics, like those of thieves and *ṭufaylīs* (uninvited guests and/or social parasites), can be the subjects of their own monographic *adab* works.[34]

Anecdotes about al-Mu'taḍid appear (with slight exceptions) in the

---

[30] Ibn al-Ǧawzī, *Aḫbār al-Aḏkiyā'*, ed. Muḥammad Mursī l-Ḫawlī (Cairo: Maṭābi' al-Ahrām al-Tiǧāriyya, 1970). On al-Mu'taḍid and the *Aḫbār al-Aḏkiyā'*, see Fedwa Malti-Douglas, "The Classical Arabic Detective", *Arabica*, XXV (1988), p. 59-91.

[31] See, for example, Ibn Manẓūr, *Lisān al-'Arab* (Cairo: al-Dār al-Miṣriyya li-l-Ta'līf wa l-Tarǧama, n.d.), v. XVIII, p. 314-315; al-Zabīdī, *Tāǧ al-'Arūs* (Beirut: Dār Ṣādir, n.d.), v. X, p. 137.

[32] See Malti-Douglas, *Structures*; Fedwa Malti-Douglas, "Structure and Organization in a Douographic Adab Work: al-*Taṭfīl* of al-Khaṭīb al-Baghdadi" *Journal of Near Eastern Studies*, XL (1981), p. 227-245.

[33] See, for example, Malti-Douglas, *Structures*, p. 14-15.

[34] On *ṭufaylīs*, see al-Ḫaṭīb al-Baġdādī, *al-Taṭfīl wa-Ḥikāyāt al-Ṭufayliyyīn wa-Aḫbāruhum wa-Nawādir Kalāmihim wa-Aš'āruhum*, ed. Kāẓim al-Muẓaffar (Najaf: al-Maktaba l-Ḥaydariyya, 1966); al-Aqfahsī, *al-Qawl al-Nabīl bi-Ḏikr al-Taṭfīl*, ed. Muṣṭafā 'Āšūr (Cairo: Maktabat Ibn Sīnā, 1989?); Malti-Douglas, "Structure and Organization"; Fedwa Malti-Douglas, "Tufayli" *Encyclopaedia of Islam*, second edition (Leiden: E. J. Brill, forthcoming). The *Kitāb al-Luṣūṣ* of al-Ǧāḥiẓ is not extant. See Charles Pellat, "Nuvel essai d'inventaire des œuvre gaḥiẓienne", *Arabica*, XXXI (1984), p. 146. On thieves, see Fedwa Malti-Douglas, "Classical Arabic Crime Narratives: Thieves and Thievery in *Adab* Literature" *Journal of Arabic Literature*, XIX (1988), p. 108-127.

section on rulers. As a result, al-Mu'taḍid is organizationally defined in two ways at the same time: as ruler and as *ḏakī*, in effect, as we shall see below, as possessor of that particular kind of *ḏakā'* associated with rule. In this sense, al-Mu'taḍid is pulled away from his historical context and placed in a professional/characterological one. But historical, chronological considerations are not missing. Within the subsection on caliphs, only seven Commanders of the Faithful have anecdotes, two Umayyads and five 'Abbasids.[35] And, these seven are arranged in chronological order. Though the chronological sequence is fragmented, since many intervening rulers are missing, it nevertheless suggests the complete series and links the *adab* context to the diachronic historical one. Among other things, this stresses the historicity of the narratives. The organization of the *Aḫbār al-Aḏkiyā'*, while it accents the synchronic division of humanity into professional and personal types, reminds the reader that the individuals in question also belong to other series.

Punishment/Torture I

In all the sources, be they historical, biographical, or strictly literary, our caliph is, as we mentioned earlier, associated with a punishment/torture nexus. All of the texts emphasize not only that al-Mu'taḍid was a concerned and just ruler, but that he was also one who fortified the caliphate and restored order in the government and in the country at large, as well as reorganizing the police. But, all sources agree, this caliph's justice was not only efficient but also swift and stern. Associated with al-Mu'taḍid's judicial severity was a reputation for violence and brutal physical punishments. Torture in this context refers not only to procedures designed to provoke confessions but to excruciating physical punishments as well.[36]

How does this leitmotif of punishment/torture manifest itself in the texts at hand? Among the chronicles, by far the fullest development of this thematic nexus is in the *Murūǧ al-Ḏahab*. By comparison, Ibn al-Ṭiqṭaqā and Ibn Kaṯīr give, in the one case, the barest allusion, in the other, a very brief and limited treatment to these topics. Al-Mas'ūdī's introductory discussion includes a description of two personal charac-

[35] Ibn al-Ǧawzī, *Aḏkiyā'*, p. 38-49.

[36] Cf. Edward Peters, *Torture* (Oxford: Basil Blackwell, 1985); Mohammed Arkoun, "The Death Penalty and Torture in Islamic Thought" in Franz Böckle and Jacques Pohier, eds., *The Death Penalty and Torture* (New York: The Seabury Press, 1979), p. 75-82.

teristics related to the caliph's public persona. The first is a spirit of economy, verging on avarice, the second, severity bordering on sadism. Here, we are told that al-Muʿtaḍid liked to shed blood and make examples of those whom he killed. Following this assessment, the text delves into habitual tortures which al-Muʿtaḍid practiced whenever he became angry at someone in his court. These include a kind of burial alive, in which the victim's head is placed in the ground first. The second form of torture which al-Masʿūdī's text details is one in which the victim's ears, nose, and mouth were plugged with cotton, and then a bellows was used to blow air into the body through the remaining orifice, which was then plugged up with cotton. The victim would become blown up like a "great camel". Then the arteries above the eyebrows were opened up and the "soul would leave from that spot". Another possibility was to have the victim, naked and bound, placed in a high spot in the palace and shot with arrows. In addition, the *Murūǧ* states that al-Muʿtaḍid had instruments of torture in special caves and that he appointed a certain Naǧāḥ al-Haramī in charge of torture.[37]

These habitual actions, placed near the beginning of the regnal account, while certainly gruesome, are nevertheless narratologically important. Their habitual nature ("he used to . . .") and their location place the remainder of the section in a specific light: al-Muʿtaḍid was a cruel ruler, who enjoyed subjecting his victims to unusual physical torture. Nor is the rest of the account devoid of references to physical cruelty. Perhaps easiest to explain are the numerous cases emanating from military expeditions or uprisings. Here, various parts of bodies were displayed or crucified on the bridges of Baghdad for the public to behold.[38]

Examining some of the anecdotal material in which the punishment/torture nexus appears can, however, shed light on what is really going on in al-Masʿūdī's text. We shall analyze three anecdotes in some detail. In the first one, a gifted storyteller, Ibn al-Maġāzilī, at whose stories listeners always laughed, was brought to the caliph by one of his eunuchs. This eunuch had listened to Ibn al-Maġāzilī and later, in the presence of the caliph, remembered the stories and anecdotes, and began to laugh. The ruler saw this and asked him about it. After the servant explained, al-Muʿtaḍid ordered him to bring the storyteller to him. The eunuch made it clear to the latter that he wanted half the

[37] Al-Masʿūdī, *Murūǧ*, v. IV, p. 260-262.
[38] See, for example, al-Masʿūdī, *Murūǧ*, v. IV, p. 275, 293, 303, 304, among others.

reward. When Ibn al-Maġāzilī was brought into the royal presence, the caliph told him that he would give him five hundred dirhams if he were able to make him laugh. But, if he could not, what should the caliph do? The storyteller replied that all he had was the nape of his neck and that the caliph could beat him there with whatever he wished and however many times he wished. The caliph agreed that he would beat him ten times.

As the narrative progresses, it becomes clear that the caliph will keep himself from laughing, and finally, the storyteller is beaten. After this is completed, Ibn al-Maġāzilī offers the caliph some advice, explaining to him the deal he had struck with the slave. The caliph breaks out in laughter and has the slave beaten. At the end of the story, Ibn al-Maġāzilī receives his financial reward, which al-Muʿtaḍid had prepared in advance.[39]

The anecdote is narratively more complex than this brief sketch would imply. For our purposes, it is the beating of the storyteller that is significant. The story has a narrative purpose, which becomes important in the context of other punishment/torture anecdotes. When al-Muʿtaḍid asks Ibn al-Maġāzilī what he is to do with him should he prove unable to make the caliph laugh, the storyteller offers the nape of his neck. And al-Muʿtaḍid accepts this offer and the punishment is inflicted in the very location chosen by the victim.

The victim's choice tends to excuse the action perpetrated by the caliph. The beating is partially deprived, for the reader, of its otherwise cruel nature. Another element reinforces this tendency: the storyteller's financial reward. These, plus the humorous context of the anecdote, liberate the *Schadenfreude* of the reader.

The attempt to excuse the caliph's cruelty by placing part of the responsibility on the victim's shoulders is also evident in the following story.

Muḥammad ibn al-Ḥasan ibn Sahl was actively campaigning for an ʿAlid uprising that would eventually kill al-Muʿtaḍid. When those who had sworn allegiance to the ʿAlid were brought in, they denied knowledge of his identity. The caliph ordered them killed, and then attempted to get the information from Muḥammad himself, who refused to divulge it. Finally, after many conversations, Muḥammad said to al-Muʿtaḍid: "If you were to broil me over a fire, I would not add to what you have heard from me", refusing once more to identify the individual in

[39] Al-Masʿūdī, *Murūǧ*, v. IV, p. 283-287.

question. Al-Mu'taḍid replied: "We will not torture you except by that which you have mentioned". The *Murūǧ* then presents two variants of Muḥammad's demise. The first was that he was impaled with an iron stick which came out of his mouth and then burned over a fire, while he cursed the caliph. The second was that he was placed between three lances, tied to their ends, and placed over the fire, while still alive, without touching it. Then he was rotated and broiled "as chicken are broiled", until his body burst. Then it was taken and crucified between the two bridges.[40]

The torture here plays an important role. On the most superficial level, it is clearly justified by Muḥammad's uprising. Furthermore, the victim had ample opportunity to confess, something he refused to do. What brings this anecdote close to that with Ibn al-Maġāzilī is that the form of torture was suggested by the victim himself. As a result, on a narrative level, the caliph is absolved of a certain amount of responsibility. On a close rhetorical examination of the text, however, it becomes clear that the victim had no such idea in mind. When he made his daring proposal, Muḥammad used the Arabic conditional grammatical structure "law . . ." (if), implying that the action would not take place.

Yet, it does. And it helps us, in turn, to define more precisely the mental structures governing torture in the *Murūǧ*. The text states that Muḥammad was broiled "as chicken are broiled". This simile serves, on the rhetorical plane, to turn the victim into an animal, thus, dehumanizing him. Further, as we shall see from the other examples below (and some of those from the beginning of the account), there is a tendency to turn the human body into an object. Finally, we almost never hear the cry of pain. Once the process begins, the victim loses his identity as an individual, and the entire procedure becomes essentially visual, a piece of theatre performed for the onlookers.[41]

Another point emerges from the comparison of Muḥammad's ordeal to that of a chicken. Chicken are consumed. Though there is no cannibalism in this particular anecdote, cannibalism is to be found in the account which al-Mas'ūdī provides of the murder of al-Mu'taḍid's father-in-law, Abū l-Ǧayš Ḫumārawayh, by some of his eunuchs. The guilty were apprehended a few miles away, then killed and crucified. Some

[40] Al-Mas'ūdī, *Murūǧ*, v. IV, p. 274-275.

[41] Cf. Michel Foucault, *Surveiller et punir: Naissance de la prison* (Paris: Editions Gallimard, 1975), p. 9-72. See, also, Elaine Scarry, *The Body in Pain: The Making and Unmaking of the World* (Oxford: Oxford University Press, 1985), p. 28.

were shot by arrows, others had their flesh torn from their legs and posteriors and eaten by Abū l-Ǧayš's black mamluks.[42]

The most elaborate anecdote in al-Masʿūdī's account of the reign of al-Muʿtaḍid involves the adventure of this caliph with a master thief who had stolen treasury money allocated for the payment of the troops. The chief guard beat the thief until he could no longer utter a word. When al-Muʿtaḍid heard of the case, he told the guard that that was no way to act. He had the guilty party brought in and said that he would pardon him, to which the man replied that he knew nothing. So al-Muʿtaḍid called in the physicians and asked them to restore the man's health, which they did. To more questioning, there was more denial. Al-Muʿtaḍid told him that if he refused to confess to the crime, he would kill him, but that if he did confess, he would be safe. The man further denied any knowledge of the crime. Al-Muʿtaḍid had him swear first by God, then by the *Qur'ān*, but the man persisted in his denial. It was then that the caliph announced that he would find the money and, because of the oaths, kill the culprit. The latter, however, continued with the same denial. Al-Muʿtaḍid had him put a hand on his head and swear on his life, which the man did, adding that he was the victim of others. At that point, the caliph declared that if the man were lying, he would kill him but be innocent of having shed his blood. The man agreed.

Al-Muʿtaḍid had thirty slaves brought in to watch over the culprit, while he remained seated, for several days, unable to rest his body. He was also not permitted to sleep. The man almost died from this ordeal. When al-Muʿtaḍid had him brought forth once again, more oaths were declared, as were more denials.

The caliph at that point announced to witnesses that the man was innocent. He asked the man to forgive him, which he did, and the caliph ordered that food and drink be provided for him. The man satiated himself, was perfumed, and given a feather bed. Just as he was about to fall asleep, he was awakened and brought before the caliph. Al-Muʿtaḍid asked him about the theft, and the culprit revealed all, after which he fell asleep. Al-Muʿtaḍid had the money brought and hidden. The thief was awakened and al-Muʿtaḍid asked him again about the theft, of which he denied any knowledge. But the caliph confronted the thief with the money and repeated the revelations to the culprit, who was quite surprised.

---

[42] Al-Masʿūdī, *Murūǧ*, v. IV, p. 277.

It is at this stage in the narrative that we are told about the torture inflicted on the culprit. He was subjected to the ordeal of being blown up with his orifices plugged. Al-Mas'ūdī goes into intricate detail of the torture, adding that it was the greatest spectacle of torture seen that day.[43]

The physical punishment of the criminal is, clearly, an important component of the narrative. But lest the reader assume that it testifies to the cruelty of the caliph, the text provides numerous indications of his generosity with the culprit and his willingness to give him yet one more chance. When the caliph declares that he will kill the thief, he makes it clear that he will not be guilty of his blood. The actions of the ruler are, once again, justified and excused. In addition, the *Murūğ* calls clear attention to the visual aspect of the ordeal. It is a show which the caliph (and the more strong-stomached reader) can enjoy.

It would, seem, therefore, that the anecdotes involving al-Mu'taḍid and torture in the *Murūğ al-Ḏahab* of al-Mas'ūdī all function to justify the actions of the caliph and remove blame from him. How does this fit with the general assessments of the caliph's cruelty made in the beginning of the account? Before proceeding any further, we should point out that there are more references to the frightful aspects of the ruler's character towards the end of the account as well. When an apparition began to be seen in the royal palace, some attributed it to a good genie who, having observed al-Mu'taḍid's bloodthirsty behavior, was attempting to dissuade him of it. Others thought it a servant sneaking about to meet a slavegirl. The caliph became so disturbed that he had many of his male and female servants put to death.[44] When on his own death-bed, al-Mu'taḍid heard a clamor, he asked what it was, to which he was told that it was the servants making a fuss with the vizier, and that they were given a donation. "He glowered and snarled in his agony of death", and those around him almost died of fear.[45]

Al-Mas'ūdī has provided two types of information about al-Mu'taḍid's behavior. On the one hand, there is the general material which frames the account, and which states that the ruler was cruel and frightening. On the other hand, there are the anecdotal narratives which absolve him of moral responsibility.

---

[43] Al-Mas'ūdī, *Murūğ*, v. IV, p. 279-283.

[44] Al-Mas'ūdī, *Murūğ*, v. IV, p. 293-294.

[45] Al-Mas'ūdī, *Murūğ*. v. IV, p. 308. This also links the caliph's death with the potential death of his companion and, thus, with those caused by his severity, bringing up again the religious reality that he will be responsible for his actions.

These two characterizations point to different aspects of the ruler as historical individual. The generalities framing the account describe his personality. The anecdotes, the specifics, demonstrate that the caliph was absolutely within his rights when putting these traits into practice. What we have is a legitimized sadism. It is noteworthy that it is only the apparently sadistic, the unusual torments, that seem to need justification. No specific excuse is given for the execution of the slaves near the end of the account. Elsewhere, al-Mas'ūdī tells us that, in another work, he has discussed the reasons for the caliph's imprisonment and threatened disfiguring of al-Muqtadir's mother.[46]

Al-Mas'ūdī wants us to understand three separate points: 1) the caliph's bloodthirsty temperament; 2) the effects of this temperament on his activities as caliph; and 3) the legal and moral justification of the way in which the caliph expressed his temperament through his official actions.

Punishment/Torture II

A different manipulation of material relating to the punishment/torture nexus takes place in al-Ṣafadī's biography of the 'Abbasid caliph. That there might have been a cruel streak in al-Mu'taḍid's character is never stated as such by al-Ṣafadī. There are, however, clear indications in the notice by the Mamluk official that this aspect of the ruler's personality was far from being outside the mind of the compiler. We are told, for example, that he was courageous and fear-inspiring. In two places in the biography, al-Ṣafadī compares al-Mu'taḍid to the founder of the 'Abbasid line, al-Saffāḥ, "the Blood-Shedder", supposedly so named because he liked to shed blood. When recounting al-Mu'taḍid's accomplishments and activities as caliph (#4 in the outline above), the text notes that he was called "al-Saffah the Second" because he renewed the rule of the 'Abbasids, restoring the power and integrity of the caliphate.[47] While this explanation of the comparison must certainly be accepted, since the biographer proposes it, the other signifieds of the signifier, al-Saffāḥ, cannot be dismissed. Lest the reader miss the connection with the first 'Abbasid, it is made once again when al-Ṣafadī mentions that al-Mu'taḍid was one of four caliphs whose father was not a caliph, and that another was al-Saffāḥ.[48]

---

[46] Al-Mas'ūdī, *Murūǧ*, v. IV, p. 294.
[47] Al-Ṣafadī, *al-Wāfī*, v. VI, p. 429.
[48] Al-Ṣafadī, *al-Wāfī*, v. VI, p. 429.

The anecdotal material in al-Ṣafadī, however, takes this possible severity, reassesses it, and redefines it. Indeed, the three anecdotes which punctuate the notice are all, fundamentally, about the character of this ʿAbbasid ruler. The first story shows al-Muʿtaḍid in the face of adversity. Here, the courage of the caliph is displayed as he kills a lion alone, his hunting companion having declined to face the animal. The narrator adds that the ruler never told the story himself, it is understood out of modesty on his part.[49] The second anecdote, on the other hand, shows a caliph who might seem too severe, as he kicks his physician to death when the latter is examining him.[50]

But it is the third anecdote, closing al-Ṣafadī's notice, which decides the issue. Ibn Ḥamdūn, the caliph's companion, states that the ruler had made it a condition that if someone saw some behavior on his part which did not make sense, he was to ask him about it. Ibn Ḥamdūn had himself wondered about something for years, and he finally conquered his fear and asked the caliph (who reassured him that he should not be afraid) why it was that when certain of his slaves had taken some melon while in Persia, the caliph had ordered them beaten and imprisoned. That would have been enough, Ibn Ḥamdūn added, but the caliph had then ordered them crucified, though their sin did not merit this. Al-Muʿtaḍid, thereupon, asks him if he thought that those who were crucified were those same slaves. How would he have faced God on the Judgment Day, he asks, if he had crucified them for having stolen melon? Rather, al-Muʿtaḍid explains, he had ordered that a group of highway men, who deserved to be executed anyway, be taken out and dressed like the slaves, so as to frighten the soldiers who would then say that if he crucified his slaves for having stolen melon, how would he be with something else? "And as such I ordered that they be vailed," says al-Muʿtaḍid, "so that their secret would be kept from the public".[51]

This anecdote is extremely important for the characterization of al-Muʿtaḍid as ruler. It raises the complex issues relating to his cruelty, justice, and punishment. The narrative shows that al-Muʿtaḍid is truly a just ruler, and this at the risk of appearing unjust to his subjects. But this appearance is only important in the eyes of men and not in the eyes of God, to whom ultimately the caliph feels he must answer. It is he, after all, who invokes the divine judgment. The political moral is

---

49 Al-Ṣafadī, *al-Wāfī*, v. VI, p. 428-429.
50 Al-Ṣafadī, *al-Wāfī*, v. VI, p. 429.
51 Al-Ṣafadī, *al-Wāfī*, v. VI, p. 429-430.

clear: as the subjects are responsible to the ruler, so is he to the deity.

But the political message of the anecdote goes further. Al-Mu'taḍid deliberately creates the impression of injustice (while secretly remaining just), not for ethical reasons but for motives of public policy. A reputation for undue severity is good for the order of the state. Subjects must be led more by terror than by fairness. Hence, the caliph who wishes to do his job of maintaining order and justice is obliged to give himself the appearance of injustice, while guarding himself from its reality. In these terms, al-Mu'taḍid's performance is a virtuoso one.

As a result, this story of the punishment of the melon swipers casts an entirely new light on al-Mu'taḍid's reputation for cruelty. First, it reminds lesser mortals that they cannot judge the behavior of a caliph. Second, it suggests that al-Mu'taḍid's reputation for cruelty was just that, and that it was a product of a careful public policy. As such, also, the Ibn Ḥamdūn anecdote redefines all the rest of the material about al-Mu'taḍid in the biographical notice. Its ability to do so is strengthened by its location—standing alone at the end of the notice. The other anecdotes are partial statements; this is a definitive one.

Like al-Mas'ūdī, al-Ṣafadī justifies al-Mu'taḍid and eliminates the potential contradiction between his concern for justice and his reputation for cruelty. If the *Murūǧ* does this by morally and legally legitimizing an undenied personal sadism, *al-Wāfī* disposes of the moral problem completely by denying any real severity and explaining away the reputation for bloodthirstiness. In doing so, the Mamluk scholar is also refuting the positions of his predecessor.

Punishment/Torture III

If both al-Mas'ūdī and al-Ṣafadī show a tension, a potential contradiction, within the character and actions of al-Mu'taḍid, Ibn al-Ǧawzī presents a consistent image of our caliph as crimefighter and provider of justice.

There are five anecdotes centering on al-Mu'taḍid in the *Aḫbār al-Aḏkiyā'*. Two (the first and the last) deal with problems of money and need not concern us further here, except as a reminder that al-Mas'ūdī had paired al-Mu'taḍid's excessive economy with his severity. The three central anecdotes show al-Mu'taḍid's crimefighting abilities and his skills at smoking out and punishing criminals.

As I have shown elsewhere, al-Mu'taḍid in these narratives behaves as a classical detective.[52] He uncovers a crime and goes about discovering the identity of the criminal, ending with the punishment of the culprit. Indeed, this is the most important element in his *ḏakā'*, or cleverness, just as it is derivative from his role as ruler.

Al-Mu'taḍid's behavior as a detective also distinguishes him from the other rulers in the *Aḫbār al-Aḏkiyā'*. Many of them are clever at ferreting out secrets, some distinguish themselves as crime fighters, but none consistently acts as detective the way al-Mu'taḍid does. In one story, the ruler uncovers the murderer of a slavegirl, parts of whose body had been fished out of the Tigris.[53] In another, al-Mu'taḍid discovers not only the criminal but even the crime which would otherwise have gone undetected, when he realizes that the behavior of a slave is not what it should be under the circumstances.[54] In the latter case, the slave is beaten until he confesses to the crime. In the third case, al-Mu'taḍid discovers, through the culprit's excited heart-beat, which slave has just been engaged in illicit sexual activity. He then brings out the torture machines, the slave confesses and is killed.[55]

Hence, we do see a torture/punishment nexus. Two culprits are tortured until they confess, and all three criminals are punished. But, there is neither cruelty nor sadism. The tortures themselves are either unspecified or unimaginative, as in the case of the slave who is beaten. For punishment, two of the criminals were killed, and one was imprisoned or killed.

The justice of particular punishments is also evoked, but in a context which displays the cleverness of the caliph. The slave whose crime al-Mu'taḍid had to uncover through torture asked the ruler whether he would be forgiven if he told the truth. Al-Mu'taḍid answered that he would be except for what the law required. The slave did not understand this answer and confessed. We then conclude that the caliph was justified when he subsequently ordered the execution of the guilty slave.

In truth, however, Ibn al-Ǧawzī is clearly not concerned, as al-Mas'ūdī and al-Ṣafadī were, with justifying al-Mu'taḍid. The role he presents, that of crimefighter, of bringer of justice, obviates any such need. The *adab* organization of the *Aḫbār al-Aḏkiyā'* further simplifies

---

[52] Malti-Douglas, "Detective".
[53] Ibn al-Ǧawzī, *Aḏkiyā'*, p. 47-48.
[54] Ibn al-Ǧawzī, *Aḏkiyā'*, p. 46-47.
[55] Ibn al-Ǧawzī, *Aḏkiyā'*, p. 47; Malti-Douglas, "Detective"

this problem. The section in question presents examples of caliphal *ḏakā'*. The writer is under no obligation to place these actions in the context of other actions by the caliph, other facets of his character, or other events of his reign. Instead, the *ḏakā'* — displaying action is reinforced through the context of other, similar actions. In the process, al-Mu'taḍid's association with torture and punishment is subsumed into his role as detective.

Conclusion

Different writers, different sources, present different images of al-Mu'taḍid. One almost feels at times as if they are carrying on a debate about the nature of this caliph and of caliphal authority in general.

Yet, the differences in the texts go farther than this. By their differing modes of organizing material, they create different conceptions of society, politics, and the historical process. Their asides, their juxtapositions of material, their evocations of syntagmatic and paradigmatic series express varied and frequently complex historical visions.

But, the confrontation of the image of this one 'Abbasid caliph in historical sources of three very different literary types — the historical chronicle, the biographical dictionary, and the *adab* work — deepens our view of the medieval Muslim conception of history. For an educated medieval Muslim, the intended audience of all of these works, the history of his culture could not be subsumed by only one of these genres. It had to be understood as being expressed through all of them.

Different literary forms stressed different aspects of historical understanding. The chronicle, whether annalistic or not, defined the historical event as part of an essentially linear sequence which unfolded in time. The biographical dictionary, like our own biographies, attached events to those who made, or were submitted to, them, and thus to the larger coherence which is the life of an individual. The *adab* work, by contrast, conceptualizes the historical event as a typical manifestation of a common character type or action. As such, it is a way of calling attention to common features and patterns of human activity, and, hence, of historical events, that transcend temporal and personal boundaries.

History, the way a culture understands its past, lay in the literary intertext, in the space between the conceptions embodied by distinctive literary forms. Indeed, we may find in this a distinctive characteristic of the medieval Islamic genius: a preference for truth in diversity over truth in unity.

IX

CLASSICAL ARABIC CRIME NARRATIVES: THIEVES AND THIEVERY IN *ADAB* LITERATURE

> En effet le vol—et ce qui s'y rattache: les peines de prison avec la honte du métier du voleur—etait devenu une entreprise désintéressée, sorte d'oeuvre d'art active et pensée ne pouvant s'accomplir qu'à l'aide du langage.
>
> Jean Genet, *Journal du voleur*

Whether or not theft is an art, and whether or not it depends on language, writing about it certainly is and does. Crime literature has long been a popular and extensive branch of mass literature in the West.[1] But crime narratives also represent an important part of the elite classical Arabic literature of the medieval Islamic world.[2]

The presence of thieves in medieval Islamic society has been amply noted by scholars.[3] But how are thieves portrayed on the literary plane? And what are the dynamics governing the literature on thieves in classical Arabic? This study will investigate these questions in relation to the literary category of thieves in classical Arabic *adab* works: largely anecdotal texts, designed at once to be edifying and entertaining. We shall not concern ourselves with beggars or other lumpenproletariat, grouped with thieves in some of the scholarly literature. Thieves in classical Arabic literature form an autonomous and self-conscious literary category which displays important similarities with other *adab* anecdotal categories, such as those of uninvited guests (*ṭufaylīs*), or clever madmen (*ʿuqalāʾ al-majānīn*).[4] It must be remembered, however, that these are literary categories, and not necessarily social-historical ones.

---

[1] On crime literature in general, see the excellent survey by John G. Cawelti, *Adventure, Mystery, and Romance* (Chicago: University of Chicago Press, 1976).

[2] On detective narratives in classical Arabic literature and the general problem of detective stories in medieval Arabic, see Fedwa Malti-Douglas, "The Classical Arabic Detective", *Arabica*, forthcoming.

[3] See, for example, Ira Lapidus, *Muslim cities in the Later Middle Ages* (Cambridge: Harvard University Press, 1967); C.E. Bosworth, *The Medieval Islamic Underworld: The Banū Sāsān in Arabic Society and Literature* (Leiden: E. J. Brill, 1976); Muḥammad Rajab an-Najjār, *Ḥikāyāt ash-Shuṭṭār wal-ʿAyyarīn fī at-Turāth al-ʿArabī* (Kuwait: al-Majlis al-Waṭanī lith-Thaqāfa wal-Funūn wal-Ādāb, 1981).

[4] Only in recent years have *adab* anecdotal categories become the subject of serious literary scholarship. See Yūsuf Sadān, *al-Adab al-ʿArabī al-Hāzil wa-Nawādir ath-Thuqalāʾ* (Tel Aviv: Maṭbaʿat as-Sarūjī, 1983); Ulrich Marzolph, *Der Weise Narr Buhlūl* (Wiesbaden: Franz Steiner Verlag, 1983); Fedwa Malti-Douglas, *Structures of Avarice: The Bukhalāʾ in Medieval Arabic Literature* (Leiden: E.J. Brill, 1985); Fedwa Malti-Douglas, "Structure and Organization in a Monographic *Adab* Work: *al-Taṭfīl* of al-Khaṭīb al-Baghdādī", *Journal of Near Eastern Studies*, 40, 3 (1981), 227-245.

Of the medieval literature on thieves, much, like the *Kitāb Ḥiyal al-Luṣūṣ* of al-Jāḥiẓ, is not extant.[5] There are, however, chapters on thieves in multi-subject *adab* works. We shall examine chapters in three *adab* works, the *Akhbār al-Adhkiyā'* of Ibn al-Jawzī, the *Muḥāḍarāt al-Udabā' wa-Muḥāwarāt ash-Shu'arā' wal-Bulaghā'* of ar-Rāghib al-Iṣbahānī, and the *Kitāb al-Faraj ba'd ash-Shidda* of at-Tanūkhī.[6]

Each of these three works presents its thieves in a different context. The *Akhbār al-Adhkiyā'* of Ibn al-Jawzī is as, as its title implies, concerned with those who display *dhakā'*, cleverness or wit. By implication, thieves, like other groups within the work, fall into the larger category. The chapter on thieves is entitled "*Fī Dhikr Ṭuraf min Fiṭan al-Mutalaṣṣiṣīn*," (Mention of Anecdotes about the Cleverness of Thieves).

Ar-Rāghib al-Iṣbahānī, on the other hand, has embedded his chapter on thieves within a larger one on courage. The encyclopedic framework of ar-Rāghib's work, however, defines his chapter less specifically than does the *dhakā'* of Ibn al-Jawzī's text. Ar-Rāghib's chapter title reflects this greater generality: "*Wamimmā Jā'a fī at-Talaṣṣuṣ wa-mā Yajrī Majrāhu*," (And From What Was Said About Thievery and What Is Analogous to It). This chapter has, in turn, been subdivided into fourteen microsections. Though a few of these respresent types of thief actions (and, hence, anecdotal morphologies), their general organizational significance is limited.[7]

At-Tanūkhī is the odd man out in this group. His chapter on thieves forms part of a larger work which, though subdivided into character types, is based on the plot of relief after adversity. Hence, the chapter on thieves is not generically concerned with demonstrating the wit of thieves, as is for example Ibn al-Jawzī, but with stressing the manner in

---

[5] Charles Pellat, "Nouvel essai d'inventaire de l'oeuvre ǧāḥiẓienne", *Arabica*, XXXI (1984), 146, lists only an apparent fragment.

[6] Ibn al-Jawzī, *Akhbār al-Adhkiyā'*, ed. Muḥammad Mursī al-Khawlī (Cairo: Maṭābi' al-Ahrām at-Tijāriyya, 1969), 194-209; ar-Rāghib al-Iṣbahānī, *Muḥāḍarāt al-Udabā' wa-Muḥāwarāt ash-Shu'arā' wal-Bulaghā'* (Cairo: al-Maṭba'a al-'Āmira, 1326 A.H.), v. I, 81-84; at-Tanūkhī, *Kitāb al-Faraj ba'd ash-Shidda*, ed. 'Abbūd ash-Shālijī (Beirut: Dār Ṣādir, 1978), v. IV, 227-267. For a detailed listing of the contents of this work, see Rouchdi Fakkar, *At-Tanûḫî et son livre: La Délivrance après l'angoisse* (Cairo: Institut Français d'Archéologie Orientale, 1955), 57-84. Ibn Ḥijja al-Ḥamawī, *Thamarāt al-Awrāq fī al-Muḥāḍarāt*, printed on the margins of al-Abshīhī, *al-Mustaṭraf fī Kull Fann Mustaẓraf* (Beirut: Dar al-Umam liṭ-Ṭibā'a wan-Nashr, 1952), v. I, 156-157, included a brief chapter on "Adhkiyā' al-Mutalaṣṣiṣīn," consisting of only one anecdote, of which a variant can be found in Ibn al-Jawzī, *Adhkiyā'*, 195-197. Chapters on thieves can be found in enclyclopedic *adab* works in manuscript. For a partial list of these, see Sadān, *Thuqalā'*, 32-34.

[7] The only general organizational principle followed in ar-Rāghib's chapter (and this not absolutely consistently) is that of the placement of non-anecdotal material (proverbs, terminology, advice, etc.) before anecdotal material.

which the victim of a theft was able to extricate himelf from that situation. Thus, the focus of the cleverness is, at least by implication, reversed. Finally, by its nature, *al-Faraj baᶜd ash-Shidda* implies a specific narrative pattern, something which neither Ibn al-Jawzī's nor ar-Rāghib's chapters do.

Yet, despite these variations in the presentations and contexts of thieves and theft, the clear similarities in the three corpora permit their analysis as a single limited anecdotal corpus: an overlap in anecdotal morphologies, common attitudes to theft and cleverness, and similarities in the images of the thieves themselves.

These chapters explicitly characterize themselves as being about thieves. Hence, material within them is automatically defined as being in some sense exemplary of the image (or one of the images) of the thief in *adab* literature. For the same reason, we are not considering stories which might have thieves in them but which are present in other sections of these works.[8] Such narratives, by their context as well often as by their nature, do not as effectively transmit the literary image of the thief as a consciously delineated category.[9]

As I have shown in other studies, the most fruitful methodology for analyzing an anecdotal corpus on a given *adab* character type is through the isolation of morphological categories designed to delineate the characteristic actions and hence the nature of the character type in question. The isolation of morphological categories itself proceeds from the isolation of functions in the anecdotes, a function understood in the Proppian sense as the act of a personage in its relation to the unfolding of the narrative. The narrative is thus considered to be a sequence of functions and it is the position within a sequence which gives a function its morphological significance. Using the Bremondian reconception of the Proppian function, we can further define this as an interface between action and role. Such an analysis exposes, therefore, not only the narrative structure of the anecdotes but the roles played by thieves within them as well.[10]

---

[8] See, for example, the story in at-Tanūkhī, *Faraj*, v. II, 330. Thieves are also present in crime-fighting anecdotes on other sections of Ibn al-Jawzī. See, for example, Ibn al-Jawzī, *Adhkiyā*ʾ, 46-47, 55. See, also, Malti-Douglas, "Detective"

[9] The image of thieves, or other criminals, as they appear in non-thief sections or chapters, represents an interesting, though distinct, subject for analysis. For criminal behavior in the context of anecdotes about crime-fighters, see Malti-Douglas, "Detective".

[10] For a complete dicussion of this methodology, see Malti-~~Douglas~~, *Structures of Avarice*, 21-28. For the application of this methodology to another *adab* category, see Malti-Douglas, "Structure and Organization"

Let us begin with the following anecdote:

Ibn al-Jawzī relates that a man went to sleep in a mosque and under his head was a bag of fifteen hundred dinars. He suddenly felt someone pulling the bag from under his head and he awoke in alarm to discover that a young man had taken the bag and begun to run. So the man got up to run after the thief but his foot had been tied with rope to a pole at the end of the mosque.[11]

This anecdote represents the simplest morphological type within the corpus of thief anecdotes, the Theft = *Dhakāʾ* anecdote. The thief has an active role and taken the goods from a victim whose role is passive. Hence, the thief is the agent in the anecdote in that he perpetrates the action that permits him to be defined as a thief, while the party who is stolen from is the patient of the act, and its victim. There is, therefore, an act which clearly defines the thief in this anecdote: his appropriation of the goods. This act represents a function. Is it the only act, the only function in this anecdote? The thief in this Jawzian anecdote is also defined by his act of *dhakāʾ*, embodied in the ruse of tying the man's foot, prevent ing him from running after the thief. While this act is essentially linked to the act of thieving, it is nonetheless analytically distinct from it. Because the effective combination, or existing together, of these two potentially distinguishable actions characterizes this anecdotal morphology, it consists of a single function with a dual nature, both theft and *dhakāʾ*.

This inherent binarism in the functional nature of the first category is characteristic of the anecdote in which the act of theft is closely related to the use of *dhakāʾ* by the thief. A similar phenomenon is evident in the following anecdote, also from Ibn al-Jawzī. A thief who had set out to steal a riding animal from someone finally entered the house of the owner. The owner and his wife sat down to eat in darkness, and the thief, finding himself hungry, decided to join them. He reached out for the bowl and the man, unaware of the thief's hand, grabbed it. So the thief grabbed the woman's hand with his other hand. She then asked her husband what he was doing with her hand. The husband, thinking that he had grabbed his wife's hand, released the thief's hand, who in turn released the wife's hand. Then they ate. The wife, being unaware of the thief's hand, grabbed it and he grabbed the husband's hand. The husband asked his wife what she was doing with his hand, at which point she released the thief's hand, and he released the husband's hand. The man then went to sleep and the thief took the horse.[12]

---

[11] Ibn al-Jawzī, *Adhkiyāʾ*, 204.

[12] Ibn al-Jawzī, *Adhkiyāʾ*, 202.

In this anecdote, we observe the thief in the active role in which he appropriates the goods, the riding animal. Yet, at the same time, we are also treated to thief's *dhakā*ʾ, which consists of his manipulating the eating situation in such a way that his presence remains hidden. Hence, this anecdote presents the same morphology as that observed earlier, a function displaying a dual nature, in which the thieving action is present alongside that of the *dhakā*ʾ. In this case, it is easier to distinguish the act of *dhakā*ʾ from that of theft for two reasons. First, because it is not directly related to the theft of the animal, and second, because it was only employed to keep the thief from being caught. Such a distinction only mirrors the dual classification of the anecdote itself: in a chapter on thieves, in a work on *adhkiyā*ʾ. Nevertheless, the actions are not really separate since taking the food is also a form of theft and avoiding discovery is also part of succesful thievery. This dictates the classification of the anecdote in the Theft = *Dhakā*ʾ morphology.

But the act of *dhakā*ʾ does not have to be linked to that of theft. Rather, there are anecdotes in which the thieving action is clearly distinguished from *dhakā*ʾ: the Theft + *Dhakā*ʾ morphology. A thief entered a man's house and stole the furniture. The man cried out: "How unlucky this night is!," to which the thief replied: "Not for everyone!"[13] In this anecdote, the thief still possesses the active role that he did in the earlier morphology. He takes the goods of the victim, who remains passive. The act of theft is clearly present. More interesting is the narrative location of the act of *dhakā*ʾ, embodied in the thief's reply to the victim's comment about the unlucky nature of the night. The *dhakā*ʾ is as clearly present as the theft, but distinct from the thievery and unrelated to it. Hence, this anecdote presents two functions: a theft followed by an act of *dhakā*ʾ.

The importance of the *dhakā*ʾ and its potential separation from any theft can be seen in a story involving the famous thief, Ibn al-Khayyāṭa. A money changer was asleep in Baṣra, with his doors locked, and surrounded by guards. He was suddenly awakened in his bed by Ibn al-Khayyāṭa, who proceeded to ask the money changer for a loan of five hundred dinars. The money changer gave Ibn al-Khayyāṭa the money and the latter admonished the man not to follow him, otherwise he would kill him. The money changer, unable to figure out how the intruder had entered, did not speak of the incident to anyone. A few nights later, he was awakened in the same manner and it was Ibn al-Khayyāṭa who came to repay the loan. The man objected to the repayment and Ibn al-Khayyāṭa explained that had he wished, he could easily have robbed him. The money changer then accepted the repayment and asked Ibn al-

[13] Ibn al-Jawzī, *Adhkiyā*ʾ, 207.

Khayyāṭa not to come to him in this way but rather to come to his shop in the daytime, or even to send an agent if need be, to get money. Henceforth, Ibn al-Khayyāṭa sent his agent during daylight hours and this arrangement was continued for some time, until the eventual capture of the thief.[14]

Clearly, in this anecdote, there is no theft, properly speaking. Ibn al-Khayyāṭa, while he does break into the money changer's house, does not rob him. Ibn al-Khayyāṭa was a thief famous in the literature for his superior thieving abilities, a medieval Arabic Arsène Lupin.[15] And this is part of what permits the anecdote to function in the context of a chapter on thieves. But that aside, as Ibn al-Khayyāṭa himself reminded the money changer, he could easily have robbed him once he had broken in. Yet, he did not. Therefore, clearly, it is the *dhakā*ʾ of his entry which is predominant and this *dhakā*ʾ is completely isolated from any type of thieving action. This *dhakā*ʾ is so important in its own right that it transcends the act of theft. Nevertheless, the anecdote makes little sense unless we assume that the author of this *dkahā*ʾ is also a thief. Not only is Ibn al-Khayyāṭa a famous member of this profession but the preceding anecdote in Ibn al-Jawzī recounts some of his adventures. Hence, the act of theft in this anecdote with the money changer, while not clearly present, is implicit in Ibn al-Khayyāṭa's role, bringing the anecdote as a whole within the Theft + *Dhakā*ʾ category.

In the anecdotal morphologies thus far examined, the thief has played an active role, is the agent, not only as perpetrator of the theft but also a generator of the act of *dhakā*ʾ. By extension, the victim in these same two anecdotal morphologies, the Theft = *Dhakā*ʾ and the Theft + *Dhakā*ʾ, has played the role of patient, from the point of view of both theft and *dhakā*ʾ. There is, however, in the corpus of thief anecdotes a morphology in which these roles intersect, the Victim = *Dhakī* anecdotes. Ar-Rāghib al-Iṣbahānī relates the following: A saddle bag was stolen from someone and he was told that had he recited the "Āyat al-Kursī" over it, it would not have been stolen. He replied that it had a complete *Qur*ʾ*ān* in it.[16]

In this narrative, the thief, unlike his brethren in earlier anecdotes, does not make an appearance. We are simply told of the theft: its

[14] Ibn al-Jawzī, *Adhkiyā*ʾ, 206.

[15] One point of similarity is that the larcenous ability of the heroes is so great that they can be presented showing their skills in non-theft situations without their fundamental indentity as thieves being called into question. See, for example, Maurice Leblanc, *La Cagliostro se venge* (Paris: Le Livre de Poche, 1973), in which Lupin's theft plays a very small role. Both Ibn al-Khayyāṭa and Lupin commit thefts despite their imprisonment. See Ibn al-Jawzī, *Adhkiyā*ʾ, 204-206 and Maurice Leblanc, *Arsène Lupin, Gentleman cambrioleur* (Paris: Le Livre de Poche, 1972), 35-65.

[16] ar-Rāghib, *Muḥāḍarāt*, 83.

perpetrator has been effectively occulted. From the perspective of the theft, however, the occulted thief remains in the active role, or, more precisely, the party stolen from remains in the passive one. From the point of view of *dhakāʾ*, however, the victim takes the active role, by replying to the challenge concerning the theft.

Hence, there are three functions in the Victim = *Dhakī* morphology: 1) a theft (with thief occulted); 2) a verbal challenge to the victim from a third party; and 3) the victim's display of *dhakāʾ* through his reaction to the challenge.

This morphology is visible in the following anecdote, also from ar-Rāghib. A mule was stolen from someone and one of his friends said to him that he was to blame for ignoring the mule. Then another friend observed that the blame belonged to the groom. Finally, the victim replied: "O people, and the thief has no blame?"[17] The tripartite structure of the Victim = *Dhakī* morphology is equally present in this anecdote. As a result, again, the victim regains his active role and becomes an agent vis-à-vis *dhakāʾ*. At the same time, his active role has nothing to do with the theft, which remains distinct from *dhakāʾ*. Hence, this morphology is more closely related to Theft + *Dhakāʾ* than to Theft = *Dhakāʾ*. The significance of this will become clear later.

In all three morphologies thus far examined, the thief played the active role, although in the Victim = *Dhakī* morphology, the victim of the theft displayed the *dhakāʾ*. But in all these cases, the thief got the goods he set out to steal. Not all thieves in the corpus, however, are this lucky. In the next three morphologies to be discussed, the thieves are always ultimately unsuccessful.

The simplest of these three morphologies (from the point of view of action and role) can be derived from the following anecdote in Ibn al-Jawzī:

A pious old woman had a son who was a money changer and who used to stay away from home playing and drinking. He would, however, return home at the end of the day with a money bag which his mother would then hide in a special room with an iron door. A thief one day decided to steal this bag, and with this in mind he penetrated the house of the old woman. She, however, began to eat and the thief told himself that she would soon go to sleep and he would then come and steal the goods. But she finished eating and began praying, extending this activity until half the night had passed. The thief was confused and afraid that morning might come without his having acquired the goods, so he decided to do something about it. He looked around the house and

[17] ar-Rāghib, *Muḥāḍarāt*, 83.

discovered a wrap and some incense. He wrapped the cloth around himself and lit the incense and began coming down the stairs, crying in a heavy voice to frighten the old woman. But she was strong and thought it might be a thief, and so said in a frightened voice: "Who is this?", to which the thief answered that he was the angel Gabriel come to save her dissolute son. She asked him to have pity on her son, since he was her only one. The thief replied that he was not sent to kill him but rather to take his bag and cause him pain in this way so that he would repent. When he repented, his bag would be returned to him. So the old woman told him to proceed with what he had been ordered to do and he told her to move away from the door. This she did and when he entered the room to take the goods, she closed the door on him and locked it. The thief realized what had taken place and attempted to escape but could not. So he asked the woman to let him out and allow him to warn her son. She, however, answered that she was afraid to open the door, lest her eyes be injured by his light. He insisted that he would extinguish his light to save her eyes, but she instead asked him what was keeping him from exiting through the roof or boring a hole in the wall with a feather from his wing. The thief realized her strength and began to beg for mercy, telling her that he would repent. But she told him that he would not leave until morning and she proceeded to pray. His asking to be let out and her praying continued until morning when her son returned and she informed him of what had occurred. He then brought the police chief and the thief was apprehended.[18]

There are many elements which contribute to the literary success of this anecdote, such as the nature of the ruse, how it is turned against its creator, etc. Clearly, here, the thief attempts to steal the goods from the old woman, and resorts to a stratagem for this purpose. But his attempt is frustrated by the victim, who resorts to her own *dhakāʾ* to defeat his ruse (indeed playing along with it and turning it against him) and frustrate his attempt.

Hence, there are two functions in this anecdote: 1) the theft is attempted; and 2) the attempt is frustrated by the *dhakāʾ* of the victim. We can call this the Frustrated Theft morphology. Concomitant with the frustration of the theft is a change in the narative role of the thief. He moves from an active to a passive role, from agent to patient, as he first attempts the theft and is then foiled in his attempt. By the same token, the intended victim also shifts from patient to agent, using her *dhakāʾ* as the instrument of role transformation.

---

[18] Ibn al-Jawzī, *Adhkiyāʾ*, 208-209.

This morphology can also be found in ar-Rāghib al-Iṣbahānī. An old woman sensed the presence of a thief in her tent, so she addressed herself, wondering out loud what she would do if she married and had three sons whom she would call ʿUmar, Bakr, and Ṣaqr. She then asked herself how they would fare if she were to die, and she repeated the names ʿUmar, Bakr, and Ṣaqr, raising her voice. She had neighbors with those names who came to her rescue and she told them: "Here is the thief".[19] The same structure is present as in the anecdote involving the thief who pretends he is the angel Gabriel. The theft is attempted when the thief enters the woman's tent, generating the first function in the morphology. The woman, however, through her *dhakāʾ*, foils this attempt, providing the second function.

As is clear from these two Frustrated Theft anecdotes, the *dhakāʾ* of the victim is manifested in the second function. In the anecdote involving the angel Gabriel, the victim exploits the thief's own ruse against him to keep him locked behind the door. In the second anecdote, on the other hand, the *dhakāʾ* is manifested through a verbal ruse, the woman's calling to her neighbours for help. In both cases, however, the act of *dhakāʾ* is directly used to frustrate the theft and is, hence, intimately related to theft. Often, for example, the two acts take place simultaneously and one cannot really say where the first has ceased and the second has taken over. Only their association with different figures distinguishes them. Thus, the act of *dhakāʾ* in the Frustrated Theft anecdote differs from the paradigmatically related action in the Victim = *Dhakī* anecdotes, in which the *dhakāʾ* was clearly separated from the theft.

The second function of the Frustrated Theft anecdotes provides the greatest variety in types of action. Ar-Rāghib tells the story of one Dāwūd the Afflicted who went out with some money and was accosted by a group of individuals who said to him: "Throw down what you have, O crazy one." He replied that he would do so and sat down and proceeded to defecate. Then he said to them: "I have nothing, by your life, other than this".[20] This anecdote clearly belongs to the Frustrated Theft morphology. The first function, the theft attempt, is present, as is the second function, the frustration of the attempt by means of the *dhakāʾ* of the victim. Here, however, the second function consists of both Dāwūd's act of defecation and of his comment to the thieves.

The Frustrated Theft morphology is the morphology of most of the anecdotes in *al-Faraj baʿd ash-Shidda* of at-Tanūkhī. By definition, this work deals with situations in which a victim extricates himself from a

[19] ar-Rāghib, *Muḥāḍarāt*, 83.
[20] ar-Rāghib, *Muḥāḍarāt*, 84.

tight spot, and, in the case of the thief anecdotes, this is a situation in which a thief is attempting to rob the victim.

The majority of the Tanūkhian anecdotes (including the ones classified in the Frustrated Theft morphology) distinguish themselves from the other thief anecdotes in our corpus, and this for a variety of narrative reasons. The Tanūkhian anecdotes have a tendency to be narratively longer than those in either Ibn al-Jawzī or ar-Rāghib al-Iṣbahānī. And, as a result of this longer narrative, the Tanūkhian anecdote can mask its morphology more effectively. Despite the narrative elaborations, however, the two functions in the Frustrated Theft morphology are present in *al-Faraj baᶜd ash-Shidda*, though their presentation is frequently distinctive.

For example, before the narrative statement of the first function, we often find introductory material, sometimes of considerable length, which sets the stage for the first function itself and the entire working out of the anecdote. Thus, before the poet Diᶜbil sets out on a journey (during which he will be attacked), we are told how he recited verses in court and did not recite them to anyone else. We later learn that after Diᶜbil and his party are robbed, the thief recites the opening verse of the same poem. When Diᶜbil succeeds in establishing that he is the famous poet and author of the line in question, the thief returns all that he had taken.[21]

This second function is also distinctive and representative of a characteristic common in the Tanūkhian corpus. It is not by ruse, or even really by any extended activity, that the potential victim frustrates the theft. Instead, it is merely by establishing his authorship of the verse in question. In another anecdote in *al-Faraj*, another robbery victim escapes theft by establishing his identity and relationship to the thief.[22]

The Frustrated Theft is not the only morphology, however, in which the thief does not end the anecdote with the goods he set out to acquire at the beginning. There is a second pattern in which the thief is also unable to retain the goods he steals: the Double Theft morphology.

Two thieves stole a donkey and one went to sell it. On the road, he met a man with a pan of fish who asked if the donkey was for sale. When he was told that it was, he asked the seller to hold on to his pan of fish so he could ride the donkey and test it. So the potential buyer did that and disappeared in an alley and fled. When the thief returned to his partner, the latter asked him what had transpired with the donkey, to which

[21] at-Tanūkhī, *Faraj*, 227-230.
[22] at-Tanūkhī, *Faraj*, 234-237.

the first thief answered that they had sold it for the same price for which they had bought it, and gained a pan of fish.[23]

In this anecdote, two thieves steal a donkey, which is then stolen from them, producing first one theft, followed by another. And each of the two thefts represents a function in this morphology, itself composed of two functions. Additional dynamics, however, characterize the Double Theft morphology. In the first function, the thieves steal the object from a victim, and they themselves are in the active role. In the second function, the thieves themselves become the victims, and that of another thief.

Morphologically speaking, the two thieves are acting, in the first function, as one character. Had they been one thief instead of two, the morphology of the anecdote would not have been changed. This can be seen in an anecdote involving a man who stole a donkey and then went to sell it. The donkey, however, was stolen from him in turn. When he returned home, his wife asked him for how much he had sold it, to which he replied: "for its own capital".[24]

The thief has been turned into a victim, but not by the party he is robbing. This gives us the familiar comic structure of the *voleur/volé*[25] which characterizes the morphology as a whole. But the first thief does not always express his reaction to this turn of events. In an anecdote in Ibn al-Jawzī, a man who has stolen some money from a money changer is imprisoned by a woman who does not release him until he gives her the money, after which she explains that she will not tolerate any competition in that town.[26]

In these anecdotes, the thieves lose the goods, but not to their original owners. Instead, the stolen property is acquired by a third party. But, what if the original owner of the goods reacquires them, taking the place of the second thief in the Double Theft anecdotes, in a word, stealing them back? This is the case in the Stealing Back anecdotes.

Both Ibn al-Jawzī and at-Tanūkhī present the following anecdote (with insignificant variations):

A man who was a thief in his youth repented and became a cloth seller. He went home one night after having locked his shop. A thief, dressed as the shop owner, came with a candle and some keys and called the guard. He gave the guard the candle in the dark and asked him to light it for him, for he had some work to do in the shop. The guard went to light the candle and the thief proceeded to open the locks with the keys.

---

[23] Ibn al-Jawzī, *Adhkiyā'*, 200.

[24] Ibn al-Jawzī, *Adhkiyā'*, 200.

[25] See, for example, Henri Bergson, *Le rire: Essai sur la signification du comique* (Paris: Presses Universitaires de France, 1972), 73.

[26] Ibn al-Jawzī, *Adhkiyā'*, 199-200.

He entered the shop and when the guard came in with the candle, the thief took it from him and placed it in front of himself and proceeded to examine the account books. The guard watched him, not doubting that he was the shop owner. When dawn came, the thief called the guard and spoke to him from afar and requested a porter. The guard brought a porter and he was made to carry four valuable parcels. Then the thief locked the shop and went with the porter, but not before giving the guard two dirhams. When morning came, the shop owner came to open his shop and the guard proceeded to thank him for the two dirhams. So the man did not believe what he heard and he opened his shop to find the candle wax and his account books lying on the ground. He then became aware of the four missing parcels. So he called the guard and asked who it was that had carried the packages with him from the shop. So the guard said to him: "Did you not ask me to call a porter and I brought you one?" The man then replied that indeed he had, but that he had been sleepy and that he wished to see the porter. The guard brought the porter and the man closed the shop and, taking the porter along with him, he asked him where he had carried the parcels, for he had been drunk. The porter told him the location to which he had carried the goods. Another porter who had helped carry the material was then called and they finally arrived at the door of a room, far from the river bank, close to the desert. The door was locked, so the man opened the lock and entered, whereupon he found the parcels unopened. There was a black robe hanging on a rope in the house so the cloth seller wrapped the parcels in it and called the porter and gave him the parcels. On the way out of the room, the thief met him and saw what he had. The thief was confused and followed him to the river bank, and when they arrived there and the man had called the boatman to cross the river, the porter asked for someone to take the load from him. The thief thereupon came forth as though he were volunteering, put the parcels on board of the ship with their owner, and placed the black robe over his shoulder. Then he said to the shop owner: "O my brother, may God be with you, you have received your parcels back, so leave my robe". The man then laughed and told the thief to descend and have no fear. Then he called on him to repent, and gave him a gift and dismissed him without harming him.[27]

To derive the functions in the Stealing Back morphology, let us distill the actions in this anecdote down to their essentials. A shop owner, a cloth seller who was previously a thief, is robbed by a thief who pretends to be the owner of the shop. When the cloth seller discovers the robbery, he proceeds to retrace the steps of the thief and follows them until he has

[27] Ibn al-Jawzī, *Adhkiyā'*, 201-202; at-Tanūkhī, *Faraj*, 256-258.

retrieved his goods. Since he also uses a ruse, we can say that he has stolen them back.

Hence, there are two functions in the Stealing Back morphology. First, the thief steals the goods from a victim, and second, the victim reacquires the stolen goods. In the process, the role of the thief in the anecdote has changed from active to passive. In the first function, he was the one who perpetrated the act, whereas in the second function, he is the one against whom the act is perpetrated.

This morphology resembles the Double Theft and Frustrated Theft morphologies, in which the thieves lose their active roles in the theft relationship. In all three categories, the thief is not permitted to consume the goods. But there are fundamental and important differences in these morphologies. In the Stealing Back morphology, the thief has actually acquired the goods he set out to steal, and this is the first function, which, thus, resembles the first function in the Double Theft morphology. But in the second function of the Stealing Back anecdotes, the victim reacquires his own goods from the thief, leaving him empty-handed. In this way, the second function differs from the second function in the Double Theft morphology. There, though the thief was left ultimately empty-handed, it was because he was robbed by another thief.

The cloth seller anecdote shows the relationship between the Stealing Back and the Double Theft morphologies. The victim of the thief's action in the first function, the cloth seller, is himself, we are told, a repentant thief. Each of the functions involves the taking of goods from another party. And it is perhaps his having been a thief which permits our cloth seller to retrieve the goods from the other thief. Thus, the shop owner, by his dual identity as at once victim and (former) thief, suggests a link between thief and victim. In fact, the paradigmatic relationship between the two men (and thus the two roles) is expressed narratively in the anecdote by the confusion of identity between the two figures, a point to which we shall return below.

Not all Stealing Back narratives, however, involve a repentant thief who reacquires his goods. Another shop owner kept his money in a strong box. A client, admiring his strong box, asked where he could get another just like it. Soon after, the shop owner found that the box had been emptied and the client had disappeared. The shop owner then traced down the culprit by locating the identical strong box and took back his own goods. Here again, the dual-function morphology is present: first, the thief steals the goods from the victim; and second, the victim reacquires the stolen goods.[28]

[28] This anecdote can be found in both Ibn al-Jawzī, *Adhkiyā*ʾ, 195-197, and at-Tanūkhī, *Faraj*, 244-247.

In yet another, and more complex, anecdote, the victim is only able to retrieve his stolen goods with the help of a prisoner, whom he visits in jail, on the advice of a third party. And this prisoner tells the victim the exact steps he should follow to repossess his property.[29] Despite the complexity, however, the anecdote displays the same morphology. The second function is simply more elaborate. Of course, the elaboration of the second function helps to explain the reacquisition of the goods by someone who is not a thief, repentant or otherwise.

It is evident that *dhakāʾ*, cleverness, plays an important part in the Stealing Back anecdotes. Not only does the repossession of the goods demand cleverness on the part of their owner but the initial theft frequently did as well. It is equally evident that this reliance on cleverness, whether stratagem-based or purely verbal, is characteristic of the thief anecdotes as a whole, not only where the title calls for it, as in the *Kitāb al-Adhkiyāʾ*, but also in the works of ar-Rāghib al-Iṣbahānī and at-Tanūkhī. The overwhelming majority of thefts is carried out by means of stratagems. Even when they are not, however, as in the Theft + *Dhakāʾ* anecdotes, *dhakāʾ* is attributed to the thieves anyway. Only in the Victim = *Dhakī* anecdotes is a stratagem or some other display of cleverness consistently absent. This does not really reflect on the theft, however, since we are never told, in this morphology, how it has been effected. Among the Frustrated Theft and Stealing Back anecdotes, it is those of at-Tanūkhī which place least emphasis on the cleverness of the thief, though even here it is not completely absent.

But the cleverness or wit of the thief does more than help him effect his larceny. It also, in a certain sense, justifies it. Through his cleverness, the thief has 'earned' the stolen property. This system of values is well displayed in the following anecdote.

A money changer with his sack passed a group of thieves. One of the group bragged to his fellows that he would show them how the sack should be stolen. He followed the money changer to his home. The latter threw down his sack, and asked the slave girl to bring him some water to his room. Once he had gone, the thief entered, took the sack, and returned to his friends, triumphant. But they replied that he had not really accomplished anything, because he had left the money changer to beat and punish the slave girl, not a nice act. So the thief asked what they wanted him to do, to which they replied that he must both save the slave girl from a beating and take the money. So the thief returned to the money changer's house and found the man beating his slave girl. The thief said that he was the servant of the merchant next door, and gave

[29] Ibn al-Jawzī, *Adhkiyāʾ*, 197-199.

him the following message: "My master greets you and says to you that you have changed. You throw down your sack in the shop and leave, and if we had not seen it, it would have been taken". The thief took out the bag, which the money changer recognized, praising God. The thief then told the money changer to go in and write a receipt and while the latter was doing so, the thief took the sack of money and left.[30]

Clearly, this anecdote shows the cleverness of the thief who was able to steal the sack twice. But more than that, it argues that it is not sufficient for a thief simply to gain possession of the goods. He must do so without bringing blame or physical harm upon a third party. Also worthy of note is the fact that after the first theft, the thief's companions said to him "you did not do/accomplish anything" (*mā ʿamalta shayʾan*). This is at least partly a reference to the absence of a ruse in the first theft.

Cleverness, *dhakāʾ*, legitimizes the theft. This is precisely the same attitude which V. S. Naipaul claimed to find in Trinidad and which he characterized as a "picaroon" value. After a Trinidadian woman was cheated by a fraudulent concert promoter, her nephew explained her reaction in local dialect: "She ain't feel she get rob. She feel she pay two dollars for the *intelligence*".[31]

Nor is this idea unusual in Arabic *adab* literature. In an earlier study, I showed that the cleverness of the *ṭufaylī* also legitimized his intrusions.[32] Similarly, it is also evident that the cleverness and verbal brilliance of the hero of the *maqāmāt* also constitute appropriate payment for his fraudulently acquired gains.

Of course, the anecdote with the money changer and the group of thieves also highlights another quality of our larcenous heroes, their general aversion to violence. This is partly related to the types of thieves presented, who are often burglars, a choice whose implications become particularly clear in ar-Rāghib al-Iṣbahānī. This author included in his non-anecdotal discussion of types of thieves mention of those who strangled their victims and the ruses employed to cover their screams. The same section includes an account of a group of thieves who strangled their victim. But one page later, ar-Rāghib presents an anecdote in which a master thief, Sulaymān, permits a group of his cohorts to rob pedestrians, but only on condition that they employ no violence. The other thieves reply that only cowards would do such a thing.[33] The thieves in *al-Faraj* are a partial exception to this, because many of them

---

[30] Ibn al-Jawzī, *Adhkiyāʾ*, 207-208.

[31] V S. Naipaul, *The Middle Passage* (New York: Vintage, 1981), 76; emphasis in original.

[32] Malti-Douglas, "Structure and Organization", 233-235.

[33] ar-Rāghib, *Muḥāḍarāt*, 81-82.

are highway robbers and a few of them employ violence or the threat of it. This would seem to be, at least partly, a consequence of the *al-Faraj baʿd ash-Shidda* format. Here, the greater the danger to the hero, the more dramatic his escape. But even these thieves (and even more so those of Ibn al-Jawzī and ar-Rāghib) distinguish themselves very clearly from the thieves and criminals who can be found in detective or crime-fighter anecdotes, present in some of the same *adab* works. As I have shown in another study, these last criminals generally follow theft with murder, often under brutal circumstances.[34]

This crucial difference shows that the non-violence of the thief anecdotes cannot simply be understood as reflecting the criminal mores of the time. Rather, these non-violent thieves form part of a literary system that governs anecdotes in chapters about thieves. Without question, the relative non-violence of these thieves supports the legitimacy of their activities.[35] But this literary legitimization is reinforced by another characteristic: the paradigmatic relationship between the thieves and their victims. If we look at the totality of the thief morphologies functioning as a system, we can see that almost all the same actions tend to be performed on both sides of the theft relationship, the thieves and the victims. We find both in active and passive roles. There are thieves whose *dhakāʾ* is distinct from their theft (Theft + *Dhakāʾ* morphology) just as there are victims whose *dhakāʾ* is distinct from their victimization (Victim = *Dhakī* morphology). There are victims who imitate thieves to reacquire their goods (Stealing Back anecdotes) just as there are thieves who become victimized themselves (Double Theft anecdotes). Finally, in the Frustrated Theft anecdotes, the *dhakāʾ* of the victim is pitted against that of the thief. In fact, the Frustrated Theft anecdote operates as a Theft = *Dhakāʾ* anecdote in which the *dhakāʾ* has passed from the side of the thief to that of the victim.

By making the roles of thief and victim so similar, so potentially interchangeable, these anecdotes make theft less a violation of law or an injustice perpetrated by one individual on another than a kind of game played according to its own rules and in which the sides could be potentially changed.

In some anecdotes, this paradigmatic relationship goes even further, creating what is, in effect, a transmorphological discourse on identity. It is easiest to initially isolate this discourse in an anecdote from the Stealing Back morphology, the one involving the repentant thief who became a

---

[34] Malti-Douglas, "Detective"

[35] As do references to proper behavior, correct treatment of women, etc. See ar-Rāghib, *Muḥāḍarāt*, 82.

cloth seller. It will be remembered that the thief in this anecdote perpetrated his action by making believe that he was the shop owner, and this by dressing like him.

We already noted a kind of paradigmatic relationship between the thief and the victim in this narrative, since the victim was previously a thief. But, in fact, the anecdote goes further and creates a virtual fusion of identity between the thief and his intended victim, the shop owner. When we are initially introduced to the thief, we are told that he was dressed in the attire of the shop owner. Then, of course, he proceeds to inspect the books as the owner would, another way in which he attempts to take on the identity of the owner. The guard does not doubt that he is indeed the owner and he follows the thief's orders to bring in the porter. All these actions indicate that the thief was successfully playing the role of the shop owner.

But this does not effect a complete identity, because it only involves the thief attempting to be the other party. In fact, the reverse also takes place, as the shop owner accepts the thief's identity. This transpires when the owner returns to his shop in the morning and discovers the theft. When the guard reminds him that he called for the porter, the owner, rather than denying that he had done so, in fact, asserts that he did and that he was merely drowsy. He has accepted the actions of the thief as his own. This continues as the owner asks the porter where he carried the goods.

In effect, a very subtle game of identity and difference, of appearance and reality, is being played out. The thief pretends to be the owner. But the owner pretends to be the thief pretending to be the owner, something very easy for him to do since he is, indeed, the owner. The circle is complete. The imitation of imitation becomes identity.

The other characters play a crucial role in this process, especially the guard. When he thanks the owner for the two dirhams, he is not really mistaking him for the thief, since he had already mistaken the thief for the owner. Instead, he is making the figure who came the night before (a thief) and the one who came in the morning (the owner) into the same person. It is the ruse of the shop owner to prolong this identification. And he does so by claiming on one occasion to have been sleepy and on another to have been drunk, two states of weakened conciousness and, hence, identity.

It could be argued that the shop owner only performed these actions to retrieve the goods. But he could have drawn the necessary information from the guard and the porters. In addition, the problem of identity is reflected through other levels of the anecdote as well.

The owner of the shop was a cloth seller and it is through the medium of clothing (a disguise) that the thief first begins his attempt to identify himself as the shop owner. When the rightful owner finally uncovers his parcels in the thief's room, he wraps them in a cloth that is hanging in that room. Lest we think that this is unimportant, it becomes the object which the thief retrieves after he has helped to unload the parcels on the boat. Hence, there is a constant interplay between the occupation of the shop owner, the clothing of the thief that he dous to make believe that he is the owner, the clothing that is in the thief's room and which the owner uses to wrap his own parcels in, and this very piece of clothing which the thief then retrieves at the end of the anecdote. And, of course, we are not told what the stolen parcels contain, but, since the shop owner is a cloth seller, we can assume that it is cloth. This entire interplay with the cloth reinforces the identity between shop owner and thief.

We already noted that the shop owner, in order to retrieve his goods, follows in the steps of the thief, and that this contributes to the process of identity. But there is more similarity in the actions. When the thief first sets out to rob the victim, he enters by opening the locks on the shop. When the shop owner finally arrives at the culprit's door, he discovers that the door is locked and he also opens the locks to enter. The entry is identical in both the initial theft and the retrieval.

The process of identification in this anecdote goes through three phases. The first involves the thief's identification with the shop owner and cultimates in his taking the goods. The second involves the reverse process on the part of the shop owner, in which he accepts identity with the thief and follows his steps until he reaches the room. The third, and final, phase of the anecdote is its resolution: the shop owner reacquires his goods, the thief regains possession of his clothing, and the shop owner laughs, asks the thief to repent, and gives him a gift.

This ending is significant, permitting the process of identity to draw to a close. Not only does each party repossess his respective property (clothing in both cases) but the repentant thief, after laughing, asks the other thief to repent, in other words, to do as he himself had done, to replace his role as thief with the other man's role of repentant thief.

What is the significance of this entire charade with identity? Clearly, the thief has attempted to steal the victim's identity in the initial phase of the anecdote, before he steals the goods. However, the victim, by playing along with the guard, is reclaiming his own identity. It could be argued that theft of identity is more that just a ruse. It acts as a representation on a metaphysical level of the process of theft itself. Theft of goods parallels theft of identity, recapture of identity parallels recapture of property.

The importance of this discourse of identity can be documented by its appearance in other anecdotes. We see it operating, for example, in the Tanūkhian anecdote with the poet Diʿbil. After the highway robber recites the verse by Diʿbil, the poet identifies himself. It is only after the poet convinces the thief of his identity that the goods are returned to him. A continuum has been sketched between physical property and identity. The poet recovers his property but he also recovers ownership of his verse of poetry. And, while this is a kind of property, what a poet writes is also something he creates from himself, a reflection if not of his total personality at least of his existence as a poet. Finally, the poet also establishes his full identity as Diʿbil.

A similar phenomenon exists in the anecdote in which the thief who has entered clandestinely proceeds to eat with the husband and wife. This story involved an elaborate hand game in which the thief's hand was grabbed in turn by the husband and the wife and he, in order to extricate himelf, would grab the other spouse's hand. In that case also, the thief, by grabbing the hand of first the wife and then the husband, was identifying himself with each of the parties who were the victims of the theft. They each think that his hand is their spouse's. It is the confusion in identity which permits his own identity as thief to remain hidden, and allows him to consume the food along with the couple.

The usurpation of identity is, of course, not a phenomenon limited to thief anecdotes. The hero of the *Maqāmāt* of al-Hamadhānī, Abū al-Fatḥ al-Iskandarī, for example, regularly takes on other roles and disguises himself. In fact, the uncovering of his identity by the narrator is usually the dramatic highpoint of the *maqāma*.

But there is an aspect to the discourse of identity which, rather than relating the thief anecdotes to their *adab* cousins, distinguishes them. The discourse of identity acts as an extreme case of the paradigmatic relationship, observed above, between thief and potential victim. Theft of identity is, after all, the ultimate demonstration of a paradigmatic relationship. This implied equivalence between thief and victim, is, in fact, unique to thief anecdotes in the *adab* corpus. Neither rulers nor physicians nor *ṭufaylīs* nor women display this phenomenon. What then is its function in thief anecdotes? As we have already observed, it contributes to the legimitization of the actions of the thieves themselves. It allows them to take their place within the essentially positive literary categories of classical Arabic tricksters. Other categories either cannot achieve this or do not need the same aid. *Bukhalāʾ*, or misers, for example, employ many stratagems and clever arguments. But their actions are essentially reprehensible and they, therefore, are never really counted as tricksters. They do not appear in *adhkiyāʾ* works and when they are presented, it is generally in a manner that makes their moral condemnation clear.[36] *Ṭufaylīs*, however, despite certain similarities in some of their actions, are on the other side of the moral divide. Though they do violate certain rules of propriety and enter by deceit where they are not invited, the high value placed on hospitality by classical Arabic culture makes it impossible for their acts to be seen as essentially negative.[37] Similarly, when physicians or rulers display their cleverness, they do so in the normal and morally legitimate exercise of their professional functions.[38]

Among the Arabic tricksters, it is only the thieves whose activities are by definition illegal. Hence, it becomes necessary to dilute, if not dissolve, this moral reprobation by blurring the distinction between them and their victims. Only in this way can these literary thieves enter the pantheon of classical Arabic trickster heroes.

---

[36] Malti-Douglas, *Structures of Avarice*.
[37] Malti-Douglas, "Structure and Organization".
[38] See, for example, Ibn al-Jawzī, *Adhkiyā'*, 178-187, 38-49, 53-66.

X

YŪSUF IBN 'ABD AL-HĀDĪ AND HIS AUTOGRAPH OF THE *WUQŪ' AL-BALĀ' BIL-BUKHL WAL-BUKHALĀ'* *

Yūsuf ibn 'Abd al-Hādī ibn al-Mibrad (d. 909/1503) was a prolific Ḥanbalī author who left a rich collection of autograph manuscripts, many of which can be found presently in the Ẓāhiriyya Library in Damascus. Among these manuscripts is one devoted to the *Bukhalā'*, which, along with its author, will form the subject of this study.

Sources.

Extensive notices on the life and works of the author can be found in:

1) Al-Ghazzī (d. 1061/1651), *al-Kawākib as-Sā'ira bi-A'yān al-Mi'a al-'Āshira* (1).
2) Ibn al-'Imād (d. 1089/1679), *Shadharāt adh-Dhahab fī Akhbār man Dhahab* (2).
3) Ash-Shaṭṭī, *Mukhtaṣar Ṭabaqāt al-Ḥanābila* (3).

Useful information, however, has also been gleaned from:

1) As-Sakhāwī (d. 902/1497), *aḍ-Ḍaw' al-Lāmi' li-Ahl al-Qarn at-Tāsi'* (4).
2) An-Nu'aymī (d. 927/1521), *ad-Dāris fī Ta'rīkh al-Madāris* (5).
3) Muḥammad ibn Ṭūlūn (d. 953/1546), *Mufākahat al-Khillān fī Ḥawādith az-Zamān* (6).
4) Muḥammad ibn Ṭūlūn (d. 953/1546), *al-Qalā'id al-Jawhariyya fī Ta'rīkh aṣ-Ṣāliḥiyya* (7).

* I would like to thank Prof. George Makdisi for his advice, Profs. André Raymond and Thierry Bianquis of the Institut Français de Damas for their hospitality, and Drs. 'Alī Ṣandūq and Mājid adh-Dhahabī of the Majma' al-Lugha al-'Arabiyya in Damascus for their assistance and cooperation.

(1) Al-Ghazzī, *al-Kawākib as-Sā'ira bi-A'yān al-Mi'a al-'Āshira*, ed. J.S. Jabbour (Beirut, 1945), v. I, p. 316.

(2) Ibn al-'Imād, *Shadharāt adh-Dhahab fī Akhbār man Dhahab* (Beirut, n.d.), v. VIII, p. 43.

(3) Ash-Shaṭṭī, *Mukhtaṣar Ṭabaqāt al-Ḥanābila* (Damascus, 1969), pp. 74-77.

(4) As-Sakhāwī, *aḍ-Ḍaw' al-Lāmi' li-Ahl al-Qarn at-Tāsi'* (Beirut, n.d.), v. X, p. 308.

(5) An-Nu'aymī, *ad-Dāris fī Ta'rīkh al-Madāris*, ed. Ja'far al-Ḥasanī (Damascus, 1948-1951).

(6) Ibn Ṭūlūn, *Mufākahat al-Khillān fī Ḥawādith az-Zamān*, ed. Muḥammad Muṣṭafā (Cairo, 1962-1964).

(7) Ibn Ṭūlūn, *al-Qalā'id al-Jawhariyya fī Ta'rīkh aṣ-Ṣāliḥiyya*, ed. Muḥammad Aḥmad Dahmān (Damascus, 1949).

5) Muḥammad ibn Ṭūlūn (d. 953/1546), *al-Fulk al-Mashḥūn fī Aḥwāl Muḥammad ibn Ṭūlūn* (1).
6) Ismā'īl Bāshā al-Baghdādī (d. 1339/1920), *Hadiyyat al-'Ārifīn* (2).

Of the modern studies dealing with Yūsuf ibn 'Abd al-Hādī, the most extensive is that by Muḥammad As'ad Ṭalas in his edition of the *Thimār al-Maqāṣid fī Dhikr al-Masājid* (3).

ONOMASTICS.

The first difficulty which one encounters in the study of this author is his very name. One may ask, what elements of the name were most commonly used for identification in the Medieval period? Is there a *shuhra* (most common name or preferred name)? The fullest onomastic chain is presented by ash-Shaṭṭī: Yūsuf ibn Ḥasan ibn Aḥmad ibn Ḥasan ibn Aḥmad ibn 'Abd al-Hādī ibn 'Abd al-Ḥamīd ibn 'Abd al-Hādī ibn Yūsuf ibn Muḥammad ibn Qudāma Jamāl ad-Dīn Abū al-Maḥāsin (4). Ibn al-'Imād, al-Ghazzī and ash-Shaṭṭī note, however, that he was known as Ibn al-Mibrad (*ash-shahīr bibn al-Mibrad*) (5), the latter author adding that this was the nickname (*laqab*) of his grandfather. In the *Hadiyya*, we have yet another possibility, for we are told that he was known as (*al-ma'rūf bi*) Ibn 'Abd al-Hādī (6). This appellation, according to as-Sakhāwī in his notice on our author's grandfather, is how the latter was known (7). It is in his notice on Yūsuf ibn 'Abd al-Hādī's father that the author of *aḍ-Ḍaw'* mentions that the father was known both as Ibn 'Abd al-Hādī and as Ibn al-Mibrad (8). Thus, both name elements "Ibn 'Abd al-Hādī" and "Ibn al-Mibrad" were present in the family of our author, though ash-Shaṭṭī's assertion that "Ibn al-Mibrad" was the *laqab* of his grandfather would seem less convincing given the evidence in *aḍ-Ḍaw'*. It would seem, therefore, that both "Ibn 'Abd al-Hādī" and "Ibn al-Mibrad" are possible *shuhras* for our author, the latter perhaps more likely given its presence and predominance in the earlier sources. Nevertheless, the fact that both name elements were inherited, and not original with the personage himself, may well have created a situation in which they could be used interchangeably.

Perhaps it is not in the strictly biographical domain that we may be able to document how our author might have been known in the Medieval period. Ibn Ṭūlūn in his *Mufākaha* and an-Nu'aymī in his *ad-Dāris* quote extensively from the Ḥanbalī writer. Ibn Ṭūlūn names him either Jamāl ad-Dīn ibn al-Mibrad (9) or Jamāl ad-Dīn ibn 'Abd al-Hādī (10). An-Nu'aymī calls him variously by a full version of the name, Jamāl ad-Dīn Abū al-Maḥāsin

(1) IBN ṬŪLŪN, "al-Fulk al-Mashḥūn fī Aḥwāl Muḥammad ibn Ṭūlūn", in *Rasā'il Ta'rīkhiyya* (Damascus, 1930).

(2) ISMĀ'ĪL BĀSHĀ AL-BAGHDĀDĪ, *Hadiyyat al-'Ārifīn* (Istanbul, 1955), v. II, pp. 560-562.

(3) MUḤAMMAD A. ṬALAS, "Introduction", to Yūsuf ibn 'Abd al-Hādī, *Thimār al-Maqāṣid fī Dhikr al-Masājid* (Beirut, 1943), pp. 9-19.

(4) ASH-SHAṬṬĪ, *Mukhtaṣar*, p. 74.

(5) ASH-SHAṬṬĪ, *Mukhtaṣar*, p. 75; IBN AL-'IMĀD, *Shadharāt*, v. VIII, p. 43; AL-GHAZZĪ, *Kawākib*, v. I, p. 316; cf. ṬALAS, "Introduction", p. 11.

(6) AL-BAGHDĀDĪ, *Hadiyya*, v. II, p. 560.

(7) AS-SAKHĀWĪ, *Ḍaw'*, v. I, p. 272.

(8) AS-SAKHĀWĪ, *Ḍaw'*, v. III, p. 92.

(9) IBN ṬŪLŪN, *Mufākaha*, v. I, pp. 168, 181.

(10) IBN ṬŪLŪN, *Mufākaha*, v. I, p. 216.

Yūsuf ibn Ḥasan ibn Aḥmad ibn ʿAbd al-Hādī (1), or a shortened version thereof, be it Jamāl ad-Dīn ibn ʿAbd al-Hādī (2), al-Jamāl ibn al-Mibrad (3), or al-Jamāl ibn ʿAbd al-Hādī (4). Al-Jamāl is, of course, an abbreviated form for Jamāl ad-Dīn. Here, we find the *laqab* Jamāl ad-Dīn (or its abbreviated form al-Jamāl) combined indifferently with either Ibn al-Mibrad or Ibn ʿAbd al-Hādī. We can assume that the *dīn* name was employed in order to distinguish our author from his father and grandfather (5). Yet the same effect could have been produced by using the *ism* Yūsuf. Similarly, when Muḥammad ibn Ṭūlūn refers to his teacher in his autobiography, he most commonly combines a form of the *dīn* name with Ibn al-Mibrad. There is one citation, however, of the formula al-Muḥaddith Jamāl ad-Dīn Yūsuf ibn ʿAbd al-Hādī (6). This raises an interesting problem since one formula which we did not find above is Yūsuf ibn ʿAbd al-Hādī. This, however, is the name most commonly chosen by modern scholars, both Arab and non-Arab (7). One could argue, however, that there is a reason for this, and that is that the author himself has written the name Yūsuf ibn ʿAbd al-Hādī twice on the title page of the autograph manuscript. Perhaps one should distinguish between, on the one hand, the name a personage might employ when speaking about himself, as in this case on the title page, and, on the other hand, the name which others might use when making reference to that personage. In other words, while the signified remained the same, the signifier would vary according to the position of the speaker or the context of the speech. This particular personage when speaking about himself used his *ism* along with some form of a *laqab* while the others, when making reference to him, tend to use his *dīn* name in lieu of the *ism*. There is, however, the further example of the title of Ibn Ṭūlūn's biography of our author (discussed below) in which he is referred to as Yūsuf ibn ʿAbd al-Hādī. Perhaps, its use in a title required the same formal usage as the signature of a manuscript. All of these examples, nevertheless, show a paradigmatic relationship between the *ism* and the *dīn* name (8). Further, since it is the *ism* Yūsuf along with ibn ʿAbd al-Hādī which appears on the author's work, it is this combination which has achieved predominance in the modern works. Therefore, in effect, a modern *shuhra* has grown up alongside the classical one, obliging a scholar, if he wishes to be quickly understood, to make reference to this name.

Our onomastic problems do not, however, stop here. The vocalization of Ibn al-Mibrad is also open to question. Among the many morphologically possible variations, three have been employed by modern writers: Mubarrad, Mabrad and Mibrad. Ḥabīb Zayyāt,

(1) AN-NUʿAYMĪ, *Dāris*, v. I, p. 55.

(2) AN-NUʿAYMĪ, *Dāris*, v. II, p. 111.

(3) AN-NUʿAYMĪ, *Dāris*, v. I, p. 502, v. II, p. 64.

(4) AN-NUʿAYMĪ, *Dāris*, v. II, p. 109.

(5) AS-SAKHĀWĪ, *Ḍaw'*, v. I, p. 272, v. III, p. 92.

(6) IBN ṬŪLŪN, "Fulk", pp. 6, 14, 15, 18.

(7) The *Encyclopaedia of Islam* has chosen to place its article under Yūsuf b. ʿAbd al-Hādī. See, "Ibn ʿAbd al-Hādī", *EI²*, p. 674. ṢALĀḤ AD-DĪN AL-MUNAJJID in "Kitāb Ādāb al-Ḥammām wa-Aḥkāmihi", *al-Mashriq*, XLI (1947), p. 423, has also chosen Yūsuf ibn ʿAbd al-Hādī. On the other hand, AZ-ZIRIKLĪ, *al-Aʿlām, Qāmūs Tarājim* (Cairo, 1957), v. IX, p. 299 has preferred Ibn al-Mibrad. The editor of AN-NUʿAYMĪ, *Dāris*, v. I, p. 55 also states that Yūsuf ibn ʿAbd al-Hādī was known as (*al-maʿrūf bi*) Ibn al-Mibrad.

(8) The significance of this relationship will be explored in a forthcoming study.

in his discussion of the *Kitāb aṭ-Ṭibākha* in *al-Mashriq*, has doubled the "r", giving, thus, Ibn al-Mubarrad (1). This particular reading could be justified onomastically. One of the great experts in the Arabic language during the Medieval period was al-Mubarrad (d. 285/898), the author of *al-Kāmil* (2). The reading Mibrad has been chosen by the editors of the *Shadharāt* and *ad-Dāris* as well as by az-Ziriklī (3). Mabrad, on the other hand, has been chosen by Brockelmann and the editor of the *Mufākaha* (4). This is also the reading preferred by Ṭalas, who justifies his choice by referring both to Brockelmann and to the editor of the *Shadharāt* (5). This last reference, however, is incorrect since, as was shown above, the editor of the *Shadharāt* in fact read the name as Mibrad (*bil-kasr*). Thus, this last reading seems slightly more common than Mabrad. In addition, though Mibrad could also be more easily explained as meaning "file", this is a dangerous procedure with regard to Medieval Arabic names. Moreover, I have been unable to locate examples of either Mibrad or Mabrad in the specialized classical Arabic onomastic sources. Therefore, though Mibrad is used in this study, the matter must be considered as far from certain.

BIOGRAPHY.

Yūsuf ibn 'Abd al-Hādī was born on the first day of Muḥarram (6) in Damascus (7), according to Ibn al-'Imād and al-Ghazzī in the year 840/1436 (8), according to ash-Shaṭṭī in the year 841 (9), and according to as-Sakhāwī, in the year "forty and some" (10). As Ṭalas rightly points out, the date which is most likely to be correct is that given by Yūsuf ibn 'Abd al-Hādī's contemporary, as-Sakhāwī (11).

Our author stemmed from an important family. His lineage, according to ash-Shaṭṭī, can be traced back to Sālim, the son of 'Umar ibn al-Khaṭṭāb (12). His own career as a teacher and legist (13) had precedents within the family. Yūsuf's grandfather taught and transmitted *ḥadīths* (14), while his father was a judge (15). His brother, Aḥmad, was also a leading personality in *fiqh*, *ḥadīth* and *adab* (16). In fact, Yūsuf composed a biography in five folios (17) of his brother, entitled "Ta'rīf al-Ghādī bi-Ba'ḍ Faḍā'il Aḥmad ibn 'Abd al-Hādī" (18).

(1) ḤABĪB ZAYYĀT, "Kitāb aṭ-Ṭibākha", *al-Mashriq*, XXXV (1937), p. 370.

(2) C. BROCKELMANN, "Al-Mubarrad", *EI*¹, pp. 623-624.

(3) IBN AL-'IMĀD, *Shadharāt*, v. VIII, p. 43; AN-NU'AYMĪ, *Dāris*, v. I, p. 55; AZ-ZIRIKLĪ, *A'lām*, v. IX, p. 299.

(4) *GAL* Sup. II: 130; IBN ṬŪLŪN, *Mufākaha*, v. I, p. 168.

(5) ṬALAS, "Introduction", p. 11.

(6) ASH-SHAṬṬĪ, *Mukhtaṣar*, p. 75.

(7) AS-SAKHĀWĪ, *Ḍaw'*, v. X, p. 308; ASH-SHAṬṬĪ, *Mukhtaṣar*, p. 75.

(8) IBN AL-'IMĀD, *Shadharāt*, v. VIII, p. 43; AL-GHAZZĪ, *Kawākib*, v. I, p. 316.

(9) ASH-SHAṬṬĪ, *Mukhtaṣar*, p. 75.

(10) AS-SAKHĀWĪ, *Ḍaw'*, v. X, p. 308.

(11) ṬALAS, "Introduction", p. 11.

(12) ASH-SHAṬṬĪ, *Mukhtaṣar*, p. 74.

(13) See, for example, ASH-SHAṬṬĪ, *Mukhtaṣar*, p. 75.

(14) AS-SAKHĀWĪ, *Ḍaw'*, v. I, pp. 272-273.

(15) AS-SAKHĀWĪ, *Ḍaw'*, v. III, p. 92.

(16) ṬALAS, "Introduction", pp. 10-11.

(17) Damascus, Ẓāhiriyya, currently catalogued as Adab 45.

(18) AL-BAGHDĀDĪ, *Hadiyya*, v. II, p. 561.

Besides stemming from an illustrious family, our author studied with some of the more distinguished men of his day. His teachers, with a few exceptions which will be noted, are listed by Ibn al-ʻImād, al-Ghazzī and ash-Shaṭṭī (1). For the sake of convenience, the teachers have been arranged by groups dependent either on the subject they taught our author or on the type of intellectual contribution they might have made to him. In a few cases, however, the identification of the teachers has been rendered uncertain (or impossible) by the paucity of onomastic data presented by the biographers.

1. The *Qur'ān*:
   - ash-Shaykh Aḥmad al-Miṣrī al-Ḥanbalī: perhaps al-Qāḍī Shihāb ad-Dīn al-Miṣrī who died in 919/1513 (2);
   - ash-Shaykh Muḥammad al-ʻAskarī: a teacher of Qur'ānic recitation who taught in al-Madrasa al-ʻUmariyya (3);
   - ash-Shaykh ʻUmar al-ʻAskarī: a teacher of Qur'ānic recitation who also taught in al-Madrasa al-ʻUmariyya (4);
   - ash-Shaykh Zayn al-Ḥabbāl: this is probably the same as Zayn ad-Dīn ibn al-Ḥabbāl, a Qur'ānic scholar in al-Madrasa al-ʻUmariyya, cited by Ibn Ṭūlūn in his *Qalā'id*, where in one instance he is quoting from our author "al-Jamāl ibn al-Mibrad" (5).

It is at this juncture in the biographical notice that all of the sources add that Yūsuf prayed with the *Qur'ān* three times (*ṣallā bil-qur'ān thalāth marrāt*) (6).

2. *Al-Muqniʻ*, a book of Ḥanbalī law (7):
   - ash-Shaykh Taqī ad-Dīn al-Jarrāʻī: a student of Ibn Mufliḥ's (8) who taught on Saturdays in al-Madrasa al-ʻUmariyya (9);
   - ash-Shaykh Taqī ad-Dīn ibn Qundus: a *muḥaddith*, teacher and author who died in 861/1456 (10);
   - al-Qāḍī ʻAlā' ad-Dīn al-Mardāwī: a leading Ḥanbalī who died in 885/1480-1 (11).

   He also taught in al-Madrasa al-ʻUmariyya, but on Mondays and Thursdays (12).

(1) Ibn al-ʻImād, *Shadharāt*, v. VIII, p. 43; al-Ghazzī, *Kawākib*, v. I, p. 316; ash-Shaṭṭī, *Mukhtaṣar*, p. 75. Most of these teachers are listed but not identified by Ṭalas, "Introduction", p. 13.

(2) See, ash-Shaṭṭī, *Mukhtaṣar*, pp. 79-80. Al-Ghazzī, *Kawākib*, v. I, p. 316 has Aḥmad aṣ-Ṣafadī al-Ḥanbalī which is probably an error.

(3) Ibn Ṭūlūn, *Qalā'id*, p. 176. Ash-Shaṭṭī does not include him in his list of teachers.

(4) Ibn Ṭūlūn, *Qalā'id*, p. 176. Ash-Shaṭṭī does not include him in his list of teachers.

(5) Ibn Ṭūlūn, *Qalā'id*, p. 175 and pp. 176-177. He is only mentioned by al-Ghazzī.

(6) Ibn al-ʻImād, *Shadharāt*, v. VIII, p. 43; ash-Shaṭṭī, *Mukhtaṣar*, p. 75; al-Ghazzī, *Kawākib*, v. I, p. 316. I have not been able to ascertain precisely what this signifies.

(7) *GAL* I: 398.

(8) An-Nuʻaymī, *Dāris*, v. II, p. 59.

(9) Ibn Ṭūlūn, *Qalā'id*, p. 173.

(10) Ibn Ṭūlūn, *Qalā'id*, pp. 285-286.

(11) H. Laoust, "Ḥanābila", *EI*², p. 162.

(12) Ibn Ṭūlūn, *Qalā'id*, p. 173.

3. Various studies (*durūs*):
   — al-Qāḍī Burhān ad-Dīn ibn Mufliḥ: a leading Ḥanbalī author, teacher and scholar who died in 884/1479 (1);
   — ash-Shaykh Burhān ad-Dīn az-Zar'ī: this is most likely Ibrāhīm Burhān ad-Dīn az-Zar'ī ad-Dimashqī ash-Shāfi'ī, a *faqih* who died before 882/1477-8 (2).

4. Reception of *ḥadīths* from the companions of:
   — Ibn Ḥajar al-'Asqalānī: the famous scholar who died in 852/1448 (3);
   — Ibn al-'Irāqī: Walī ad-Dīn, was a *ḥāfiẓ* and author who died in 826/1423 (4);
   — Ibn al-Bālisī. Given the paucity of information, it is difficult to know which member of the Bālisī family is intended here (5);
   — al-Jamāl ibn al-Ḥarastānī: 'Abd aṣ-Ṣamad, was a Shāfi'ī jurist who died in 614/1218 (6);
   — aṣ-Ṣalāḥ ibn Abī 'Umar: Muḥammad ibn Aḥmad ibn Abī al-Ḥasan was an *imām* in al-Madrasa al-'Umariyya, founded by his grandfather. He died in 781/1379 (7);
   — Ibn Nāṣir ad-Dīn: Shams ad-Dīn Muḥammad was a *ḥāfiẓ* and leading *muḥaddith* in the Damascus area. He was also a prolific writer; he died in 842/1438 (8).

5. Reception of *ijāzas* from Egypt (9):
   — Ibn Ḥajar al-'Asqalānī;
   — ash-Shihāb al-Ḥijāzī: this is possibly Aḥmad ash-Shihāb al-Ḥijāzī, a resident of Old Cairo, who died in 893/1488 (10);
   — al-Burhān al-Ba'lī: this is most likely Ibrāhīm Burhān ad-Dīn al-Ba'lī al-Ḥanbalī who taught jurisprudence. He died in 844/1441 (11).

Aside from the foregoing teachers listed by the three most important biographers, there are three *shaykhas* (female *shaykhs*) who are not to be found in the three major sources but who must be mentioned nevertheless. As-Sakhāwī, in his extremely brief notice on Yūsuf, notes that he received the right to cite forty traditions on the authority of Khadīja bint 'Abd al-Karīm (12). This fact is also mentioned by the biographer in his notice on Khadīja. She herself was a *ḥadīth* transmitter and teacher who died either in 896/1491 or before (13).

(1) AN-NU'AYMĪ, *Dāris*, v. II, pp. 59-61; IBN ṬŪLŪN, *Qalā'id*, pp. 99-101; IBN AL-'IMĀD, *Shadharāt*, v. VII, pp. 338-339; G. MAKDISI, "Ibn Mufliḥ", *EI*², pp. 882-883.

(2) AS-SAKHĀWĪ, *Ḍaw'*, v. I, pp. 185-186, where it is said that he died before his son by a few years. The son, Aḥmad, died in 882. For his biography see, AS-SAKHĀWĪ, *Ḍaw'*, v. I, p. 208.

(3) F. ROSENTHAL, "Ibn Ḥadjar al-'Asḳalānī," *EI*², pp. 776-778.

(4) AS-SUYŪṬĪ, *Ṭabaqāt al-Ḥuffāẓ*, ed. 'Alī Muḥammad 'Umar (Cairo, 1973), p. 543.

(5) On the important Bālisī family, see IBN ṬŪLŪN, *Qalā'id*, pp. 198-199. The reference is not in ash-Shaṭṭī.

(6) AN-NU'AYMĪ, *Dāris*, v. I, pp. 389-392.

(7) IBN ṬŪLŪN, *Qalā'id*, p. 177. Ash-Shaṭṭī does not include him among the teachers.

(8) AS-SUYŪṬĪ, *Ḥuffāẓ*, p. 545; AS-SAKHĀWĪ, *Ḍaw'*, v. VIII, pp. 103-106.

(9) This particular category is only cited by ash-Shaṭṭī.

(10) AS-SAKHĀWĪ, *Ḍaw'*, v. II, p. 256

(11) AS-SAKHĀWĪ, *Ḍaw'*, v. I, p. 184.

(12) AS-SAKHĀWĪ, *Ḍaw'*, v. X, p. 308.

(13) AS-SAKHĀWĪ, *Ḍaw'*, v. XII, p. 91.

The other two *shaykhas* are not in any of the biographical sources but are listed by Ṭalas who extracted them from reading certificates on certain Ẓāhiriyya manuscripts (1). The first is Fāṭima bint Khalīl al-Ḥarastānī: ad-Dimashqiyya aṣ-Ṣāliḥiyya, the grand-daughter of at-Taqī 'Abd Allāh ibn Khalīl al-Ḥarastānī. She was a transmitter who died after the year 873/1468-9 (2). The second is al-Aṣīla Asmā' bint 'Abd Allāh ibn al-Mir'ātī. She also was a transmitter who flourished in the ninth century (3). Scholarly intercourse, and especially the reception of *ijāzas*, of this sort with learned women was common at the time (4).

Furthermore, there are two teachers who are not in any of the biographical sources, classical or modern. The two have been gleaned from quotations of our author, cited in Ibn Ṭūlūn's *Qalā'id*, and both were involved in Qur'ānic studies in al-Madrasa al-'Umariyya. The first is ash-Shaykh Khalaf who was counted among the *abdāl* (a category of saints) and who taught recitation in the western *khizāna* and the second is ash-Shaykh 'Umar al-Lu'lu'ī who taught in the eastern *khizāna* (5).

Yūsuf ibn 'Abd al-Hādī was known as a Ṣāliḥī (6), or one who lived in aṣ-Ṣāliḥiyya, a city on the outskirts of Damascus. Aṣ-Ṣāliḥiyya was a flourishing town with a marketplace, a mosque and schools, most of whose inhabitants followed the theological doctrines of Aḥmad ibn Ḥanbal (7). In fact, Yūsuf was one of the leading jurists of the Ḥanbalī school (8). He taught in al-Madrasa al-'Umariyya, in aṣ-Ṣāliḥiyya, first only on Tuesdays, but later took over on Mondays and Thursdays as well (9). Perhaps one of his most famous students was Shams ad-Dīn Muḥammad ibn Ṭūlūn (10), himself a prolific writer and scholar (11). He, in fact, composed a biography of his teacher entitled, "al-Hādī ilā Tarjamat Yūsuf ibn 'Abd al-Hādī" (12), which, unfortunately, is not extant (13).

Yūsuf ibn 'Abd al-Hādī died on Monday, the 16th of Muḥarram, in the year 909/1503 (14), in Damascus (15), and was buried in the famous cemetery at the foot of

(1) Ṭalas, "Introduction", p. 13.

(2) As-Sakhāwī, *Ḍaw'*, v. XII, p. 91.

(3) Ṭalas, "Introduction", p. 13.

(4) See A. A. al-Muhanna, "The Literary Conflict of the Fifteenth Century and the Role of Al-Sakhawi", *Faculty of Arts and Education Bulletin, University of Kuwait*, VII (1975), p. 6.

(5) Ibn Ṭūlūn, *Qalā'id*, p. 175; J.S. Trimingham, *The Sufi Orders in Islam* (London, 1971), pp. 164-165.

(6) al-Ghazzī, *Kawākib*, v. I, p. 316; ash-Shaṭṭī, *Mukhtaṣar*, p. 75; Ibn al-'Imād, *Shadharāt*, v. VIII, p. 43; as-Sakhāwī, *Ḍaw'*, v. X, p. 308.

(7) Muḥammad Aḥmad Dahman, "Introduction", to Ibn Ṭūlūn, *Qalā'id*, pp. 3-5.

(8) As-Sakhāwī, *Ḍaw'*, v. X, p. 308; az-Ziriklī, *A'lām*, v. IX, p. 299.

(9) Ibn Ṭūlūn, *Qalā'id*, p. 173. For this important *madrasa*, see Ibn Ṭūlūn, *Qalā'id*, pp. 165-183.

(10) Ibn al-'Imād, *Shadharāt*, v. VIII, p. 43; al-Ghazzī, *Kawākib*, v. I, p. 316; ash-Shaṭṭī, *Mukhtaṣar*, p. 75.

(11) W. M. Brinner, "Ibn Ṭūlūn", *EI*², pp. 957-958.

(12) Ash-Shaṭṭī, *Mukhtaṣar*, p. 75. Al-Ghazzī, *Kawākib*, v. I, p. 316 and Ibn al-'Imād, *Shadharāt*, v. VIII, p. 43 only mention that Ibn Ṭūlūn wrote a biography, but they do not give its title.

(13) Ṭalas, attempted to locate this work but was unsuccessful, see, Ṭalas, "Introduction", p. 14.

(14) Ibn al-'Imād, *Shadharāt*, v. VIII, p. 43; al-Ghazzī, *Kawākib*, v. I, p. 316; ash-Shaṭṭī, *Mukhtaṣar*, p. 77. An-Nu'aymī, *Dāris*, v. I, p. 502 gives an alternate date of 878 and al-Baghdādī, *Hadiyya*, v. II, p. 560 gives 880.

(15) Zayyāt, "Kitāb aṭ-Ṭibākha", p. 370.

the Qāsiyūn mountain on the outskirts of Damascus (1). He had given all of his books as a *waqf* to al-Madrasa al-'Umariyya (2).

Our author was, according to the sources, an extremely learned man (*'allāma*) (3). Though he was most knowledgeable in *ḥadīth* and *fiqh*, he also displayed an intellectual interest in questions of grammar, mysticism, Qur'ānic commentary (4) as well as in matters related to rhetoric (5). In addition, he appears to have taken a considerable interest in medical questions as evidenced by the fact that he wrote many works on medically related problems (6). Nonetheless, no mention of this interest is made in the primary sources whether biographical or not. Perhaps, the biographers were most concerned with painting Yūsuf as a *faqīh* and *muḥaddith* who was learned in the religious sciences and *adab*.

According to ash-Shaṭṭī, Yūsuf ibn 'Abd al-Hādī wrote more than four hundred works, the majority of which concerned the science of *ḥadīth* and related issues (7). Al-Baghdādī and ash-Shaṭṭī present the most extensive lists of these works (8). Ṭalas examined all of the author's extant works preserved in the Ẓāhiriyya Library, numbering over fifty, and has presented them in his introduction to the *Thimār* (9). He divides them into six categories including *fiqh, ḥadīth, adab* and medicine. His descriptive discussion of the manuscripts comprises in many cases the number of folios, the date of completion, a selection of chapter headings and, here and there, a discussion of the contents and the manner of their presentation. In addition, Ṭalas provides, in a note, other titles derived from Brockelmann's *Geschichte* (10). Perhaps one of the more interesting and significant of Yūsuf's compositions is a *fihrist* he compiled of the works in his own library (11). This work is fifty-nine folios in length (12). The manuscript contains around six hundred titles, many of which, as Ṭalas points out, are otherwise unknown (13). The importance of this as a document for Medieval sources cannot be denied. The work on the *Bukhalā'* with which we are concerned here is listed by al-Baghdādī (14). In addition, Ibn Ṭūlūn notes (curiously, he seems to be the only source to mention this fact) that Yūsuf ibn 'Abd al-Hādī wrote an autobiographical sketch, though, unfortunately, this does not seem to be extant (15).

(1) Ibn al-'Imād, *Shadharāt*, v. VIII, p. 43; an-Nu'aymī, *Dāris*, v. I, p. 502; ash-Shaṭṭī, *Mukhtaṣar*, p. 77; al-Ghazzī, *Kawākib*, v. I, p. 316.

(2) Ash-Shaṭṭī, *Mukhtaṣar*, p. 77. Others also had given their collections of books to al-Madrasa al-'Umariyya as *waqfs*, nor was Yūsuf's the largest collection there. See, Ibn Ṭūlūn, *Qalā'id*, p. 183.

(3) Ibn al-'Imād, *Shadharāt*, v. III, p. 43; al-Ghazzī, *Kawākib*, v. I, p. 316. See also the long list of almost hagiographical descriptives in ash-Shaṭṭī, *Mukhtaṣar*, p. 75.

(4) Ibn al-'Imād, *Shadharāt*, v. VIII, p. 43; al-Ghazzī, *Kawākib*, v. I, p. 316; ash-Shaṭṭī, *Mukhtaṣar*, p. 75.

(5) Ash-Shaṭṭī, *Mukhtaṣar*, p. 75.

(6) See, for example, ash-Shaṭṭī, *Mukhtaṣar*, p. 76-77.

(7) Ash-Shaṭṭī, *Mukhtaṣar*, p. 75.

(8) Ash-Shaṭṭī, *Mukhtaṣar*, pp. 75-77; al-Baghdādī, *Hadiyya*, pp. 560-562.

(9) Ṭalas, "Introduction", pp. 19-49.

(10) Ṭalas, "Introduction", pp. 49-50.

(11) Damascus, Ẓāhiriyya, Adab 19.

(12) Ṭalas incorrectly describes, it as being 150 pages (*ṣafḥa*), Ṭalas, "Introduction", p. 16.

(13) Ṭalas, "Introduction", p. 16.

(14) Al-Baghdādī, *Hadiyya*, p. 562.

(15) Ibn Ṭūlūn, "Fulk", p. 6.

THE MANUSCRIPT.

As was mentioned earlier, the manuscript on the *Bukhalā'* is an autograph with no other available copies. It is preserved in the Ẓāhiriyya Library, as Adab 40 (1).

Before undertaking a descriptive analysis of the contents and organization of the work, a few comments are in order about the manuscript itself. The fact that it is an autograph can be documented from the title page, which will be discussed below, as well as by the author's handwriting. Yūsuf's unusual and very characteristic script is easily recognizable from a colophon reproduced in a work by Ṣalāḥ ad-Dīn al-Munajjid as well as by two facsimiles reproduced by az-Ziriklī (2). In addition, this manuscript has the appearance of a rough draft or working copy. In many places the writer left large blank spaces on the folios (see Table I). It was common for Medieval Arabic writers to leave similar blanks in their texts so that additional information could be added if necessary. The distribution of blank spaces is not insignificant and will be discussed below. Further, there are many places in the text which have large areas crossed out, a sign that the writer had changed his mind (3).

TABLE I

BLANK AREAS IN THE MANUSCRIPT

3v	bottom	2/3
4v	bottom	1/2
7v	whole	
8r	whole	
8v	bottom	1/2
9r	bottom	1/2
9v	whole	
10r	top	1/2
11r	whole	
11v	bottom	1/3
12r	top	1/3
12r	bottom	1/3
13r	top	1/2
13v	whole	
15r	bottom	1/2

(1) *GAL* Sup. II: 131 and Sup. II: 947; ṬALAS, "Introduction", p. 46.

(2) ṢALĀḤ AD-DĪN AL-MUNAJJID, *al-Kitāb al-'Arabī al-Makhṭūṭ* (Cairo, 1960), v. I, plate 58; AZ-ZIRIKLĪ, *A'lām*, v. IX, plates 1485, 1486.

(3) On leaving spaces and reworking manuscripts generally, see FRANZ ROSENTHAL, *The Technique and Approach of Muslim Scholarship* (Rome, 1947), p. 30. See also, G. MAKDISI, "Ibn Taimīya's Autograph Manuscript on *Istiḥsān*", in G. MAKDISI, ed., *Arabic and Islamic Studies in Honor of Hamilton A.R. Gibb* (Cambridge, 1965), p. 451; AḤMED ZÉKI PACHA, *Dictionnaire biographique des aveugles illustres de l'Orient* (Cairo, 1911), p. 16.

TABLE I (cont.)

15v	top	1/3	
16r	bottom	1/2	
17r	bottom	1/3	
17v	top	1/2	(after chapter heading)
20v	bottom	1/3	
21v	top	1/2	
22r	bottom	1/3	
26r	bottom	1/2	
27r	whole		
27v	bottom	1/2	
28r	bottom	1/2	
28v	bottom	1/3	
29r	bottom	1/2	
29v	bottom	2/3	
30r	bottom	1/2	
30v	top	1/3	
30v	bottom	1/3	
31r	bottom	1/2	
31v	bottom	1/3	
32r	bottom	2/3	
32v	bottom	1/3	
33r	bottom	1/2	
34r	bottom	1/2	
34v	bottom	1/2	
35v	whole		
36r	whole		
36v	bottom	1/2	
37r	bottom	1/2	
37v	bottom	1/2	
38v	bottom	3/4	
39r	bottom	2/3	
39v	bottom	1/2	
42v	bottom	1/4	
43r	whole		
46r	whole		
53v	bottom	1/2	
56r	bottom	1/2	
56v	whole		
57r	whole		

TABLE I (cont.)

59v	bottom	1/3
61v	bottom	1/3
62r	whole	
62v	bottom	1/2
71v	whole	
72r	whole	
72v	whole	
75v	whole	
78r	bottom	1/2
83v	whole	(except for two lines)
85v	bottom	1/3
94r	bottom	2/3
94v	whole	
95r	bottom	1/4
95v	whole	
96v	bottom	1/2
100v	bottom	1/4
101v	bottom	1/4
106r	bottom	2/3
109r	bottom	1/3
110r	bottom	2/3
110v	whole	

Another difficulty which must be mentioned is the handwriting. Ash-Shaṭṭī notes that Yūsuf ibn 'Abd al-Hādī not only wrote a great deal but also wrote it quickly. He adds that few are those who are capable of reading his writing because of his way of linking letters as well as his habit of eliminating diacritical marks (1). It would appear, however, that these problems are exacerbated in the case of the *Bukhalā'* manuscript for various reasons which will be discussed presently. Ṭalas, though he examined many of Yūsuf's autographs, noted in the case of the *Bukhalā'* that the handwriting was difficult to decipher (2). This is probably due not only to the handwriting peculiarities just noted but also to the fact that the actual physical state of the manuscript is, to say the least, lamentable. The difficulties presented by the handwriting and the crossings-out are accentuated by the fact that there are many areas which are covered with blotches. These seem to be due to the spilling and splashing of the ink, though they may have been caused partially by later damage to the manuscript. In addition, the pages of the manuscript having been written recto verso, in many cases the writing of one page appears on the reverse side (see Plates II and III). This effect, which may have been due to the seepage of the ink, has resulted in the obliteration

(1) ASH-SHAṬṬĪ, *Mukhtaṣar*, p. 77.

(2) ṬALAS, "Introduction", p. 46.

of certain parts of the text. All of these characteristics, when taken together, in many places turn the manuscript into a puzzle.

The text which we have consists of 112 folios. Of course, as was shown above, many of the folios are not full, but even those which are, differ in the amount of written material they contain. In effect, Yūsuf's writing varies from relatively large characters, which permit approximately fifteen lines per page, to smaller characters permitting up to twenty-two lines per page. In addition, on certain folios, our author also added material by writing around the margins. The folios themselves are numbered from 1 to 112. The ten-page quires (*juz'*, *ajzā'*) (1), except the first, are all labelled in ordinal numbers in the author's handwriting (*thānī*, *thālith*, *rābi'*, etc.). The position of these quire labels agrees in every case with the Arabic numbering on the folios, for example, the second quire begins on folio 11, the third on folio 21, the fourth on 31, up to the eleventh on folio 101. Whoever did this numbering, it obviously reflects the original divisions of the manuscript into quires. Further, there is some evidence that the numbering was done in the author's lifetime since on folio 101 recto, an incorrect numbering is corrected by what is almost surely a stroke from the pen of Yūsuf ibn 'Abd al-Hādī.

In addition, the work appears to be unfinished. Folio 112 recto ends with a complete anecdote but no more (see Plate IV). If this were the conclusion of the work, however, Yūsuf ibn 'Abd al-Hādī would most likely have added a colophon. The possibility that the work was completed and parts of it lost would appear to be effectively countered by the fact that folio 112 is followed by four blank, unnumbered folios bound in with the manuscript. Moreover, this last, twelfth, quire is the only one not to be labelled. Might this not indicate that the author did not label the quire because he intended to finish it at some later time? Further evidence on this matter will be presented below.

Even the title page of this work is not without its problems. The title itself is partially obscured by blotchings as well as by markings showing through from the other side (see Plate I). Perhaps it is due to these factors that Brockelmann proposed two titles for the work, one of which seems to have acquired precedence, though neither one is satisfactory in view of the Arabic itself. Brockelmann at first set down two possibilities for the title: *Wuqū' al-Balā' wal-Bukhl wal-Bukhalā'* and *Wuqū' al-Balā' fī al-Bukhl wal-Bukhalā'* (2). Though he clearly seemed uncertain about which letters were actually there, his second citation of the work is simply *wal-Bukhl* (3). Al-Baghdādī, who cites the work, and Ṭalas, who discusses it, both favored the reading *fī al-Bukhl*. Arguments could be advanced for either interpretation. The problem is two-fold. On the one hand, *wal-Bukhl* does not make much sense given the Arabic grammatical construction with *Wuqū'*, whereas *fī* does. But on the other hand, the element in question does not resemble the examples of *fī* in the text, but is closer to the renditions of *wa*. The one solution which would answer both the grammatical and the orthographic objections is *bi*. In fact, if one glances at the other examples

(1) See, ROSENTHAL, *Technique*, p. 37.
(2) *GAL* Sup. II:131.
(3) *GAL* Sup. II: 947.

of *bil* in the manuscript, it can be seen that their form is the same as that on the title page. There is not, of course, a diacritical mark under the *bā'* but this is the rule rather than the exception for our author. Yūsuf does list this work in the above-mentioned *Fihrist* but merely in the shortened form, *Kitāb Wuqū' al-Balā'* (1). Therefore, the title of the work which is proposed here and which seems to be the most correct is *Wuqū' al-Balā' bil-Bukhl wal-Bukhalā'* (The Occurence of Misfortune in *Bukhl* and the *Bukhalā'*).

Below the title, the author attributes the work to himself, Yūsuf ibn 'Abd al-Hādī. Following the title and the author's name, there is a certificate of transmission of the work (see Plate I). It reads:

(line 1)	سمع مواضيع منه من لفظي أولادي عبد الهادي
(line 2)	وعبد الله وحسن وأجزت لهم أن يرووه
(line 3)	عنّي وعنهم لأولادي وكتب
(line 4)	يوسف بن عبد الهادي

My children 'Abd al-Hādī, 'Abd Allāh and Ḥasan heard topics from it in my own wording and I authorized them to transmit it on my authority and on their authority to my children. Written by Yūsuf ibn 'Abd al-Hādī.

The second mention of children in this certificate is probably a reference to the author's other children, including a daughter Fāṭima (2).

There is yet one more piece of information to be found on the title page, written in a different handwriting and having all the diacritical marks. It simply states that Muḥammad ibn Ṭūlūn received ownership of the book from the son of the writer, 'Abd al-Hādī.

THE CHAPTERS.

Before presenting the chapter titles, a few words are in order about certain orthographic problems and questions. The first problem, and one which has been mentioned several times, is the absence of diacritical marks in the text. This, of course, is not just a peculiarity with our author, but something one finds in other autographs (3). What it does, however, is to multiply the possibilities of a reading and there is no need here to set down all of these possibilities for an initial, medial or final consonant. I have not, as would be considered matter of fact in cases like this, indicated the words missing diacritical marks because what Makdisi said concerning Ibn Taymiyya's autograph is applicable to Yūsuf ibn 'Abd al-Hādī's as well: "To do so in the present case would amount to repeating in the apparatus

(1) YŪSUF IBN 'ABD AL-HĀDĪ, *Kitāb Fihrist*, Damascus, Ẓāhiriyya, Adab 19, folio 18 recto.

(2) ṬALAS, "Introduction", p. 12.

(3) See MAKDISI, "Ibn Taimīya", p. 450.

criticus almost every word of the text" (1). One instance where the issue is aggravated is that of the two prepositions *fī* and *min*. Our author has two different ways of writing *fī* and the more common of the two is at times indistinguishable from *min*. The choice of one or the other has often been made on internal syntactic criteria.

Ash-Shaṭṭī's comment about Yūsuf's manner of linkage of consonants needs further explanation in the case of the *Wuqū'*. Not only does our author link consonants within a word which would not normally be linked, such as the *wāw* or the *dāl*, but he links words together where they should clearly not be linked. An excellent example of this can be found on folio 25 recto where the suffix of the perfect third feminine singular is linked to the following word, without, needless to say, any diacritical marks.

The last orthographic convention which must be discussed is related to the *hamza*. The *hamza* is never written, either in its initial, medial or final positions. While this is not unusual for manuscripts, I have, however, included it there where the morphological pattern of the word calls for it. Thus, where in all cases the author has written, for example, البخلا, I have rendered this by البخلاء, and so on.

The chapters themselves are not numbered but are labelled as *bāb* (chapter). I have, however, taken the liberty of numbering them in order to facilitate subsequent discussion.

Following is a list of the chapter titles with their corresponding folios. When at all possible, I have avoided translating the word *bukhl* (or other derivatives of the root *b-kh-l*), an essential concept in the work. Other research has led me to conclude that the available Western translations, such as avarice, stinginess, or miserliness, do not do justice to the precise contours and range of meanings of the Arabic term (2).

(1) Makdisi, "Ibn Taimīya", p. 450.

(2) For a discussion of this problem and the definition of *bukhl*, see, Fedwa Malti-Douglas, "The *Bukhalā'* Work in Medieval Arabic Literature", Ph.D. Dissertation, Los Angeles, 1977, pp. 1-2, 254-262, 280-282. This material will be included in a major study on the *Bukhalā'* currently in preparation.

٢٨. باب ما قيل إنّ الموت أيسر من سؤال بخيل
28. Chapter: What Was Said Concerning the Fact that Death Is Easier than Asking from a *Bakhīl* 30r

٢٩. باب ما قيل إنّ البخل أضرّ شيء
29. Chapter: What Was Said Concerning the Fact that *Bukhl* Is the Most Harmful Thing 30v

٣٠. باب ما قيل إنّ البخيل يكره أن ينيل
30. Chapter: What Was Said Concerning the Fact that the *Bakhīl* Hates to Allow [Someone] to Obtain 31r

٣١. باب ما قيل إنّه لم يبق من اللذّات إلاّ ذمّ البخيل
31. Chapter: What Was Said Concerning the Fact that there Are No Pleasures Remaining except that of Censuring the *Bakhīl* 31v

٣٢. باب ما قيل إنّ البخيل لا غيبة له
32. Chapter: What Was Said Concerning the Fact that the *Bakhīl* Cannot Be Slandered (1) 32r

٣٣. باب ما قيل إنّه لا خير مع البخل
33. Chapter: What Was Said Concerning the Fact that there Is No Good Associated with *Bukhl* 32v

٣٤. باب ما قيل إنّ المذنب السخيّ خير من العابد البخيل وأخفّ على القلوب وأحبّ إلى النفوس
34. Chapter: What Was Said Concerning the Fact that the Generous Sinner Is Better than the Pious *Bakhīl* and Is Lighter on the Hearts of Men (i.e. More Acceptable) and More Beloved to the Souls 33r

٣٥. باب ما قيل [إنّ] النظر إلى البخيل يقسي القلب وإنّ بقاء البخيل كرب على قلوب المؤمنين
35. Chapter: What Was Said Concerning the Fact that Looking at a *Bakhīl* Hardens the Heart and that the Existence of the *Bakhīl* Grieves the Hearts of the Believers 33v

٣٦. باب ما قيل إنّ البخيل باخل بماله جائد بعرضه والجواد جواد بماله باخل بعرضه
36. Chapter: What Was Said Concerning the Fact that the *Bakhīl* Is Stingy (*bākhil*) with His Money, Generous with His Honor, but the Generous Man Is Generous with His Money, Stingy (*bākhil*) with His Honor 34r

(1) This reading, which might appear odd, is borne out by the passage.

٤٦. باب ما قيل في أنّ سؤال الشريف البخيل غاية الذلّ
46. Chapter: What Was Said Concerning the Fact that the Noble Person's Asking for Something from the *Bakhīl* Is the Ultimate Disgrace 40v

٤٧. باب في وصف جماعة من البخلاء
47. Chapter: The Description of a Group of *Bukhalā'* 41r-42v

٤٨. باب فيما وقع من التصحيف للبخلاء من شدّة الوهم
48. Chapter: The Types of Grammatical Errors *Bukhalā'* Make Due to the Strength of Their Self-Deception 42v

٤٩. باب في أخبار جماعة من البخلاء
49. Chapter: Some Stories about a Group of *Bukhalā'* 43v-44v

٥٠. باب قيل إنّ الأصمعيّ كان من البخلاء
50. Chapter: It Was Said that al-Aṣmaʿī (1) Was a *Bakhīl* 45r-45v

٥١. باب وصف عدة من البخلاء
51. Chapter: The Description of a Number of Bukhalā' 46v-47r

٥٢. باب من البخلاء مروان بن أبي حفصة
52. Chapter: Among the *Bukhalā'* Is Marwān Ibn Abī Ḥafṣa (2) 47r-48r

٥٣. باب في وصف عدة من البخلاء
53. Chapter: The Description of a Number of *Bukhalā'* 48v-52r

٥٤. باب يُعدّ من البخلاء زبيدة بن حميد الصيرفيّ
54. Chapter: Zubayda Ibn Ḥumayd aṣ-Ṣayrafī (3) Is Counted Among the *Bukhalā'* 52r-52v

٥٥. باب ما قيل على ألسن قدور البخلاء
55. Chapter: What Was Said by the Tongues of the *Bakhīls'* Cooking Pots 53r-53v

٥٦. باب في ذكر نبذة من أخبار البخلاء وهجوهم
56. Chapter: Mention of Part of the Stories about the *Bukhalā'* and the Lampoons Written against Them 54r-56r

(1) The celebrated philologist who died in 213/828. See, B. Lewin, "Al-Aṣmaʿī", *EI²*, pp. 717-719.

(2) The poet who died in 182/798 or before. See, among others, Ibn al-ʿImād, *Shadharāt*, v. I, p. 301.

(3) An important money-lender who lived in Baṣra. See, Ṭāha al-Ḥājirī, "Notes" to al-Jāḥiẓ, *Kitāb al-Bukhalā'*, ed. Ṭāha al-Ḥājirī (Cairo, 1971), pp. 298-299.

(1) The famous poet who died in 210/825 or 211/826. See, A. Guillaume, "Abū 'l-'Atāhiya", *EI*², pp. 107-108.

(2) The explanation for the presence of the pronominal suffix *hā* seems obscure, though the element is clearly present in the chapter title. It seems particularly odd in view of the fact that it is the only example of its presence, though the formula is a common one in the chapter titles. Perhaps it is the result of a slip of Yūsuf ibn 'Abd al-Hādī's pen. G. Makdisi has suggested to me that this might represent an understood object of the verb "to mention".

٦٥. باب فيمن مدح بخيلاً رجاء العطاء فانعكس عليه مراده ولم يعطه او أعطى نزراً او غير ما أمل فعاد بالذمّ والهجاء

65. Chapter: Concerning He Who Praised a *Bakhil* in Expectation of a Gift but Whose Desire Was Turned Back upon Him or to Whom the *Bakhīl* Did Not Give or Gave Him Little or Other than What He Had Hoped for and Who therefore Responded with Censure and Lampoons 73r-75r

٦٦. باب فيمن استضاف رجلاً فأساء قراه فحمله ذلك على أن ذمّه وهجاه

66. Chapter: Concerning He Who Invited Someone but Was Inhospitable and thus Prompted the Guest to Censure Him and Lampoon Him 76r-78r

٦٧. باب في ذكر نبذة من أخبار البخلاء

67. Chapter: Mention of a Few Stories about the *Bukhalā'* 78v-82v

٦٨. باب وممّن شُهر بالبخل من المتقدّمين أبو الأسود الدؤليّ

68. Chapter: Among the Early Muslims Known for Their *Bukhl* Was Abū al-Aswad ad-Du'alī (1) 82v-83v

٦٩. باب ما ذكر من بخل الحسن بن مخلّد

69. Chapter: What Was Mentioned about the *Bukhl* of al-Ḥasan ibn Mukhallad (2) 84r-85v

٧٠. باب في ذكر جماعة من البخلاء وأخبارهم

70. Chapter: Mention of a Group of *Bukhalā'* and Their Stories 86r-86v

٧١. باب وقد كثر الهجاء بالبخل على الطعام إذ كان من أقبح صفات اللئام

71. Chapter: There Already Exists Much Lampooning of *Bukhl* over Food since It Is One of the Ugliest Characteristics of the Misers *(al-li'ām)* 86v-92r

٧٢. باب المذكورون بأنّهم أبخل الناس

72. Chapter: Those Who Are Mentioned as Being the Most Miserly *(abkhal)* of People 92r-93v

(1) A government official who died in 69/688-9. See, J.W. Fück, "Abū 'l-Aswad al-Du'alī", *EI*², pp. 106-107. For the *nisba* the manuscript has الدئلي which is either an error in the *hamza* chair or a reference to the variant of the nisba, ad-Dīlī. I have corrected it to the more common form. See, as-Sam'ānī, *al-Ansāb* (Hyderabad, 1966), v. V, pp. 405-408.

(2) An 'Abbāsid vizier, see, Ibn 'Abd Rabbihi, *al-'Iqd al-Farīd*, eds. Aḥmad Amīn, Aḥmad az-Zayn and Ibrāhīm al-Abyārī (Cairo, 1965), v. IV, p. 166.

(1) Probably a reference to the city in Persia in the Zagros mountains and not the city of the same name south of Cairo. See, L. Lockhart, "Ḥulwān", *EI²*, pp. 571-572 and J.M.B. Jones, "Ḥulwān", *EI²*, p. 572.

(2) The city in Iraq.

(3) The city in Iraq.

(4) The city in Iraq.

٨٣. باب ما ذُكر في بخل أهل مرو وأهل خراسان

83. Chapter: What Was Mentioned about the *Bukhl* of the People of Merv (1) and the People of Khurāsān 108v-109r

٨٤. باب قال صاحب العقد ومن البخلاء هشام بن عبد الملك

84. Chapter: The Author of *al-'Iqd* (2) Said: Among the *Bukhalā'* Is Hishām Ibn 'Abd al-Malik (3) 109r

٨٥. باب قال صاحب العقد ومن البخلاء عبد الله بن الزبير

85. Chapter: The Author of *al-'Iqd* Said: Among the *Bukhalā'* Is 'Abd Allāh Ibn az-Zubayr (4) 109v

٨٦. باب قال صاحب العقد ومن اكابر البخلاء محمّد بن الجهم

86. Chapter: The Author of *al-'Iqd* Said: Among the Most Important *Bukhalā'* Is Muḥammad Ibn al-Jahm (5) 110r

٨٧. باب قال ابن عبد ربّه

87. Chapter: Ibn 'Abd Rabbihi Said 111r-112r

As can be seen from the above listing of the chapters and their respective folios, most are extremely short. As will be shown, the entire work, with the exception of a passage here and there, was taken from other sources. Nevertheless, the chapter divisions themselves are, for the most part, original. A few of the chapter titles were taken from one of Yūsuf's sources (al-Khaṭīb al-Baghdādī, to be discussed below), but most are original. They, thus, show what Ibn 'Abd al-Hādī considered most important about the material he collected.

SOURCES FOR THE *Wuqū'*.

The delimitation of the author's sources has been a rather complicated process. What is meant here by "source" is neither the ultimate or first authorship of a text nor the last person from whom Yūsuf may have received an *ijāza* to transmit material, but rather the written text or collection from which our author actually drew the texts he copied. This delimitation of sources, thus, permits an examination of the way the author went about the composition of his work. When the source could be identified with a published text, I have merely indicated the citation. In other cases, the material has been described or summarized.

(1) The city in Khurāsān.

(2) This and the following chapters make reference to *al-'Iqd al-Farīd* of Ibn 'Abd Rabbih.

(3) The Umayyad Caliph who died in 125-6/793. See, F. GABRIELI, "Hishām", *EI*², pp. 493-495.

(4) An early claimant to the caliphate who died 73-4/692. See, H.A.R. GIBB, "'Abd Allāh b. al-Zubayr", *EI*², pp. 54-55.

(5) On this governor and theologian who flourished in the 2nd/9th century, and on his reputation, see the very interesting article by GÉRARD LECOMTE, "Muḥammad b. al-Ğahm al-Barmakī", *Arabica*, V (1958), pp. 263-271.

Of course, by far the clearest indication of the provenance of certain of these sections is having the author inform us directly, as he does, for example, when he writes in the chapter title *qāla ṣāḥib al-'Iqd* or *qāla Ibn 'Abd Rabbihi*, clear references to *al-'Iqd al-Farīd* and its author, Ibn 'Abd Rabbihi (d. 327/940). But this, he does in only four of the eighty-seven chapters.

The sources for the remaining eighty-three chapters were derived, when possible, from internal evidence. The actual arrangement of the material within each chapter provided important clues. It should first be pointed out that what we are dealing with are self-contained potentially independent micro-units, be they *ḥadīths*, anecdotes, poetry, etc., which are generally set off one from the other by a chain of transmitters. Given in some instances the narrow scope of the descriptive titles, some of the chapters consist of only one unit.

The first unit of a chapter, assuming for a moment that the entire chapter comes from one source, is preceded by a chain of transmitters which can, for analytical purposes, be divided into two parts. The first would be transmitters from the source of the unit, for example al-Khaṭīb al-Baghdādī, up to Yūsuf ibn 'Abd al-Hādī himself, while the second would be the transmitters of the unit itself from its original creator (e.g., the Prophet in the case of a *ḥadīth*) up to Yūsuf's source. This, however, would be our author's normal procedure only with the first unit of a given chapter. In the second unit, he does not repeat the first part of the chain (i.e., from the source to himself) but simply states: *wa-bihi ilā*, followed by his source. In the case of al-Khaṭīb, for example, he writes, most of the time, *wa-bihi ilā al-Khaṭīb*. This expression is then followed by whatever *isnāds* al-Khaṭīb might have had in his text and the unit. This procedure is followed for however many units the chapter might include. On occasion, no name is given after *wa-bihi*.

If, however, the chapter comes from two different sources, for example al-Khaṭīb al-Baghdādī and al-Bukhārī, then the procedure outlined above will be modified to account for the second source. In this case, whenever the first unit from the second source is presented, it will have the complete two-part *isnād*, one from the source to Yūsuf, another from the unit to the source. But the same procedure will be followed for the subsequent units, for example, *wa-bihi ilā al-Bukhārī*, followed by an *isnād* and a *matn*.

In other words, if the same source is used for more than one unit in any one chapter, it is possible to identify that source by the presence of the formula *wa-bihi ilā*, followed by the repetition of the source. The essential factor would then be the actual break in the chain of transmitters, allowing for the isolation of the source.

The problem arises when a source is only used once. It is then embedded within a long *isnād*, and becomes indistinguishable from any other transmitter in the chain. If all of the *isnāds* going up to our author were the same, then it would be conceivable by close textual comparison to derive the exact level at which a new element appears and then perhaps have a more certain idea of who the source might be. However, the transmitters vary and there are several possible chains, each of which goes up from a given source to Yūsuf ibn 'Abd al-Hādī.

In this manner, it has been possible to establish some of our author's sources with varying degrees of certainty. To be certain of the provenance of a unit, the unit was compared with the source on a word to word basis. There were minor internal variants which will be discussed following the presentation of the sources. By far the most important source for Yūsuf's *Wuqū'* is a work on the same subject, entitled *al-Bukhalā'*, by al-Khaṭīb al-Baghdādī (d. 463/1071) (1). Ibn 'Abd al-Hādī's work follows quite closely and repeats most of the material in al-Khaṭīb's *Bukhalā'* and is, further, in substantially the same order, as can be seen from Table II below. Yūsuf, however, calls his source by various names. The formula *wa-bihi ilā* is usually followed by the same appellation, the *laqab* al-Khaṭīb. When, on the other hand, the reference is in the middle of a two-part chain of transmission, the following appellations are used: al-Khaṭīb, al-Ḥāfiẓ Abū Bakr Aḥmad ibn Thābit, al-Ḥāfiẓ Abū Bakr, al-Ḥāfiẓ Abū Bakr al-Baghdādī, al-Ḥāfiẓ Abū Bakr al-Khaṭīb and Abū Bakr al-Baghdādī.

There were other sources which were established with certainty and where therefore it was possible to do a close textual comparison between the unit in Ibn 'Abd al-Hādī and that in the source. These include *al-'Iqd al-Farīd* by Ibn 'Abd Rabbihi (2) mentioned above, and *aṣ-Ṣaḥīḥ* by al-Bukhārī (d. 256/870) (3). In these sources, the degree of certainty is the same as that in al-Khaṭīb. The unit as well as its surrounding *isnād* was verified for textual equivalence.

The following table lists the chapters in the manuscript along with the number of units per chapter and their corresponding source. The volumes, if any, for the source are indicated in Roman numerals, followed by the page numbers. Where the source has not been delimited, a dash will follow and that particular material will be discussed after the presentation of the table. The units and their sources are given in their order of appearance in Yūsuf's text.

(1) AL-KHAṬĪB AL-BAGHDĀDĪ, *al-Bukhalā'*, eds. Aḥmad Maṭlūb, Khadīja al-Ḥadīthī and Aḥmad al-Qaysī (Baghdad, 1964).

(2) *Al-'Iqd al-Farīd*, cited above.

(3) AL-BUKHĀRĪ, *aṣ-Ṣaḥīḥ*, in AL-KIRMĀNĪ, *Sharḥ Ṣaḥīḥ al-Bukhārī* (Cairo, 1939).

TABLE II

MAJOR SOURCES FOR THE *Wuqū'*

Kh = al-Khaṭīb al-Baghdādī, *al-Bukhalā'*
B = al-Bukhārī, *aṣ-Ṣaḥīḥ*
I = Ibn 'Abd Rabbihi, *al-'Iqd al-Farīd*

Chapter	*Units*	*Source*	*Pages*
1	3	Kh	25-27
2	1	Kh	27
3	1	Kh	27-28
4	1	—	
5	1	Kh	28
6	3	Kh	28-30
	5	B XXII	160; 163; 163-164; 164; 166
	2	—	
7	2	B VII	199
8	1	B VII	205
9	1	—	
10	1	B XX	13
	1	B X	63-64
11	4	Kh	30-32
12	5	Kh	32-35
13	2	B VII	205-207
	3	Kh	35-36
14	1	Kh	36-37
15	13	Kh	37-44
16	3	Kh	44-45
17	4	Kh	45-46
	1	—	
18	6	Kh	46-49
	1	—	
19	10	Kh	50-57
20	3	Kh	57-58; 65-66
21	1	Kh	57-58
22	1	Kh	58-59
23	2	Kh	59-60
24	1	Kh	60
25	2	Kh	60-61
26	1	Kh	61-62

TABLE II (cont.)

Chapter	*Units*	*Source*	*Pages*
27	1	Kh	62
28	1	Kh	62-63
29	1	—	
30	1	Kh	63
31	2	Kh	63-64; 70
32	1	Kh	64
33	2	Kh	64
34	2	Kh	64-65; 65
35	2	Kh	64-65; 65
	1	—	
36	2	Kh	66
37	1	—	
	1	Kh	66
38	2	—	
	1	Kh	66-67
39	1	Kh	67
40	1	Kh	67-68
41	1	Kh	68
42	1	—	
	5	Kh	69; 107-108
43	1	Kh	70
44	1	Kh	70-71
45	1	—	
	1	Kh	71
46	2	—	
47	9	Kh	71-74
48	2	Kh	74-75
49	7	Kh	75-78
50	4	Kh	78-79
51	4	Kh	79-80
52	5	Kh	80-82
	1	I VI	177-178
53	15	Kh	83-94
54	1	Kh	94-95
	1	I VI	178
55	4	Kh	95-96
56	9	Kh	96-100
57	1	—	
	4	Kh	100-102

TABLE II (cont.)

Chapter	*Units*	*Source*	*Pages*
	1	—	
	1	Kh	102-103
58	1	Kh	103
59	5	Kh	103-104; 105-106; 111
60	4	Kh	104-105; 106
61	2	Kh	106-107
62	1	Kh	107
63	24	Kh	108-110; 111-119
64	17	Kh	120-131
65	7	Kh	132-136
66	13	Kh	137-142
67	10	Kh	143-149
68	5	Kh	149-151
69	1	Kh	155-158
70	2	Kh	158-159
71	41	Kh	160-176
72	5	Kh	179-184
73	1	Kh	185
74	2	Kh	185-186
75	3	Kh	186-187
76	5	Kh	187-188
	1	—	
	1	I VI	183
77	9	Kh	189-190; 195-196
78	2	—	
79	3	—	
80	2	—	
81	1	—	
82	1	—	
	2	Kh	160; 119
	7	—	
83	1	I VI	174-175
84	1	I VI	176
85	2	I VI	176; 177
	2	—	
86	1	I VI	177
87	1	I VI	179-180
	1	—	
	4	I VI	180; 182

The material whose source was not indicated in the above table will now be discussed. This material can be divided into four groups. The first group is material which can be found repeated elsewhere in the *Wuqū'* and whose ultimate source was generally al-Khaṭīb al-Baghdādī. When our author presents this material, however, he does not usually include the long chain of transmitters. The units in this category are the following:

1) The last unit in Chapter 35: taken from the surrounding sayings attributed to Bishr ibn al-Ḥārith.
2) The unit in Chapter 37: repeats the *ḥadīth* concerning the Banū Salama and their leader, a *bakhīl*. Many variants of this were presented in Chapter 15.
3) The first unit in Chapter 38: two lines of poetry simply introduced by: *wa-anshadūnā fī ma'nā dhālika*. An almost identical version of this poem appears in al-Khaṭīb, p. 196, and in the *Wuqū'*, Chapter 77. In this case, the first hemistich of the second verse has been changed. It is impossible to say whether our author considered this a variant or simply made an error in copying.
4) The first unit in Chapter 42: this constitutes the last line of the poem which ends Chapter 41.
5) The last unit in Chapter 79: this is a *ḥadīth* from al-Bukhārī, which was presented in Chapter 8.

The second group involves units which had some possible indication of a source, be it that the source was stated or that it could be isolated given the existence of a divided line of transmission preceded by the formula *wa-bihi ilā*. In all of the cases, however, it was impossible to identify the source with certainty or compare the texts:

1) The unit in Chapter 9: here, Yūsuf starts the unit with *qāla Ya'qūb ibn Yūsuf al-Baghdādī fī Fawā'idihi* and proceeds with the transmitters and the unit. Brockelmann lists no *Fawā'id* by this author but Yūsuf cites a *Fawā'id* by Abū Sa'd al-Baghdādī in his *Fihrist* (1). The unit is a statement by Abū 'Abd Allāh Aḥmad ibn 'Aṭā' to the effect that writing *ḥadīth* is contrary to ignorance and that sufism negates *bukhl*.
2) The unit in Chapter 76: this unit is a variant of a preceding anecdote in the same chapter. Our author introduces this variant by the following: *wa-wajadtu fī Ta'ālīq Aḥmad ibn 'Īsā ibn ash-Shaykh Mufawwaq ad-Dīn*, probably a reference to a work cited in Brockelmann, the *Ta'ālīq libn 'Īsā al-Maqdisī*, and listed in the author's *Fihrist* (2).
3) The two units in Chapter 78: in this instance we have the two-part *isnāds*, broken in the second unit with *wa-bihi ilā*. The source would, therefore, appear to be a certain Abū Muḥammad ibn Zubayr (or Zabr, as the writing is not overly clear), whom I was unable to locate. The first unit is an anecdote about two couples of

(1) Yūsuf ibn 'Abd al-Hādī, *Fihrist*, folio 37 verso.

(2) *GAL* Sup. I:250; Yūsuf ibn 'Abd al-Hādī, *Fihrist*, folio 37 recto.

whom one man and one woman (each from a different couple) show themselves to be *bakhīls*, while their mates show themselves to be generous. It turns out that the generous man and woman are brother and sister and the two *bakhīls* are also brother and sister. A narratologically identical, but rhetorically variant, version of this anecdote can be found in *al-Mustaṭraf fī Kull Fann Mustaẓraf* by al-Abshīhī (d. 850/1446) (1). The second unit is an anecdote involving two bedouin brothers, one of whom becomes an urbanite by entering the service of al-Ḥajjāj ibn Yūsuf and the attempt of the other brother to obtain hospitality from him.

4) The first unit in Chapter 79: the source for this anecdotal unit is most likely Ibn Abī ad-Dunyā (d. 281/894) (2). While the chain of transmitters is not broken, Ibn Abī ad-Dunyā's name does appear among the transmitters and, as will be shown below, he was probably used as a source by Yūsuf. His *Fihrist* lists many titles by this famous *adīb* (3). The anecdotal unit concerns a man who would not eat a loaf of bread he had and eventually died without eating it.

5) The two units in Chapter 80: the source for these may be Abū Bakr ad-Dīnawarī (d. 310/922) (4). Again, the problem is that the chain of transmitters is not broken. Nevertheless, this author is clearly indicated as the source for other units, as will be shown below. In the first anecdote, a man is accused of being extremely avaricious (*la'īm*) by a woman who does not believe that *laban* should be bought or sold. In the second unit, a man demonstrates his *bukhl* by dressing his son in an old dirty coat, scorning the spending habits of others, etc.

6) Units 7 and 8 in Chapter 82: once again, we have two units from the same source with a broken *isnād* for the second unit with the phrase *wa-bihi ilā* followed by ad-Dīnawarī, certainly the Abū Bakr ad-Dīnawarī mentioned above. Both units are made up of verse. The first is simply a recopying of the same poem already taken from al-Khaṭīb, in Chapter 53 (al-Khaṭīb, pp. 83-84). The second unit states that though *bukhl* is very bad, it is better than poverty that would oblige one to beg from a *bakhīl*.

7) Units 9 and 10 in Chapter 82: here, as before, the second unit shows the broken *isnād* with the formula *wa-bihi ilā* followed by Ibn Abī ad-Dunyā, a reference to Ibn Abī ad-Dunyā al-Qurashī, mentioned earlier. This author was mentioned above as a possible source for another unit. Both units are in verse. The first seems to indicate that date pits and bad water are better than begging. In the second unit, the poet laments that though he associated with people, they have not all been praiseworthy.

In the third group, we have materials whose source could not be traced. In all cases, the *isnāds* were not broken at any point and, therefore, the source could not be determined.

(1) Al-Abshīhī, *al-Mustaṭraf fī Kull Fann Mustaẓraf* (Beirut, n.d.), v. I, p. 176.

(2) *GAL* I:153-154 and *GAL* Sup. I:247-248.

(3) See Yūsuf ibn 'Abd al-Hādī, *Fihrist*, folios 25 verso, 28 recto, 28 verso, 29 recto, 30 verso, 31 verso, 36 recto, 38 recto, 38 verso, 40 verso, 42 verso, among others.

(4) *GAL* I:154 and *GAL* Sup. I:249.

Among the *ḥadīths* for which a written source could not be determined are some which were located in the standard *ḥadīth* collections and some which could not be located in these standard works (or the C.I.T.M.). Again, the units are presented by chapters:

1) The unit in Chapter 4: this is a *ḥadīth* which could not be located in the *ḥadīth* collections. It states that the generous man is close to God and Muḥammad is his companion, while the *bakhīl* is in Hell and Iblīs is his companion.
2) The last two units in Chapter 6: these units add still two more variants to the eight other variants of the same *ḥadīth* already present in this chapter. The second of these two units is identical to a *ḥadīth* in the *Sunan* of an-Nasā'ī (d. 303/915) (1).
3) The unit in Chapter 17: this unit is also a *ḥadīth* which states that there are two things (*shay'āni*) which do not come together in a believer, *bukhl* and a bad nature. There is a variant of this in the *Sunan* of at-Tirmidhī (d. 279/892) whose content is the same. The one difference in the Arabic is the replacement of *shay'āni* by *khaṣlatāni* (two characteristics) (2).
4) The last unit in Chapter 18: this unit is also a *ḥadīth* and is a variant of the other units in the chapter. It is not, however, listed in any of the *ḥadīth* collections.
5) The unit in Chapter 29: the unit involves Chosroes who asks his companions what the worst thing is for men. The answer is that it is poverty. But he replies that avarice (*shuḥḥ*) is worse than poverty because when the poor man finds something he is well off whereas the avaricious man is not.
6) The two units in Chapter 46: the first unit is a list of five disgraceful actions. The second unit is a *ḥadīth* concerning men whose faces are human but whose hearts are those of devils. The unit is not entirely legible.
7) The first unit in Chapter 57: this unit is a statement that charity (*muwāsāt*) was mentioned in front of someone who answered that it was a path on which boxthorn (*'awsaj*) grew.
8) The second unit in Chapter 79: this unit has no transmitters and simply starts with *qāla ba'ḍ al-'ulamā'*. It is a statement to the effect that the *bukhl* of the *bukhalā'* makes them feel responsible for possessions and a proof of that is he who is keen and base in gathering things.
9) The unit in Chapter 81: this unit has an *isnād* which begins with the same chain of transmitters as another unit on folio 22 verso. The difference in transmitters starts for the unit under question here with Ibn al-Jawzī. While this would seem like an ideal source, given that Ibn al-Jawzī (d. 597/1200) authored many *adab* works and received many citations in Yūsuf's *Fihrist* (3), there is not enough in-

(1) AN-NASĀ'Ī, *Sunan an-Nasā'ī* (Cairo, 1965), v. VIII, p. 226,

(2) AT-TIRMIDHĪ, *Sunan at-Tirmidhī*, ed. 'Abd ar-Raḥmān M. 'Uthmān (Cairo, 1965), v. III, p. 231.

(3) *GAL* I:500-506 and *GAL* Sup. I:914-920; YŪSUF IBN 'ABD AL-HĀDĪ, *Fihrist*, folios 2 recto, 2 verso, 11 verso, 18 verso, 19 recto, 20 recto, 25 recto, 29 recto, 30 verso, 42 recto, 43 recto, 44 verso, 54 recto, 57 verso, among others.

formation to conclude. The unit is a statement by a certain Abū Ja'far Muḥammad ibn 'Alī that his father cautioned him against keeping the company of and befriending five types of people, among whom, of course, is the *bakhīl*.

10) The first unit in Chapter 82: this unit is in verse and represents the reproach of a poet who was not given hospitality.
11) The fourth unit in Chapter 82: this unit is also in verse and seems to be another such reproach.
12) The fifth unit in Chapter 82: this unit, which is also in verse, describes a *bakhīl* who blocks up his door to avoid giving hospitality.
13) The sixth unit in Chapter 82: this unit is in verse and in it the poet Abū al-'Atāhiya (1) declares that he has used magic incantations against the *bukhl* of someone.
14) The unit in Chapter 87: though this anecdote is in a chapter attributed to Ibn 'Abd Rabbihi, I have not been able to locate it in *al-'Iqd*. The anecdote concerns a *shaykh* who hid a bowl of soup under his clothing with amusing results.

The fourth group is composed of materials whose source would appear to be Yūsuf ibn 'Abd al-Hādī himself. These units are not preceded by *isnāds*:

1) The first unit in Chapter 45: this unit is, in effect, an elaboration of the chapter title. It is a known fact, Yūsuf writes, that a generous man has people indebted to him even when he dies whereas a *bakhīl* dies leaving his debts.
2) The sixth unit in Chapter 57: our author praises the *umma* of the Prophet Muḥammad.
3) The two last units in Chapter 85: in the first unit, Yūsuf summarizes in his own words a passage from the *Ṣaḥīḥ* of al-Bukhārī about Ibn az-Zubayr and 'Ā'isha (2). In the second unit, our author states that there is material in the *Ṣaḥīḥ* which contradicts the evidence he has already presented in the chapter that Ibn az-Zubayr was a *bakhīl*. For this purpose, Yūsuf notes, from al-Bukhārī, that Ibn az-Zubayr gave people dates to eat (3).

Composition and Organization.

It should be noted that even when Yūsuf ibn 'Abd al-Hādī took a unit from another source, he did not always copy it exactly. When copying the *isnāds*, for example, our author would occasionally drop off a name element from one of the personages (usually *nisbas* and *laqabs*) or a place name, either through oversight or because he considered it superfluous for the establishment of the transmission. His *isnāds* display another interesting characteristic. This is the tendency to leave short blank spaces in the middle of the *isnād* itself. The

(1) The two lines are not in the *dīwān* of Abū al-'Atāhiya. See, *Dīwān Abī al-'Atāhiya* (Beirut, 1964).

(2) Al-Bukhārī, *aṣ-Ṣaḥīḥ*, v. XXI, pp. 206 ff.

(3) For this passage, see, Al-Bukhārī, *aṣ-Ṣaḥīḥ*, v. XI, p. 25.

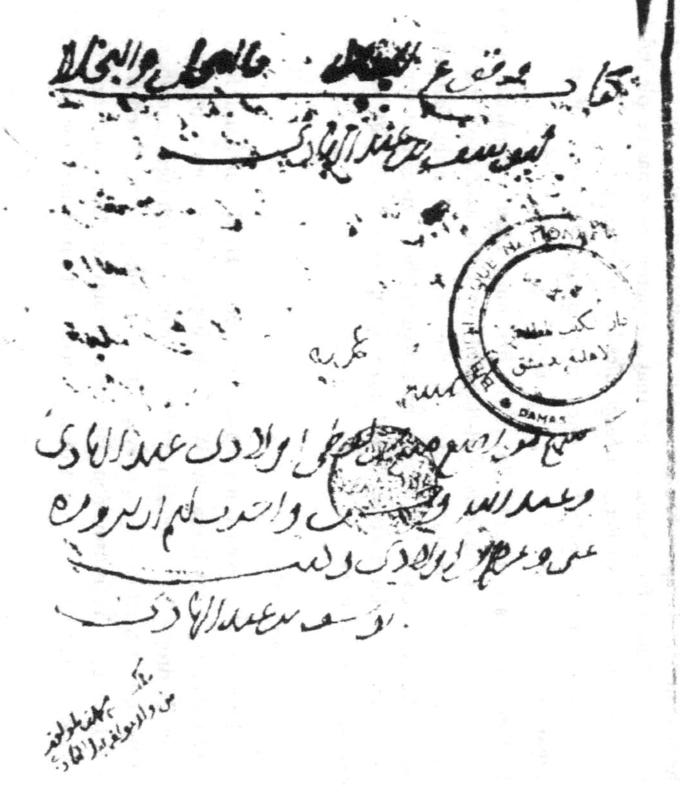

X

PL. II

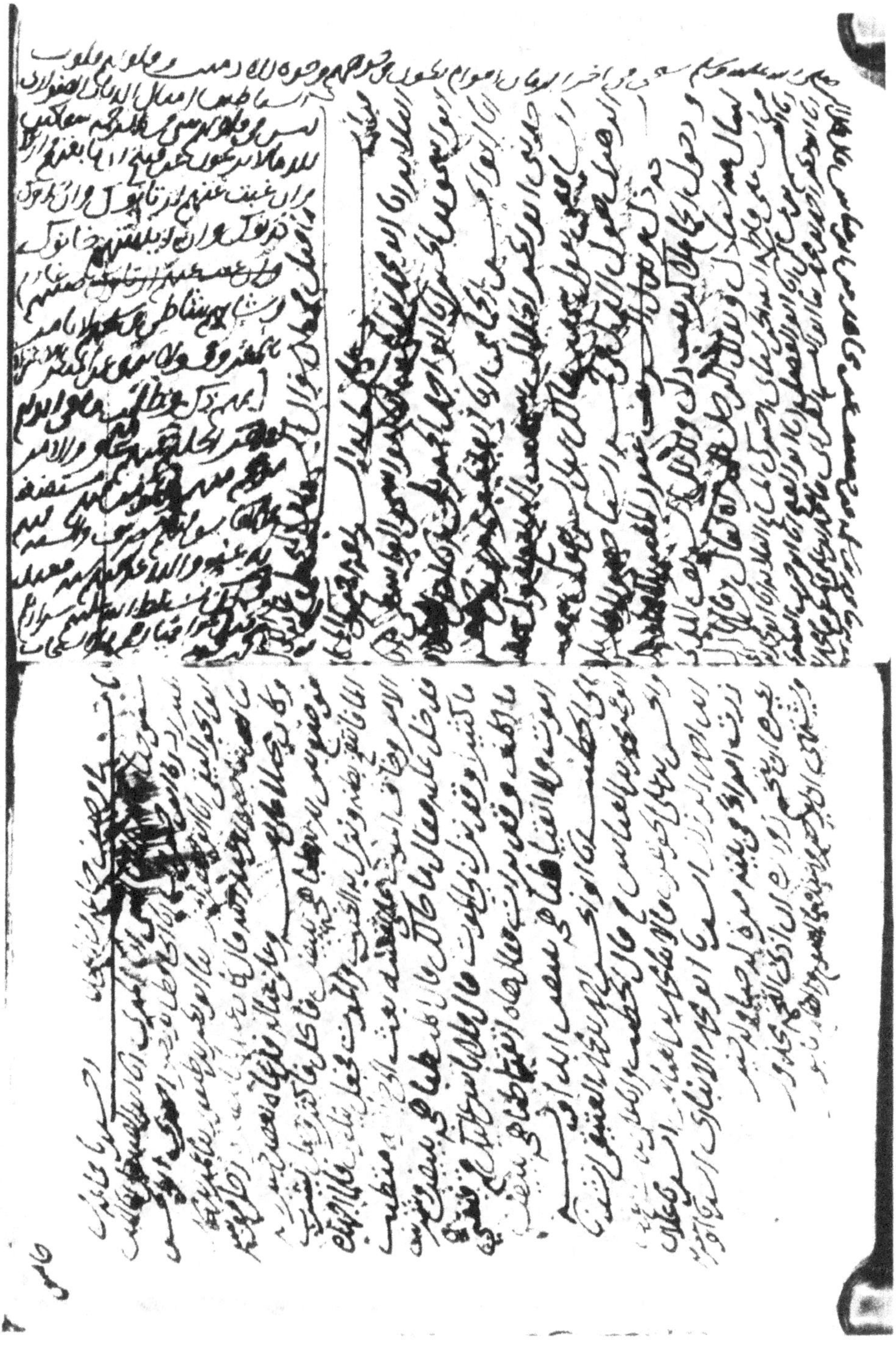

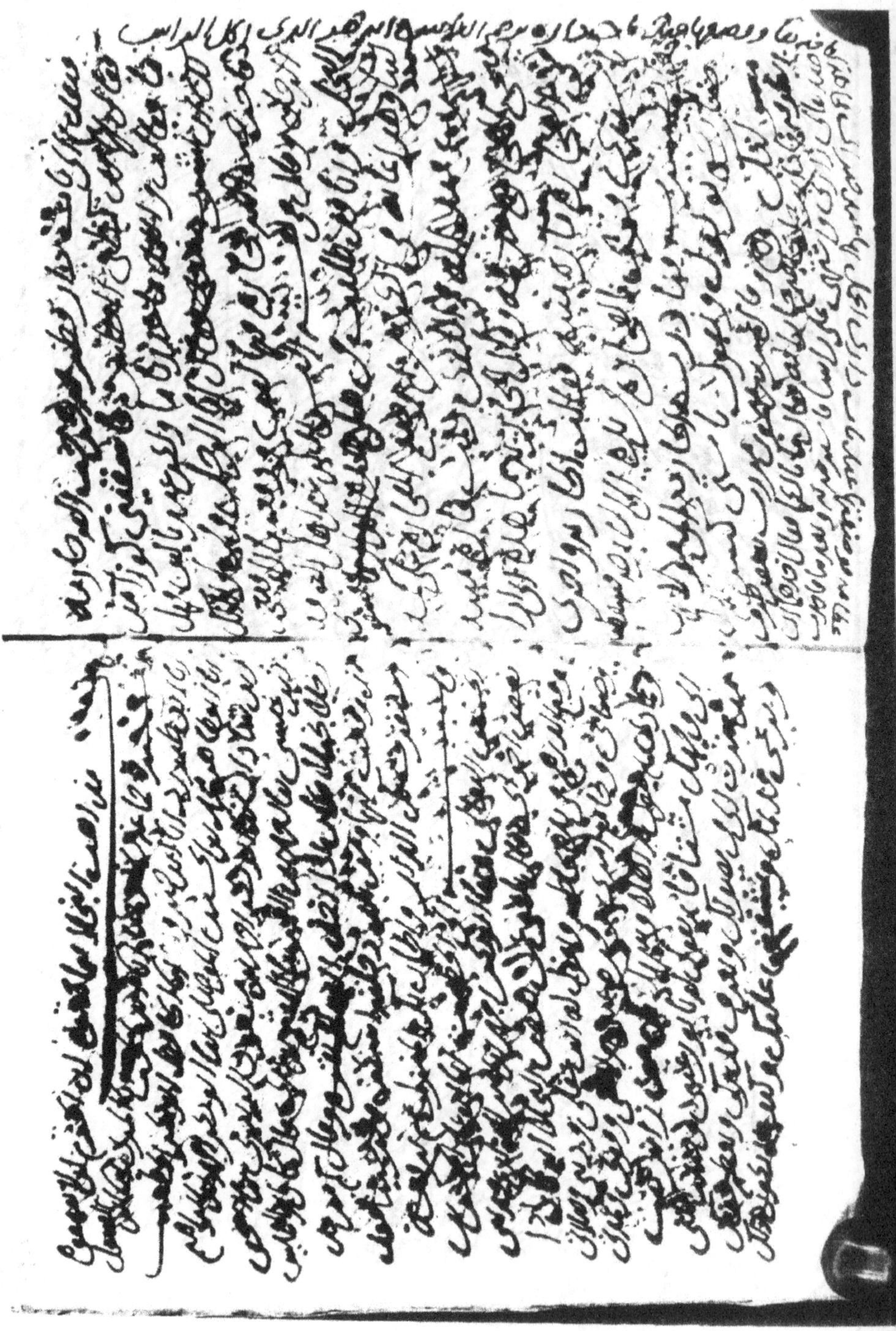

Pl. III

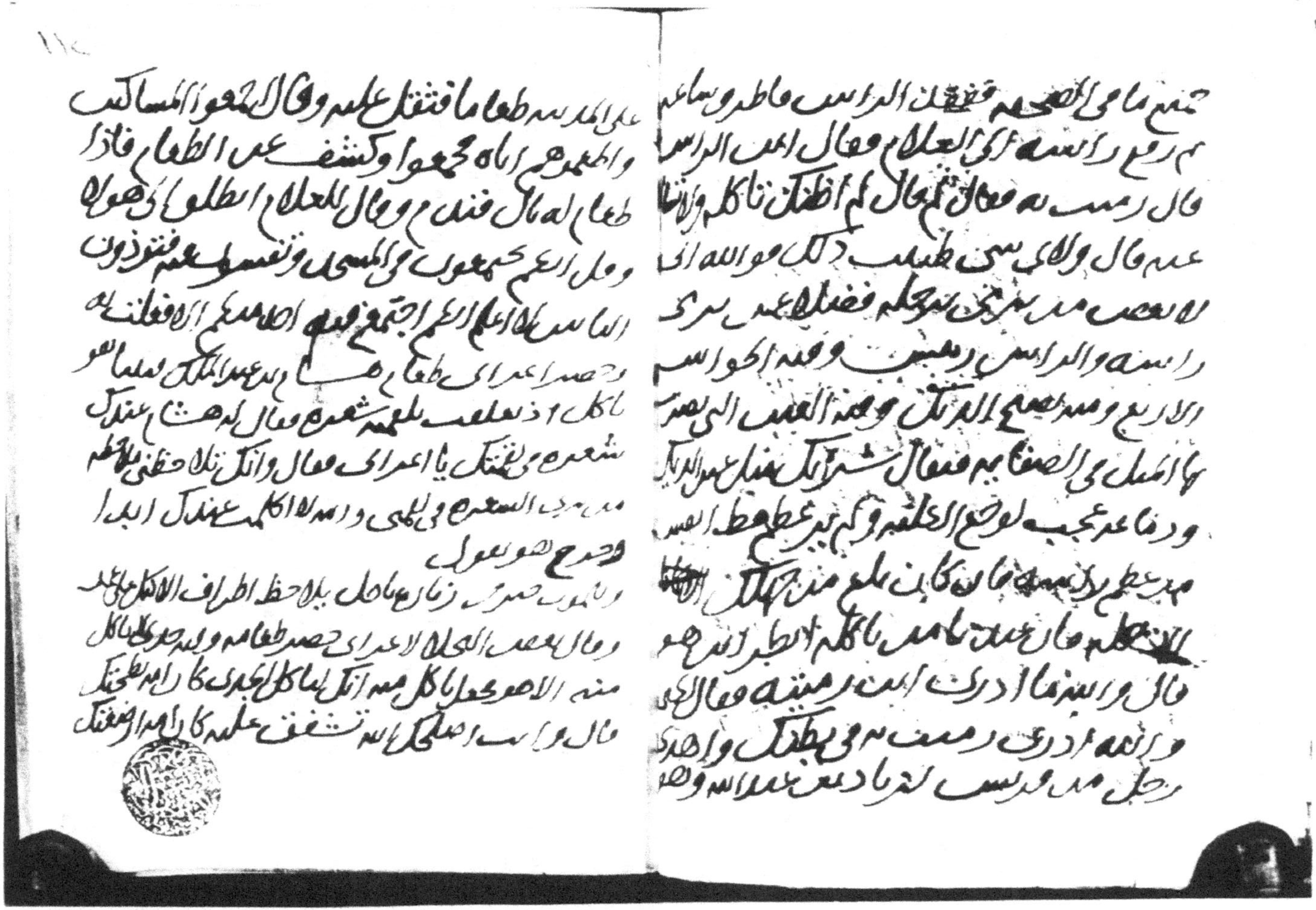

positions in which these spaces were left indicate clearly that they were not meant to be permanent but that the author intended to return to them. On folio 2 recto, for example, an *isnād* has been copied from al-Khaṭīb. In the third line of the *isnād*, Yūsuf has left a space after حبيب and begins writing again with حدثنا شعبة. The missing element is حدثنا ابو داود. In the following line, our author has written عمرو بن followed by a space. The missing name is مرة. A little further, another space is left where the elements "Ibn al-Ḥārith" should go (1). In addition, on folio 103 recto, Yūsuf has left approximately one line and a half where he obviously intended to copy the *isnād* from al-Bukhārī. These spaces pose several questions: was our author composing from memory and planning to check his lapses against a written text at some future time? Or, was he working from a written text which was not entirely legible? It seems clear, however, that he wrote the text in great haste. Finally, these spaces strengthen the argument that the text was never completed. Was work on it interrupted by the death of the author? We have no way of knowing. Even the fact that this text is mentioned in another, that is the *Fihrist*, need not necessarily argue against this hypothesis since the *Fihrist* itself may have been drawn up late in Yūsuf's life in connection with his donation of his library as a *waqf* to al-Madrasa al-ʿUmariyya.

In effect, the dependence of Yūsuf ibn ʿAbd al-Hādī's *Wuqūʿ* upon the earlier work by al-Khaṭīb al-Baghdādī is so great that a complete edition of the former text would be superfluous. For this same reason, however, the autograph of the *Wuqūʿ* may add vital new information to the manuscript evidence on the *Bukhalāʾ* of al-Khaṭīb al-Baghdādī and may show important new variants to be considered in any re-edition of al-Khaṭīb's work (2).

The above, however, does not mean that the organization of Yūsuf's work is without interest. Indeed, the fact that we are dealing with an autograph makes it possible for us to examine both the organization and, to a limited degree, the procedures of composition. Though Yūsuf made many changes in the order of presentation of al-Khaṭīb's material, he generally took care to preserve the basic organizational principles of al-Khaṭīb's work. These may be succinctly stated as follows:

1) No introduction but a short invocation.
2) An initial section composed of non-anecdotal material, chiefly *ḥadīths*, followed by a second section composed of prose anecdotes and verse units which are almost exclusively narrative in structure.
3) A short closing section made up almost exclusively of *ḥadīths* (3).

(1) See, AL-KHAṬĪB, *al-Bukhalāʾ*, p. 26.

(2) To take but one example, on page 66 of al-Khaṭīb's *Bukhalāʾ*, the editors have chosen *wa-mawākibī* and, in a note, explain that the original had *wa-marākibī* which in turn had been corrected in a marginal note to *wa-mawākibī*. Yet the editors note that *wa-marākibī* is "not far from correct". The *Wuqūʿ* (folio 34v) has *wa-marākibī*.

(3) For a discussion of the organization of al-Khaṭīb's work, see, F. DOUGLAS, "The *Bukhalāʾ* Work", pp. 103-116. This material will be included in the above-mentioned study on the *Bukhalāʾ*, in preparation.

The last principle has not been followed since part of the last section in al-Khaṭīb's work can be found in Chapter 77 of the *Wuqū'*. In addition, since we apparently do not have a completed work, we do not know how our author would have finished his work. Yūsuf's selection from his predecessor was not haphazard. In fact, his adherence to the fundamental division between *ḥadīth*, on the one hand, and anecdote and verse, on the other, can be seen even more clearly if one examines the nature of the non-Khaṭībian material in the *Wuqū'*, as discussed above.

For the most part, new material has been inserted where it belonged, *ḥadīth* with *ḥadīth* and anecdote with anecdote, variant with variant. For example, the sections taken from *al-'Iqd al-Farīd* in Chapters 83 to 87 are all anecdotal, though there are non-anecdotal materials in the corresponding chapter of *al-'Iqd* which our author could have chosen had he so wished (1). Further, in Chapters 52, 54 and 76, for example, variants have been added from other authors to the units from al-Khaṭīb. In certain cases, there can be no doubt from the writing that they were added at a later time (see, for example, folio 98 verso). In fact, the arrangement of the material in the manuscript indicates that the composition of the work was begun with both the works of al-Khaṭīb and al-Bukhārī in hand, while material from Ibn 'Abd Rabbihi was added later. Finally, even the distribution of blank spaces is significant. A glance at Table I will show that a far larger number of spaces was left in the first forty-five folios of the text, which are those made up essentially of *ḥadīths*, and this despite the fact that some non-Khaṭībian materials have already been added. This is almost certainly to allow the integration of new or variant *ḥadīths*. New anecdotes could, however, be placed at the end of the text and new variants of an anecdote were less likely to appear than new variants of a *ḥadīth*.

Yūsuf ibn 'Abd al-Hādī, thus, though he borrowed his materials from a small number of earlier authors, apparently recognized and certainly recreated a general organizational principle which was also present in the work of his predecessor. There is every reason to believe, therefore, that his organizational principle, which in terms of form separated *ḥadīths* on the one hand from anecdote and verse on the other, and in terms of content went from the sacred to the profane, constituted at least one culturally established organizational principle for monographic *adab* works. Naturally, the importance and degree of extension of this principle can only be ascertained by the analysis of other works of Yūsuf ibn 'Abd al-Hādī and of other Medieval Arabic *adab* writers as well.

(1) See, IBN 'ABD RABBIHI, *'Iqd*, v. VI, pp. 174-204.

XI

STRUCTURE AND ORGANIZATION IN A MONOGRAPHIC *ADAB* WORK: *AL-TAṬFĪL* OF AL-KHAṬĪB AL-BAGHDĀDĪ

AL-KHAṬĪB AL-BAGHDĀDĪ, about whom Ibn Khallikān stated that had he only written the *Ta ͗rīkh Baghdād* it would have sufficed,[1] has fortunately left for posterity more than the justly famed biographical compendium of the notables of Baghdād. This noted *muḥaddith* of the eleventh century was, in his own right, a distinguished *adīb* as well.[2]

When one examines the chapters devoted to character types in medieval encyclopedic *adab* works, one discovers that the *ṭufaylīs*, loosely translated, party crashers, or uninvited guests, frequently follow the *bukhalā ͗*, or misers.[3] It is, therefore, no surprise that al-Khaṭīb al-Baghdādī, author of a *Kitāb al-bukhalā ͗*,[4] should also write a book on the *ṭufaylīs*, *Al-taṭfīl wa-ḥikāyāt al-ṭufayliyyīn wa-akhbāruhum wa-nawādir kalāmihim wa-ashᶜāruhum*.[5] It is the latter work which will concern us here. Our discussion will, as the title indicates, center on organization and structure in this monographic *adab* work and on how the two reinforce their individual literary effects.

The distinction between organization and structure is a vital one for any structuralist analysis of a literary text. This distinction has been drawn most clearly by Jean Pouillon who explained organization as the visible combination of elements in a text,

1 Ibn Khallikān, *Wafayāt al-aᶜyān*, vol. 1, ed. Iḥsān ᶜAbbās (Beirut, n.d.), p. 92.

2 For the life and works of al-Khaṭīb al-Baghdādī, see Yūsuf al-ᶜIshsh, *Al-Khaṭīb al-Baghdādī: mu ͗arrikh Baghdād wa-muḥaddithuhā* (Damascus, 1945); R. Sellheim, "Al-Khaṭīb al-Baghdādī," *EI*², pp. 1111-12. For a discussion of the biographical tradition, see my article, "Controversy and Its Effects in the Biographical Tradition of al-Khaṭīb al-Baghdādī," *Studia Islamica* 66 (1977): 115-31.

3 See, for example, the relative placement of the sections on the *bukhalā ͗* and those on the *ṭufaylīs* in Ibn ᶜAbd Rabbihi, *Al-ᶜiqd al-farīd*, vol. 6, ed. Aḥmad Amīn, Ibrāhīm al-Abyārī, and ᶜA. S. Muḥammad Hārūn (Cairo, 1949), pp. 174-204 and 204-15; al-Nuwayrī, *Nihāyat al-arab fī funūn al-adab*, vol. 3 (Cairo, n.d.), pp. 294-323 and 323-37.

4 Al-Khaṭīb al-Baghdādī, *Al-bukhalā ͗*, ed. Aḥmad Maṭlūb, Khadīja al-Ḥadīthī, and Aḥmad al-Qaysī (Baghdad, 1964). For discussions of this work, see my forthcoming book, *Structure of Avarice: The* Bukhalā ͗ *Work in Medieval Arabic Literature*. See also my article "Humor and Structure in Two *Buḫalā* Anecdotes: al-Ǧāḥiẓ and al-Ḫaṭīb al-Baġdādī," *Arabica*, forthcoming.

5 Al-Khaṭīb al-Baghdādī, *Al-taṭfīl wa-ḥikāyāt al-ṭufayliyyīn wa-akhbāruhum wa-nawādir kalāmihim wa-ashᶜāruhum*, ed. Kāẓim al-Muẓaffar (Najaf, 1966). Apparently, the only other extant monographic *taṭfīl* work is that of Ibn al-Jawzī, preserved in manuscript. See *GAL*, Supp. 1, p. 916; ᶜĪsā Iskandar al-Maᶜlūf, "Min Nafā ͗is al-Khizāna al-Taymūriyya," *Revue de l'Académie Arabe de Damas* 3 (1923): 342. Al-Jāḥiẓ also appears to have written a work on this subject, which is, unfortunately, not extant. See *GAL*, Supp. 1, p. 245; Charles Pellat, "Ǧāḥiẓiana III. Essai d'inventaire de l'oeuvre ǧāḥizienne," *Arabica* 3 (1956): 177. Given the striking differences between the *Kitāb al-bukhalā ͗* of al-Jāḥiẓ and that of al-Khaṭīb, there is no reason to assume that the *Kitāb al-taṭfīl* of al-Khaṭīb would have been based on that of his predecessor.

For additional material on *taṭfīl* and *ṭufaylīs*, see the two encyclopedic *adab* works cited above and Ibn Ḥujja al-Ḥamawī, *Thamarāt al-awrāq fī al-muḥāḍarāt*, printed on the margins of al-Abshīhī, *Al-mustaṭraf fī kull fann mustaẓraf*, vol. 1 (Beirut, n.d.), pp. 154-56; al-Ḥuṣrī, *Zahr al-ādāb wa-thamar al-albāb*, vol. 4, ed. Zakī Murbārak and Muḥammad ᶜAbd al-Ḥamīd (Beirut, 1972), pp. 979-81; Ibn al-Jawzī, *Akhbār al-adhkiyā ͗*, ed. Muḥammad Mursī al-Khawlī (Cairo, 1970), pp. 188-93.

whereas structure refers to more limited configurations of elements which define (one might say determine) the text, both in its uniqueness and its comparability.[6]

The structural analysis to be undertaken here is a narratological micropoetic one based on a methodology originally designed for the *Bukhalā͗* works of al-Jāḥiẓ and al-Khaṭīb al-Baghdādī.[7] This methodology is based upon the isolation, and then recombination into a corpus, of the literary microunits which make up the bulk of the work, i.e., *ṭufaylī* anecdotes. For the purpose of this study, the *ṭufaylī* anecdote has been defined as a self-contained narrative unit which demonstrates that a person, persons, group, or class of people illustrate the characteristic of *taṭfīl*. As with the *bukhalā͗* anecdotes, it is the narrative quality of the unit which determines its status, and not necessarily the type of discourse employed. Therefore, both prose and verse units are considered to be anecdotes.

In this definition, the essential quality of the anecdote is its ability to embody an action, its quality as a narrative. Hence, the structural analysis will be based on a readaptation of the Proppian/Bremondian definition of the function. Propp described the function as the action of a personage, defined from the point of view of its significance for the unfolding of the narrative. In the process, Propp stressed that it was the action and not the personage performing it which defined the nature of the function. Claude Bremond, on the other hand, in his *Logique du récit*, redefined the Proppian function as not simply an action, which he called "*processus*," or process, but as the relation of a "personnage-sujet" to a "processus-prédicat." For him, thus, the structure of the narrative rests on a sequence not of actions but of roles. If the concept of "role" is understood as a character defined by an action which he performs, is subjected to, or is likely by his nature to perform, then the *ṭufaylī*, like the *bakhīl*, is a person so defined. Further, it will be necessary to note that the *ṭufaylī* anecdote, *qua* anecdote, represents only one incident or sequence of events. Thus, rather than being a chain of functions, it frequently contains only one function or, at most, a sequence of two. In effect, therefore, the function is more often defined paradigmatically than syntagmatically.[8]

To say that an *adab* work is composed of literary microunits means, in effect, that it is composed, almost exclusively, of what Abd el-Fattah Kilito has called "discours rapporté" or reported discourse.[9] For this reason, the selection and arrangement of the units is what gives the *adab* work its character. If selection can be related to structure, arrangement is the major tool of organization.

6 Quoted and discussed in Jean-Marie Auzias, *Clefs pour le structuralisme* (Paris, 1975), pp. 14-15.

7 For this methodology, see my book *Bukhalā͗ Work*, chap. 1 and my article "The Micropoetics of the *Bukhalā͗* Anecdote," *Journal Asiatique* 247 (1979): 309-17.

8 See again my *Bukhalā͗ Work*, and "Micropoetics," cited above, and Vladimir Propp, *Morphologie du conte*, trans. Marguerite Derrida (Paris, 1970). This translation has been used because it is based on the second, corrected Russian edition (Leningrad, 1969); this edition not only corrects factual and technical errors present in the first edition but completes the text on many important points. The second edition of the English translation, *Morphology of the Folktale* (Austin, 1968), is based on the first Russian edition of the work. See "Note de l'éditeur," Propp, *Morphologie*, and "Appendix I: The Problem of 'Tale Role' and 'Character' in Propp's Work," in Heda Jason and Dimitri Segal, eds., *Patterns in Oral Literature* (The Hague, 1977), pp. 313-20. See also Claude Bremond, *Logique du récit* (Paris, 1973), pp. 132-34.

9 Abd el-Fattah Kilito, "Le genre 'Séance': une introduction," *Studia Islamica* 63 (1976): 34.

The organization of the work will be dealt with first. The *Kitāb al-taṭfīl* consists of twenty-six chapters, including an introduction. This short introduction which, interestingly enough, has a number of Jāḥiẓian qualities, orients the reader to the types of material which the author has gathered in his work. It also contains a discussion of humor and of the appeal of anecdotes.[10]

Following the introduction, the reader is first presented with a philological discussion of the root *ṭ-f-l*, and its derivatives, *taṭfīl* and *ṭufaylī*. The latter is explained as someone who comes in uninvited, taken from the verb *ṭafala* and its verbal noun, representing the process by which the darkness of night conquers the day. The actions of the *ṭufaylī* are related to this verb in that they harm people, given that no one knows who invited him or how he entered. A second etymology is given: *ṭufaylī* as a nisba to Ṭufayl, a man of Kūfa who attended receptions without an invitation. Further, this particular appellation was the one employed by the common people. Interestingly enough, there is a distinction made, at least in the philological tradition, between one who comes in uninvited while people are eating, a *wārish*, and one who comes in uninvited while people are drinking, a *wāghil*. This distinction does not manifest itself in the anecdotal material, where only the generic term *ṭufaylī* is to be found. There is one practice mentioned in the philological exposition which does appear in the anecdotes, and which could be said to be the ancestor of the modern "doggy bag": *al-zall*, or carrying out food from receptions.[11] Following this linguistic discussion, we are given the names under which the *ṭufaylī* was known in the Jāhiliyya.[12]

These philological discussions are followed by the first two anecdotal chapters. The anecdotes in these two chapters are, however, different from those in the rest of the work, and, as will be shown, below, this difference has major organizational significance. The first of the two chapters contains anecdotes which show that the Prophet, when invited, in certain cases brought someone along who had not been invited, including ʿĀʾisha. The anecdotes themselves are prefixed by a statement to the effect that the *sunna* permits this type of action. The next chapter is composed entirely of

10 Al-Khaṭīb, *Taṭfīl*, pp. 1-3. cf. al-Jāḥiẓ, *Al-bukhalāʾ*, ed. Ṭāha al-Ḥājirī (Cairo, 1971), pp. 1-8.

11 Al-Khaṭīb, *Taṭfīl*, pp. 4-6. These two derivations of the term *ṭufaylī* are standard in the lexicographical tradition, along with a third, omitted by al-Khaṭīb in his philological section but alluded to in a humorous *risāla* at the end of the work pp. 113-14), which relates the *ṭufaylī* to he who comes uninvited at the time of day called *ṭafal* (here, near sunset). These three are the only derivations to be found in the lexicographical and philological traditions. See, for example, al-Zabīdī, *Tāj al-ʿarūs*, vol. 7 (Cairo, 1888-90), pp. 417-19; Ibn Manẓur, *Lisān al-ʿarab*, vol. 13 (Cairo, n.d.), pp. 426-29; al-Fīrūzābādī, *Al-qāmūs al-muḥīṭ*, vol. 4 (Cairo, n.d.), p. 7; al-Thaʿālibī, *Thimār al-qulūb fī al-muḍāf wal-mansūb*, ed. Muḥammad Abū al-Faḍl Ibrāhīm (Cairo, 1965), pp. 108-9; Ibn Sīda, *Al-mukhaṣṣaṣ*, vol. 1 (Beirut, n.d.), p. 67; al-Azharī, *Tahdhib al-lugha*, vol. 13, ed. Ahnad al-Bardūnī and ʿAlī al-Bijāwī (Cairo 1966), pp. 347-50. Cf. Edward W. Lane, *An Arabic-English Lexicon*, vol. 5 (London, 1874), pp. 1859-60.

It is, of course, logically and morphologically possible that the term *ṭufaylī* was derived, either directly or ultimately, from the other verb based on the root *ṭ-f-l*, *ṭafula*, whose basic meaning is to be soft or tender (as in *ṭifl*, child, diminutive: *ṭufayl*). Nevertheless, as was noted above, there is no mention of such a derivation in the literature. Nor would it seem likely that the name Ṭufayl al-ʿarāʾis (or al-Aʿrās) need be interpreted as showing a connection (other than historical coincidence) between the idea of coming uninvited and *ṭufayl* understood as the diminutive of child. Not only do the sources give no other *ism* for this man, but the name Ṭufayl was by no means uncommon in the period, as can be seen in Guidi's index to the *Kitāb al-aghānī*. I. Guidi, *Tables alphabétiques du Kitāb al-aġānī* (Leiden, 1900), pp. 415-16.

12 Al-Khaṭīb, *Taṭfīl*, pp. 7-8.

variants of the same anecdote, in which the Prophet, though invited, brings someone along who was not.[13]

Technically, these units, since they relate the actions of the Prophet, are *ḥadīths*. Nevertheless, their narrative nature makes them also anecdotes, and, if another personage had been substituted for the Prophet in them, one would not hesitate to classify them as anecdotes. An important question can then be asked, however: are they *ṭufaylī* anecdotes? If so, of course, the Prophet would then be encouraging *taṭfīl*, and his companions would be *ṭufaylīs*. On the one hand, the title of the second chapter reads: *dhikr man ṭaffala ᶜalā ᶜahd rasūl allāh min al-ṣaḥāba* [Mention of he who came in uninvited at the time of the Prophet from among the Companions], clearly making reference to the root *ṭ-f-l*. On the other hand, al-Khaṭīb specifically noted that the bringing of another, uninvited, guest was a permissible act. Therefore, although, in a certain sense, these guests came in "uninvited," they were clearly not guilty of wrongdoing. For this reason, the anecdotes in these two chapters could be considered "morally excused *ṭufaylī* anecdotes." Structurally, all of these anecdotes display the same morphology: a bringing-along morphology, distinct from the other anecdotal morphologies in the text. Finally, if we treat these two chapters as a literary unit, however, we have a statement that a certain kind of action is permissible according to the *sunna*, followed by the evidence to that effect.

Following these two chapters, we are given a series of *ḥadīths* and other normative sayings to the effect that he who enters without an invitation enters as a thief and leaves as an aggressor. Further, he who eats food to which he was not invited, eats that which is unlawful.[14] The *ḥadīths* among these, since their literary role is that of normative statements condemning *taṭfīl*, are not being considered anecdotes.

It is directly after this normative material that the *ṭufaylī* anecdotes themselves begin. Most of the rest of the work consists of a series of nineteen chapters, made up almost entirely of *taṭfīl* anecdotes. The major organizational principle used in ordering the chapters is the division between those chapters devoted to a number of different *ṭufaylīs* (chap. 7 to 16)[15] and those centering around the archetypical *ṭufaylī*, Bunān (chaps. 17 to 25).

Almost all of the relatively small number of non-anecdotal units interspersed throughout the rest of the work constitute various sayings, attributed to or transmitted by Bunān, regarding food and eating. In one, he tells us the best ways to eat eggplant,[16] for example; in another, he advises chewing a lot because it strengthens gums and teeth.[17]

The *Kitāb al-taṭfīl* concludes with a six-page *risāla* in which detailed advice is given a *ṭufaylī* on how to conduct himself to maximize his *taṭfīl*.[18] Not only does this text form a sharp break with the shorter anecdotal units which preceded it but, by bringing in virtually all the stages, devices, and aspects of *taṭfīl*, it evokes and integrates the subjects which were dispersed in separate anecdotes across the work.

To recapitulate, the organization of the *Kitāb al-taṭfīl* can be most easily seen as a division into seven parts: 1) an introduction in a relatively light tone of about three

13 Ibid., pp. 9-16.

14 Ibid., pp. 17-24.

15 The chapter divisions are given in the edition. I have taken the liberty of numbering them, labeling al-Khaṭīb's introduction the first chapter.

16 Al-Khaṭīb, *Taṭfīl*, p. 98.

17 Ibid., p. 100.

18 Ibid., pp. 112-17.

pages; 2) a philological discussion of about five pages; 3) a series of anecdotes about the Prophet and the Companions of about eight pages; 4) a set of normative statements sharply condemning *taṭfīl* of about seven pages; 5) anecdotal material about various *ṭufaylīs* of about sixty pages; 6) anecdotal material centering on Bunān of about thirty pages; and 7) a six-page *risāla* giving advice to the prospective *ṭufaylī*.

But, what is the significance of this organization? On one level, it displays a certain literary organizational sense. Viewed this way, one could speak of an introductory section consisting of parts 1 through 4; a body, parts 5 and 6; and a literary conclusion which recapitulates, in an entertaining way, the actions in the body of the work. While such a view is clearly not without merit, it fails to account for the arrangement of parts 1 through 4, and, in particular, the sandwiching of the normative statements between two different groups of anecdotes.

The significance of the arrangement can best be seen when compared with that of al-Khaṭīb's *Kitāb al-bukhalāʾ*, a book by the same author, in the same genre, and on a very similar topic. Al-Khaṭīb's *Bukhalāʾ* displays a fairly simple organization. The work has no introduction but begins with a long series of *ḥadīth*s which either condemn *bukhl* directly, or place *bukhl* in the garden of vices.[19] These *ḥadīth*s act as a normative introduction and set a clear moral tone for the work. They are followed by the anecdotal sections of the work. Al-Khaṭīb's *Bukhalāʾ* concludes with a short section composed of *ḥadīth*s which also condemn *bukhl* but which are more practical and less theoretical in orientation.[20]

In this context, it is easier to see the unique features of the organization of the *Kitāb al-taṭfīl*. The *Taṭfīl* does not begin with a moralizing or normative introduction but rather with a morally neutral general introduction and philological discussions which represent those parts of the *adab* ideal which relate more exclusively to literary than to ethical concerns. The presence of anecdotes about the Prophet and the Companions preceding those about later individuals is somewhat reminiscent of *ṭabaqāt* organization. What is distinctive here is that they are separated from the other anecdotes by the normative condemnatory statements. This positioning is clearly not fortuitous. Had the normative section begun the work, or in any way preceded the anecdotes about the Prophet, it might have suggested that the Prophet's actions were improper or, at the very least, have confounded the Prophet's actions with those of the *ṭufaylīs*. Instead, this normative passage forms a sharp moral boundary between the licit actions of the Prophet and the illicit actions of the *ṭufaylīs*.[21]

A number of conclusions about the nature of the work can be drawn from this organization. The first is that the organization itself is essentially linear. Materials precede other materials which they are supposed to define. The condemnation of *taṭfīl* is meant to apply to the actions which follow it, not to those which precede it. This, in turn, suggests that the book was meant to be read in order, that is, from the beginning

19 To be taken in the sense of Foucault's "Le Fou au jardin des espèces," Michel Foucault, *Histoire de la folie à l'âge classique* (Paris, 1972), pp. 193-225.

20 Al-Khaṭīb, *Bukhalāʾ* and also my *Bukhalāʾ Work*, pp. 95-116. This organizational scheme has been followed, with slightly variant contents, by the Ḥanbalī author Yūsuf ibn ʿAbd al-Hādī (d. 909/1503). See my article "Yūsuf ibn ʿAbd al-Hādī and His Autograph of the *Wuqūʿ al-Balāʾ bil-Bukhl wal-Bukhalāʾ*," *Bulletin d'etudes orientales*, 31 (1979): 17-50.

21 There is one exception, the incomplete *ḥadīth* found on p. 21 (of *Al-taṭfīl*). It is clear from al-Khaṭīb's comments, however, that he considered this a special case imposing special ethical/religious problems.

to the end. For this reason, I would argue, it is fundamentally wrong to treat works of this type as mere collections of anecdotes, virtual entertainment reference works, lacking in compositional unity.

The other major conclusion to be drawn from this organization concerns the moral orientation of the work. Had the *Kitāb al-taṭfīl* begun with a clear moral statement, such an arrangement would have tended to set the tone for the entire work. Instead, it is not until the fourth section (seventeen pages into the work) that a clear moral position is expressed regarding *taṭfīl*. In effect, by beginning this work with more essentially literary introductions, the author is giving preference to the literary character of his work and, while a moral position is taken, it is done in a subordinate way. When the *Kitāb al-taṭfīl* is compared to the *Kitāb al-bukhalāʾ*, the former can be seen as a less moralizing work. Though both works are based on characters, and in both cases these characters embody negative traits, our author treats *bukhl* as a more important moral issue, as more inherently immoral, and more in need of clear condemnation. In a way, *bukhl* could be seen, at least for al-Khaṭīb al-Baghdādī, as relating more to *adab* as ethics and correct behavior, while *taṭfīl* would relate more to *adab* as literature and entertainment.

As was observed above, the bulk of the text is comprised of *taṭfīl* anecdotes. In effect, they form a corpus of 129 anecdotes. As our analysis will show, *taṭfīl* can, in fact, be seen as taking place at different levels, and under different circumstances. It should be remembered, however, that the process being employed is not the division of an a priori concept of *taṭfīl* into concrete categories but the isolation of morphological patterns. In these cases, thus, structure is identified not on the basis of any actions which might be present in the anecdote but on those related to the role of *ṭufaylī*. Structure, then, is the interface of a *taṭfīl* action and a *ṭufaylī*. Thus, attention will be paid not only to the nature of the *taṭfīl* act but also to what I, following Claude Bremond, will call the agent or patient status of the *ṭufaylī*. In this distinction, the agent is the person who performs the action, whereas the patient is the person who is subjected to it.[22]

Since the basic meaning of *taṭfīl* is generally considered to be party crashing or coming uninvited, it is not surprising that the most numerous category of anecdotes (forty-six or 35.7 percent of the corpus) involves the practical problem of entry for the *ṭufaylī* or uninvited guest. These are the Entry anecdotes. They comprise one function, represented by an action through which the *ṭufaylī* succeeds in entering some kind of gathering or party, against the implied unwillingness of the host. In this category of anecdotes, thus, the *ṭufaylī* is clearly the agent while the host is a patient. In terms of the dynamics of what I have called elsewhere a hospitality situation,[23] that is the relationship between a host and a guest, this morphology could also be defined as one in which the *ṭufaylī* has initiated the relationship of host and guest.

Many of the qualities of this category can be seen in the following anecdote.

The proverbial Bunān passed by a wedding party and naturally wanted to get in. Upon being denied entry, he went to a grocer and gave him his ring in exchange for ten cups of chewable honey[24] and came to the gate and asked the *bawwāb* (gatekeeper)

22 Bremond, *Logique*, pp. 137 ff.

23 See my *Bukhalāʾ Work*, chap. 4.

24 See the editor's comments on Ibn al-Jawzī's version of the anecdote. Ibn al-Jawzī, *Adhkiyāʾ*, pp. 188-89 and n. 7.

to open for him. The *bawwāb* asked him who he was. Bunān replied: "I see you do not know me. I am the one whom they sent to buy the cups." So the *bawwāb* let him in. Bunān entered and ate and drank with the people. When he finished, he took the cups and called the *bawwāb*, saying: "Open for me, they want the pure honey, so I can return these." Then he went out, returned the cups to the grocer, and took his ring.[25]

It is clear that the function-generating action in this anecdote is the ruse, or stratagem, by which the *ṭufaylī* gains physical entry to the party. Once physically inside, he is free to partake of the food and drink which is there. Thus, two of the striking qualities of this anecdote are: on the one hand, physical entry and on the other, the stratagem. Nevertheless, though many of the anecdotes in this category display both of these features, neither is structurally essential.

Let us take first the problem of physical entry. There are anecdotes in which, without the question of physical entry being at issue, the *ṭufaylī* initiates the guest/host relationship.

The *ṭufaylī* Ibn Darrāj came to Baghdād and passed by a dinner-party. He entered, but lo and behold the owner of the house had placed a ladder, and whenever he saw someone he did not know, he would say: "Please go up." So Ibn Darrāj went up to a furnished room in which thirteen *ṭufaylī*s collected. Then the host took the ladder away and the tables were set below. The *ṭufaylī*s were truly confused and proclaimed that the likes of this had never happened to them before. Upon asking them what their occupation was, Ibn Darrāj was told that they were *ṭufaylī*s and that, in fact, they had no stratagem (*ḥīla*) for the occasion. Thereupon, Ibn Darrāj made them promise that they would allow him to teach them the tricks of the trade if he were able to come up with a ruse to get them food. He then addressed the host saying: "What would you prefer? That you bring us a large platter of food which we will eat and then leave or that I throw myself head first so that a slain man is taken out of your house, and your wedding party becomes a funeral?" At this point, Ibn Darrāj began pulling up his pants as though he were about to run and jump. Upon this, the host began imploring him to have patience and not to do it. He then hurried his servants saying: "This one is a madman." Food was brought up, and the *ṭufaylī*s ate and left.[26]

This anecdote clearly belongs to the Entry category; yet there is no physical entry. The *ṭufaylī*, indeed all the *ṭufaylī*s, have already entered the host's house, though this action did not have the desired effect of initiating their status as guests. In fact, the only movement which takes place is on the part of the food which was transported to the room where the *ṭufaylī*s were staying, rather than their being brought to the food. This anecdote, then, shows that entry in this category must be understood as the initiation by the *ṭufaylī* of the hospitality situation and not merely a physical entry into the host's home. This concept of entry as initiation means, in turn, that, while the crossing of a spatial boundary is frequently crucial in defining the nature of the function-generating action, space as such is not the criterion actually used in delineating the anecdotal morphologies.

It was, of course, noticed that this anecdote about Ibn Darrāj, like the earlier one about Bunān, embodied a stratagem. Indeed, such stratagems are present in the

25 Al-Khaṭīb, *Taṭfīl*, p. 62. In the interest of brevity, the English versions of these anecdotes have sometimes been condensed slightly in the process of translation.

26 Ibid., p. 67.

majority of Entry anecdotes. In fact, Chapter 13, entitled, "Stories about Those Who Were Prevented from Entering, and Who Therefore Used Stratagems [Deceit] and Gave Reasons to Enter," is composed, as the title suggests, exclusively of stratagem-based Entry anecdotes.[27] Further, as this title itself indicates, the stratagem implies deceit. Yet, one of the distinguishing characteristics of the stratagems in the Entry category is their tendency to be distributed along a continuum. The two poles of the continuum are represented by, on the one hand, pure stratagems, like the ones just discussed, and, on the other hand, cases of what could be called purchase or open exchange.

The idea of purchase is best displayed by the following anecdote in which a group of people were sitting and drinking. A man entered, they greeted him, but one of them asked him to leave. The *ṭufaylī*, however, replied with some nice lines of poetry, whereupon the company decided to let him stay and partake of the drinking since he was so witty (*ẓarīf*).[28]

Clearly, in this anecdote, though we can speak of a device, or action, by which the *ṭufaylī* succeeded in gaining entry to the gathering, we cannot properly speak of a ruse since no one was fooled. Through his eloquence, the *ṭufaylī* could be said to have purchased his right of entry.

What this anecdote, on the one hand, and the anecdotes about Bunān and Ibn Darrāj, on the other hand, have in common is a relationship between cleverness and the delivery of the goods. In each case, we can see that an equation was set up with cleverness on one side and fulfillment on the other (see fig. 1 below). In addition, in all cases, the *ṭufaylī* acts as an agent (horizontal axis) using cleverness to extract the goods from the host, who is a patient. If one focuses, however, on the host's attitude and behavior (vertical axis), then the principal distinction between purchase and the stratagem can be seen as one between a host who goes along by his own free will and a host who is fooled, i.e., knowledge vs. deceit.

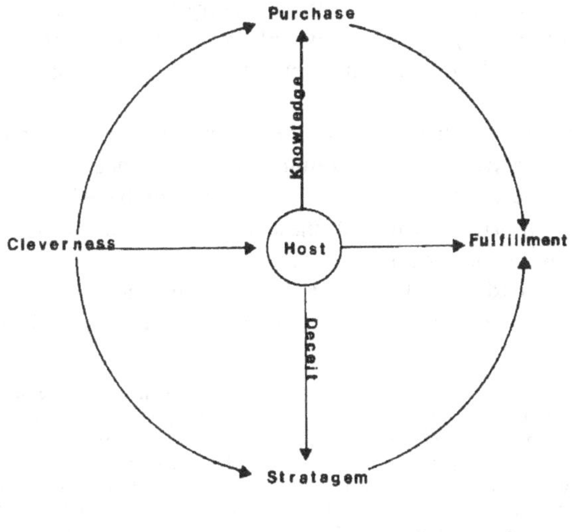

[27] Ibid., pp. 62-68.

[28] Ibid., pp. 41-42.

That this connection between the two types of relationship, that of purchase and that of the stratagem, is one of a continuum can best be illustrated by the following anecdote.

A *ṭufaylī* came to a wedding party but was prevented from entering. He knew, however, that the bride's brother was absent. So he went and took a piece of paper which he designed like a letter but with nothing inside. On the outside he wrote: from the brother to the bride. Then he came and said: "I have a letter from the brother of the bride to her." So he was permitted to enter, and he proceeded to give her the letter. But people said: "We have never seen the likes of this, there is no one's name on it." The *ṭufaylī* answered: "But more wondrous than that is the fact that there is not even a single consonant inside the letter, because he was in such a hurry." So the people laughed and realized that he had used a ruse to enter, and then they received him.[29]

Though the anecdote itself speaks of a ruse, the story is far from being a case of a stratagem relationship. True, the *ṭufaylī* does enter by means of a stratagem, that of the bogus letter. However, by the time he has been brought to say: "But more wondrous than that is the fact that there is not even a single consonant inside the letter, because he was in such a hurry," he is no longer really fooling anyone since, though this remark pretends to answer the question put about the letter, it does not really do so. In effect, it plays a double role. On the one hand, it exposes the stratagem, while, on the other hand, it constitutes a witty remark in its own right. Taking the anecdote as a narrative, one can speak of a stratagem which had to be abandoned in the encounter and replaced by a witty remark. Put another way, this anecdote shows the central position of knowledge in the distinction between purchase and the stratagem. Once the stratagem is discovered, it ceases to act as a stratagem but, by the same token, it can then be appreciated for its innate cleverness. The *ṭufaylī*'s second remark not only seeks to purchase entry through its own cleverness but also effects the conversion by which the stratagem becomes a piece of cleverness and, thus, an object of appreciation. From a literary point of view, one could say that the cleverness of the stratagem, which is only appreciated by the reader in the Ibn Darrāj and Bunān anecdotes, is also appreciated by the guests in the bogus letter anecdote.[30]

It was noted above that, given the basic meaning of *taṭfīl* as party crashing, it was not unexpected that many anecdotes should reflect this meaning, and these were the Entry anecdotes. Nevertheless, there are anecdotes not based on entry or crashing. One of the most important group of these is constituted by the Inside anecdotes (twenty-five or 19.4 percent of the corpus).

Jaʿfar ibn Muḥammad al-Kūfī related that he was once at a nobleman's dinner-party with Bunān. They were sitting at a table with a group of scribes, and one of the

[29] Ibid., p. 64.

[30] There is every reason to believe that this equation between cleverness and gain, with its continuum between the poles of purchase and stratagem, possesses a significance which goes well beyond al-Khaṭīb's *Taṭfīl*. Elements of it can be found, for example, in the *Bukhalāʾ* works of both al-Jāḥiẓ and al-Khaṭīb al-Baghdādī. This relationship may, in fact, be one of the most important recurring structural elements in medieval Arabic *adab* and fiction. It appears to operate in *The Thousand and One Nights*, for example, and in the *Maqāmāt*. Cf. Mia Gerhardt, *The Art of Story-Telling* (Leiden, 1963), pp. 397 ff; Tzvetan Todorov, "Les Hommes-récits," in Tzvetan Todorov, *Poétique de la prose* (Paris, 1971), pp. 78-91. I plan to explore this question more thoroughly in a study currently in preparation.

guests had in front of him a plump chicken. Bunān proceeded to hit the other fellow on the hand and to grab the chicken from in front of him. When Ja^cfar asked him what he was doing, Bunān answered that the chicken was joint property (*mushā*^c)[31] and could not be divided.[32]

In this anecdote, Bunān is the *ṭufaylī*, and his *taṭfīl* does not consist in his entry or his crashing the dinner-party. In fact, what Bunān has done in this anecdote has been to grab the chicken from one of the other diners, thereby increasing his own allotment of food. His action has taken place inside a gathering, after a clear hospitality (or host/guest) relationship has already been established. The *taṭfīl* action, thus, does not consist in initiating the hospitality relationship but in maximizing the benefit to be derived from it. In this situation, it is technically irrelevant whether or not the *ṭufaylī* has been invited or has crashed. In this particular example, we do not know whether or not Bunān is invited.

The function of the Inside anecdote is, therefore, the action by which a guest maximizes his share of whatever goods are presented. Implicit in this is the idea that the *ṭufaylī* receives more goods than he would have otherwise obtained. The *ṭufaylī* is, in fact, the agent, while either the other guests or the host are the victims.

The structural irrelevance to this morphology of whether or not the *ṭufaylī* was invited, and hence the clear distinction between the nature of *taṭfīl* in the Inside anecdote and the idea of *taṭfīl* as party crashing can best be seen in another Bunān anecdote. Our proverbial *ṭufaylī* is quoted as advising that when one is invited to a dinner-party, one should sit on the right of the house in order to have easier access to the food and more control of the general circumstances of the dinner-party.[33]

Clearly, since it is explicitly stated that the hypothetical guest has been invited, one can perform a *taṭfīl* action and hence be a *ṭufaylī*, without crashing. The fact that the Inside anecdotes describe a type of *taṭfīl* which does not fit into the common definition of *taṭfīl* as coming uninvited should lead us, at least initially, to question this definition.

Another distinctive feature of this anecdote is the nature of the action which takes place within it. In fact, the action itself has never occurred but is only recommended. Morphologically, this recommendation is not the significant element since the act of recommending actions, as abstracted from the actions recommended, would not by itself make someone a *ṭufaylī*. Hence, it is the nature of the action recommended and not the act of recommendation which determines the structure of the anecdote.

This literary device of couching an action in the form of a recommendation is a favored one in the Inside category. Sometimes, as in the case mentioned above, the recommendation is simply presented as a quote from the recommender. It can, however, form part of a more complex narrative. Wakī^c was eating with Bunān at a table when Bunān began reprimanding him for eating eggplant the cost of which was one hundred for a *dāniq* (one sixth of a *dirham*), and leaving the chicken breasts, when a single chicken was selling for one *dīnār*.[34]

As these anecdotes suggest, the art of being a *ṭufaylī* on the "inside" involves more than a selfish taking from others, but also considerable attention on the *ṭufaylī*'s part

31 See Joseph Schacht, *An Introduction to Islamic Law* (Oxford, 1964), pp. 138-39.

32 Al-Khaṭīb, *Taṭfīl*, pp. 99-100.

33 Ibid., p. 97.

34 Ibid., p. 87.

to his own actions, lest one of these be wasteful. *Ṭufaylīs* are told, for example, when sitting at a table, never to talk while eating, and if addressed by someone who must be answered, then only to answer with yes (*naʿam*). The reason for this is that talking distracts you from eating, and saying *naʿam* is like chewing.[35] The guest is not only advised to stay away from cheaper foods and vegetables but also to beware of filling himself up by drinking too much water.[36]

The other distinctive quality of the anecdotes in the Inside category that in virtually all cases, the function-generating action is based on a stratagem. Here, the stratagem involves some unusual eating practice designed to maximize the benefit to the *ṭufaylī*.

In effect, the Entry and Inside categories can be seen as reflecting two different stages in the development of the hospitality situation. A third stage in this development is represented by the Overstaying-Welcome category. This category, though quite small (two anecdotes, or 1.6 percent of the corpus), is nevertheless very interesting in its stratagems and in its manipulation of agent and patient roles. In this category, the guest shows his *taṭfīl* not by entering uninvited or over the resistance of the host, not by maximizing his consumption, but by overstaying his welcome, that is, by refusing to leave.

A man from Baṣra came to stay at a friend's house in Medina. But he exasperated his host by the length of his stay. So the host said to his wife: "Tomorrow, I will ask our guest how many cubits he can jump. I myself will jump from the courtyard to the gate. But when the guest jumps, close the door after him." So the next day, the host said to the guest: "How is your jumping?" He said: "Good." So the host jumped a few cubits from inside the house to the outside. Then he told the guest to jump. So he jumped two cubits to the inside. The host thereupon said to him: "I jumped a few cubits to the outside but you jumped two cubits to the inside!" The guest replied: "Two cubits to the inside is better than four to the outside."[37]

In this anecdote, clearly, the guest has shown his *taṭfīl* by overstaying his welcome and refusing to leave. Here, however, the agent and patient relationships have been changed, as has the role of of the stratagem. The host tries to use a stratagem to get his guest to leave: the host is then the agent, the guest, the patient, and if the stratagem were successful, the intended victim. In this morphology, however, the hosts's stratagem does not succeed, as is shown in this anecdote by the *ṭufaylī*'s clever reply. In effect, in Overstaying-Welcome anecdotes, the basic agent/victim relationship implicit in *taṭfīl* in which the *ṭufaylī* is an agent is actualized through a narrative structure in which it is reversed, at least initially, the host becoming the agent and the *ṭufaylī* the patient. However, we see that the host has failed because the *ṭufaylī* has nullified the stratagem of the host with a counterstratagem. This last reverses the agent/patient roles of the anecdote creating or restoring the *ṭufaylī*-agent host-victim role structure implicit in *taṭfīl*.

Hence, the Overstaying category has two functions, each represented by a stratagem. In the first, the host attempts to rid himself of his guest through a stratagem, and in the second, the guest, who is a *ṭufaylī*, foils the host's plan through a stratagem of his own.

35 Ibid., p. 57.
36 Ibid., pp. 74-75, 76-77.
37 Ibid., p. 25.

In another anecdote, a host and his wife decide to pretend that they are having an argument in order to try the following ruse upon a guest who has overstayed his welcome. After the couple argued, the wife said to the guest: "By He who blesses your leaving tomorrow, which one of us is more unjust?" The guest answered: "By He who blesses my staying with you a month, I do not know."[38]

The existence of each of these two stratagems, that of the host and that of the guest, is suggestive. The obligation of the host to resort to a stratagem implies that he did not feel free to simply evict the guest. In these anecdotes some sort of a hospitality taboo seems to be operating, whose rule is similar to that of the taboo on the outright refusal of hospitality in the *Bukhalā*ᵓ works, which obliged hosts to turn to stratagems.[39] But the second stratagem, that of the *ṭufaylī*, is also suggestive. For us to see that the *ṭufaylī* did not wish to leave, and, in fact, remained despite the attempts of his host to dislodge him, it would have sufficed for the host's stratagem to fail without the *ṭufaylī* responding with a second stratagem. A situation like this obtains in certain Jāḥizian *bukhalā*ᵓ anecdotes in which a host employs a stratagem to deprive a guest and the stratagem fails, either through chance or through a weakness in the stratagem itself.[40] In the Overstaying-Welcome morphology, by contrast, we are reminded that the *ṭufaylī* is a prince of tricksters who bests the stratagems of his opponents with superior stratagems of his own.

It should also be noted that the Overstaying-Welcome category, like the Inside category, reflects a concept of *taṭfīl* distinct from coming in uninvited. In fact, in the jumping-contest anecdote just discussed, it was stated that the *ṭufaylī* was a friend of the host's and, hence, it is very likely that he was invited, or, at least, welcome when he came.

In all of the morphologies discussed so far, we have seen the *ṭufaylī* triumph over all obstacles and maintain his status as an agent. There are anecdotes, however, in which the *ṭufaylī* becomes a patient, indeed a victim. These are the Ṭufaylī = Victim anecdotes (ten or 7.8 percent of the corpus).

In the following anecdote, our victim is none other than our hero Bunān himself. Bunān came to Baṣra and he was told of a group of *ṭufaylī*s who operated with a Master (*ᶜarīf*) who would clothe them and guide them to certain actions, and, in turn, would divide the spoils with them. So Bunān went to him and he was given the same amenities as the other *ṭufaylī*s. He stayed with the leader three days, and on the fourth day he went out with the group and came to a dinner-party. Thereupon he ate, and took out a great deal of food, of which the Master took half and gave Bunān the other half. So Bunān sold his half for a *dirham*. He continued in this manner for several days until one day, he came to a very nice wedding party. There, he ate and took out a substantial amount of food. What he did, however, was to sell it for a *dīnār* to someone whom he met. This he kept for himself and did not mention the affair to the group leader. The latter called together his *ṭufaylī* followers and said to them: "This Baghdādī (meaning Bunān) has betrayed us, and thought that I would not know everything he has done, so beat him while telling him what he has kept from us." The *ṭufaylī*s began beating Bunān. While one would say: "He has eaten a stew," and would

38 Ibid., p. 24.

39 See my *Bukhalā*ᵓ *Work*, chaps. 4 and 5; and my articles "Micropoetics," pp. 315-16 and "Humor."

40 See, for example, al-Jāḥiẓ, *Bukhalā*ᵓ, pp. 123-24, 148-49.

hit him, another would smell his hand and say: "He has eaten a vegetable dish," and still another would say: "He has eaten semolina." This they did until they had identified everything Bunān had eaten, without making a single mistake. Then a *shaykh* among them gave Bunān a nice slap saying: "He has sold that which he took for a *dīnār*." Then another beat him, saying: "Give me the *dīnār*." So Bunān gave him the money and they took his clothes which had been given him and threw him out. Bunān after this swore that he would never stay in a city whose *ṭufaylīs* knew the hidden (*al-ghayb*).[41]

In this anecdote, what has effectively taken place is that Bunān, because of his greed, tried to take advantage of the other *ṭufaylīs*. But they were too clever to be taken in, discovered his ploy, and punished him for it. Thus, there are two functions in this anecdote, and, therefore, in the Ṭufaylī = Victim morphology. In the first, the *ṭufaylī* takes some action and, in the second, we see not only that he was not successful but that he suffers for it. In this schema, the first action is motivated by *taṭfīl*, that is, is a *taṭfīl* action. Thus, we can see that the *ṭufaylī* became involved in this situation through his *taṭfīl*, and it is, thus, as a *ṭufaylī* that he is victimized. We can say, therefore, that in these anecdotes the role of *ṭufaylī* and that of victim have become fused. Obviously, a victim is a type of patient so we can see the agent/patient status of this morphology as being one in which the *ṭufaylī* starts the anecdote as an agent and ends it as a patient. In the above story, Bunān's *taṭfīl* is really a form of greed, independent of the taking advantage of hosts at parties.

In the Overstaying-Welcome anecdotes, the *ṭufaylīs* bested their hosts in the contests of cleverness and stratagems. Here, the *ṭufaylī* has himself been bested but, characteristically enough, by other *ṭufaylīs*. A similar situation is found in the following story.

A *ṭufaylī* had a dinner-party which was crashed by two other *ṭufaylīs*. But he recognized them and took them up to a room and kept them there until he had fed those whom he wanted. Then he let them go without giving them anything to eat.[42]

Here, the subjects of the anecdote, and the victims, are the *ṭufaylīs*. They have been defeated by a host, but this host was himself a *ṭufaylī*. In these two anecdotes, thus, when a *ṭufaylī* is defeated by someone more clever than he, that someone is a *ṭufaylī*. In fact, this last anecdote can be compared with the story about Ibn Darrāj which was discussed earlier. In both narratives, the host uses the stratagem of isolating the *ṭufaylīs* upstairs. However, the host who is also a *ṭufaylī* succeeds, while the host who is not is outwitted.

This is not to say that all *ṭufaylī* victims are victimized by other *ṭufaylīs*. They can be victimized by bad luck, or an error on their part. Such is the case in the following highly complex anecdote:

Al-Maʾmūn commanded that ten *zindīqs* whose names had been given to him be brought from Baṣra. So they were gathered, and a *ṭufaylī* spotted them. He said to himself: "These people have undoubtedly gathered for a meal." So he ran after them and joined them. The group was taken to a boat which had been prepared for them, and they boarded it. At this, the *ṭufaylī* said to himself: "It is an excursion," and he entered the boat with them. But it was not very long before the people were put in irons, and the *ṭufaylī* with them. So he said: "My *taṭfīl* has brought me to chains." Then he was taken along with them to Baghdād and they were brought to al-Maʾmūn.

41 Al-Khaṭīb, *Taṭfīl*, pp. 90-91. 42 Ibid., p. 66.

One by one, he had the *zindīqs* executed until all ten had been killed, with the *ṭufaylī* remaining. Al-Maʾmūn asked what this last man was doing there. The *ṭufaylī* answered that he knew nothing of the sayings of the others, that he only knew God and the Prophet, and that he was just someone who had seen them gathered and who had assumed that they were going to a meal. So al-Maʾmūn laughed and invited him to a feast.

Here the narrative shifts as the story we have been following becomes the frame for another. A courtier takes the occasion to relate an anecdote exemplifying the generosity of a host to a *ṭufaylī*. After hearing this story, al-Maʾmūn released our original hero and rewarded him.[43]

Despite the happy ending, this man was indeed victimized through his own *taṭfīl*, as he himself recognized. The victimization, however, was entirely self-imposed. Indeed, we would say that it was the strength of his desires which misled him. Finally, if he did in the end get a meal, this was in no way the result of his cleverness but merely of the magnanimity of the caliph.

Self-victimization even more clearly resulting from the psychological state of the *ṭufaylī* can be seen in the case of a *ṭufaylī* who was asked why he was pale. He explained that it came from being between courses and for fear that the food had come to an end.[44] This *ṭufaylī* is a victim because he is afraid, and the anecdote represents a pure case of self-victimization. What is also quite interesting in this example is that *taṭfīl* has been reduced to an extreme desire, that is, a mere psychological abstract of the *taṭfīl* action. Such abstraction, with its concurrent emphasis on the psychology of the *ṭufaylī* and the psychological states which underlie *taṭfīl* actions, is similar to the abstract, psychological treatment typical of so many Khaṭībian *bukhl* anecdotes.[45] It should be noted, however, that the tendency to psychological abstraction was greater in the *Kitāb al-bukhalāʾ* of al-Khaṭīb than in his *Kitāb al-taṭfīl*.

In the Ṭufaylī = Victim category, this psychological element, while occasionally present, was not morphologically essential. There are anecdotes, however, in which the psychological attachment of the *ṭufaylī* constitutes the function-generating, and hence morphologically essential, action in the narrative. It was stated about a certain *ṭufaylī* that he loved wine from his companions and hated that money leave him.[46] In this brief anecdote, we are not told of any action which the *ṭufaylī* has taken. Instead, we are shown his attachment to the goal of *taṭfīl*: drinking other people's wine. Therefore, the action in the anecdote which shows that the subject is a *ṭufaylī* is an action which shows his attachment. Such anecdotes are, therefore, called Attachment anecdotes (thirty-four or 26.4 percent of the corpus).

The precise objects of the attachment can vary. Often, it is to invitations and dinner-parties. ʿAbbās the *ṭufaylī* was asked what he would love most to have befall him. He answered: "an invitation nearby on a rainy day."[47] More often, anecdotes in this category go directly to the root of the matter, i.e., they show an attachment to food.

43 Ibid., pp. 44-46. This is the only case in the *Kitāb al-taṭfīl* of a narratologically complete anecdote which also serves as the frame for another story.

44 Ibid., p. 57.

45 See, for example, al-Khaṭīb, *Bukhalāʾ*, pp. 71, 75, 145, 172. See also my *Bukhalāʾ Work*, chap. 5.

46 Al-Khaṭīb, *Taṭfīl*, p. 26.

47 Ibid., p. 58.

This attachment to food can be shown in a variety of ways. About one *ṭufaylī* it was stated that if he saw bread in the clouds, he would fly in the air with the eagle.[48] Sometimes, the *ṭufaylīs* themselves admit this attachment. A certain *ṭufaylī* was once asked if he loved Abū Bakr and ᶜUmar. He answered that food had not left any love in his heart for anyone.[49] Even more impious were Bunān's views on a similar subject. Our hero once heard a man explain that the antichrist would come in a year of famine with bread and various types of food. Bunān replied that this was a man who deserved to be listened to and obeyed.[50]

Among the most interesting Attachment anecdotes are those which seek to demonstrate an attachment bordering on obsession by showing the subject's preoccupation with the object. One *ṭufaylī* was heard to say: "I waited for him the time it takes a man to eat a loaf of bread." The same *ṭufaylī*, when asked what two times two was, answered: "Four loaves of bread."[51] In other cases, the arithmetic was not so precise. Abū Saᶜīd al-Ṭufaylī was asked what four times four was. He answered: "Two loaves of bread and a piece of meat."[52]

These anecdotes are important for a number of reasons. By shifting the perspective from the stratagems of the *ṭufaylī* to his motivation, they provide a sketch of the psychological states which motivate, and, thus, in a certain sense explain, the actions of the *ṭufaylī*. By themselves, and even more so when combined with the abstracted psychological anecdotes in al-Khaṭīb's *Bukhalāʾ*, they argue against the idea suggested by some scholars that literature of this sort tends to be a-psychological.[53] The other major effect of these anecdotes is to shift somewhat our image of the *ṭufaylī*. He is not merely a clever trickster and master of stratagems, but also someone with a considerable attachment to, if not an obsession with, other people's food.

As the Attachment category shows, there are actions characteristic of a *ṭufaylī* which do not involve physical attempts to maximize his consumption. Another such type of action is that in which the *ṭufaylī*, rather than recommending any one specific *taṭfīl* action, defends the practice of *taṭfīl* or preaches it to others. The anecdotes involving this type of action constitute the Preaching category (twelve anecdotes, or 9.3 percent of the corpus).

A man asked his father, who was a *ṭufaylī*, if he were not ashamed of his *taṭfīl*. The father replied: "What do you disapprove in it?" "After all," he added, "the children of Israel had practiced *taṭfīl*, having said," (and here follows a Qurᶜānic quote): "Our Lord, send down upon us a Table out of heaven, that shall be for us a festival."[54] This use, one might say misuse, of a quote from the Qurʾān is typical of a tendency to try to exploit religious texts or maxims to defend *taṭfīl*. Similar uses are made of religious examples in al-Jāḥiẓ by *bakhīls* attempting to defend their vice.[55]

48 Ibid., p. 27.

49 Ibid., p. 57.

50 Ibid., p. 108.

51 Ibid., p. 60.

52 Ibid.

53 Charles Pellat, "Bukhl," *EI²*, p. 1297; Todorov, "Hommes-récits," pp. 78 ff.

54 Al-Khaṭīb, *Taṭfīl*, p. 34. Interestingly enough, there are several discrepancies in the citation. First of all, the entire verse has not been repeated. The *ṭufaylī*'s quote began: "rabbanā ʾanzil . . . ," while the Qurʾānic verse begins: "qāla ᶜIsā ibn Maryam allahumma rabbana ʾanzil . . . (Sūrat al-Māʾida, verse 113). And yet, the *ṭufaylī* had attributed the remark to the Children of Israel instead of Jesus. For the translation, see A. J. Arberry, *The Koran Interpreted*, vol. 1 (New York, 1974), p. 146.

55 See, for example, al-Jāḥiẓ, *Bukhalāʾ*, pp. 9-16, 185-86, 192-94.

To return to the Preaching anecdotes in al-Khaṭīb al-Baghdādī's *Kitāb al-taṭfīl*, arguments were also framed to rebut specific objections. To refute the saying, presented earlier in the work as a *ḥadīth*, that he who comes in to eat without being invited enters as a thief and leaves as an aggressor, Bunān employed the following argument: such food is *ḥalāl*, because the host, if he wants to serve a hundred people, tells the majordomo to prepare enough for two hundred. This is because those he wishes will come along with those whom he does not wish. "And I," explained Bunān, "belong to the group whom he does not wish."[56] Similarly, a *ṭufaylī* interpreted al-Khiḍr's advice to Moses not to walk without a need as meaning that he should not walk to any place where he could not chew something.[57]

These anecdotes do not contain stratagems, if stratagem is used to mean a trick designed to obtain some physical result for the perpetrator. Their clever arguments, however, are almost verbal and intellectual stratagems which distort the original meanings and significance of normative statements in order to make them support a vice. Thus, they, like the stratagems, contribute to the image of *ṭufaylīs* as men (in fact, no women are mentioned)[58] who put cleverness at the service of a less than noble cause.

A number of points emerge clearly from this morphological analysis. One has already been alluded to. This is the problem of the definition of *taṭfīl*. Even if we were to exclude, for analytical purposes, the Attachment and Preaching anecdotes as not necessarily representing precise *taṭfīl* actions or, at least, concrete actions, the problem would still remain. In the sequence of morphologies which relate to the hospitality situation, only the Entry category fits the definition of *taṭfīl* as coming uninvited to a party. In the Inside and Overstaying Welcome categories, not only are the morphologically significant actions independent of the question of invitation but in many cases, we know that the *ṭufaylī* was invited. This tendency of the idea of *taṭfīl* to extend far beyond the notion of crashing would be even further strengthened if one were to include the Attachment anecdotes as showing a quality which suffices to define a *ṭufaylī*. In effect, if one were to attempt to draft a definition of *taṭfīl* and the *ṭufaylī* based upon the actions of the *ṭufaylī* expressed in the *Kitāb al-Taṭfīl*, one would arrive at the following: *taṭfīl* represents the abuse by a guest of his rights in a hospitality situation. This abuse can then be seen as taking place at different stages. Entry would be the abuse of initiation, that is, coming without being invited; the Inside anecdote would represent the abuse of the rights to food and drink which the guest normally possesses; and Overstaying would be the failure to leave at the appropriate time.

And yet, the definition of *taṭfīl* as coming uninvited is the only one formally presented by al-Khaṭīb al-Baghdādī in his philological discussion. The only other remark indicating another, or broader, definition of *taṭfīl* is the statement found in the normative condemnatory section of the work to the effect that he who overstays his

56 Al-Khaṭīb, *Taṭfīl*, p. 35.

57 Ibid., p. 57.

58 This is in contrast to the fact that there are a few female *bakhīlāt*, al-Jāḥiẓ, *Bukhalā'*, pp. 30, 33-34, 37. The problems which would be posed by a woman attempting to practice *taṭfīl* are well illustrated by the following normative statement cited by al-Khaṭīb: the person most deserving of one slap is he who comes to a meal uninvited. The person most deserving of two slaps is he to whom the owner of the house says: "Sit here," and who answers: "No. I would rather sit here." The person most deserving of three slaps is he who is invited to a meal and then says to the master of the house: "Call the lady of the house to eat with us." Al-Khaṭīb, *Taṭfīl*, p. 23.

welcome is of the rank (*manzila*) of the *ṭufaylīs*.[59] A similar situation obtains in the lexicographical and philological sources. Without exception, the notices devoted to *taṭfīl* itself define the term exclusively as coming uninvited.[60]

The question becomes somewhat more complicated when one considers the synonyms given for the *ṭufaylī*. In effect, al-Khaṭīb gives four: the *immaᶜa*, the *wāghil*, the *wārish*, and the *rāʾish*. When these are checked in other sources, it becomes clear that the first two refer exclusively to coming uninvited (remembering that *wāghil* refers to drink). In addition, while most of the sources examined identify the verb *warasha* as coming uninvited, they also indicate that it can be used to refer to covetousness over food, while *rāʾish* refers to one who eats a lot. Interestingly enough, except for a single occurrence of *wāghil* in the closing *risāla*, these four terms do not appear in the non-philological sections of the *Kitāb al-taṭfīl*.[61] There are also a number of terms listed as synonyms for *ṭufaylī* in both the *Lisān al-ᶜArab* and the *Tāj al-ᶜArūs*. Of these, two, *wārish* and *wāghil*, have already been discussed. A third, *zallāl*, refers, as was noted above, to carrying out food from feasts.[62] Of the remaining words, five, *rāshin*, *naṭīl*, *dāmiq*, *zāmij*, and *dāmir*, refer exclusively in this context to one who comes or enters uninvited. Of the other synonyms listed by the *Lisān* and the *Tāj*, *mukzim*, *laᶜmaẓ* or *luᶜmūẓ*, *qasqās*, and *arsham*, all revolve around covetousness of food or overeating. It is also said that *laᶜmaẓa* equals *taṭfīl*.[63]

In effect, the lexicographical definition of *taṭfīl* and *ṭufaylī*, both within the *Kitāb al-Taṭfīl* of al-Khaṭīb al-Baghdādī and in other sources, focuses on the idea of coming uninvited, while at the same time showing some relation between the terms in question and the notion of what we have called attachment to food. This focusing on coming uninvited was sharper in the case of al-Khaṭīb than, for example, in the *Lisān* or the *Tāj*. Hence, there is some variation between the lexicographical definitions and that derived from the anecdotal morphologies, and which was described as the abuse by a guest of his rights in a hospitality situation. The lexicographical definition gives a

59 Al-Khaṭīb, *Taṭfīl*, p. 23.

60 Al-Zabīdī, *Tāj*, vol. 7, pp. 417-19; Ibn Manẓūr, *Lisān*, vol. 13, pp. 426-29; al-Fīrūzābādī, *Al-qāmūs*, vol. 4, p. 7; Ibn Sīda, *Al-mukhaṣṣaṣ*, vol. 1, p. 67; al-Azharī, *Tahdhīb*, vol. 13, pp. 349-50; Lane, *Lexicon*, vol. 5, pp. 1859-60.

61 Al-Khaṭīb, *Taṭfīl*, pp. 4-8, 113; al-Zabīdī, *Tāj*, vol. 4, pp. 364-65; vol. 5, p. 268; vol. 8, pp. 158-59; Ibn Manẓūr, *Lisān*, vol. 8, pp. 198-200, 265-66; vol. 9, pp. 349-50; vol. 14, pp. 258-60; al-Thaᶜālibī, *Fiqh al-lugha* (Cairo, n.d.), p. 221; al-Azharī, *Tahdhīb*, vol. 8, ed. ᶜAbd al-ᶜAẓīm Maḥmūd and Muḥammad ᶜAlī al-Najjār (Cairo, 1966), pp. 196-97; vol. 11, ed. Muḥammad Abū al-Faḍl Ibrāhīm and ᶜAli al-Bijāwī (Cairo, 1966), pp. 407-9; Ibn Sīda, *Al-mukhaṣṣaṣ*, vol. 1, p. 67; vol. 3, p. 101; Ibn Sīda, *Al-muḥkam*, vol. 2, ed. ᶜA. S. Aḥmad Farrāj (Cairo, 1958), pp. 150-51; vol. 6, ed. Muḥammad ᶜAlī al-Najjār and Murād Kāmil (Cairo, 1973), pp. 40-41; al-Tibrīzī, *Kanz al-ḥuffāẓ*, ed. L. Shaykhū (Beirut, 1895), pp. 256-57, 617; al-Suyūṭī, *Al-muzhir fī ᶜulūm al-lugha wa-anwāᶜihā*, vol. 1, ed. Muḥammad A. J. al-Mawlā, Muḥammad Abū al-Faḍl Ibrāhīm, and ᶜAlī al-Bijāwī (Cairo, 1945), p. 549.

62 Al-Zabīdī, *Tāj*, vol. 7, pp. 358-59; Ibn Manẓūr, *Lisān*, vol. 13, pp. 325-28; al-Azharī, *Tahdhīb*, vol. 13, pp. 163-67.

63 Al-Zabīdī, *Tāj*, vol. 5, p. 262; vol. 6, pp. 348-49; vol. 8, pp. 126-27, 313; vol. 9, pp. 45-46, 216; al-Zabīdī, *Tāj al-ᶜarūs*, vol. 6, ed. ᶜA. S. Aḥmad Farrāj et al. (Kuwait, 1969), pp. 17-18; vol. 11 (Kuwait, 1972), pp. 309-13; vol. 16 (Kuwait, 1976), pp. 370-78; Ibn Manẓūr, *Lisān*, vol. 3, p. 114; vol. 5, pp. 376-77; vol. 8, pp. 56-59; vol 9, p. 341; vol. 11, pp. 392-93; vol. 14, pp. 167-68; vol. 15, pp. 133-34, 421-22; vol. 17, p. 40; al-Thaᶜālibī, *Fiqh*, p. 221; al-Tibrīzī, *Kanz*, pp. 255-56; Ibn Sīda, *Al-mukhaṣṣaṣ*, vol. 1, pp. 66-67; Ibn Sīda, *Al-muḥkam*, vol. 2, p. 324; vol. 6, pp. 67-69, 200; al-Azharī, *Tahdhīb*, vol. 3, ed. ᶜAbd al-Ḥalīm al-Najjār and Muḥammad ᶜAlī al-Najjār (Cairo, 1966), pp. 196-97; vol. 11, ed. 60; vol. 9, ed. ᶜA. S. Hārūn and Muḥammad ᶜAlī al-Najjār (Cairo, 1966), pp. 44-45; vol. 10, ed. ᶜAlī Ḥasan Hilālī and Muhammad ᶜAlī al-Najjār (Cairo, 1967), pp. 103-4, 628-29; vol. 9, pp. 341, 362-63; vol. 14, ed. Yaᶜqūb ᶜAbd al-Nabī and Muḥammad ᶜAlī al-Najjār (Cairo, 1966), pp. 122-23.

primacy to the notion of coming uninvited, which primacy is not reflected in the same degree in the morphological definition. This contrast represents, in my view, not so much a conflict as a difference of emphasis. The lexicographical definition is meant to distinguish and scientifically define the basic meaning of the word within a philological tradition. What we have called the morphological definition is really an *adab* definition, representing the *ṭufaylī* and *taṭfīl* both as a character type and as a subject category in *adab* literature.

But these anecdotal morphologies do more than define *taṭfīl*. They also present an image of the *ṭufaylī*. One of the most striking characteristics of these morphologies is their tendency to rely on stratagems. Two of the most important categories, the Entry and Inside categories, which together represent over half of the corpus, are largely based on stratagems, as is the Overstaying-Welcome category. This tendency of *taṭfīl* actions to represent cleverness is further strengthened if one includes the Preaching anecdotes, which rely on verbal and intellectual stratagems.

As a character type, therefore, the *ṭufaylī* is clearly someone who lives by his wits.[64] This can be seen in the first place by the stratagems which he uses to achieve his goals. But, as we saw, these actions do not always involve deception. Even where they do not, as when the *ṭufaylī* is received into the company because of his wit, it is still the *ṭufaylī*'s cleverness which earns him his daily bread. The fact that in many anecdotes the assembled company admires the cleverness of the *ṭufaylī* is also significant, since it contributes to the reader's own admiration for the stratagems, both those which are exposed and those which remain hidden. In effect, the reaction of the audience within the text conditions that of the audience outside the text. The notion of purchase which, as far as the participants in the anecdote are concerned, only operates where there is knowledge and no deception, tends to become extended by the reader (who, after all, has full knowledge) to the stratagems involving deception. Thus, unlike the stratagems of the *bukhalāʾ*, which generally appear either absurd, odious, or ridiculous, many of those of the *ṭufaylīs* are presented as entertainingly clever.

It is not out of place, therefore, to speak of the *ṭufaylī* as a kind of hero,[65] not unlike perhaps the heroes of the *maqāmas*: independent and resourceful men, who survive by their cleverness and not without deception. It is altogether congruent with this "heroic" status that *Bunān* should be presented as an expert on fine foods. Nevertheless, another side to the *ṭufaylī*'s character was shown, though less prominently. This is the image of a man obsessed by a desire for food and dominated by his greed.[66]

64 This helps to explain why he is often included among the *adhkiyāʾ* (the clever or sharp-witted). See, for example, Ibn al-Jawzī, *Adhkiyāʾ*, pp. 188-93; Ibn Ḥujja al-Ḥamawī, *Thamarāt*, vol. 1, pp. 154-56.

65 Cf., for example, von Grunebaum's provocative suggestion that a miser might be a hero, G. E. von Grunebaum, "The Hero in Medieval Arabic Prose," in *Concepts of the Hero in the Middle Ages and the Renaissance*, ed. Norman T. Burns and Christopher J. Reagan (Albany, 1975), p. 90. While it would seem more difficult to consider a miser a hero than it would, for example, a *ṭufaylī*, the entire problem of the relationship between medieval Arabic character types and the idea of a hero or anti-hero is one which needs further study.

66 Such a view is, of course, in contradiction with the interpretation put forth by the editor of the volume. After describing ʿAbbāsid society as one knowing great contrasts between wealth and poverty, he explains that *taṭfīl* "is the twin brother of poverty, hunger, and privation." *The ṭufaylī*, driven by hunger and destitution, is led to ignore polite usages and crash meals, "Editor's Introduction," in al-Khaṭīb, *Taṭfīl*, pp. *jīm-hāʾ* There are many problems with this interpretation. No mention is made in the book of the destitution or poverty of the *ṭufaylī*. Nor is there necessarily any marked class distinction

These conclusions derived from the structural analysis of the anecdotes support those drawn from the study of the organization of the work. It was already noted above that the organization of the materials in the text reflected a certain moral ambivalence which condemned *taṭfīl* but which did not make this condemnation a dominating element. One reason for the more tolerant treatment given to *taṭfīl*, especially when compared with *bukhl*, might be that for the medieval Arabs, the obligations of the host were so important that abuses on the part of the guest were more easily tolerated.[67]

It is entirely consistent with the nature of *adab* literature that its messages should be delivered in these two ways, through the recurring patterns which inform the units selected, that is, their structure; and through the arrangement of the units, that is, their organization. It is equally a generic feature that both the structures and the organization also obey literary criteria, fusing the message with its entertaining package.

---

between the *ṭufaylī* and his host. Often, they are friends; in one case, both the host and guests are described as *ṭufaylīs*. It is true that some *ṭufaylīs*, like Bunān, are marginal social types, but their marginality is not that of destitution and poverty. The hunger which draws the *ṭufaylī* towards food is not that of starvation or deprivation but that of gluttony and gourmandise.

67 This argument, namely that the moral condemnation of *taṭfīl* must be nuanced by the recognition that the hospitality shown by a host in such a situation is in itself a great virtue and a mark of nobility of character, is displayed in the story told by the courtier to al-Maʾmūn discussed above. In this story, the courtier told how he had once come uninvited and was nevertheless treated with great cordiality and generosity by the host. Al-Maʾmūn agreed that this host indeed had a noble character and this story formed part of the motivation for his rewarding the original *ṭufaylī*, al-Khaṭīb, *Taṭfīl*, pp. 44-46.

XII

MAQĀMĀT AND *ADAB*: "AL-MAQĀMA AL-MAḌĪRIYYA" OF AL-HAMADHĀNĪ

THE *MAQĀMĀT*, OR ASSEMBLIES, OF BADĪᶜ AZ-ZAMĀN AL-HAMADHĀNĪ (d. 398/1008)[1] represent, without doubt, one of the masterpieces of classical Arabic literature. As is well known, the *Maqāmāt*, as a text, is a collection of adventures most of which concern a rogue hero, Abū al-Fatḥ al-Iskandarī, narrated by ᶜĪsā ibn Hishām, in rhymed prose (*sajᶜ*).

Much of the scholarly attention paid to the *Maqāmāt* of al-Hamadhānī has been devoted to the question of origin. Was Badīᶜ az-Zamān the originator of the *maqāmāt* genre? Some scholars have also noted the fact that some of these *maqāmas* possess literary appeal, though without investigating the exact nature of this appeal. In this regard, one of the *maqāmas* most frequently singled out has been "al-Maqāma al-Maḍīriyya." Yet, any reading of the *Maqāmāt* of al-Hamadhānī will show that this *maqāma* differs in important ways from most of the others in the collection. This difference leads, in turn, to the question of the nature of the relationship of that *maqāma* with others in the corpus of al-Hamadhānī.

It will be the purpose of this study to demonstrate that these issues are, in fact, interrelated. An analysis of the appeal of "al-Maqāma al-Maḍīriyya" will lead us to an assessment of its position in the corpus of *maqāmāt* in the text of al-Hamadhānī, thus investigating the relationship of this particular piece with other *maqāmas*. In addition, the question of appeal and that of textual relationship will be shown to be connected to the question of progenitors, since much of the appeal of this *maqāma* is derived from the creative use of preexisting literary roles, techniques, and situations.

* * *

The *Maqāmāt* are probably the most clearly delimited and distinct of all medieval Arabic prose genres. Their apparent virtual creation ex-nihilo by al-Hamadhānī has long attracted the interest of literary critics, both medieval and modern.

The most thorough recent discussion of this problem can be found in A. F. L. Beeston's "The Genesis of the *Maqāmāt* Genre."[2] The study itself contains two

* James T. Monroe's important study, *The Art of Badīᶜ az-Zamān al-Hamadhānī as Picaresque Narrative* (Beirut: American University of Beirut, 1983), was not available to me until after this article was already in press. The reader will find that his analysis of "al-Maqāma al-Maḍīriyya," pp. 145–60, displays significant parallels with, but also clear differences from, my own.

[1] Badīᶜ az-Zamān al-Hamadhānī, *al-Maqāmāt*, ed. Muḥammad ᶜAbduh (Beirut: Dār al-Mashriq, 1968).

[2] A. F. L. Beeston, "The Genesis of the *Maqāmāt* Genre," *Journal of Arabic Literature*, II (1971), pp. 1–12. We are not considering in this study arguments without foundation, like

major points. The first is a dismissal of an argument by Zakī Mubārak that Ibn Durayd (d. 321/933) was the originator of the *maqāmāt* genre. The second point, to which the bulk of the article is devoted, is the claim that stories in *al-Faraj ba*ᶜ*d ash-Shidda* of at-Tanūkhī (d. 384/994) constitute the most important literary progenitors of the *maqāma*. Both of these points are important enough to be treated separately.

Discussing the first of these two points, Beeston refers to the "flurry of controversy" between Zakī Mubārak and Muṣṭafā Ṣādiq ar-Rāfiᶜī over the question of al-Hamadhānī's 'invention' of the genre.[3] In *al-Muqtaṭaf* in 1930, Zakī Mubārak announced his discovery that al-Hamadhānī was not the inventor of the *maqāmāt* genre, as al-Ḥarīrī (d. 516/1122) had stated in the introduction to his own later collection of *Maqāmāt*, and as had generally been assumed since that time. Mubārak based his argument on a passage in the *Zahr al-Ādāb* by al-Ḥuṣrī (d. 413/1022). In this work, al-Ḥuṣrī wrote that Ibn Durayd had composed forty stories which he had invented himself (*istanbaṭahā min yanābī*ᶜ *ṣadrihi wa-stankhabahā min ma*ᶜ*ādin fikrihi*), and which he had presented in unusual language. This had incited Badīᶜ az-Zamān, according to al-Ḥuṣrī, to counter Ibn Durayd's stories with his *Maqāmāt*.[4]

It will be easier to follow the issues in question and the positions of the different critics if we begin by noting that this passage by al-Ḥuṣrī contains, in effect, three separate, and potentially independent, statements: 1) the existence of stories by Ibn Durayd written in unusual language; 2) that Ibn Durayd invented these stories himself; and 3) that it was these stories which instigated al-Hamadhānī to compose his own *Maqāmāt*.

On the suggestion of Ṭāhā Ḥusayn, Zakī Mubārak looked for these stories in *al-Amālī* of al-Qālī (d. 356/967). Then, upon finding stories attributed to Ibn Durayd in *al-Amālī*, and assuming that these stories were the stories in question, Mubārak concluded that Ibn Durayd was, indeed, the inventor (*mubdi*ᶜ) of the genre.[5]

In answer to Zakī Mubārak, Muḥammad Ṣādiq ar-Rāfiᶜī belittled the importance of this "discovery." He noted, among other things, that the passage in question by al-Ḥuṣrī had already been quoted by ash-Sharīshī (d. 619/1222) à propos of al-Ḥarīrī's statement that al-Hamadhānī was the originator of the *maqāmāt* genre, and that this information had been discussed numerous times since.[6] Aside from the issue of the novelty of Mubārak's thesis, there is no question but that, at the least, he has seriously overstated his case. As both ar-Rāfiᶜī and Beeston point out, the passage from al-Ḥuṣrī does not really suggest that Ibn Durayd was the inventor of the *maqāmāt* genre, nor does it contradict the statement by al-Ḥarīrī.[7] In fact, ash-Sharīshī himself cited the passage from al-Ḥuṣrī without any suggestion that it contradicted al-Ḥarīrī's position, almost certainly because he was aware of the distinction between inventing a genre and inspiring it. Because, in effect, there are two issues: whether Ibn Durayd invented the *maqāmāt* genre and whether his stories were both the closest literary progenitors and the inspiration of al-Hamadhānī's *Maqāmāt*. Disposal of the first argument leaves the second still standing. Indeed, both Muḥammad Rushdī Ḥasan and Shawqī Ḍayf have adopted the position that al-Hamadhānī was inspired by the Ibn Durayd stories presently to be found in *al-Amālī*.[8] To properly assess this position,

---

that of Jūrjī Zaydān, who credits al-Hamadhānī's teacher, Ibn Fāris (d. 390 A.H.), with the creation of the genre. As Muḥammad Rushdī Ḥasan points out, there is no evidence for this whatsoever. See Jūrjī Zaydān, *Kitāb Ādāb al-Lugha al-*ᶜ*Arabiyya* (Cairo: Maṭbaᶜat al-Hilāl, 1930), II, pp. 275–276, 309; Muḥammad Rushdī Ḥasan, *Athar al-Maqāma fī Nash*ᵓ*at al-Qiṣṣa al-Miṣriyya al-Ḥadītha* (Cairo: al-Hay'a al-Miṣriyya al-ᶜĀmma lil-Kitāb, 1974), p. 13.

[3] Beeston, "Genesis," p. 1.

[4] Zakī Mubārak, "Iṣlāḥ Khaṭaᵓ Qadīm Marrat ᶜalayhi Qurūn fī Nashᵓat al-Maqāmāt," *al-Muqtaṭaf*, April (1930), pp. 418–420; and idem, "Aḥādīth Ibn Durayd," *al-Muqtaṭaf*, May (1930), pp. 561–564; al-Ḥuṣrī, *Zahr al-Ādāb wa-Thamar al-Albāb*, ed. Muḥammad Muḥyī ad-Dīn ᶜAbd al-Ḥamīd (Beirut: Dār al-Jīl, 1977), I, pp. 305–306. Two dates are available for the death of al-Ḥuṣrī, 413 and 453. 413 is that preferred by the *Encyclopaedia of Islam*, second edition, and by ᶜUmar Riḍā Kaḥḥāla, *Mu*ᶜ*jam al-Mu*ᵓ*allifīn* (Damascus: al-Maktaba al-ᶜArabiyya, 1957), I, p. 64.

[5] Mubārak, "Iṣlāḥ Khaṭaᵓ," pp. 418–420.

[6] Muḥammad Ṣādiq ar-Rāfiᶜī, "Khaṭaᵓ fī Iṣlāḥ Khaṭaᵓ," *al-Muqtaṭaf*, May (1930), pp. 588–590; ash-Sharīshī, *Sharḥ Maqāmāt al-Ḥarīrī*, ed. Muḥammad Abū al-Faḍl Ibrāhīm (Cairo: al-Muᵓassasa al-ᶜArabiyya al-Ḥadītha, 1969), I, p. 24.

[7] If we were to judge from Beeston's notes, he referred only to the articles by Zakī Mubārak and ar-Rāfiᶜī and not to al-Ḥuṣrī.

[8] Ḥasan, *Athar al-Maqāma*, pp. 10ff.; Shawqī Ḍayf, *al-Maqāma* (Cairo: Dār al-Maᶜārif, 1980), p. 20.

however, we have to examine the stories in *al-Amālī* in relation to al-Ḥuṣrī's statement.

Since the stories of Ibn Durayd do not exist in an independent collection, it has generally been assumed that the stories transmitted on the authority of Ibn Durayd in *al-Amālī* of al-Qālī are those referred to by al-Ḥuṣrī. As Zakī Mubārak noted, the number of stories transmitted by Ibn Durayd in *al-Amālī* exceeds the number mentioned by al-Ḥuṣrī.[9] The question then becomes, to which stories was al-Ḥuṣrī referring? What is clear from an examination of the text of al-Qālī is that the narratives transmitted by Ibn Durayd are spread throughout the work. In other words, they are not presented as a coherent whole by al-Qālī, but rather as separate units which he happens to include in his text. Furthermore, while some of these texts contain the unusual language to which al-Ḥuṣrī referred, in the form of rhymed prose, or *sajᶜ*, not all of them do so.[10]

On the face of it, we have, therefore, no way of being sure that these stories are the ones referred to by al-Ḥuṣrī. Further doubt is created if we consider al-Ḥuṣrī's second point, that these stories were the invention of Ibn Durayd himself. Indeed, none of the stories attributed to Ibn Durayd in *al-Amālī* is attributed to Ibn Durayd alone. That is, Ibn Durayd is only the last transmitter in the chain. This means that if we accept the chains of transmission as they are presented in *al-Amālī*, then none of these stories is the original invention of Ibn Durayd. Mubārak deals with this problem by claiming that the chain of transmission is spurious, an invention of Ibn Durayd. As evidence for this, he states that the authorities listed are unknown people (*nās majhūlīn*).[11] It is not completely unheard of for medieval Arabic writers to falsely attribute stories. Al-Jāḥiẓ (d. 255/868–869), among others, apparently did so.[12] But the creation of a fictional chain of authorities would be more extraordinary, and, in any case, quite exceptional. Do we have any reason to believe that this is the case in these stories? Are Ibn Durayd's authorities unknown people? On the contrary, the great majority of stories are transmitted on the authority of ᶜAbd ar-Raḥmān ibn ᶜAbd Allāh, who himself transmitted on the authority of a variety of well known lexicographers and philologists, including Abū Ḥātim as-Sijistānī (d. 255/869), Abū ᶜAmr ash-Shaybānī (d. 205/820), Abū ᶜAmr ibn al-ᶜAlāʾ (d. 154/770), Abū ᶜUbayda (d. 209/824–825), Ibn al-Kalbī (d. 204 or 206/819 or 821), etc.[13]

There is, therefore, no reason to doubt these chains of transmission and, either these are not the stories in question or al-Ḥuṣrī was wrong about their being the invention of Ibn Durayd, or about the entire story. This last position has been adopted by ar-Rāfiᶜī who argues essentially that there is no source other than al-Ḥuṣrī for this information, and that no such original stories are listed among the works of Ibn Durayd.[14] While it is possible that al-Ḥuṣrī erred, this does not seem likely, given that our knowledge of the writings of this period is far from complete and al-Ḥuṣrī himself showed a considerable predilection for the *Maqāmāt* of al-Hamadhānī.[15] In all fairness, we must conclude that there is a considerable possibility that the *Maqāmāt* of al-Hamadhānī were instigated by a series of stories by Ibn Durayd, apparently no longer extant. Unfortunately, however, since we do not possess these stories (or have no way of knowing whether the ones we do possess are the ones in question), we are not in a position to compare the literary qualities of these stories with the *Maqāmāt* to determine whether they are closer than other potential literary progenitors of the genre. We have only the word of al-Ḥuṣrī that they were the actual instigators.

This brings us to the article by A. F. L. Beeston. The British scholar, as we saw before, dismissed Mubārak's argument without much ado and suggested an alternate source of inspiration in the creation of the genre, and that is at-Tanūkhī. The latter's work, *al-Faraj baᶜd ash-Shidda*, according to Beeston, "contains more than one tale which, apart from the style of diction could easily have figured as one of B.'s [Badīᶜ az-Zamān] *maqāmāt*."[16] Beeston isolated one particular story in at-Tanūkhī's anecdotal collection which represents for him "a *maqāma* in embryo, showing already some of the features which emerge as

[9] Mubārak, "Aḥādīth Ibn Durayd," pp. 562–563.

[10] Al-Qālī, *al-Amālī* (Cairo: al-Hay'a al-Miṣriyya al-ᶜĀmma lil-Kitāb, 1975). See, for example, v. I, pp. 32, 36, 37, 54, 55, 61, 169, 315; v. II, pp. 301–302, 345, 346.

[11] Mubārak, "Aḥādīth Ibn Durayd," p. 563.

[12] Such is the case apparently with the *risāla*s in the *Kitāb al-Bukhalāʾ*. See Fedwa Malti-Douglas, *Structures of Avarice: The Bukhalāʾ in Medieval Arabic Literature* (Leiden: E. J. Brill, forthcoming), Chapter III.

[13] See, for example, al-Qālī, *al-Amālī*, I, pp. 38, 57, 169, 315; II, pp. 180, 301.

[14] Ar-Rāfiᶜī, "Khaṭaʾ," p. 589.

[15] Al-Ḥuṣrī in his *Zahr al-Ādāb* includes an unusually large number of these *maqāmas* for a work of this type.

[16] Beeston, "Genesis," p. 2.

typical" in al-Hamadhānī.[17] The story in question is "Qiṣṣat Ḥā'ik al-Kalām," (The Story of the Weaver of Words).[18] The similarities between this story and the *maqāmas* lie, for Beeston, in several areas. The first concerns the presence of the man in rags, who, nevertheless, turns out to be "a miracle of cleverness and eloquence," and at the end "proves to be something other than he appears."[19] Beeston also calls attention to the presence of what he considers "social satire" in at-Tanūkhī's story, and states that social satire is also present in some of Badī' az-Zamān's *maqāmas*, such as "al-Maqāma al-Maḍīriyya." On a more formal level, Beeston points to the use of poetry in the story as resembling that in many of the *maqāmas*.

For Beeston, given all this, the originality of al-Hamadhānī rests in his use of *saj'* and in the "frank admission that his stories are fictional." This last aspect leads Beeston to say: "I would hazard a guess that this is the point of Ḥarīrī's word 'invented' (*abda'a*)."[20]

After enumerating his points, Beeston discusses some other aspects of the *maqāma*, especially the poetry, claiming that Badī' az-Zamān "has no poetic gifts," and that the small fragments of poetry at the end of the *maqāmas* are "a feature imitated from Tanūkhī's story."[21] Finally, Beeston notes that at-Tanūkhī's work should have been in circulation about the time when al-Hamadhānī was composing his *Maqāmāt*, and that this text, more than any other, served as model and inspiration for Badī' az-Zamān.

Beeston's argument is persuasive in that the story he has examined probably bears more similarities to the most common type of *maqāma* than any other story that has been brought forward. Our discussion of the problem of Ibn Durayd's instigation of Badī' az-Zamān has shown, however, that no exclusively comparative analysis can ever completely contradict al-Ḥuṣrī's historical statement.

But more fundamentally, and more significantly for our discussion, there is no doubt that Badī' az-Zamān al-Hamadhānī was deeply conscious of writing within a well-developed Arabic literary tradition and especially that part of the tradition usually described as *adab* literature. As such, he undoubtedly borrowed and reworked material from many literary predecessors. For Shawqī Ḍayf, while al-Hamadhānī was influenced on the level of form (*ash-shakl*) by Ibn Durayd, he was influenced on the level of content by the writings on beggars (*ahl al-kudya*) of al-Jāḥiẓ and other authors.[22] Muḥammad Rushdī Ḥasan has echoed this position, while Mārūn 'Abbūd has pointed to the "Ḥadīth Khālid ibn Yazīd" from al-Bukhalā' of al-Jāḥiẓ with its stories of beggars as a literary progenitor of the *Maqāmāt*.[23]

The breadth of al-Hamadhānī's debt to previous anecdotal literature is further increased, however, if we turn our attention from the mere subject of beggars and beggary to the nature of the character that al-Hamadhānī has created and the roles this character is called upon to play. In this context, one can see a similarity between Abū al-Fatḥ al-Iskandarī and other trickster heroes of Arabic anecdotal literature. Like the hero of the *maqāma*, the *ṭufaylī*, or professional party crasher, is a socially marginal character who lives by his wits.[24] And, as I have noted elsewhere, there is often a sense in the *Taṭfīl* literature, as in the

[17] Beeston, "Genesis," p. 8.

[18] At-Tanūkhī, *Kitāb al-Faraj ba'd ash-Shidda*, ed. 'Abbūd ash-Shālijī (Beirut: Dār Ṣādir, 1978), III, pp. 306–313.

[19] Beeston, "Genesis," p. 7.

[20] Beeston, "Genesis," p. 9. Beeston attributes the term "abda'a" twice (p. 2 and p. 7) to al-Ḥarīrī. Whereas al-Ḥarīrī's text, as given by ash-Sharīshī and quoted by Mubārak, is "ibtada'a." The term *abda'a*, however, is used by ar-Rāfi'ī in his discussion (but not citation) of this issue. See ash-Sharīshī, *Sharḥ*, I, p. 21; Mubārak, "Iṣlāḥ Khaṭa'," p. 418; ar-Rāfi'ī, "Khaṭa'," p. 588.

[21] Beeston, "Genesis," p. 11. Obviously, such an appreciation can be called into question but a proper investigation of it would demand another study.

[22] Ḍayf, *al-Maqāma*, p. 20.

[23] Ḥasan, *Athar al-Maqāma*, pp. 11–12; Mārūn 'Abbūd, *Badī' az-Zamān al-Hamadhānī* (Cairo: Dār al-Ma'ārif, 1980), p. 35. See, also, al-Jāḥiẓ, *al-Bukhalā'*, ed. Ṭāhā al-Ḥājirī (Cairo: Dār al-Ma'ārif, 1971), pp. 46–53.

[24] See Fedwa Malti-Douglas, "Structure and Organization in a Monographic *Adab* Work: *al-Taṭfīl* of al-Khaṭīb al-Baghdādī," *Journal of Near Eastern Studies*, 40 (1981), pp. 227–245. The most important extant source of *taṭfīl* anecdotes is that of al-Khaṭīb al-Baghdādī, *at-Taṭfīl wa-Ḥikāyāt aṭ-Ṭufayliyyīn wa-Akhbāruhum wa-Nawādir Kalāmihim wa-Ash'āruhum*, ed. Kāẓim al-Muẓaffar (Najaf: al-Maktaba al-Ḥaydariyya, 1966). Though this was written after al-Hamadhānī, it is based upon earlier materials, and representative selections of *taṭfīl* literature can be found in earlier encyclopedic works like that of Ibn 'Abd Rabbihi, *al-'Iqd al-Farīd*, VI, eds. Aḥmad Amīn, Ibrāhīm al-Abyārī, and 'A. S. Muḥammad Hārūn (Cairo: Maṭba'at Lajnat at-Ta'līf, 1949), pp. 204–215.

maqāma, that this trickster has earned a moral right to his reward because of his cleverness.[25]

As we said initially, the relationship between the *Maqāmāt* of al-Hamadhānī and earlier anecdotal literature (especially the *ṭufaylīs* and *bukhalā*ʾ) can be seen most clearly in the case of "al-Maqāma al-Maḍīriyya." This *maqāma* has also generally been recognized both as one of the most appealing of those written by al-Hamadhānī and, at the same time, as somehow different from the others. Muḥammad Rushdī Ḥasan considers it one of a small number of "story-like" (*qiṣaṣiyya*) and "humorous" (*fukāhiyya*) *maqāmas*, placing "al-Maḍīriyya" in the latter category.[26] The contradiction is hardly insoluble, of course, the *maqāma* being both a good story and humorous. What the contradiction represents, however, is that neither author gave a systematic explanation of the appeal of the *maqāma*, which explanation would show the literary solidarity of the story and its humor.

In the process, nonetheless, these critics have called attention to a vital literary problem, and that is the relationship between "al-Maḍīriyya" and the other *maqāmas* with which it forms a corpus. Among the generic qualities that clearly distinguish the *Maqāmāt* from its literary predecessors, one is the consistent use of rhymed prose (*saj*ʿ). The other is the nature of the *Maqāmāt* as a corpus. Because the *maqāmas* display a strictly uniform discourse and fiction, and because they describe the continuing adventures of the same two characters,[27] they form a single literary unit. In other words, although each *maqāma* forms a potentially independent narrative unit which can stand on its own from a literary point of view, it must, nevertheless, be examined in the light of other *maqāmas* in the corpus to yield its full significance. Hence, in the case with which we are dealing, the difference between "al-Maḍīriyya" and the greater number of its fellows dictates its relationship to the others and its specific appeal.

But, both the relationship between "al-Maḍīriyya" and other *maqāmas*, and the nature of its appeal relate to earlier anecdotal literature. Thus, the examination of those elements that al-Hamadhānī took from earlier writers and the ways in which he transformed them is also the best explanation of his appeal.

* * *

"Al-Maqāma al-Maḍīriyya" takes its title from *al-maḍīra*, the stew which will instigate the *maqāma* itself. The narrator, ʿĪsā ibn Hishām, recounts the adventure of the rogue hero, Abū al-Fatḥ al-Iskandarī, at which he is also present. ʿĪsā was in Basra with Abū al-Fatḥ. The two were invited to a dinner party, at which a very nice *maḍīra* was served. Abū al-Fatḥ recoiled in horror, cursed the stew, and refused to come near it. Everyone thought that he was simply joking but the matter was quite serious. So the *maḍīra* was pulled away with everyone's hearts and eyes following. They then asked Abū al-Fatḥ about the affair.

Abū al-Fatḥ then related that while he was in Baghdad, a merchant invited him to a *maḍīra*, and he kept persisting in his invitation until Abū al-Fatḥ accepted. On the way to the house, the merchant praised his wife, especially her cooking talents, including her very movements around the oven. From there, the merchant proceeded to explain why he loved her, and that she was, in fact, more generous than he. He continued to elaborate on her qualities until they arrived at the quarter. Then he began a long praise of the quarter until they arrived at the door of the house. Then the merchant began to lavish his praise on the house, including its windows and the intricacy of their workmanship, proceeding to the door and its manufacturer and his excellence. This, in turn, brought on admiration for the door knocker and its origin. Once inside the vestibule, the host began explaining how he acquired the house and the ruses he had to employ to get it. He then followed this story with another case of a clever purchase, proceeding to a description of the mat and the matmaker.

Then declaring that they should return to talking about the *maḍīra*, since noontime had arrived, the merchant called for the slave to bring the basin and water. Abū al-Fatḥ, at this point, praised God and told himself that perhaps relief had come. The slave came forth and the merchant then proceeded to discuss the slave, bidding him to show off various parts of his body, including his head, leg, arm, and teeth. Of course, the slave did what his master told him, which provoked the merchant to tell Abū al-Fatḥ about the provenance of the slave. The merchant then asked the slave to put down the basin and bring the pitcher. Then follows a description of the basin, with the host inciting Abū al-Fatḥ to ask him when he bought it, and proceeding to answer his own question without

[25] Malti-Douglas, "Structure and Organization," pp. 234–235.

[26] Ḥasan, *Athar al-Maqāma*, p. 27; ʿAbbūd, *Badī*ʿ *az-Zamān*, pp. 80, 86.

[27] Of course, Abū al-Fatḥ al-Iskandarī, though present in most of the *maqāmāt*, is not present in all of them. ʿĪsā ibn Hishām, as narrator, is present in all the *maqāmas*.

any response from the guest. When the slave brought forth the pitcher, the merchant lavished praise on it, claiming that that particular pitcher was only proper for that basin, and that basin was only fit for that specific part of the house, which was in turn only fit for that house itself, which in turn was beautified by the presence of that guest.

The host then called for the servant to bring out the water, since it was time to eat. The water then spurred more praise, which led to praise of the vessel, in turn leading to the napkin, and how it was made.

Then the merchant asked the slave to bring out the table, since time had passed and it was now time for the food. So the slave brought out the table, which incited the merchant to begin its praise, urging Abū al-Fatḥ to admire its form. Abū al-Fatḥ, instead, asked when the food was coming out, to which the merchant replied: "Now." Then the host asked the slave to hurry up with the food, adding one more observation about the virtues of the table.

At this point, Abū al-Fatḥ became angry and replied that there still remained the bread and its various attributes, including how it was made, which baker was brought, as well as the wood and the flour, not to mention the salt and the vinegar and so on. Of course, after this, Abū al-Fatḥ added, one still had the *maḍīra* itself, how its meat was purchased, how the proper cooking pot was had, how the fire was lit, and so forth. And this, indeed, was a never-ending affair.

Then Abū al-Fatḥ got up and the merchant asked him where he was going. Abū al-Fatḥ answered that he had to fulfill a need. So the merchant took this opportunity to begin lavishing praise on his toilet, describing its floor and its ceiling. The construction of the privy is so excellent and its materials of such quality that the tiny ants slid off its walls and the flies slip when they walk on it. This led to a description of its door, ending with the exclamation that "the guest wishes that he could eat in it." So Abū al-Fatḥ replied that the merchant himself should eat there, and that the toilet was not part of the deal.

Abū al-Fatḥ went to the door, in a hurry to leave. He ran out with the merchant following and yelling: "Abū al-Fatḥ, the *maḍīra*." (*Abū al-Fatḥ, al-maḍīra*). The boys thought that "*al-maḍīra*" was a nickname for Abū al-Fatḥ, and began to call it out. So, out of excessive anger, he threw a stone at one of them, which instead hit a man in his turban and penetrated his skull. Abū al-Fatḥ was then beaten with sandals and taken to jail, where he spent two years. He vowed after this that he would never eat a *maḍīra* as long as he lived.

Our hero at this point asked the members of the original dinner party if he was unjust in this. So ʿĪsā ibn Hishām states that they accepted his excuse and made the same vow, concluding that the *maḍīra* had sinned against the free-born and preferred base people over the good.[28]

This *maqāma* can be analyzed on several levels. Let us begin wih the level of organization, that is, the visible arrangement of materials. From that point of view, the *maqāma* can be divided into ten sections.

1. The frame with ʿĪsā and Abū al-Fatḥ. This includes the presence at the initial dinner party and the presentation of the *maḍīra*, as well as Abū al-Fatḥ's reaction and the removal of the stew.

2. The narration by Abū al-Fatḥ of the beginning of his misadventure, including the invitation of the merchant and the latter's persistence. Here, we also have the initial part of the merchant's speech in praise of his wife, his quarter, his house, including its window, its door, its door knocker, the staircase, and the mat.

3. The mention of the *maḍīra* and noontime, and the call to bring out the water. This is, of course, followed by the praise of the slave, the basin, and the pitcher.

4. The second mention of food, and that the time to eat has come. This is followed by the praise of the water, the vessel, and the napkin.

5. The merchant's request to bring forth the table, with the third mention that it is time to eat. The arrival of the table and the merchant's subsequent praise of it.

6. Abū al-Fatḥ's confrontation of the merchant about the arrival of the food. This is followed by the merchant's order to hurry up the bringing out the food, with an attempt to return to the praise of the table.

7. The reaction of anger on Abū al-Fatḥ's part, which he follows by a speech about the remaining objects which have not yet received their proper praise, including the bread, the flour, and finally the *maḍīra* itself.

8. The attempt by Abū al-Fatḥ to use the privy, which elicits the response of praise by the merchant, culminating in his statement that a guest would want to eat there. This is followed by Abū al-Fatḥ's reaction to this.

9. The running out of Abū al-Fatḥ, with the merchant at his heels yelling out to him "Abū al-Fatḥ,

[28] For the complete Arabic text, see al-Hamadhānī, *Maqāmāt*, pp. 104–117. For a full English translation, see *The*

al-Maḍīra." This brings on the yells of the boys, provoking Abū al-Fatḥ to throw a stone. Abū al-Fatḥ's bad luck with this act and his punishment.

10. The return to the frame, and the reaction of the guests at the initial dinner party.

Several points about this organization bear mention. While the merchant's various speeches of praise form a major part of the *maqāma* (sections 2 to 8), the speeches themselves are broken at crucial points by the mention of the impending arrival of the food. Furthermore, all the speeches of the merchant are confined to the praise of non-food items, although he does sing the praises of the vessels and the food-linked items, such as the napkin. On the other hand, Abū al-Fatḥ's response when he gets angry and mentions the objects still to be praised is centered on food, including the bread and the *maḍīra* itself. We will discuss the significance of these points for the overall literary effect of the *maqāma* below.

It is also evident that the *maqāma* consists of one story, that of Abū al-Fatḥ and the merchant, enframed within another story, that of Abū al-Fatḥ, ᶜĪsā ibn Hishām, and the company. This use of the technique of the frame story is far more than a mere compositional flourish or ornament. It is, indeed, crucial to the construction of the *maqāma* as a whole. To see this, and in particular to see the relationship between the two stories, the framing and the enframed, we need to go beyond the organizational level of analysis and investigate the narrative structure of the *maqāma* itself.

Both stories are about dinner parties, and they both, in fact, mirror each other. Although the frame story takes place in Basra and the enframed takes place in Baghdad, both involve invitations from a "a merchant," (*baᶜḍ at-tujjār*).[29] Furthermore, both stories center around the non-consumption of a *maḍīra*, with, of course, one major difference. In the frame, the *maḍīra* is presented and then pulled away with the yearning eyes following it, whereas in the enframed story, the *maḍīra* is never presented, but with the yearning nevertheless present on the part of Abū al-Fatḥ. Clearly, the frame story is used to set up and explain the story which it enframes.

This enframed story possesses a narrative structure taken directly from *adab* anecdotal literature and which finds its clearest expression in *bukhalā*ᵓ literature. One of the most common types of *bukhalā*ᵓ anecdotes is the Hospitality anecdote which possesses a structure which, it will immediately become evident, is also the structure of the enframed story. This structure involves a hospitality situation, that is, a situation in which a host and guest are both present and in which, thus, hospitality is enjoined upon the host. This Hospitality morphology consists of two functions. In the first, the demand for hospitality, either implicit or explicit, and either provoked by the host or merely submitted to by him, is created. In the second, the host somehow avoids fulfilling whatever is implied by the demand for hospitality, but he must do so without violating the taboo on the outright refusal of hospitality, that is, he must do so through some sort of stratagem or ruse.[30]

Clearly, in the enframed story with Abū al-Fatḥ and the merchant, these forces are at play. The merchant has gone so far as to invite Abū al-Fatḥ to partake of the *maḍīra*. Not only that, but he persists in the invitation until the guest agrees to go along. In other words, the demand for hospitality has been set up, and explicitly at that: it has been instigated by the host, the merchant. Thus, the first function in a Hospitality anecdote is present. Of course, as we know from the *maqāma* itself, the *maḍīra* is never produced. In other words, the guest never had the opportunity to consume the promised dish. However, the host, the merchant, does not at any time refuse to serve the stew. Instead, he resorts to delaying tactics, in this case, speech-making, terminating in a reference to eating in the toilet, which provokes the departure of the guest. The fact that the merchant peppers his long speech with the constant references to the impending arrival of the food implies that he was, at the very least, thinking about his obligation. Nevertheless, the *maḍīra* never makes its appearance and the stratagem of the host is successful. The second function in a Hospitality anecdote is, thus, present. Therefore, if we take the enframed story in isolation, we can observe that it would make an excellent *bukhalā*ᵓ anecdote. And even the stratagem employed by the host is built upon elements present in the stratagems of the *bukhalā*ᵓ, for whom delaying, speech-making, and the idea

Maqámát of Badíᶜ al-Zamán al-Hamadhání, trans. W. J. Prendergast (London: Luzac & Co., 1915), pp. 88–97.

29 Al-Hamadhānī, *Maqāmāt*, pp. 104, 106.

30 For a definition and discussion of the Hospitality anecdote, see Fedwa Malti-Douglas, "The Micropoetics of the *Bukhalā*ᵓ Anecdote," *Journal Asiatique*, CCLXVII (1979), pp. 314–316; idem, "Humor and Structure in Two *Buḫalā*ᵓ Anecdotes: Al-Ǧāḥiẓ and al-Ḫaṭīb al-Baġdādī," *Arabica*, XXVII (1980), pp. 310–311; and idem, *Structures of Avarice*, Chapter IV.

of eating in toilets are characteristic.[31] Yet, nowhere in the *bukhalāʾ* literature, either in al-Jāḥiẓ or al-Khaṭīb al-Baghdādī or the encyclopedic *adab* works, do we find this particular stratagem. This last point is important because it shows that, although the enframed story would make an excellent *bukhalāʾ* anecdote, al-Hamadhānī did not simply take one of the many anecdotal plots already in circulation but instead constructed his own, original story.

But, of course, the enframed story does not stand on its own, and it is not simply a story of how a host cheated a guest of nourishment. The frame shifts the focus from the actions of the host to the reactions of the guest. As we said, the enframed story, taken in isolation, would function as a *bukhalāʾ* anecdote, that is, in effect, an anecdote about a *bakhīl*, and in which the *bakhīl*, in this case the host, is the central character. On the most superficial level, what the frame story accomplishes is to place in the foreground Abū al-Fatḥ al-Iskandarī, casting him as the central character of the *maqāma* as a whole and, therefore, also, as a result, of the enframed story. In the process, however, the frame story has also altered the morphological significance of the actions within the enframed story, creating, thus, a different structure for the *maqāma* as a whole.

Instead of a story of a host cheating a guest, we have a story of a guest victimized by a host. While this difference might seem artificial, it is, as we shall see, crucial for an understanding of the *maqāma*, both structurally and from a literary point of view generally. Thus, though "al-Maqāma al-Maḍīriyya" exploits the narrative strategies of *bukhalāʾ* Hospitality anecdotes, its morphology, seen as a whole, is not that of a Hospitality anecdote but of that sort of a literary microunit in which a central figure who normally possesses an active role is forced into the passive one of victim. This kind of narrative structure can be found only in Bakhīl = Victim anecdotes but even more clearly in Ṭufaylī = Victim anecdotes.

The Bakhīl = Victim anecdote was a type of anecdote found in the *bukhalāʾ* literature, characterized by two functions: in the first, something is done to the *bakhīl*, and in the second, we see that he has suffered because of it.[32] The Ṭufaylī = Victim anecdote is similar in that the *ṭufaylī* (or uninvited guest) takes some action, which is not only unsuccessful but from which he also suffers.[33] As we shall see, it is this last type of anecdote which is closest in structure to "al-Maqāma al-Maḍīriyya."

This similarity becomes clearer when we look at the problem of roles. There is, in fact, a considerable similarity between the roles normally played by the *ṭufaylī* and those of the hero of the *maqāma*. Both could be characterized as rogue heroes who live by their wits. And, thus, when both are victimized, the same process takes placed in each case. This is a process of role transformation in which a character starts out with an active role and is then forced into a passive one. Of course, this role transformation from active to passive does not take place within "al-Maqāma al-Maḍīriyya." Abū al-Fatḥ starts out passively, that is reacting to events, from the very first scene. The role transformation can only be seen when this unit is replaced in its proper literary context, that is, the corpus of al-Hamadhānī's *Maqāmāt*. It is only because we know that Abū al-Fatḥ normally outtricks his opponents that we can see a role reversal in this case. In other words, the other *maqāma*s in the collection have familiarized us not only with the figure of Abū al-Fatḥ but also with a characteristic role, one in which he manipulates others. It is this radical difference in role that constitutes the most important difference between "al-Maqāma al-Maḍīriyya" and the rest of the *maqāma*s in the collection. This *maqāma* is one in which the role which we have come to expect from the other *maqāma*s is reversed, the manipulator has become the manipulated, or, in structural terms, the hero's role has shifted from active to passive, from agent to victim.

But this is nothing new, since we find this same phenomenon in the relationship between Bakhīl = Victim and Ṭufaylī = Victim anecdotes and their respective corpora.[34] In all three cases, the reader better appreciates the victimization and role transformation because he has become accustomed to a preceding dominant plot structure. Thus, on a certain level, the full implications of the role transformation which we

[31] See Malti-Douglas, *Structures of Avarice*, Chapter IV. See, also, Malti-Douglas, "Humor," pp. 309–316. See, also, for example, al-Jāḥiẓ, *al-Bukhalāʾ*, pp. 123–124; al-Khaṭīb al-Baghdādī, *al-Bukhalāʾ*, eds. Aḥmad Maṭlūb, Khadīja al-Ḥadīthī, and Aḥmad al-Qaysī (Baghdad: Maṭbaʿat al-ʿĀnī, 1964), pp. 173, 187–188.

[32] See Malti-Douglas, "Humor," p. 311; idem, *Structures of Avarice*, Chapter IV.

[33] See Malti-Douglas, "Structure and Organization," pp. 238–240.

[34] Malti-Douglas, *Structures of Avarice*, Chapter VI; idem, "Structure and Organization," pp. 238–240.

witness with Abū al-Fatḥ al-Iskandarī can only be understood in the presence of the other *maqāmas* in the corpus.

And, this structural relationship between "al-Maḍīriyya" and the other *maqāmas* is also crucial to its literary appeal. The dominant literary effect of this *maqāma* is, of course, humor, and the above-mentioned structure carries with it a potent source of humor. This derives first of all from the shift of roles which constitutes a reversal of expectation, which, as I have shown in other studies, is a familiar humor-producing technique.[35] In the case of "al-Maqāma al-Maḍīriyya," of course, we have the particular type of reversal of expectation, which Bergson has described as the *voleur/volé* syndrome, a phenomenon in which a character is victimized by the precise sort of action he usually performs.[36] Clearly, this is the case in the *maqāma* at hand. And, as in the cases of *bukhalā*ᵓ and *ṭufaylīs* who are victimized through their own tricks, Abū al-Fatḥ's punishment is also condign. Indeed, he is a trickster who generally wins his way with grandiose speeches. It is perfectly appropriate that he is outmaneuvered here by another speech. In the process, of course, the trickster has been outtricked. Nor does al-Hamadhānī permit the reader to forget this. The merchant not only outtricks Abū al-Fatḥ through his own speech but also virtually tells Abū al-Fatḥ, and, hence, the reader that he, the merchant, is the great trickster, by placing within his own speech accounts designed to show his own cleverness. This demonstration is presented fairly early on in the *maqāma*, in section 2.

In fact, however, we have been introduced to this phenomenon at the very beginning of the *maqāma*. In the opening line, ʿĪsā ibn Hishām states that he was in Basra with "Abū al-Fatḥ al-Iskandarī, the man of eloquence, he calls it and it answers him, and of rhetoric, he orders it and it obeys him."[37] Structurally, we can see that this line helps to cement the relationship between "al-Maḍīriyya" and the other *maqāmas*. It reminds the reader of the role usually played by Abū al-Fatḥ. The line serves as a linking device between this *maqāma* and the others. And, as we saw, the knowledge of this preceding role is essential to the appreciation of the *maqāma*.

Characterizations of Abū al-Fatḥ with phrases even close to this are extremely rare in the *Maqāmāt*.[38] And this fact is doubly significant because, taken in the context of "al-Maqāma al-Maḍīriyya," this phrase is richly ironic. It is, of course, the opposite of what takes place. The images in this phrase are those of power: Abū al-Fatḥ calls upon and orders eloquence and rhetoric, they answer him, and even more important, obey him. It is precisely this relationship which is overturned. Not only are eloquence and rhetoric the instruments of Abū al-Fatḥ's undoing but we could even say that, in a certain sense, he calls upon them and they do not answer, he orders them and they do not obey.

We can see this more clearly if we examine the precise appearance of eloquence or speech-making in the *maqāma*. Typically, in the *Maqāmāt*, we have a speech or series of speeches by Abū al-Fatḥ himself. In "al-Maqāma al-Maḍīriyya," we do not simply have a single speech by one speaker, in this case, the merchant. If we are to look for the paradigmatic equivalent of the usual *maqāma* speech or display of eloquence in "al-Maḍīriyya," we find, instead, an interesting phenomenon. This could be conceived as a single long panegyric shared by two speakers. Such a shared speech is apparently an innovation on the part of al-Hamadhānī, since, for example, in structurally similar *bukhalā*ᵓ anecdotes, the *bakhīl*/host is the sole carrier of the speech.[39]

Despite its dramatic tension, the shared speech does not function as a dialogue. Instead, we have a speech that is begun by the merchant. Abū al-Fatḥ attempts to gain control over the flow of discourse through an interjection in section 6, and then his own speech in section 7 about food preparation. It is the merchant, however, who finally reestablishes control over the discourse, terminating it with his own words about the toilet, which defeat Abū al-Fatḥ. We are reminded

35 For complete definitions of the following humoristic techniques and an integrated model, along with a critique of earlier theories, see Malti-Douglas, "Humor," pp. 300–308. For the role reversal, see Malti-Douglas, "Humor," p. 312, and idem, *Structures of Avarice*, Chapter VI.

36 See Malti-Douglas, "Humor," p. 306, and idem, *Structures of Avarice*, Chapter VI.

37 Al-Hamadhānī, *Maqāmāt*, p. 104.

38 In fact, there is only one phrase in the text close to the one under discussion. This is in "al-Maqāma al-Ḥamdāniyya," when someone says that he knows a man who "treads on eloquence with his sandals." Al-Hamadhānī, *Maqāmāt*, p. 151.

39 See, for example, al-Jāḥiẓ, *al-Bukhalā*ᵓ, pp. 123–124, which anecdote is discussed in Malti-Douglas, "Humor," pp. 309–316.

also of the merchant's control over the discourse by his repeated rhetorical questions on the pattern of "and ask me . . " or "how do I know this?"[40] The eight such questions which punctuate the merchant's talk show that it is the merchant and not his interlocutor who is dictating the direction of the conversation, to the point of putting questions into the mouth of his guest.

All these literary devices, since they revolve around the *voleur/volé* syndrome, could be said to be morphologically related. But, if we examine this syndrome carefully, we can see that part of its appeal lies in the victimization of the hero. Indeed, just as in Bakhīl = Victim and Ṭufaylī = Victim anecdotes, one of the major sources of humor in this *maqāma* is *Schadenfreude*, or sadistic humor: pleasure taken in the suffering of others.[41]

In the case of this *maqāma*, this is the suffering of the hero, Abū al-Fatḥ, which results from his victimization. That this effect is meant to dominate the *maqāma* can be seen even from its literary organization. The first emotion which we encounter in Abū al-Fatḥ is the cry of horror and pain when he is presented with the *maḍīra* in the frame story. All the other victimizations are from the point of view of *Schadenfreude* subordinate to this one, since they explain it. Hence, every time in the course of the *maqāma* that Abū al-Fatḥ is victimized, we can read his suffering through the suffering felt in the initial response at the beginning of the *maqāma*. Thus, it is not necessary for us to be told that Abū al-Fatḥ has suffered each time he is victimized. We know this already and hence, the reader can bring *Schadenfreude* to all the successive incidents of Abū al-Fatḥ's victimization.

We see here also one of the literary uses of the frame story. It places in the foreground Abū al-Fatḥ's suffering which is, therefore, present throughout the *maqāma* to a far greater degree than would have been the case were we presented with the enframed story alone.

Within the enframed story, Abū al-Fatḥ is victimized concretely on two principal occasions: the first being his denial of the stew and the second being his imprisonment. In a sense, of course, these two create a third, because in the frame story, Abū al-Fatḥ is also unable to enjoy his meal. Al-Hamadhānī has so constructed his *maqāma*, however, that the first of these two victimizations, the denial of the *maḍīra*, echoes throughout the *maqāma*. The principal means to deny the meal, of course, was the speech of the merchant. In other words, the guest receives talk instead of nourishment. And the host's speech is organized in such a way as to stress this phenomenon. The host repeatedly mentions the food, suggesting that it is about to arrive but then returns to his praise of various objects. Each time this takes place, the expectations of the guest are raised and then dashed; in effect, a series of victimizations. In the process, we also see Abū al-Fatḥ's mounting impatience and anger. The victimization through the speech is, thus, reemphasized each time that the host repeats this phenomenon.

There is another level of victimization present in the enframed story, and it is related to what can be seen as Abū al-Fatḥ's attachment to the meal which he is never permitted to consume. In a sense, this attachment is self-induced by Abū al-Fatḥ himself, and it, of course, contributes to the *Schadenfreude* since it increases his suffering. This attachment is embodied in the speech which Abū al-Fatḥ addresses to the host. As we pointed out earlier, the speeches of praise on the part of the host did not include food. The area of food was covered by Abū al-Fatḥ in his speech in answer to his host (no. 7 in the organization). The fact that our hero chose to address himself to this area demonstrates his level of attachment to the food. Structurally speaking, there was no need for him to go on at length about the various aspects of the meal. This type of self-victimization, especially through an overwhelming attachment to food, is present not only in the *bukhl* literature but in the *taṭfīl* anecdotes as well.[42] Its literary effect there is the same as that in the *maqāma*, to increase the victimization of the *bakhīl* or the *ṭufaylī*, thereby increasing the *Schadenfreude*.

To a degree, of course, the expectation of, and the longing for, the *maḍīra* are also shared by the reader. Here again, the frame story sets up and increases the emotional reactions within the enframed story. In the opening narrative, after a superb *maḍīra* is served, it is taken away, and "the hearts rose with it and the eyes traveled after it."[43] That is, both the lack of the *maḍīra* and the longing for it have already

---

[40] See, for example, al-Hamadhānī, *Maqāmāt*, pp 108, 109, 113, 114.

[41] For a fuller discussion of the psychological conditions for this emotion, see Malti-Douglas, "Humor," pp. 306–307.

[42] Malti-Douglas, "Humor," pp. 309–323; idem, "Structure and Organization," pp. 238–240; and idem, *Structures of Avarice*, Chapters IV and V.

[43] Al-Hamadhānī, *Maqāmāt*, p. 105.

been created, making it easier to perceive these phenomena in the enframed story.

All these phenomena reinforce and echo Abū al-Fatḥ's primary victimization throughout the *maqāma*. But this victimization is further strengthened by being linked to a second one, that of Abū al-Fatḥ's imprisonment. Al-Hamadhānī has constructed this last episode, which extends from our hero's leaving the house of the merchant, in such a way as to create further echoes of victimization. In fact, we have a series of five events, all of which are victimizations of Abū al-Fatḥ:

1. The merchant runs after him, calling out "Abū al-Fatḥ, al-Maḍīra," which is, of course, a reminder of what he did not receive.

2. The children mistake "al-Maḍīra" for a nickname and repeat the words of the merchant. This merely increases the victimization in number 1, and the suggestion that "al-maḍīra" could be a nickname for Abū al-Fatḥ only further associates him with the object of his undoing. The cries of the children become almost like jeering.

3. Abū al-Fatḥ throws a stone at the children and misses, hitting a passerby instead. The throwing of the stone shows Abū al-Fatḥ's reaction, his anger at the preceding, while his having missed shows him as a failure in even this action and deprives him of the satisfaction he would have received if the stone had struck its intended victims.

4. Abū al-Fatḥ is beaten. The victimization is obvious.

5. Abū al-Fatḥ is imprisoned. Again, the victimization is obvious.

In this chain of events, it is the act of the children who have mistaken "al-maḍīra" for a nickname which forms the link between the two basic victimizations. Up to that time, we have only a relationship between host and guest. It is the children who, by misunderstanding the merchant's words, project Abū al-Fatḥ's victimization from the original situation into a new one.

Of course, when we speak of role reversal, or of *Schadenfreude* generally, we are speaking of elements essential to the unfolding of the plot of the *maqāma* itself. There are other types of humoristic elements, however, which are independent of the structure of the anecdote and more or less independent of the plot. Among these are the purely technical devices of suspense and repetition, and our discussion thus far makes it evident where the author has employed these. Suspense begins with the frame story, since the reader does not know the reasons for Abū al-Fatḥ's adverse reaction to the *maḍīra*, and it continues throughout the speech of the merchant. This last device is, of course, similar to the suspense created by the prolix speech of the *bakhīl* in an anecdote of al-Jāḥiẓ about Maḥfūẓ an-Naqqāsh.[44] We showed the use of repetition in our discussion of the victimization of Abū al-Fatḥ.

By far the most important non-morphological source of humor in "al-Maqāma al-Maḍīriyya" is what Arthur Koestler called bisociation, that is, the bringing together of elements from different spheres not normally associated with one another.[45] On one level, it is possible to see this *maqāma* as revolving around a series of bisociations. The most important of these is a bisociation familiar from earlier anecdotal literature, that of food and excretory or eliminatory functions.[46] After all, it is the merchant's suggestion that the guest might want to eat in his toilet that puts Abū al-Fatḥ to flight. A mild echo of this bisociation can be seen in the merchant's story of how his napkin and his wife's underdrawers (*sarāwīl*) were made from the same material.[47] But force, and humor, is added to the basic bisociation of eating in the privy by the merchant's description of his toilet. A humoristic highpoint is his statement that it is so well constructed that "the tiny ants slide off its wall and cannot cling to it. And the flies walk on its floor and slip."[48] First of all, this strengthens the major bisociation by stressing the disgusting nature of a toilet filled with ants and flies; and this repulsiveness is reinforced through the physical image of the vermin struggling to hold on to the surfaces. But, secondly, this phrase creates a second humorous bisociation between the praise of the toilet and evocation of these undignified creatures.

Of course, the description of the toilet itself reflects the basic incongruity between elaborate praise and its object, which is, after all, a toilet. This is brought out by further bisociations like the one created when the host states, to show the magnificence of his toilet, that "it belittles the spring residences of the prince and the autumn ones of the vizier."[49]

---

[44] Malti-Douglas, "Humor," pp. 314–315.

[45] For discussion, see Malti-Douglas, "Humor," p. 301.

[46] See Malti-Douglas, *Structures of Avarice*, Chapter VI. See, also, among others, al-Jāḥiẓ, *al-Bukhalā'*, pp. 131, 150–151; al-Khaṭīb al-Baghdādī, *al-Bukhalā'*, pp. 71, 167–168, 168, 172.

[47] Al-Hamadhānī, *Maqāmāt*, p. 114.

[48] Al-Hamadhānī, *Maqāmāt*, p. 117.

[49] Al-Hamadhānī, *Maqāmāt*, p. 116.

In fact, the entirety of the merchant's speech creates a constant set of bisociations between food and other irrelevant subjects. He begins talking about food but ends up praising his wife, his wash basin, his neighborhood, etc. The bisociation is maintained by the fact that while we and the hero are thinking about food, the merchant is talking about everything else. And this is achieved in the text itself by the constant references to the impending arrival of the food. But, there is also a more general bisociation operating, that between the meal which Abū al-Fatḥ is expecting and the speech which he is receiving. Speech has replaced eating, oral functions both, in a pattern also found in the *bukhalā*ʾ and *ṭaṭfīl* literature.[50]

It is not, however, merely food which is the focus for bisociations, but one dish in particular, the *maḍīra*, whose presence hangs over the entire *maqāma*. When in the frame story the *maḍīra* first appears, ʿĪsā ibn Hishām describes it as one which "extolls civilization, quivers in the pot, heralds good health, and testifies to the imamate of Muʿāwiya."[51] At first glance, these compliments are obviously too strong for their object, a pot of stew. The reference to the caliph Muʿāwiya constitutes a humorous bisociation between an important religious issue and the totally profane subject of food. But even more significant than these bisociations, which are not unprecedented in anecdotal literature,[52] is the fact that the *maḍīra* is being described almost as if it were alive. Not only does it "quiver" but it "heralds" and "testifies." One such phrase taken by itself might be a mere rhetorical artifice, but their combination carries a flavor of anthropomorphization.[53] Anthropomorphization is suggested again by the bisociation created when Abū al-Fatḥ is effectively given the nickname of "al-Maḍīra." The name of a person is a reflection of his essence. To call a person "al-Maḍīra," is to make that word mean both a person and a stew. These examples, however, only suggest anthropomorphization, they do not demand it. One finds a clear expression of the anthropomorphization of the *maḍīra* in the very last line of the *maqāma*. After hearing Abū al-Fatḥ's story, the assembled company agrees that the *maḍīra* has "sinned against the free-born and preferred base people over the good."[54] These are obviously actions that can only be taken by sentient beings. In effect, the *maḍīra* has been made into another character. And the anthropomorphized *maḍīra* has been given the credit for victimizing Abū al-Fatḥ, which chiefly belongs to the merchant.

Narratively, therefore, this judgment is erroneous. But, it reflects a psychological truth. The *maḍīra* has defeated Abū al-Fatḥ because it represents his weakness, his Achilles heel. The chief qualities we associate with him are unusual degrees both of wiliness and eloquence. In "al-Maqāma al-Maḍīriyya," we are introduced to his attachment to fine food, and one could argue, from a psychological point of view, that it is this attachment which has permitted his victimization by the merchant. Thus, "al-Maqāma al-Maḍīriyya" completes our portrait of the character of the rogue hero, Abū al-Fatḥ al-Iskandarī. It gives him, along with his verbal skills, an attachment to food which relates him to one of his predecessors in Arabic literature, the *ṭufaylī*.

---

[50] This can be seen not only in the tendency of *bakhīl*s to present speeches instead of food but also in the advice given to *ṭufaylī*s not to speak, lest it get in the way of their eating. See Malti-Douglas, "Humor," pp. 312ff.; and idem, "Structure and Organization," p. 237.

[51] Al-Hamadhānī, *Maqāmāt*, p. 104.

[52] See, for example, al-Jāḥiẓ, *al-Bukhalā*ʾ, pp. 31–32; and, for discussion, Malti-Douglas, *Structures of Avarice*, Chapter VI.

[53] Muḥammad ʿAbduh, in his commentary on the text, explains these phrases in ways that can be understood as attributes of a dish, which is, of course, correct for one level of the text. But this, of course, does not eliminate the literal meaning which is semantically present.

[54] Al-Hamadhānī, *Maqāmāt*, p. 117.

XIII

Playing with the Sacred: Religious Intertext in *Adab* Discourse

Four-letter words seem to have a fascination for the West, and the Arabic word *adab* is no exception. Appealing and elusive at the same time, this innocuous term has caused more ink to be spilled than perhaps any other word in the history of Arabic literary criticism. Since I have done so elsewhere, I will not review this discussion here.[1] Suffice it to say that *adab* can be understood as a spirit,

Author's note: An earlier version of this study was delivered at the colloquium on "Medieval and Renaissance Humanism," at the Rockefeller Foundation Bellagio Study and Conference Center, Bellagio, Italy, November 28, 1989.

1. For an analysis of the discussions of *adab*, see my *Structures of Avarice: The Bukhalāʾ in Medieval Arabic Literature* (Leiden: Brill, 1985) 7–16. The recent work by George Makdisi, *The Rise of Humanism in Classical Islam and the Christian West with Special Reference to Scholasticism* (Edinburgh: Edinburgh University Press, 1990), effectively defines *adab* as a collection of separate subjects, that are then equated with Western humanism, understood as a collection of similar subjects.

but more concretely as a discourse (itself based on characteristic ways of manipulating texts of certain kinds) that could be said to express this ideal. *Adab* literature is an intertextually rich anecdotal and narrative literature designed to be at once didactic and entertaining. A mixed form that combines prose and poetry, the *adab* work includes Qurʾānic verses, *ḥadīths*, poetic selections, and anecdotes. One of the key issues in an examination of *adab* as cultural focus has been its relationship to the Islamic religious tradition. Despite the attention to this problematic in discussions of the meaning of *adab*, the matter has not been subjected to a systematic investigation based on the texts themselves.[2] It is clear that any understanding of *adab* as a worldly counterpart to the otherworldly focus of the religious sciences (a dichotomy that is highly questionable in the Islamic context anyway) needs, at the least, to be carefully nuanced, if for no other reason than the systematic and consistent presence in prototypical *adab* works of religious materials, like the aforementioned *ḥadīth* and Qurʾānic citations. In the overwhelming majority of cases, these religious materials are presented in a manner consistent with the way they would be used in religious works, for example, *ḥadīth* works, works of moral theology, and so forth.[3] Religious materials play other roles in *adab* texts, however. They are sometimes assimilated into the *adab* texts in ways that apparently subordinate them to the *adab* spirit. From a world of authority, they enter a world of play.

A close examination of the religious intertext in a representative group of *adab* anecdotes will allow us to examine this distinctive use of sacred materials. The authors of these anecdotes are some of the greatest names in Arabic prose and are certainly representative of the major strands of Arabic *adab* literature: al-Jāḥiẓ (d. 255/869), Ibn Qutayba (d. 276/889), al-Thaᶜālibī (d. 429/1038), al-Khaṭīb al-Baghdādī (d. 463/1071), and Ibn al-Jawzī (d. 597/1200). The dynamics of the *adab* discourse has a certain consistency, as we shall see throughout the analysis.

Western critics have called ample attention to the need for a reexamination and a rereading of the Western cultural and literary corpus. The provocative

2. For a discussion and references, see my *Structures*, 9. See also, Mohammed Arkoun, *Essais sur la pensée islamique* (Paris: Maisonneuve et Larouse, 1973) 210–16; cf. Makdisi, *Rise of Humanism*, 113–15. On *adab* anecdotal literature, see also, Yūsuf Sadān, *al-Adab al-ᶜarabī al-hāzil wa-nawādir al-thuqalāʾ* (Tel Aviv: Maṭbaᶜat al-sarūjī, 1983); Ulrich Marzolph, *Der Weise Narr Buhlūl* (Wiesbaden: Franz Steiner, 1983).

3. See, for example, Ibn al-Jawzī, *Akhbār al-ḥamqā wa-l-mughaffalīn* (Beirut: al-Maktab al-tijārī li-l-ṭibāᶜa wa-l-nashr wa-l-tawzīᶜ, n.d.) 21; Ibn ᶜAbd Rabbihi, *al-ᶜIqd al-farīd* (ed. Aḥmad Amīn, Aḥmad al-Zayn, and Ibrāhīm al-Abyārī; Cairo: Maṭbaᶜat lajnat al-taʾlīf wa-l-tarjama wa-l-nashr, 1965) 1.232, 235; al-Rāghib al-Aṣbahānī, *Muḥāḍarāt al-udabāʾ wa-muḥāwarāt al-shuᶜarāʾ wa-l-bulaghāʾ* (Beirut: Manshūrāt dār maktabat al-ḥayāt, n.d.) 1.121, 142, 403.

Rewriting the Renaissance is only one such effort.[4] Critics have also investigated the literary properties of religious texts, as has been done, for example, by Northrop Frye in his masterful *Great Code.*[5] This essay differs. Rather than subjecting the Islamic holy texts, such as the Qurʾān or the *ḥadīth*, to critical investigation (as Mohammed Arkoun does in his *Lectures du Coran*, for example),[6] I propose to analyze the permutations of religious material in *adab* works: how is the religious intertext used or misused? How does this help us to understand *adab* discourse?

The controversial eleventh-century religious traditionist al-Khaṭīb al-Baghdādī authored works ranging from *ḥadīth* criticism to history and *adab.*[7] His anecdotal corpus includes a delightful work on uninvited guests (*ṭufaylīs*), in which the following appears.[8] Al-Ḥasan ibn al-Sabbāḥ al-Nisāʾī relates that he went to Jaʿfar ibn Muḥammad, who asked him his opinion of sweets. The guest replied that he did not pass judgment on something absent, upon which the host called for an etched bowl in which was an almond pastry. Following a description of the pastry, the guest uttered a verse from the second *sūra* of the Qurʾān, "Your God is one God,"[9] upon which the host presented him with one piece of pastry. The guest then followed with another verse of the Qurʾān that exploits the number two and received a second piece of pastry. The narrative continued in this way, with the guest bringing forth a verse from the holy book containing the appropriate number, at which point he was given yet another piece of pastry. At the number twelve, followed by the twelfth piece of pastry, the guest jumped to the number twenty, at which the host threw the bowl at him, telling him to eat and addressing him with an insult. The guest merely replied that had the host not thrown the bowl, he would have said (again quoting the Qurʾān): "Then We sent him unto a hundred thousand, or more."[10]

4. Nancy J. Vickers, Margaret W. Ferguson, and Maureen Quilligan (eds). *Rewriting the Renaissance: The Discourses of Sexual Difference in Early Modern Europe* (Chicago: The University of Chicago Press, 1986).

5. Northrop Frye, *The Great Code: The Bible and Literature* (New York: Harcourt Brace Jovanovitch, 1982).

6. Mohammed Arkoun, *Lectures du Coran* (Paris: Maisonneuve et Larose, 1982).

7. For a biographical assessment of al-Khaṭīb and the controversy surrounding him, see my "Controversy and Its Effects in the Biographical Tradition of al-Khaṭīb al-Baghdādī," *Studia Islamica* 46 (1977) 115–31.

8. Al-Khaṭīb al-Baghdādī, *al-Taṭfīl wa-ḥikāyāt al-ṭufayliyyīn wa-akhbāruhum wa-nawādir kalāmihim wa-ashʿāruhum* (ed. Kāẓim al-Muẓaffar; Najaf: al-Maktaba al-ḥaydariyya, 1966), and for the anecdote, pp. 53–54. On this work, see my "Structure and Organization in a Monographic *Adab* Work: *al-Taṭfīl* of al-Khaṭīb al-Baghdādī," *JNES* 40 (1981) 227–45.

9. Sūrat al-Baqara, 2:163; A. J. Arberry (trans.), *The Koran Interpreted* (2 vols.; New York: Macmillan, 1974) 1.48.

10. Sūrat al-Ṣaffāt, 37:147; Arberry, *The Koran Interpreted*, 2.155.

This would seem a relatively straightforward anecdote. The *ṭufaylī* will stop at nothing to achieve his goal, including the exploitation of the Holy Book. His reply to the host's insult at the end of the anecdote illustrated this well: if necessary, he would have recited numbers into the thousands. And without a doubt, the tactic worked: each Qurʾānic verse brought forth pieces of pastry. This is obviously not the original signification of the verses in their Qurʾānic context. The *ṭufaylī* was redirecting the religious text to fulfill his physical (and psychological) desires for the food. He could not have done better than to begin on his gluttonous path with the assertion of the unity of God, present in the verse.[11]

Other dimensions add to the complexity of the narrative and help redefine the presence of the religious intertext. An underlying orality permeates the narrative: something emanating from the mouth (the verse from the Qurʾān) brings forth something that enters the mouth (the piece of pastry). That this orality is not a random component can be seen if one examines the guest's initial description of the pastry, which appears before the recitation of the first verse leading to the host's offer of the pastry. The guest has not yet partaken of the delicacy, but nevertheless describes elements of it that can only be assessed after he has sampled it. The description of the external physical appearance is followed by the sounds the piece of pastry makes as first it is pulled out (a squeaking like that of Sindī sandals)[12] and then put into the mouth (a sizzling like that of iron being taken out of the furnace). Both of these images create interesting but certainly unsavory bisociations: the first with sandals and the second with iron.

The religious text is here used to produce food. In another Khaṭībian anecdote, this one drawn from his book on misers, the dynamics are reversed. If, as its name suggests, the *Kitāb al-taṭfīl* is about uninvited guests (and by extension about guests who abuse their rights), the *bukhalāʾ* or miser literature tends to concentrate on the problem of hospitality and, therefore, to a considerable degree on hosts who may be niggardly with their guests. We are on opposite sides in the tug-of-war between host and guest. A Bedouin came to visit a man, who happened to have a platter of figs in front of him. Seeing the visitor, he covered the platter with his garment. This did not go unremarked upon by the newcomer, who then sat in front of the man. The latter asked the guest if he knew something from the Qurʾān well, to which the latter replied "Yes." Told to recite, he proceeded with the following: "By the olive and the

11. For the interpretation of this verse, see, for example, al-Bayḍāwī, *Tafsīr al-Bayḍāwī* (Beirut: Dār al-kutub al-ʿilmiyya, 1988) 1.97.

12. On this type of sandal, see al-Jāḥiẓ, *Kitāb al-tarbīʿ wal-tadwīr* (ed. Charles Pellat; Damascus: Institut Français de Damas, 1955) 84–85.

Mount Sinai."[13] The man then asked where the fig was, to which the guest replied, "Under your garment."[14]

This anecdote only makes sense if one knows that the protagonist has changed the Qur'ānic text. Recited properly, the verses should be: "By the fig and the olive and the Mount Sinai."[15] The textual play does not work, however, the guest not receiving any figs for his trouble. The circumstances of the fruit hidden under the man's robe would certainly suggest a sexual implication, and figs have been associated with male organs in other traditions.[16] But in Arabic, the term *tīna* (the noun of unity as opposed to *tīn*, the collective, in the Qur'ānic verse) signifies the behind or anus, which does not fit the anecdote.[17]

In another example, a *ṭufaylī* was asked about his knowledge of the Qur'ān. Replying that he was one of the most learned people in it, he was then requested to interpret a part of the following verse: "Enquire of the city wherein we were."[18] He replied that it referred to the people of the city, adducing as proof that when one says that one ate the table of so and so, he means he ate what was on it.[19]

This *ṭufaylī* is at once learned, as he himself claimed, and creative. His explanation of the Qur'ānic verse from the *Sūrat Yūsuf* concords with its traditional interpretations, hence showing his knowledge of *tafsīr* (Qur'ānic exegesis).[20] His creativity, spurred clearly by his one-track mind (centered as it is on food), lies in his analogical reasoning. One synecdoche has been replaced by another; and in the process, the holy text is placed in an associative relationship with the *ṭufaylī*'s object of desire. There is clearly nothing in the Qur'ānic text itself that calls up this bisociation, and the relationship between the divine original and its anecdotal context remains external, artificial. Hence, the Qur'ānic text is in no sense redefined; there has been no real semantic interference between intertext and context.

In effect, this has been the case with all the anecdotes thus far discussed. The first with numbers is a perfect example. The use of the Qur'ānic citations

13. Sūrat al-Tīn, 95:1–2; Arberry, *The Koran Interpreted*, 2.343.

14. Al-Khaṭīb al-Baghdādī, *al-Bukhalā'* (ed. Aḥmad Maṭlūb, Khadīja al-Ḥadīthī, and Aḥmad al-Qaysī; Baghdad: Maṭba'at al-'ānī, 1964) 75–76. On this book, see my *Structures*.

15. Sūrat al-Tīn, 95:1–2; Arberry, *The Koran Interpreted*, 2.343.

16. I am grateful to Speros Vryonis and the participants in the colloquium on "Medieval and Renaissance Humanism" for this information.

17. See, for example, al-Zabīdī, *Tāj al-'arūs* (Beirut: Dār ṣādir, n.d.) 9.154.

18. Sūrat Yūsuf, 12:82; Arberry, *The Koran Interpreted*, 1.263.

19. Al-Khaṭīb, *al-Taṭfīl*, 56.

20. See, for example, al-Bayḍāwī, *Tafsīr*, 1.493; Jalāl al-Dīn al-Maḥallī and Jalāl al-Dīn al-Suyūṭī, *Tafsīr al-Qur'ān al-karīm*, printed on the margins of *al-Qur'ān* (2 vols.; Cairo: Muṣṭafā al-Bābī al-Ḥalabī, 1966), 1.274.

is anecdotal. There is a genuine semantic identity in the case of the occulted fig, but this relationship remains superficial and has no influence on the semantic field of the Qurʾānic verse. (It should also be noted that the alimentary interpretation of the fig and the olive is doubled with a geographic one in the exegetical tradition.)[21] This does not mean that the games played here remain exclusively rhetorical. The Qurʾān retains its status as normative text (to say the least), and its use in this context opens up questions about the relationship between its inherent textual truth and its exploitation (in both senses of the term) in situations of varied and occasionally dubious morality. The bisociation with food, so natural in the context of *ṭufaylī* and *bukhalāʾ* literature, does nevertheless expand the horizons of the holy texts into another domain, suggesting implicit redefinition.

The interpretation of a religious text, however, can be perverted. Al-Jāḥiẓ, the acknowledged master of medieval Arabic prose, provides us with a good example. In his defense of avarice included in al-Jāḥiẓ's famous *Kitāb al-bukhalāʾ*, Ibn al-Tawʾam reinterprets a *ḥadīth* of the Prophet in which the latter advises someone to hold on to his money, turning it into a justification for not spending and effectively, therefore, for avarice (*bukhl*).[22] The argument is clever (and not without echoes in al-Jāḥiẓ's *Bukhalāʾ*), but it is fundamentally dishonest because it confuses the virtue of economy with the vice of avarice. In the process, it has altered the meaning of the sacred text (here a *ḥadīth*). However, it is the semantic similarity between sacred text and context that permits this transformation. As we shall see, other anecdotes exploit varying levels of semantic similarity to effect different kinds of reinterpretation.

This ingenious technique is also evident in the case of the *ṭufaylī* who was asked if he were not ashamed of his behavior. What is wrong with it, he replied, since even the Israelites practiced it, for they said (again citing the Qurʾān): "O God, our Lord, send down upon us a Table out of heaven, that shall be for us a festival"?[23]

Here, the brief interpretation is presented first in the justification of the asocial behavior. The Qurʾānic verse is both evidence and clarification of the interpretation, adding, of course, the weight of the divine word. This clever protagonist is, however, not as honest (or as learned?) as some others of his type, for the speaker in the Qurʾānic verse is actually Jesus and not the col-

21. See, for example, al-Bayḍāwī, *Tafsīr*, 2.607.

22. Al-Jāḥiẓ, *al-Bukhalāʾ*, (ed. Ṭāhā al-Ḥājirī; Cairo: Dār al-maʿārif, 1971) 186. On these missives, for and against miserliness, see my *Structures*, 51–52. This text is textually attributed to Ibn al-Tawʾam, but there is no reason why it could not have been written by al-Jāḥiẓ himself. See ibid., chap. 3.

23. Sūrat al-Māʾida, 5:114; Arberry, *The Koran Interpreted*, 1.146; Al-Khaṭīb, *al-Taṭfīl*, 34.

lectivity of Israelites. A sort of mangling of the Qurʾānic text is effected. The shift alters the implications of the verse since Jesus, not here asking for himself, could in no sense be acting as a *ṭufaylī*; and even without this change, the *ṭufaylī's* interpretation constitutes a moral hijacking of the Qurʾānic intent.

The area of bisociation need not be limited to food. The Ḥanbalī theologian and polyhistor Ibn al-Jawzī, in the chapter on *ṭufaylīs* in his *Akhbār al-adhkiyāʾ* ("Stories of the Clever and Witty"), relates an anecdote about the prototypical uninvited guest, Bunān. The latter came to a banquet and the door was locked before he could enter. So he rented a ladder and placed it on the man's wall, looking out on the man's family and daughters. The man said to him: "O you, do you not fear God? You have seen my family and daughters." Bunān replied: "O *shaykh*, [and here the Qurʾānic citation begins] 'Thou knowest we have no right to thy daughters, and thou well knowest what we desire.'"[24] The man laughed and told Bunān to come down and eat.[25]

In this concise narrative, it is as though we had come full circle. The Qurʾānic verse alludes to the people of Lot, whose homosexual inclinations are part of what causes their downfall. But Bunān is not interested in the sexual; his appetites lie elsewhere. He borrows this Qurʾānic allusion and redirects it to his own desires. Clearly, the anecdote revolves around a tension between sexual and alimentary desires. And this is manifest from its very beginning. The closing of the door, the climbing of the ladder, Bunān's scopic activity—these all form part of the sexual discourse in the anecdote. Pulling at this is the alimentary component: the banquet, implying food. When the host confronted the prospective *ṭufaylī* with the sexual (the scopic), Bunān replied with a verse about sexuality but shifted it to a nonsexual use.

The manipulation of sexuality and the religious intertext is a fairly consistent element in the anecdotes about women in the *adab* corpus. Relatively atypical is the case of the woman who passed by a group of men from the Banū Numayr, who persisted in staring at her. She admonished them with both a verse from the Qurʾān directed against looking ("Say to the believers, that they cast down their eyes")[26] and with a line of poetry of similar import. The men were ashamed and bowed down their heads.[27] The female speaker in this anecdote uses the verse from the holy book in the exact way it was intended: as an admonition against looking. Her goal is achieved: the men lower their

24. Sūrat Hūd, 11:79; Arberry, *The Koran Interpreted*, 1.248.

25. Ibn al-Jawzī, *Akhbār al-adhkiyāʾ* (ed. Muḥammad Mursī al-Khawlī; Cairo: Maṭābiʿ al-ahrām al-tijāriyya, 1970) 189.

26. Sūrat al-Nūr, 24:30; Arberry, *The Koran Interpreted*, 2.49.

27. Ibn Qutayba, *ʿUyūn al-akhbār* (4 vols. in 2; Cairo: Dār al-kutub, 1963) 4.85.

eyes. But the religious intertext does more. It reverses the power of the sexual situation, which begins with the male scopic in a superior position. The male gaze has been deflected by the religious text.[28]

More typical is an anecdote relating that when a man who wished to buy a slave girl asked her price, she replied: "And none knows the hosts of thy Lord but He."[29] Her refusal to answer a prospective buyer was effected through the holy book. She silenced the male voice by using a verse whose content in no way denoted sexuality and was essentially irrelevant.

Two women, one a virgin and one not, were shown to a buyer and he favored the virgin. The nonvirgin then asked him why he preferred the virgin, given that there was only one day between them. The virgin then replied: "And surely a day with thy Lord is as a thousand years of your counting."[30] The man liked both women and bought them both.[31] Here, the virgin responded to her colleague's question, which the latter had addressed to the male buyer. Through the use of the verse, she created a bisociation between the religious and the sexual—and one that played up to the sexual power of the man. The Lord in the Qurʾānic verse became the lord and master of the house. His sexual possession of the woman is compared with the deity's domination of the universe. Patriarchal religion, one might say, has been reduced to patriarchy. The response does more, however. The verse from *Sūrat al-Ḥajj* is embedded in a section on the punishments inflicted by the deity. This context of punishment serves to reinforce the negative implications of the loss of virginity.

This kind of dialogue mediated through a religious intertext is even more prominent in a story found in the *Laṭāʾif al-luṭf* by al-Thaʿālibī, one of the most indefatigable scholars of his time. The vizier al-Faḍl ibn Yaḥyā explained to the ʿAbbāsid caliph Hārūn al-Rashīd that he was consorting with two of his slave girls, one Meccan and one Medinan. The Medinan aroused him and proceeded to the sexual act, at which point the Meccan slave girl overpowered her. The Medinan replied that she had more right to this, adducing the *ḥadīth*, according to which the Prophet said: "He who revives a dead land, it belongs to him."[32] But the other responded with another *ḥadīth*: "The quarry belongs

28. For the dynamics of this problematic in *adab* chapters on women, see my *Woman's Body, Woman's Word: Gender and Discourse in Arabo-Islamic Writing* (Princeton: Princeton University Press, 1991) 29–53.

29. Ibn al-Jawzī, *Adhkiyāʾ*, 238. The verse is Sūrat al-Muddaththir, 74:31; Arberry, *The Koran Interpreted*, 2.311.

30. Sūrat al-Ḥajj, 22:47; Arberry, *The Koran Interpreted*, 2.33.

31. Ibn al-Jawzī, *Adhkiyāʾ*, 236.

32. This *ḥadīth* is a reasonably popular one, as evidenced by A. J. Wensinck, *Concordance et indices de la tradition musulmane* (8 vols; Leiden: Brill, 1936–88) 1.539. See, for example, Mālik ibn Anas, *Kitāb al-muwaṭṭaʾ* (ed. Fārūq Saʿd; Beirut: Dār al-āfāq al-jadīda, 1983) 637–38.

not to the one who arouses it but to the one who hunts it."[33] The caliph laughed and the two slave girls were given to him.[34] A change of registers is effected here through the use of the nonsexual *ḥadīth* in a clearly sexual context. The interchange between the women is restricted to the two religious texts. Through this exploitation, the female speakers succeed in turning the male into a sexual being, if not into a merely sexual object. But it is precisely their verbal skills, their ability to manipulate the religious discourse, that makes them desirable females, themselves objects of desire, as they are the property first of one male and then of another.

These anecdotes, thus, vary in the degree to which they reinterpret or redefine the religious text. Of course, this reinterpretation is in no sense absolute. The orthodox or received interpretations of these verses or *ḥadīths* are never really eliminated. In fact, the authoritative nature of the *ḥadīth* or Qurʾānic citations is key to their use in the power plays of the anecdotes. The religious texts are assimilated into the systems of *adab* anecdotes: the struggles over food and sex, the clever stratagems, the displays of wit. They show us that *adab* must be understood not (or at least not exclusively) on the basis of the nature of the materials included in it, still less their origin, but in terms of the specific ways in which these materials are presented, exploited, or manipulated.

33. I have not been able to locate this *ḥadīth* in the standard compilations.
34. Al-Thaᶜālibī, *Laṭāʾif al-luṭf* (ed. ᶜUmar al-Asᶜad; Beirut: Dār al-masīra, 1980) 99–100.

INDEX